NOAH'S ARK:
A Feasibility Study

John Woodmorappe

M. A. Geology, B. A. Geology, B. A. Biology

Institute for Creation Research
Santee, California

NOAH'S ARK: A Feasibility Study
John Woodmorappe

Institute for Creation Research
P.O. Box 2667, El Cajon, California 92021
10946 Woodside Avenue North, Santee, California 92071

Phone: 619/448-0900
Customer Service: 800/628-7640
www.icr.org

First printing, 1996
Second printing, 2003

Library of Congress Catalog Card Number: 95-081877

ISBN: 0-932766-41-2

Printed in the United States of America

This work is dedicated to the observance of the 25th anniversary of the founding of the Institute for Creation Research.

– John Woodmorappe

Acknowledgments

I would like to thank Drs. George Howe, Jerry Bergman, and Walter ReMine for reviewing earlier versions of this work. I also thank Dr. Chris Ledvina and Janet Howe for technical assistance.

Table of Contents

Foreword

In this unique volume, John Woodmorappe has provided an amazingly complete and compelling response to the many critics of the Biblical record of the Flood and Noah's Ark. While not questioning the possibility of God's miraculous activity in connection with the gathering and care of the animals in the Ark, Woodmorappe has shown that the Genesis record makes perfect sense even if no miracles at all were involved.

As with all his earlier studies (see, for example, the collections of articles in *Studies in Flood Geology*, published by ICR in 1993), his documentation is so thorough and so incisively applied that critics of the Biblical account henceforth will have to rely solely on sophistry and *ad hominem* arguments if they are to continue to reject and ridicule it. Noah did build a great seaworthy vessel, and it did house representatives of all kinds of land animals for an entire year to preserve life on the land during the awful global cataclysm of the great Flood.

This fact, of course, strengthens even further the strong case for flood geology, so capably supported in Woodmorappe's earlier volume, and, therefore, of the divinely inspired and infallible Genesis record of recent literal creation of all things.

The author of this unique volume has been a diligent researcher in topics both scientific and Biblical, especially in the fields of geology, biology and paleontology, for over twenty years. He has a B.A. in biology, a B.A. in geology, and an M.A. in geology. He has been a university research fellow and a science teacher in public schools.

The careful and thoughtful reader will find this book remarkably persuasive in its logic and authoritative documentation. I am glad to recommend it.

Henry M. Morris
President, ICR
October 1995

Introduction

Keywords

Noah, Ark, Apologetics, Genesis, Flood, Vertebrate Taxonomy, Vertebrate Zoology, Vertebrate Husbandry.

Abstract

This work is a systematic evaluation of the housing, feeding, watering, and waste-disposal requirements of some 16,000 animals on Noah's Ark. It is also a comprehensive rebuttal to the myriads of arguments that have been made against the Ark over the centuries. It is shown that it was possible for eight people to care for 16,000 animals, and without miraculous Divine intervention. Proven solutions are offered to the problems of animals with special diets, such as the panda and koala. The bulk of hay poses no problem, and neither do the climatic requirements of animals.

The latter part of this work considers the immediate post-Flood world. It answers, among other things, arguments related to salinity tolerances of organisms in floodwater, seed survival and germination through the Flood, and a host of genetics "problems" of post-Flood population bottlenecks.

Rationalistic Attacks on the Ark: A Brief History

Attacks on the credibility of the Ark account go back to classical antiquity. Allen (1963, pp. 70-91) and Browne (1983, pp. 3-27) offer comprehensive histories of these criticisms. I provide a brief summary of them. Apelles, a disciple of the heretic Marcion, is listed as one of the first critics of the Ark. He asserted that the Ark was barely large enough for four elephants! The early church fathers responded to some of these criticisms. However, it is noteworthy that various apologists of the early Church (e.g., Origen, Augustine, Ambrose, Procopius) were all too eager to disregard Scriptural specifications for the Ark's size and shape in favor of their own rather imaginative ideas. At the same time, pagan critics of the Bible had been trying to reduce the Flood to a local phenomenon, and there were a few early believers (e.g., Pseudo-Justin) who went along. However, most commentators (e.g., Tertullian, Pseudo-Eustatius, Procopius) recognized and strongly supported the universality of the Flood.

Allen (1963, p. 84) contends that questions related to the Ark and the Flood were largely forgotten during the Middle Ages. However, during the Renaissance and 17th century, interest in the Ark enjoyed a revival (Allen 1963, p. 78-79). Even so, many theologians during this time, impatient with questions about the Ark, preferred to "spiritualize" it and to relegate all

Flood-related questions to the miraculous and rationally unknowable. Nevertheless, it was during this time that Buteo (see below) provided the first scientific study of the Ark and its contents.

The Believers' Sellout of the Ark. The Flood account was commonly accepted until about the middle of the 18th century (Browne 1983). Up to that time, only a few hundred mammalian species were known (Wilson and Reeder 1993), and no problem was seen in the housing and care of this small number of animals. However, Allen (1963, p. 88-9) cites some critics who did not believe that the Ark could house even the animals that were known by the year 1690, and asserts that "enlightened men" by the late 17th century already "knew" that the Flood, if it occurred at all, could only have been local.

Currently, nearly 5000 mammalian species are known (Wilson and Reeder 1993). The growth in knowledge of animal numbers over the last few centuries has been particularly dramatic in certain groups. For instance, only 27 species of bats were known at the time of Linnaeus, whereas the number as of 1947 was about 1,950 (Ryberg 1947, p. 2). Largely because of this ever-increasing number of animals known, there came about a growing prejudice that the Ark could not house them all.

This false notion motivated believers to engage in various revisionisms of Scripture, such as the local flood copout (for further discussion of this, see Allen 1963, and Whitcomb and Morris 1961, pp. 107-9). This Scripture-twisting gymnastic relegated the Noachian Deluge to a glorified river flood of the Tigris-Euphrates. Of course, such a trivialization of the Biblical account has no validity. For instance, Allen (1963, p. 90) dismisses the change in position (from a global Flood to a local flood) as little more than a progressive retreat from believers' attempts to find rational support for the Bible. Contemporary humanistically-dominated science ascribes no more credibility to Scripture owing to the local-flood copout than it did for the global Flood (see, for instance, the modernist Bailey 1989).

The compromising-evangelical Young (1995, p. 60), a modern advocate of the local-flood copout, falsely supposes that the 16th and 17th-century defenders of the Ark were successful in upholding its cargo-carrying capabilities only because of their awareness of a small number of animals. In this work I demonstrate the capability of the Ark to house 8,000 kinds of animals, with room to spare, which is many times the animals known two or three centuries ago.

In recent decades, the literal Ark and global Flood have enjoyed emphasis as a result of the modern scientific creationist revival. This, in turn, has triggered a rather vitriolic backlash against the Ark by anti-creationists. Most of the arguments that have surfaced are nothing but the same old chestnuts dusted off and re-used by infidels and modernists. They then are accepted as gospel truth by compromising evangelicals (e.g., Youngblood 1980, Morton 1995), who naively repeat them also. Probably the most comprehensive recent parody of the Ark account is provided by Moore (1983), who has recycled many old arguments, and added a few of his own. More recently, Moore (1995) has smeared fundamentalism as a "scientific absurdity." Babinski (1995, p. 220), evidently very impressed by Moore's diatribe against the Ark, felt compelled to abandon the faith. Recently, Moore's many assertions have been all resurfaced by Plimer (1994), who in turn has embellished some of them with his own absurdities. It is shown throughout this work that Moore's arguments, while superficially impressive to the uninitiated, are completely devoid of merit.

Defamation of the Bible. Along with the rest of Scripture, the Biblical Flood account itself has been subject to constant attacks by rationalists. For instance, modernists right up to the present (e.g., Bailey 1989) continue to adhere to the JEPD Hypothesis. While Moore (1983, p. 37) and Plimer

(1994, p. 88) have exalted this hoary modernistic edifice to godlike status, other unbelievers are becoming disenchanted with it. For instance, the modernist Armstrong (1993, p. 12) remarks:

> This form of criticism has come in for a good deal of harsh treatment, but nobody has yet come up with a more satisfactory theory which explains why there are two quite different accounts of key Biblical events, such as the Creation and the Flood, and why the Bible sometimes contradicts itself.

In actuality, the contradictions and supposed duplicate accounts about the Flood do not exist, but are simply imagined difficulties manufactured by the JEPD hypothesis and the rationalistic worldview to which it is beholden (for a detailed refutation of the JEPD hypothesis with regards to Genesis 6-8, see McDowell 1975, pp. 139-141). Likewise, the words of our Lord have also been subject to incessant rationalistic attacks, including His teachings on the Flood. The most recent of these manifestations of modernism has been the so-called Jesus Seminar which, predictably, denied the authenticity of most of our Lord's teachings and actions. For a refutation of the many false and baseless claims of the "Jesus Seminar," see the papers in Wilkins and Moreland (1995).

The Study of Ark Logistics. The 16th century Buteo (Allen 1963, p. 78-9) is mentioned as being the first to study the Ark and its logistics from a scientific viewpoint. He showed that the Ark could have carried several hundred cow-sized and sheep-sized animals, in addition to many smaller creatures. A variety of 17th-century writers then followed Buteo's lead (for a listing of them, with references, see Young 1995, p. 60). The most notable of these was the 17th Century Jesuit Athanasius Kircher (see Diamond 1985, for a description of Kitcher's work). By contrast it appears that little work has been done by believers over the last two centuries to solve the real or imagined scientific problems related to the Ark itself, at least in any kind of systematic manner. Diamond (1985) has challenged modern creationists to study the Ark and its logistics. I have accepted the challenge, and this work is the result. A small foretaste of this research had been orally presented at the Third International Conference on Creationism (Woodmorappe 1995).

The Role of Miracles. Whitcomb (1988, p. 21) has called attention to the presence of both Divine miraculous and providential actions with regard to the Flood and the Ark. Yet Scripture does not give us details about the manner or extent of supernatural involvement during the Flood. Since we do not know and cannot know, this side of eternity, about miracles connected with the Ark, I focus almost exclusively on non-miraculous solutions to alleged problems with the Ark account.

Moore (1983, p. 38) and Morton (1995, p. 72), repeating many earlier critics, have alleged that the Ark account, in order to work as described in Scripture, would have required an endless profusion of ad hoc Divine miracles. This work thoroughly demonstrates the contrary. In fact, most "problems" regarding the Ark not only have naturalistic solutions, but have *several* such solutions, assuming that the "problems" are genuine to begin with.

Why No Noachian Rapture? Why was the Ark needed at all if God could have judged and destroyed the world miraculously? To understand this question, note the impossibility of pinning God down to one *modus operandi*. For instance, when God has provided food for His creatures, He has done it through methods as diverse as the miraculous creation of food (Exodus 16:4; 1 Kings 17:14-16; John 6:11), miracles of providence (1 Kings 17:6), and usually through indirect means (Matthew 5:45; Acts 14:17). Saying, as Moore (1983, p. 37) does, that God "should" have just dispensed with the Ark (and taken Noah's family to heaven, destroyed the earth, and then replaced Noah's family on earth) is as foolish as it is presumptuous. Clearly, the fact that God chooses to work miraculously in one situation does not in any way prevent Him from working through naturalistic means in other cases (in fact, in the vast majority of cases).

Another unrealistic theological issue has been raised by Morton (1995, p. 70). He contends that the extinction of animals would imply "poor planning" on God's part because animals would be taken on the Ark "for absolutely no reason" in view of God's foreknowledge that some of them would go extinct. Using Morton's "logic," dare we suppose that God creates certain infants in vain when He foreknows that many of them will die young—even before their first birthday? Of course not! God decides who lives and for how long (Acts 17:26). The brevity or otherwise of the lifespan is His decision, and is otherwise irrelevant to their creation. The same applies to animals' lives—including those taken on the Ark. Since animal kinds are nothing but collections of animal individuals, the extinction of kinds is subject to the same divine will. And nothing God does is in vain!

My Previous Flood-Related Research. Being both a biologist and geologist, I have spent the last 20 years doing intensive research related to Creation and the Flood. My collected works have recently been published in a single volume (Woodmorappe 1993). In it, I have refuted many long-held objections against the Flood. For instance, my paper *A Diluviological Treatise*... provides a detailed explanation of how one Flood accounts for fossils in their stratigraphic order. Another paper, *Causes for the Biogeographic Distribution*... addresses the question of why modern animals are so varied on different continents even though they all originated from one point (the Ark on Ararat). It also dispels the oft-repeated canard (e.g., Moore 1983, 35; Morton 1995, p. 70) about the animals (e.g., Australian marsupials) returning to the same locations from where they had lived before the Flood.

Part I

A Complete Inventory of the Animals and Supplies on the Ark

Chapter 1

Which Part of the Animal Kingdom was on the Ark?

The Living Cargo: Mammals, Birds, and Reptiles

Did the Ark actually have to carry *every* type of animal in existence? Modern anti-creationists continue to resurrect long-discredited tomfooleries about the overcrowded Ark. For instance, although it was shown long ago (Whitcomb and Morris 1961; Jones 1973) that the Ark was not required to carry every member of Kingdom Animalia, recent critics (e.g., Futuyma 1983, McGowan 1984, Moore 1983, Skehan 1986, Plimer 1994, and Morton 1995) continue to burlesque the Ark by placing just about every imaginable living thing on it. Morton (1995, pp. 68-9) has visions of snails and earthworms struggling for thousands of years to make it to the Ark in time. Moore (1983, p. 16) fantasizes that the Ark carried deep-sea fish. McGowan (1984, p. 57), not to be outdone, puts whales and sharks on the Ark. Futuyma (1983, pp. 202-3) adds to the farce by repositing all the millions of plant and animal species onto the Ark. Schneour (1986) and Plimer (1994) take rationalistic arguments against the Ark to new heights of absurdity by insisting that it had to carry cultures of microorganisms!

At the other extreme, we have compromising evangelicals (e.g., Hugh Ross 1990) who want to "save" the Flood by insisting that Noah only had to carry a few common domesticated animals on the Ark. Needless to say, Scripture does not limit the contents of the Ark to domesticated animals (Jones 1973). Neither, for that matter, does Jewish tradition (Friedler 1967, p. 5; Ginzberg 1909, 1988, p. 328).

Let us now consider what Scripture *does* say concerning the types of animal life taken on the Ark. It is clear that the contents of the Ark were limited to all living and extinct land mammals, birds, and land reptiles (Jones 1973), as elaborated and shown here in Tables 1 and 2. The Hebrew terminology in the Genesis account rules out invertebrates having been taken on the Ark (Jones 1973). The same holds true for marine and amphibious vertebrates (Hasel 1978, pp. 86-7). Let us consider the main inhabitants of the Ark in more detail.

Birds. Terrestrial birds were undoubtedly on the Ark. By contrast, many types of seabirds spend less than 10% of their lives on land, and for this and similar reasons can be considered marine creatures (see Ainsley 1980). It is thus very unlikely that they were on the Ark, but I have included them in the totals. The distinction between true seabirds, and shore-birds, is discussed in detail in the section *Carnivores and Piscivores*.

Dinosaurs. Most if not all dinosaurs were present on the Ark, as they were clearly terrestrial creatures (Bakker 1986, pp. 105-124). When Moore (1983, p. 9) ridicules some earlier creationists who had suggested that dinosaurs were aquatic animals and could have survived the Flood outside the Ark, he had better reserve his scorn for his fellow evolutionists. After all, it is they who suggested that dinosaurs were too heavy to walk on land without their massive bodies being supported by water. This notion had been widely prevalent in both popular and scientific depictions of dinosaurs (in fact, Bakker 1986, p. 116, called it an "eighty-year orthodoxy"). For instance, the classic Charles Knight paintings of dinosaurs, displayed in the Field Museum in Chicago and reprinted in countless books, depicted dinosaurs as swamp creatures. Bakker (1986, p. 124), has shown that the dinosaurs' anatomy is completely incompatible with even a swampy habitat.

Although many terrestrial vertebrates can swim continuously anywhere from several hours to a few days (see Johnson 1978, and references cited therein), it is quite impossible that they could have survived the Flood outside the Ark once the floodwaters had prevailed on the earth. However, many land animals must have temporarily survived while the Floodwaters were still cyclically advancing and retreating. As the waters buoyed them up, they swam. At the same time, the sediments were deposited beneath them. When the waters temporarily retreated, the animals were stranded on the sediment, and made footprints. Such a cycle must have repeated itself up to several times, thus generating the successive layers of footprint horizons we now find in the geologic record. Note that footprint horizons found near the top of the sedimentary column (e.g., Late Cretaceous) should not be mistakenly thought of as late-Flood deposits. Any local stratigraphic sequence containing footprint horizons is probably entirely early-Flood in origin (e.g., Oard 1995). Although land animals certainly drowned, sooner or later, the same need not have been true of their eggs. For instance, while lizards were on the Ark, lizard eggs, notably resistant to seawater (Carlquist 1974, p. 9), may have survived the Flood in a viable state.

Amphibians? Possibly the more terrestrial amphibians were on the Ark (Jones 1973). But since they were few in number (Carroll 1988; Duellman 1979) and were mostly small in size (Carroll 1988; Jenkins and Walsh 1993; Pough 1989), their inclusion could only have had a negligible effect on the calculations of Ark inventory. Furthermore, I have erred on the side of amphibious animals by including, on the Ark, many mammalian and reptilian genera that may have been or actually are aquatic or semi-aquatic. This was necessary because various members of otherwise-terrestrial vertebrate families are aquatic, and an unknown number of extinct genera may have been capable of prolonged life in water without necessarily bearing any skeletal features indicative of such capabilities.

Unknown Animals. We can be confident that we have discovered nearly all genera of extant land animals. However, there is no way of determining, or even intelligently guessing, the numbers and sizes of unknown extinct animals. A number of estimates for the numbers of specific unknown types of extinct animals do exist (e.g. dinosaurs: Dodson 1990). However, the computations involved all presuppose the validity of organic evolution and the geologic time scale in their calculations, and thus have no meaning in the creationist-diluvialist paradigm.

When considering unaccounted-for extinct animals, we must remember that there is plenty of extra space on the Ark beyond that accounted for in this study (as quantified and discussed in: *The Engineering and Infrastructure of the Ark*. Secondly, by choosing the kind as equal to the genus instead of the family, I already have placed up to eight times the actual number of animals on the Ark.

Furthermore, the existence of unknown extinct animals is partly offset by the fact that a substantial fraction of all provisionally-accepted extinct genera, all of which are placed on the Ark in this study, are of dubious validity (Carroll 1988). Indeed, since its inception, vertebrate paleontology has suffered from a proliferation of invalid generic names based on nondiagnostic material, and an exaggeration of the numbers of putatively valid generic names derived from more complete material. In recent decades, a considerable number of extinct genera have been "sunk," and this process continues today. For example, a recent study (King and Rubidge 1993) has drawn several long-accepted therapsid genera into synonymy.

Since all my calculations are much more numerically sensitive to the needs of the fewer large animals than to those of the numerous smaller ones, it follows that dubious genera of the large-sized animals are the ones that appreciably exaggerate the inventory and logistics of the Ark. For instance, for purposes of this study, I have included all 87 commonly-cited sauropod dinosaur genera as valid, and placed them on the Ark (as juveniles). Yet, according to sauropod specialist McIntosh (1992, p. 345), only twelve sauropod genera can be regarded as "firmly established" and an additional twelve "fairly well established." Likewise, a significant fraction of the thousands of extinct medium to large sized hoofed-mammal genera are of questionable validity. This is illustrated by the fact that, in recent decades, the rate of discovery of extinct large-mammal genera has only modestly exceeded the rate of the suppression of invalid generic names within most large-bodied mammalian orders (Peczkis 1989).

Why Animal Destruction? Some critics (e.g., Moore 1983) question why God chose to destroy the animals along with humans during the Flood, reasoning that animals are not conscious entities and cannot be morally culpable of anything. Scripture does not tell us God's precise motives for including the destruction of animals, other than the fact that the whole earth was polluted (Genesis 6:11). Thus the Flood was not only punitive but also cleansing in character. The destruction of animals, then, need not have had anything to do with their ostensible moral culpability (any more than does the mass extermination and cremation of diseased animals, or the shooting of man-eating lions). Animals are incapable of moral instruction (Psalm 32:9). However, if animal consciousness is at all relevant, it is important to point out that we do not know what kind of mental states animals are capable of. Present-day neurobiology is incapable of discerning which neural processes result in conscious thought (of whatever type) and which do not (Glynn 1993, p. 607). At the same time, numerous studies (e. g., Barber 1993) suggest that at least some animals are sentient beings.

Taxonomic Rank of the Created Kind

Calculating the numbers of animals on the Ark requires not only an analysis of their taxonomic identity, but also taxonomic rank. Despite years of work by creationists demonstrating that the created kind must be broader than the species, anti-creationists (e.g. Moore 1983) perpetuate the old objection about the Ark being grossly overcrowded with every *species* of animal. Clearly, the anti-Biblicists will seek to discredit the Ark account at any cost. To make it even worse, the anti-creationists—Awbrey (1981), Moore (1983), along with the compromising evangelical Hugh Ross (1994, p. 73)—have the audacity to level the false charge that creationists have invented the concept of the created kind as an *ad hoc* device to reduce the numbers of animals on the Ark. These critics seem willingly ignorant of the many evidences of the created kind being broader than the species (see below). Already in the 17th century (Allen 1963, p. 80; see also Young 1995, p. 58), English Bishop John Wilkins had pointed out that the tiresome controversy about the roominess of the Ark would be ended if men would stop calling every animal by five names!

There is a very fundamental reason why the created kind must, at minimum, be at the generic and not specific level. The genus is the smallest division of plants and animals that can usually be identified without scientific study (Cain 1956, p. 97). Since Scripture was written to be understood without modern scientific training or other knowledge unavailable to the ancients (or even outside of Scripture itself), the created kind could not possibly refer to species, but must be broader than the species. Furthermore, the created kind is not some vague ethereal entity as the anti-creationists make it out to be, but is well founded by creationist scholarship. For instance, there is a wealth of evidence that, at minimum, the created kind is broader than the species of conventional taxonomy (see below). In fact, many biologists use the term *syngameon* (see Templeton 1991a, p. 20, and earlier-cited works) to refer to the most inclusive unit of interbreeding among plants and animals. The *syngameon* is usually broader than the species and even, in many cases, the genus. Moreover, Jones (1972a), has shown that the Hebrew term for creation kind, *min,* is a real entity and not simply that "like begets like." Any putative difficulty in the discovery of a one-to-one correspondence between a specific taxonomic rank and the created kind in no way negates the concept of the kind. It merely reflects the limitations of man-made taxonomy (ReMine 1993, p. 513), although quantitative studies of animal morphology (Wyles et al. 1983) support the position that conventional taxonomic divisions are not merely convenient labels, but have some objective validity.

Can the created kind ever be above the family level? Gish (1993) recently pointed out that he had been misrepresented by anti-creationists, and had never suggested that the created kind may be as high as the order of conventional taxonomy. In his decades-long studies of turtles, Frair (1991; and earlier-cited works) did suggest that the created kind among turtles may be as high as the order. However, the Testudines may be an atypically homogenous group, at least at the ordinal level (Karl et al. 1995, p. 265). Furthermore, members of different families within Testudines do not freely interbreed with each other (Frair, personal communication). Following the interbreeding criteria discussed below, it follows that the kind among turtles must be below the ordinal level.

Identifying the Created Kind. Jones (1972b), largely using Scriptural evidence (e.g., the animal lists in Leviticus), demonstrated that the created kind is approximately equivalent to the subfamily or family, at least in the case of birds and mammals. Recently, Scherer (1993) has arrived at the same conclusion, but on the basis of scientific evidence. This evidence includes numerous documented cases of interbreeding between individuals of different species and genera, as well as interbreeding with a third species or genus in situations where two species or genera do not themselves interbreed. Thus, Scherer's definition of the kind is very similar, if not identical, to Templeton's (1991a, p. 20) aforementioned term *syngameon.*

The many instances of interbreeding which Scherer (1993) cites can be multiplied greatly. For instance, Hubbs (1955) and Smith (1992) provide a large inventory of known instances of trans-specific and trans-generic breeding among fish. McAllister and Coad (1978) have presented a matrix depicting all known instances of trans-generic breeding in the fish family Cichlidae. (This matrix is quite similar to the one by the creationist Scherer (1986) for trans-generic breeding within the avian family Anatidae). Almost all the genera of the marine turtle family Cheloniidae can form fertile hybrids with each other (Karl et al. 1995).

Of course, there are countless examples of hybridization within the genus, as between fish species (e.g., McClure and McEachran 1992; Meagher and Dowling 1991), reptiles (Bailey 1942; Frye 1991; Huff 1980; von Mertens 1968), and amphibians (Oliveira et al. 1991; Wilson et al. 1974). Breeding among different species of birds is exceedingly common, and also occurs between genera (Tatarinov 1986). For a bibliography of all papers providing similar examples, in just several issues of only one journal of avian biology (*Auk*), see (Monroe 1991). There is also a recent survey (Close and Lowry 1990) of such occurrences among marsupial mammals. Finally, instances of hybrid zones among different species of plants and animals have recently been tabulated (Harrison 1990; see also Minelli 1993, pp. 75-6).

The above-cited examples hardly exhaust the possibilities for interbreeding between species and genera. Indeed, it is a fact that most species are named according to morphological differences between animals and not closure of the gene pool:

> . . . the fact that only a tiny percentage of recognized species have been tested, naturally or otherwise, for reproductive isolation from other apparently closely related forms. . . . (Archer 1981, p. 130)

Does Rapid Post-Flood Speciation Accredit Organic Evolution? Anti-creationists commonly raise doubts if new species and genera could arise in only the few thousand years since the Flood. In doing so, they only display their ignorance of both creationist and evolutionist research along these lines. In fact, the release of single pairs and seven pairs of animals must have facilitated the rapid origin of new species and genera, a matter examined in detail in the section *rapid speciation*.

When confronted with the evidence for rapid speciation, anti-creationists (Moore 1983, p. 18; Morton 1995, p. 68; Plimer 1994, p. 103) then try to confuse the issue by asserting that creationists are accepting or supporting organic evolution to a more intense extent than do most evolutionists! The absurdity of their argument centers on the claim that recognizing the origin of a new species or genus is the same as admitting the origin of a new order, etc. In reality, the origins of the different taxonomic ranks are *not* comparable:

> Most of the differences between species evolved in the diversification of species and genera, the lower categories of taxa, and are presumed to be adaptive specializations without any obvious advance in overall grade of complexity. These changes can be called *lateral radiations* (Bullock 1991; Harvey and Pagel 1991). Another kind of evolutionary change is the relatively rare increase in general complexity, such as characterizes the differences between some phyla, classes, and orders, and possibly a few families. I have already referred to these changes as *vertical grades* of complexity (italics in original). (Bullock 1993, p. 90)

The evolutionist Bullock re-states what scientific creationists have been saying all along, and even uses much the same vocabulary (i.e., lateral radiations, which is very similar to what scientific creationists have called horizontal variation, or variation within a kind). Most definitely, speciation does not equal organic evolution.

Making the Crowded-Ark "Problem" More Challenging. If, as the preponderance of evidence (Jones 1972b; Scherer 1993) shows, the created kind was equivalent to the family (at least in the case of mammals and birds), then there were only about 2,000 animals on the Ark (Jones 1973). In such a case it is obvious that there was no problem in housing all the animals on the commodious Ark.

However, in order to make this exercise more interesting, I have deliberately made the problem of animal housing on the Ark much more difficult by adopting the genus as the taxonomic rank of the created kind. This necessitates, as shown below, nearly 16,000 animals on the Ark. This number is based on land animals of whose existence we know (either as live animals or fossils). Because I have intentionally made the Ark-crowding problem so much more difficult than it actually was, all other possible sources of error, individually and collectively, are rendered trivial by comparison. This makes it unnecessary to provide error bars for the various tables in this work.

Which Animals Were Clean?

Did Noah take seven individuals or seven pairs of clean animals on the Ark? Jones 1973) has surveyed over forty Bible commentaries on this matter and found them about evenly divided as to whether Scripture indicates seven pairs or seven individuals. In this work, I accept seven pairs, although, as shown below, this has little effect on the overall calculations.

Accounting for clean animals on the Ark may at first seem problematic for several reasons. In the first place, the concept of a clean animal at the time of Noah may not have been the same as it was millennia later with the Levitical system (H. Morris 1976, pp. 190-191). However, considering the perspicuity of Scripture, I will, in the absence of evidence to the contrary, assume that the concepts of clean animals were the same during the time of Noah as they were after the inception of the Law of Moses. In fact, as shown below, if we let the Bible be its own interpreter, it becomes evident that the number of clean animals is not only knowable, but is also quite small.

Since, in this work, we are setting the created kind at the level of the genus, we must first question the number of valid genera involved because of the high degree of interbreeding between genera of clean animals. This can be especially seen in the families Bovidae (Wall et al. 1992) and Cervidae (Van Gelder 1977). Among the birds, hybridization is commonly seen between the genera in Galliformes (various chickens, turkeys, quail, and pheasants: Amundsen and Lawrence 1955; McGrath et al. 1972; Prager and Wilson 1975); Anseriformes (i.e. many genera in Anatidae: Prager and Wilson 1975; Scherer 1986); and, to a lesser extent, in Passeriformes (i.e., finches: Roberts 1973). Considering generic-level taxonomy further, we need to note that not all genera of Anseriformes and Galliformes are accepted as clean according to certain Jewish traditions (Forst 1993). Furthermore, there is the usual problem of taxonomic lumping versus splitting, and this, of course, impacts the numbers of valid clean genera. For instance, in the Bovidae, some authors split *Bos* and *Bubulus* each into two genera (Wall et al. 1992, p. 263).

Let us now consider which specific reptiles, mammals, and birds are clean animals. First of all, no reptiles are candidates for clean animals, as Scripture informs us that they are all unclean (Rabinowitz 1972, p. 33), as are all the smaller mammals (e.g., rodents, shrews: Huttermann 1991, p. 185). The sole clean mammals include those which possess cloven hooves and chew continuously (Deuteronomy 14: 4-6). Indeed, motion photography shows that the typical cow chews 30,000-50,000 times during each 24-hour period (Welch and Hooper 1988, pp. 108-9). The Bible specifically lists the clean mammals as consisting of, in terms of modern taxonomy, approximately thirteen bovid/cervid genera (Jones 1972b). According to Jewish tradition (for example, Maimonides: Grunfeld 1972, p. 49-50), this Scriptural list is exhaustive; so no other live or extinct mammal is to be accepted as clean, even if it chews again and divides the hoof.

This fact imposes a major constraint on the number of possible clean animals, in that the *simanim* (sign) of cloven hoofs and chewing again is a necessary but not sufficient condition for a land mammal to be accepted as clean (Forst 1993). For instance, the giraffe divides the hoof and chews again, but there is no clear Jewish tradition of it being kosher (Rabinowitz 1972). According to some other Jewish traditions (Dresner and Siegel 1959, 1966), all clean animals are necessarily domesticated (or perhaps at least in a loose symbiotic relationship with humans). This conclusion is also supported by Morris (1995, pp. 22-23). Thus, the number of candidates for clean animals is drastically reduced, as only a few tens of genera of mammals and birds are commonly reckoned as domesticated (for a list of these genera, see Fowler 1986, p. 1067). This is despite the fact that many other animals are apparently no less suitable for domestication (Loosli and McDowell 1985, p. 4).

All the foregoing considerations indicate that the clean animals are a rather small and exclusive circle of animals which can be known, ruling out the possibility that just any wild (and also any extinct) bovid, giraffid, or cervid genus is a clean animal. The number of potential clean animals is further reduced once we recognize that Scripture is a complete, self-contained revelation. Since the Word of God requires no extra-Biblical sources of information to be understood properly, it follows that only animals individually specified in Scripture as clean can be regarded as such. As noted earlier, this amounts to, for mammals, approximately thirteen bovid/cervid genera (Jones 1972b).

The Clean Birds. Scripture lists numerous birds which are unclean (see Jones (1972b) for listing along with taxonomic analysis), and only several types of birds, belonging to a few tens of genera at most, are mentioned in the Bible in relation to human use (Rabinowitz 1972). If Jewish tradition is considered, one needs to add only a few additional birds, not mentioned in the Bible, to our list of clean birds (Rabinowitz 1972). These are all strongly granivorous and, as mentioned, consist of several members of Galliformes, Anseriformes, and Passeriformes.

Having already discussed the clean members of the first two orders, I now focus on the passerine birds. By analogy with the other clean birds, all of which are dominantly seed-eating, note that only the 122 genera comprising the following families are dominantly granivorous: Estrildidae, Ploceidae, Fringillidae, and Emberizidae (Inskipp 1975, p. 21). Jewish tradition restricts this further to only sixteen passerine genera having a definite tradition of being clean (Rabinowitz 1972, p. 30). However, taking into account all of the signs of cleanliness, and letting the Bible be its own interpreter, we are left with only the genus *Passer*. This is about the only member of Order Passeriformes mentioned in Scripture (Psalm 84:3; Proverbs 26:2; Matthew 10:29). Notably, it is *Passer domesticus* which has a close symbiotic relationship with man, accounting for its spread around the world wherever man has sown cereal crops (Summers-Smith 1988, p. 137).

Clean Animals and Sacrifice. Various commentators have suggested a connection between Noah's sacrifice after the Flood (Genesis 8:20) and the identity of the clean animals, but Scripture does not indicate how many animals were sacrificed by Noah (Jones 1973). However, keeping in mind the Hebrew terminologies and usages in Scripture, and being consistent with Biblical terminology, we can note that Noah's sacrifice was a burnt offering (Hebrew *olah*: Rainey 1971, p. 601). This type of sacrifice, according to other examples in Scripture, is limited to bulls, sheep and goats, and birds (Rainey 1971, p. 601-2). Jewish tradition about Noah himself indicates that he sacrificed only those animals which he had taken by seven pairs (namely: an ox, a sheep, a goat, two turtle doves, and two young pigeons: Ginzberg 1909, 1988, p. 333), because he reckoned that he had been commanded by God to take those animals by seven pairs for precisely that reason.

Only a Few Clean Animals on the Ark. Our discussion of the nature and identity of the clean animals dispels the absurdity that there were thousands or tens of thousands of clean animals on the Ark (Morton 1995, pp. 67-8). Let us now examine how the presence of clean animals affects the logistics of the Ark.

The inclusion of the seven pairs of approximately thirteen bovid/cervid genera (Jones 1972b) increases the values quoted in Tables 1 and 2 by less than one-half of one percent, and the logistics (Tables 3-4 and 6-7) by only 2–3%. As for the seven pairs of clean birds, the overall calculations are so insensitive to the numbers of these small-bodied animals that even putting tens of extra small animals on the Ark changes the quoted values by far less than 1%. It is evident that the calculations pertaining to the logistics of the Ark are only slightly affected by the addition of the clean animals, even if they were in seven pairs and not seven individuals. For this reason, the quoted values in all the tables of this work do not include the clean animals, whose impact is negligible.

The Ark Animals by Body-Mass Category

In common with all scientific measurements, all data in this work have been converted to, and expressed in, the metric system. To avoid any confusion, however, I use the expression "metric ton" interchangeably with 1000 kilograms, and with the megagram. All of the calculations in this work involving the Ark assume a short cubit of 45.72 cm (Wright 1985, p. 419). This is a conservative figure. For instance, the Jewish scholar Ben-Uri, in his study of the Ark, accepts a cubit of 50 cm (Friedler 1967, p. 5), and other commentators have cited even larger values.

In order to derive a complete inventory of animals on Noah's Ark, I have compiled and computed body-mass estimates for all the living and known extinct genera of land vertebrates (Table 1). These can be broken down into eighty-eight orders of live and known extinct land vertebrates (the twenty-five largest of which are shown in Table 2). Note that the distribution of their constituent genera is highly asymmetric, and there is a sharp asymptotic drop-off of constituent genera per order when the orders are listed from largest to smallest (Table 2). Indeed, merely the three largest orders (Passeriformes, Squamata, and Rodentia) collectively account for nearly half of the 16,000 animals on the Ark (Table 2). At the other extreme (not shown), forty-four orders have ten pairs or fewer, and thirty-five have five or fewer pairs.

Methodology Used. May (1978), in his study of insect body sizes, has found a similar asymmetry to the one which I have discussed in the previous paragraph in relation to land vertebrates. Therefore, I have used a similar methodology to the one that he has used to calculate the body-size (in my case, body mass) distribution of genera within the land-vertebrate orders, which is described in the ensuing paragraphs.

Table 1. Ark Animals: Their Numbers by Mass and Vertebrate Class									
LOG BODY MASS IN GRAMS:									
		0-1	1-2	2-3	3-4	4-5	5-6	6-7	7-8
ALL MAMMALS	7428	466	1,570	1,378	1,410	1,462	892	246	
ALL BIRDS	4,602	630	2,272	1,172	450	70	4		
ALL REPTILES	3,724	642	844	688	492	396	286	270	106
TOTALS	15,754	1,738	4,686	3,238	2,352	1,928	1,188	516	106

Table 2. Ark Animals: Distribution of Genera by Order and Mass										
		LOG BODY MASS IN GRAMS:								
Order—Class/diet			0-1	1-2	2-3	3-4	4-5	5-6	6-7	7-8
PASSERIFORMES—Av	2236		380	1700	146	10				
SQUAMATA—Rv	1938		642	764	402	116	12	2		
RODENTIA—Mh	1746		100	858	562	178	42	6		
ARTIODACTYLA—Mh	1144				14	244	456	424	6	
CARNIVORA—Mc	696				86	332	238	40		
THERAPSIDA—Rv	508			10	90	166	122	96	14	
MARSUPIALIA—Mh	468		4	100	126	104	94	38	2	
PERISSODACTYLA—Mh	436					20	150	130	136	
CHIROPTERA—Mv	412		216	180	16					
PRIMATES—Mh	412			44	158	148	58	6		
INSECTIVORA—Mc	404		110	204	86	4				
SAURISCHIA—Rv	390				4	22	72	78	108	106
GRUIFORMES—Ah	280			78	122	58	22			
ORNITHISCHIA—Rh	278				4	30	46	50	144	
APODIFORMES—Ah	276		242	34						
NOTOUNGULATA—Mh	252				26	90	96	40		
EDENTATA—Mh	250			6	38	48	72	80	6	
CHARADRIIFORMES—Ah	208			74	132	2				
CONDYLARTHA—Mh	198			2	56	86	52	2		
GALLIFORMES—Ah	176			4	106	66				
FALCONIFORMES—Ac	170			6	86	78				
PSITTACIFORMES—Ah	164			70	92	2				
CAPTORHINIDA—Rh	152			40	80	10		22		
THECODONTIA—Rc	144			8	24	26	54	32		
PICIFORMES—Ac	128		4	94	30					
(ADD REMAINING 61 LAND-VERTEBRATE ORDERS)										
TOTALS	15754									

Since the few large orders by themselves contain the overwhelming majority of all the genera, it is obvious that the calculations of body-mass distribution on the Ark are insensitive to the precise body-mass distributions of the many small orders but highly sensitive to the body-mass distribution of the considerably fewer but larger orders. Therefore, it is necessary to have a detailed body-mass breakdown of only the larger orders. For the many smaller orders, it is sufficient to simply assign a characteristic value for body mass to each small order, or just provide a rough estimate of the body-mass distribution of its constituent genera.

Constructing the Ark-Animal Database. We need to specify all the live and extinct vertebrate genera in terms of body sizes (masses). No such comprehensive database exists, so I assembled one by using existing smaller databases, supplemented with careful extrapolation. As shown in Tables 1 and 2, each animal was assigned to an order-of-magnitude body-mass category. This reflects the fact that adults vary greatly in body mass within a genus, so a single value for body mass would have little meaning.

Body mass estimates are available for nearly all extant land mammal genera (Damuth 1987; Nowak and Paradiso 1983), and for most extant avian genera (Dunning 1993; Ritland 1982). This is not the case for reptiles, so I compiled body mass estimates for nearly half of all extant reptilian genera. For tortoises, I converted carapace sizes available for various genera (Ernst and Barbour 1989) into body masses. For squamate genera, I first tallied the relatively comprehensive estimates of body masses that are available (Andrews and Pough 1985; Guyer and Donnelly 1990; Nagy and Peterson 1988, p. 127; Pough 1973, 1977; Seymour 1987; and Stevenson 1985). I then expanded this data base by converting tabulated snout-vent lengths (Censky and McCoy 1988; Dunham et al. 1988; Henderson et al. 1988; Shine 1991; Shine and Greer 1991; and Witten 1985) into body masses by means of a regression (Pough 1980).

Extrapolating Within Extant Vertebrate Families. The distributions of body masses obtained for numerous reptilian genera were subsequently extrapolated, within each respective extant reptilian family (listed by Duellman 1979), to the total number of extant squamate genera (enumerated by Duellman 1979) and extinct ones (enumerated by Carroll 1988) that occur within each extant family.

As for extinct genera in modern families of birds, I simply extrapolated the available body-masses of genera to the grand total of genera (live plus extinct) of each family. For mammals, I followed a somewhat different methodology. Peczkis (1988) has found that 67% of mammalian genera tend to occur in the modal body-mass category of the typical mammalian family, and 90% of genera occur in the two largest weight categories of the given family. Utilizing this information, I identified the modal and next-largest body weight category of each of the extant mammalian families. I then totaled the number of live and extinct genera in each family, and then apportioned this total in each family according to the ratios found by Peczkis (1988). It should be noted that the vast majority of all the extinct mammalian genera are members of still-living families, which is also the case with extinct avian genera, but not with extinct reptilian genera.

Large Extinct Mammalian and Avian Orders. Following the same methodology as described above, I needed only to subject the larger extinct mammalian and reptilian orders to detailed body-mass analyses, as the smaller ones have very little impact on the calculations. There are no large extinct orders of birds to consider. Now let us consider the relatively large extinct mammalian orders (e.g., Notoungulata and Condylartha; Table 2). I am not at liberty to reveal the sources which I used to determine the modal and next-largest body-mass categories of each of their constituent families because they are the subject of a forthcoming paper.

Large Extinct Reptilian Orders. For Order Therapsida, I generated a body-mass breakdown (shown in Table 2) of its genera through the use of skull (and sometimes whole-skeleton, or thigh-diameter). The data was culled from several sources (principally Anderson and Anderson 1970, Chart 1; Baur and Friedl 1980, p. 260, Brink 1982, and Kemp 1982), along with general comments on their distribution by body mass (Peczkis 1995).

For the dinosaur orders (Saurischia and Ornithischia), a body-mass apportionment is available for over two-thirds of all known and putatively-valid dinosaurian genera (Peczkis 1995). I extrapolated the body-mass distribution within each dinosaurian family, tabulated by Peczkis (1995), to the total number of genera of each respective dinosaur family (enumerated by several authors in the Wieshampel et al. 1992 volume). The totals were then apportioned with respect to the two dinosaur orders, and are shown in Table 2.

Small Extinct Vertebrate Orders. I now consider the remaining extinct orders of mammals, birds, and reptiles. Since, as noted earlier, there is no need for great detail with respect to the apportionment of their genera according to body mass, I arrived at a general distribution of their respective genera by utilizing several comprehensive sources (especially Carroll 1988, and Potts and Behrensmeyer 1992) along with an overview of their mean and maximal body sizes (Benton 1990, p. 288).

Enumerating the Animals on the Ark. There were nearly 16,000 animals on the Ark (Table 1), spanning eight orders of magnitude of body mass, ranging in size from hummingbirds (i.e., a few grams per individual) to sauropods (up to perhaps 80 megagrams when adults). I have based all the ensuing calculations on the Ark logistics by using the arithmetic mean of each respective small body-mass category (e.g., assuming in calculations that all animals in the 1-10 gram category weigh 5 grams, etc.). For animals larger than 100 kg, I used the geometric mean of each category (e.g., letting every animal in the 100–1000 kg category weigh 316 kg for purposes of calculations). My reason for using the geometric mean for the larger animals is the fact that there are more smaller than larger animals in each respective large-bodied category. This follows from the fact animals follow a log-normal distribution of genera relative to body-mass categories (Maurer et al. 1992), with the larger animals being part of the tail end of this distribution.

With respect to medium and large animals (that is, all animals greater than 10 kg as adults), I have represented them on the Ark as juveniles (for details, see: *Large Animals as Juveniles . . .*). However, for purposes of census, I have tabulated the large-bodied animals as adults in Tables 1 and 2. In all the other calculations (e.g., Tables 3,4,6,7), I have represented the medium to large animals as juveniles, also using JF (Juvenile Factors) to convert adult food/water intake to growing-juvenile intake for the 371-day interval. Details on calculating JF are also provided in the *Large Animals . . .* chapter).

Mass Distribution of the Animals on the Ark. As can be seen from the census (Tables 1 and 2), the vast majority of the animals on the Ark were small. Without allowing the representation of large animals as juveniles, the median animal on the Ark would have been the size of a small rat (about 100 grams: Hendrickson 1983, p.70). It is obvious that Whitcomb and Morris (1961) have been overly generous to their compromising-evangelical detractors when they had suggested that the average animal on the Ark was the size of a sheep. In fact, from the tabulation, it can be seen that only about 11% of the animals on the Ark were substantially larger than sheep.

Chapter 2

Floor Space Allotments for the Animals

How much floor space should be allowed for each size of animal on the Ark? I discuss this matter in detail in the section *Implications of Animal Crowding*. In this chapter, I only provide a brief rationale for the particular values I quote and use (Table 3). We might naturally suppose that there is an analogy between the Ark and situations where modern animals are transported en masse on ships. However, such animals are at sea usually only a few days or weeks, so the duration is not comparable enough for a meaningful comparison with the year-long Ark experience.

Moore (1983, p. 16) has claimed that animals require large floor areas, based on the experiences of zoos, and the transport of animals to zoos. However, the zoo is a very inappropriate and misleading analogy for the housing requirements of the animals on the Ark. First of all, the zoo is a facility intended for the public display of captive animals, as well as for the relatively comfortable confinement of animals on a permanent basis. Enclosures must generally also be spacious enough

Table 3. Ark Animal Housing: Floor-Space Areas Required			
BODY MASS CATEGORY (Log G.)	**CATEGORY ANIMAL COUNT**	**AREA REQUIRED (Sq. Meters per animal)**	**CUMULATIVE PERCENTAGE (of 3 Ark Floors)**
5-6	1,188	1.11 (JUVENILE)	13.9
4-5	1,928	0.56 (JUVENILE)	25.4
6-7	516	1.77 (JUVENILE)	35
3-4	2,352	0.28	42
7-8	106	2.51 (JUVENILE)	44.8
2-3	3,238	0.04	46.2
1-2	4,686	0.01	46.7
0-1	1,738	0	46.8

for animals to breed in captivity. By contrast, the Ark represents *temporary* confinement of animals, in an *emergency* situation, without their necessarily breeding during the stay on the Ark. The Ark was most certainly not a floating zoo, but a floating Flood shelter. Since we only need consider the minimum floor space for animals to survive in reasonable health for one year, we must orient ourselves not according to modern zoos, but according to modern examples of animals kept under conditions of extreme confinement. The closest modern analogues to the Ark are not the zoo but the laboratory animal situation and the intensive livestock unit, commonly known as the factory farm (Johnson 1991). In the latter, we have up to 100,000 animals, living under very crowded conditions under one roof, and cared for by a handful of people. The intensive confinement of animals is not new. For instance, the ancient Romans used to fatten hares by keeping them in small cages (Varro 36 B.C., p. 320), and they fattened dormice by keeping them in jars (Varro 36 B.C., p. 321).

Moore (1983, p. 17) has berated Whitcomb and Morris (1961) for comparing the confinement of animals on the Ark to that of livestock on railroad cars, owing to the fact that livestock are allowed to leave the cars, during railroad stops, for exercise. Moore is clearly clutching at straws, because the extreme confinement of animals in railroad cars is not unique, and the exercise of animals is irrelevant. Indeed, the situations of intensive animal confinement (namely factory farms and laboratory-animal situations), discussed and quantified below, reflect long-term intensive animal confinement, for months or years, commonly with few or no opportunities for animals to leave their enclosures.

Animal Housing: Requisite Ark Floor-Space. I have constructed Table 3 for the purpose of estimating the minimum floor space needed for all the animals on the Ark. For the smaller animals (i.e., 1 gram to 10 kg in mass) I have accepted the standard floor-space areas recommended for the housing of laboratory animals (Simmonds 1991, pp. 186-7). For larger animals (i.e., greater than 10 kg as juveniles), I quoted the values for floor spacing of intensively-housed livestock (Esmay 1977, p. 72; ILAR 1978, pp. 34-5), which are also comparable to those allotted for large animals under conditions of laboratory housing (Jennings 1974, p. 91). Since all the larger animals were represented on the Ark as juveniles, it is necessary for the floor-space allowance for the larger animals to reflect this fact. For our purposes, a 50 kg animal was taken as a representative juvenile of a 1,000–10,000 kg adult, and a several hundred kg (or more) animal was a representative juvenile of a 10,000–100,000 kg sauropod dinosaur.

We can see from Table 3 that less than half the cumulative area of the Ark's three decks need to have been occupied by the animals and their enclosures. Furthermore, this assumes no tiering of the enclosures, which of course *maximizes* the Ark floor space needed for animal housing, but also allows at least some of the food and water to be stored overhead. There is plenty of room left over to account for the Ark infrastructure, and passageways between the animal enclosures, although the latter need not consume much additional floor area. For instance, in coal mines, alleys only 1.5 meters wide between mule stables have proven wide enough for large feed trucks to pass through (Greer 1916, p. 999), and those on the Ark could, of course, have been much smaller.

Chapter 3

Quantities of Water and Provender Required

This chapter provides calculations for the 371-day total of drinking water and feedstuffs for the nearly 16,000 animals on the Ark. Owing to the difficulty of quantifying the possible effects of hibernation and torpor in the reduction of these requirements (as discussed under *Dormancy of Animals . . .*), I assume, for purposes of calculation only, that no suspended animation of any kind ever took place among the animals on the Ark.

As for Moore's (1983, p. 28) rationalistic prejudice against the possibility of God having provided a superconcentrated diet for the animals, let us keep in mind such miraculous foods as the manna (Exodus 16:14-36), the inexhaustible food of the widow of Zeraphah (1 Kings 17:14-16), and the possible miraculous provision of a supernutritious oil for the starving believers in a German concentration camp (TenBoom 1971, p. 202-3). However, in keeping with the rest of this work, I assume that the food on the Ark was naturally provided, as evidently taught in Scripture (Genesis 6:21).

I do not discuss specialized animal diets in this chapter, but do so in *Feeding Challenges I . . . II*. However, it should be noted at the outset that most of Moore's (1983) arguments about specialized diets are very outdated and inaccurate, particularly his citation of the European zookeeper Hediger regarding wild animal diets needing to be as close to natural diets as possible. This traditional approach is not usually followed any longer by American zoos (M. Morris 1976, p. 13), nor in at least some European ones (Prins and Dornhof 1984, p. 131). Indeed, in the vast majority of cases, captive animals' diets do *not* have to closely resemble their natural ones:

> Until about 30 years ago there were considerable misconceptions about how to feed even the most easily-kept mammals. With the exception of a few zoos the diets given were traditional, based on long-standing, unquestioned practice. . . . Monkeys were fed on fruit and vegetables, because it was assumed that was what they ate in the wild. . . . *The majority of mammal species kept in captivity can be maintained adequately on diets which have primarily been designed for domestic farm stock, domestic pets, and laboratory animals* (emphasis added, Jones 1985, p. 92).

In a similar vein, Douglas (1981, p. 112) has criticized some softbilled-bird keepers for persisting in outdated traditional methods of feeding, which, again, assume an obligatory close duplication of natural diets. We now realize that the feeding of wild birds cannot be tied down to hard-and-fast rules (Roots 1970, p. 31).

Inventory of Food on the Ark. Since food-intake rates varies greatly according to the type of food consumed, it first must be standardized. This is done by expressing it in terms of dry matter intake, which scales closely according to animal body mass (Nagy 1987). I first calculated the dry-matter intake of all the animals on the Ark (Table 4) and then converted it to the intake of actual possible foods (Table 5). The total dry-matter intake on the Ark comes out to 1990 tons (Table 4). To arrive at this value, I first accounted for gross differences in animal food intake. Mass for mass, endotherms (birds and mammals) require up to ten times more food per unit time than do ectotherms (reptiles). We do not know the thermal physiology of therapsids nor dinosaurs, both of which are extinct with no close relatives in the extant fauna. (I defer discussion of their respective growth rates and food intake until the section: *Large Animals as Juveniles . . .*). As for the extant land vertebrates, I calculated their dry-matter intakes, accounting for different body masses and thermal physiologies, using the regressions in Nagy (1987). However, owing to the fact that the large mammals' food consumption dwarfed that of all the remaining animals combined (i. e., the birds, reptiles, and smaller mammals), only the large-mammal dietary requirements needed to be calculated in detail (Table 4).

It should be pointed out that my use of Nagy's (1987) equations probably overestimates the food intake of the animals on the Ark, for the following reason. Nagy's calculations are based on the foods whose digestibility is comparable to that which animals usually eat. If, by contrast, concentrate diets were the primary food on the Ark, the corresponding digestibilities would have been significantly higher. For instance, the digestibilities of grains is usually at or near 80% (Levi 1957, p. 461), which is higher than that of most forages.

In order to convert the 1990 tons of dry matter intake (Table 4) to the actual tonnage of food on the Ark (Table 5), we need to know what fraction of the food, on average, was dry matter. Because of the need for preservation and the assumed absence of refrigeration, most food on the Ark must have been dry. Almost all grain-based foods are at or near 90% dry by mass (Levi 1957, p. 461; Zink

Table 4. Ark Food Inventory I: Dry Matter Equivalents		
CATEGORY	**LOG BODY MASS (G)**	**371-DAY FOOD INTAKE: DRY MATTER EQUIVALENT**
MAMMALS	5-6	(371)(898)(7.79 KG)(0.34 JF)=882 TONS
MAMMALS	4-5	(371)(1462)(1.71 KG)(0.45 JF)=417 TONS
MAMMALS	6-7	(371)(246)(51.7 KG)(0.05 JF)=236 TONS
MAMMALS	3-4	(371)(1410)(0.258 KG)=135 TONS
DIN/THER	5-6	(371)(162)(7.79 KG)(0.5)(0.34 JF)=80.0 TONS
(ADD REMAINING 27 CATEGORIES)		
....		
		TOTAL FOOD DRY MATTER ON ARK: 1990 TONS

Table 5. Ark Food Inventory II: Net Volumes of Feedstuffs			
TYPE OF PROVENDER (Each row depicts the *entire* 1990 ton dry-matter intake in the form indicated)	**NUTRIENT DENSITY (KG/L)**	**BULK FOOD VOLUME (CUBIC METERS)**	**ARK VOLUME TAKEN**
MAIN FOODS ON THE ARK:			
Settled barn-dried hay (Zerfoss 1947)	0.09	21,800	50.5%
Lightly-compressed hay pellet (Butler 1959). Sunflower seeds	0.28	7,060	16.3%
Doubly-compressed hay (Earle 1950). Heavy oats	0.37	5,410	12.5%
Pelleted horse food (Earle 1950). Pelleted cattle food (Moore 1964)	0.66	3,030	7.01%
Dried fruits (Adams 1975). GRAIN FEEDS (e. g. peas, lentil and gram seeds, rice) (see text)	0.68	2,930	6.78%
RELATIVELY UNCOMMON FOODS ON THE ARK:			
Fresh meat (FAO 1990)	0.3	6,633	15.4%
Dried meat (not compressed) (Ensminger 1991)	0.5	3,980	9.22%
Dried meat (compressed) (FAO 1990; Jensen 1949; Mann 1960)	1.04	1,923	4.5%
Dried fish (Adams 1975)	0.16	12,800	29.5%

1935, p. 440). Both hay and compressed-hay pellets can also be over 90% dry by mass (Poore et al. 1968, p. 527), and a similar value is reached (or exceeded) by dried meat (Levi 1957, p. 502; Sharp 1953, p. 3). Any foods on the Ark much above 10% moisture were negligible in terms of overall bulk mass (although they are important for individual animals, as discussed in *Feeding Challenges*).

There must have been a great diversity of foods on the Ark, because Noah had been commanded to take food aboard in great variety (Genesis 6:21), and because a variety of foods tends to forestall nutritional disorders in animals. If the feedstuffs on the Ark averaged 80% dry by mass, their total mass on the Ark was 2,500 tons. However, were the feedstuffs even drier, the total mass was correspondingly lower (e.g., 2,200 tons if the feedstuffs averaged 90% dry).

There are, of course, many variables to consider when calculating food intake (digestibilities, individual differences, moisture content, etc.). However, all these uncertainties are numerically dwarfed by the requirements of the larger animals (particularly mammals), which, as we have seen, account for the vast bulk of food intake on the Ark (Table 4). Furthermore, since most of the medium to large animals were herbivores, it is hay which ordinarily would have been their primary food. For this reason, and because hay requires so much storage space (and is therefore the subject of many arguments against the Ark in and of itself), I devote an entire section of this work, *The Colossal Bulk of Hay . . .* , to the volumetric requirements of the feedstuffs on the Ark. In that section, I also document the fact that merely 3–6 thousand cubic meters of volume, which is 6–12% of the interior Ark volume, sufficed for the 371-day supply of food for the 16,000 animals.

Inventory of Water on the Ark. Some commentators have suggested that Noah could have collected rainwater from atop the Ark for the animals. Indeed, the know-how for collecting rainwater for agricultural purposes goes back to early antiquity (Senft 1991, p. 25). However, in this study, I will make the pessimistic assumption that all the water needed during the Ark voyage had to be carried aboard.

As is the case with food, growing animals need drinking water in a proportion greater than a simple fraction of their respective adult weight (Esmay 1977, p. 54). For this reason, I use the same Juvenile Factors (JF) to calculate water consumption (Table 6) of the young of large animals as I have done when calculating animal food intake (Table 4). Based on the animals and their sizes quoted above, and various equations for water intake of captive animals (Calder 1984, p. 136), I estimate (Table 6) that the total amount of potable water on the Ark was 4.07 ML (million liters). This comprised only 9.4% of total Ark volume, which was 43,169 cubic meters.

Table 6. Inventory of Drinking Water on the Ark		
CATEGORY	**LOG BODY MASS (G)**	**371-DAY WATER INTAKE (ML=MEGALITERS; KL=KILOLITERS)**
MAMMALS	5-6	(371)(892)(17.6 L)(0.34 JF)=1.98 ML
MAMMALS	4-5	(371)(1462)(3.35L)(0.45 JF)=818 KL
MAMMALS	6-7	(371)(246)(140 L)(0.05 JF)=639 KL
MAMMALS	3-4	(371)(1410)(0.421 L)=220 KL
DIN/THER	5-6	(371)(162)(17.6 L)(0.5)(0.34 JF)=180 KL
(ADD REMAINING 22 CATEGORIES)		
		TOTAL: 4.07 ML, OR 9.4% OF ARK VOLUME

Moore (1983, p. 29) and his parrot, Plimer (1994, p. 127), raise another bogus issue when they claim that any drinking water would have splashed out of drinking vessels owing to the movement of the Ark. In reality, to the extent that the movement of the Ark had been a significant factor at all, drinking water could have been provided in properly-contoured vessels in order to eliminate any potential problems with splashing. Nor is this some kind of modern technology. For instance, the ancient Romans provided water for pigeons in troughs. These were covered by boards with holes only big enough for the birds to put their heads in for drinking (Varro 36 B.C., p. 283, 293).

Chapter 4

Waste Management

The Accumulation of Excreta, and Vermin Control

This section considers the alleged problems of dealing with animal excreta when under the stipulation that animal waste is allowed to accumulate in the Ark. Had animal enclosures being cleaned daily (or nearly so), and the waste dumped overboard, potential problems with manure gasses, odors, and vermin would have been almost nonexistent. Such prompt removal of animal excreta, along with the manpower requirements involved, are discussed in the section *Manpower Studies* in the chapter *Manure Handling and Disposal*.

To quantify the daily production of urine on the Ark, I could consider the use of the mathematical regressions for calculating the urine production of mammals as a function of their body mass (Adolph 1949, Edwards 1975). The non-mammalian urinary production can be neglected. Furthermore, most reptiles do not produce liquid urine but produce urates, whose amount is usually very small per given reptilian body mass (Loumbourdis and Hailey 1991). As it turns out, the urine production of even the large mammals need not be quantified in detail, as the amounts of it produced daily can be added to and subsumed by the water content already present in their feces. Consider, for example, hogs. Their feces is 80–82% water by weight, which rises to only 87% when daily amounts of urine are included (Robinson 1961, p. 9). As for cattle, the amount of urine produced is overshadowed by the inherent variability of moisture inherent in bovine excreta (10–20%; Overcash et al. 1983, p. 201). Specifically, cattle feces alone is 85% water (by weight), cattle urine alone is 95% water, while mixed cow excreta is 87.5% water (Sobel 1966, p. 27). In addition, urine production appears to scale linearly with body weight of growing animals (Overcash et al. 1983, p. 201), so no special allowance needs to be made, in terms of urine production, for the juvenile animals on the Ark.

Let us now consider animal excreta as a whole (manure and urine combined). Much data exists on the masses and volumes of animal excreta for various wild animals (Hanski and Cambefort 1991, p. 375-6; MacDonald and Davis 1966, p. 66-7; Overcash et al. 1983, p. 231; Welch 1982, p. 205), and domesticated ones (e.g., Grundey 1980, p. 42; Loehr 1977, p. 376; Taiganides 1987, p. 96; Weller and Willets 1977, p. 30). However, it must be kept in mind that the amounts of excreta produced per animal vary greatly according to diet, with concentrated and highly digestible feeds resulting in considerably less manure per animal per day than feeds with the opposite characteristics (for several examples, see Weigelt 1989, p. 7).

Keeping all this information in mind, note that we do not need to calculate the excreta production of all the animals on the Ark in detail, for the following reasons. Only the excreta produced by the large mammals is of numerical importance, because the amounts generated by smaller mammals (and all non-mammals collectively) is negligible by comparison. Moreover, the waste production of the reptiles becomes even more minute in comparison with that of mammals once it is remembered that ectotherms eat much less than do the equivalently-sized endotherms, producing proportionately less excreta. Birds, while endothermic, are almost all small, so their collective production of excreta is likewise negligible.

Quantities of Excreta Produced Daily. Therefore, in our calculations of daily animal waste production on the Ark, we need only to have gross values for the mass of excreta produced daily by a large herd of captive ungulates (expressed as mass of excreta per total mass of ungulates). Thus, using such data given by Taiganides (1987, p. 99), I compute that the 16,000 animals on the Ark produced 12 megagrams of wet excreta daily. This is a maximum value (since it is applicable to the Ark animals at their maximal size, which is just before disembarkation), and is based on the 241 megagrams of endothermic-equivalent Ark biomass, out of the 411 megagrams of total Ark biomass. (The derivation of the 241-ton value is given under *Ventilation*, whereas the derivation of the 411-ton maximal biomass (as well as the 111-ton minimal biomass) is given under *Large Animals as Juveniles . . .*). In addition, in my calculation, I allow a 12% greater manure production for young ungulates in relation to an equivalent mass of adult ungulates. This is in accordance with data available on growing ungulates (Grundey 1980, p. 42).

Let us put the twelve tons of daily excreta in perspective. This value is comparable to the daily production of excreta in many intensive poultry houses (Mason and Singer 1990, p. 120), in contrast to 430 tons daily in some intensive swine units (Mason and Singer 1990, p. 120). However, the actual daily mass of excreta on the Ark was probably somewhat smaller than the twelve tons quoted, because the Ark animals were probably fed a more concentrated diet than are comparably-sized animals in feedlots, on whose experience my calculations are based. In terms of volume, the daily production of animal excreta on the Ark was nearly twelve cubic meters, since the density of excreta is very close to that of water (1.00; Sobel 1966, p. 28), or slightly above (1.04; Taiganides 1987, p. 99).

Assuming that the average water content (by weight) of the twelve tons of daily animal excreta was 87%, the Ark animals excreted a total of 1.57 tons of dry matter daily. This comes out to a 70.5% digestibility of their 5.32 ton dry-matter daily food intake (the 1990 tons total dry matter intake (Table 4) divided by the 371 days). Digestibilities of various foods, vary, of course, but this value of 70.5% is very much in line with other information on the digestibilities of various concentrated feeds. It is the digested of the food consumed by the large animals (particularly herbivores) to which the calculations are the most sensitive. Hence, it is significant that 70% is a common value for the digestibility for various common feeds given to large farm livestock (Noton 1982, p. 78) as well as relatively exotic feeds given to the same (Lekule et al. 1988, p. 323). Ordinarily, the digestibility of foods eaten by wild ungulates vary between 50 and 62%, but even this improves considerably when grain-based feeds are added (Wallach and Boever 1983, p. 238). Thus, the figure of 70% overall digestibility of feeds is often approached or reached by a wide variety of captive wild ruminants (see Table 20.7: p. 338 in Soest 1982), especially if the food is in concentrate and/or pelleted form, as probably was the case on the Ark (as discussed in the chapter *The Colossal Bulk of Hay. . .*).

Despite the fact that the smaller animals collectively accounted for a negligible quantity of food intake on the Ark, it is nevertheless interesting to note that the digestibilities of foods by smaller animals commonly exceed 70%, if only because smaller animals tend to be concentrate selectors during feeding. Digestibilities well in excess of 70% are common for the foods typically eaten by various mostly-small mammals (Peters 1983, p. 151), birds (Ricklefs 1974, p. 167), and reptiles (Iverson 1979, p. 279; Nagy 1982, p. 57; Zimmerman and Tracy 1989, their Table 2).

Dealing with Animal Waste. Moore (1983, p. 29) has cited Neubuser (1968, p.170) regarding the "almost insuperable difficulties" zoos have in dealing with animal waste, and then imagined that the same situation must have been applicable to the Ark. As far as zoos are concerned, there is no doubt that many of them have problems with waste management because, as noted earlier, they lack even the most basic labor-saving practices. Indeed, Neubuser (1968, p. 170) is speaking, in context, about the problems of manure removal where stables are cleaned *one at a time*. By contrast, livestock-housing farms and intensive livestock units can readily deal with large quantities of animal waste rather expeditiously, by *not* cleaning animal enclosures one at a time. So could the Ark crew, as shown below.

Let us begin by considering the animal waste produced by the smaller animals. Animal droppings are commonly allowed to accumulate over long periods of time in indoor animal enclosures without any problems. For instance, excreta from captive pigeons dries and becomes odorless (Levi 1957, p. 443). Accumulations of bat guano in buildings can give off a pungent odor, but are not dangerous (Hill and Smith 1984, p. 172). Moreover, unless allowed to stay damp, bat guano in buildings usually dries and becomes nearly odorless (Mitchell-Jones et al. 1986, p. 321). Poultry droppings commonly are allowed to accumulate in poultry houses. For instance, Kimbark (1968) describes a situation where the manure from 16,000 caged laying hens (note that the Ark contained nearly 16,000 animals) was allowed to accumulate for five years without problems. In other hen houses, poultry excreta has accumulated without removal for as much as fifteen years (Adams 1971, p. 28). Animal waste in rabbitries also has been allowed to accumulate to great thicknesses, being removed only on an annual basis (Cheeke et al. 1987, p. 60).

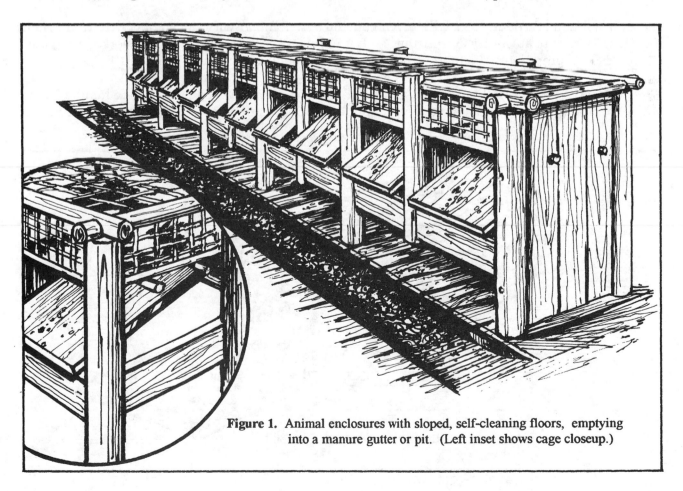

Figure 1. Animal enclosures with sloped, self-cleaning floors, emptying into a manure gutter or pit. (Left inset shows cage closeup.)

I now consider the larger animals. Moore (1983, p. 29) has cited the vast amounts of time needed to replace the soiled litter or bedding in enclosures of captive large animals. The fallacy in his argument is the implied premise that bedding must be used and, if used, must be replaced daily. In reality, if bedding is used, it need not be replaced daily, or even annually (see below). Furthermore, there are types of animal housing, as shown in Figures 1 and 2, which do not utilize *any* bedding (for an early reference to such a system, see Hopkins (1913). p. 50). Figure 1 depicts a sloped, non-bedded floor, such as used in rabbitries, and is redrawn after a photograph in Cheeke et al. (1987, p. 25). The self-cleaning floor eliminates the use of bedding entirely (Dumelow 1993, p. 209), and the slatted floor (Fig. 2) usually does also. Let us consider these two arrangements in some more detail.

Sloped, Self-Cleaning Floors (Fig.1). In this arrangement, the excreta is not in a position to accumulate in the cage, because it flows down a slanted board or chute into: a gutter that is periodically cleaned out (with the excreta dumped overboard), a manure pit where it accumulates (Dumelow 1993, p. 210; Morrison et al. 1966, p. 43) for the duration of the Ark voyage, a manure pit in which it is continuously destroyed by vermicomposting (see *Vermicomposting*). The arrangement is not only used in rabbitries (Fig. 1), but also in the intensive housing of larger animals (e.g., cattle). In the latter case, the animal enclosure consists of a bare sloped floor, which allows excreta to flow into a central channel or gutter solely by gravity flow (with perhaps occasional or sporadic assistance with a rod). A grade or slope of the floor of 0.5 to 2.0% is sufficient for the waste to flow in this manner without becoming fractionated into its liquid and solid components (Dumelow 1993; Robinson 1961, p. 25; Morrison et al. 1966, p. 43).

It is not at all difficult to visualize Noah having been familiar with sloped floors, as their origins clearly go back into antiquity. For instance, a Late Bronze Age livestock shed, discovered in England, possesses a sloping floor which empties into a central manure tank (Trow-Smith 1957, pp. 25-6).

The Slatted Floor (Fig. 2). The slatted floor is a major labor-saving device used to handle animal waste in intensive animal housing of just about any-sized animal. Figure 2 depicts the non-bedded

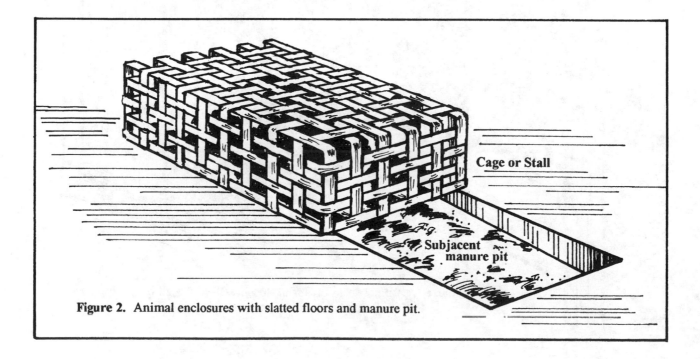

Figure 2. Animal enclosures with slatted floors and manure pit.

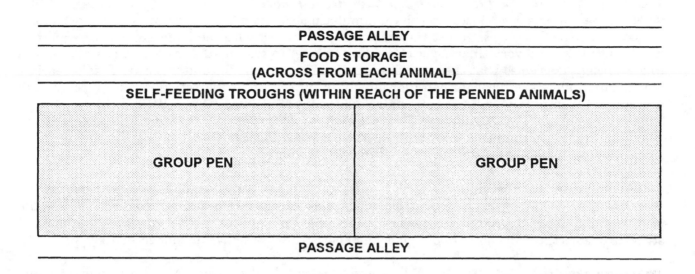

Figure 3. Group Housing of Large Animals.

battery hen cages, and is redrawn from Overcash et al. (1983, p. 145). The droppings do not build up in the cage, but fall through a slatted cage floor into a storage pit below, where they meet one of the three fates stated in the previous paragraph. In the case of larger animals, they simply trample the manure through narrow openings in the floor, or through a trellis of woodwork (Baxter 1984a, p. 17), into storage pits below. For this arrangement to function, the large animals must have little room to move, so their hooves keep working the excreta through the slats. In fact, the values I quoted for enclosure floor space per large animal (Table 3) are largely based on this need (Jennings 1974, p. 91).

Although, as noted earlier, the excreta in the pits can be dumped overboard, or destroyed by vermicomposting, it can also be allowed to accumulate for long periods of time without notable problems. This is done, for instance, in traditional Norwegian barns (Turnbull 1967, p. 33). The semi-solid cattle excreta accumulates in storage pits. Gravity causes it to separate, and the more liquid fraction drains away through openings (Turnbull 1967, p. 33). (On the Ark, the liquid fraction could be drained overboard through, for example, grated outfalls). Long-term accumulation of large-animals' excreta routinely occurs without major problems in modern intensive livestock units. In fact, despite their liquid-slurry removal systems, the manure sometimes accumulates in storage tanks without ever being removed (Turnbull 1967, p. 33).

No one knows when the slatted floor was first invented, although it was certainly used in Iceland for the last 200 years (Turnbull 1967, p. 33). In ancient Israel (Frankel 1987, p. 64), the olive oil from olive pulp was allowed to drain on perforated boards that had been placed over oil-collecting vats. It would have taken little imagination to notice that animals could stand on such boards so that their urine runs through and, then, as suggested by Baxter (1984a, p. 258) someone would note that, with appropriately sized and spaced holes in the boards, the animals would also trample their manure through the board into the pit below.

Yearlong Sanitary Bedding with No Excreta Removed. It is possible to design a situation where large animals are housed and the accumulating excreta *and bedding* are not removed for a period of a year. The key is to get the excreta out of contact with the lying animal. One method involves the use of a very thick layer of bedding or litter to soak up the urine and absorb manure to a sufficient degree so that the animals don't lie in a stinking, unsanitary mire. This is feasible when the animals are not confined individually in narrow stalls, but are allowed to freely walk around and trample the manure into a great thickness of bedding (Duley 1919, p. 14; Salter and Schollenberger 1939, p. 30). Figure 3 depicts such an arrangement. Provided that the stocking density of the large animals is not excessive, the thick bedding can absorb both urine and feces for a year (Duley 1919, p. 14)—the duration of the Ark habitation.

A variety of bedding material, such as different types of straw, could have been used on the Ark. However, sawdust, softwood wood shavings, and—especially—peat moss, would have been the best bedding materials, required anywhere from a half to a quarter of the corresponding mass of straw to absorb the same amount of liquid animal waste (Salter and Schollenberger 1939, p. 10-11).

Yearlong Sanitary Bedding with Frequent Removal of Excreta. A much thinner bedding could have been used if the manure droppings had been removed daily or nearly so, with the urine from the larger animals being allowed to drain through the floor and then be piped away and disposed (Salter and Schollenberger 1939, p. 10). Note that the urine drains right through the bedding, as the bedding itself does not absorb urine (McBane 1993, p. 57). The draining-away of urine in modern horse stables is accomplished through the laying of the bedding on top of brick (McBane 1993, p. 57-8). This technique goes back to antiquity, having found a use in Roman stables (Toynbee 1973, p. 318). McBane (1993, p. 165) elaborates:

> As mentioned, deep litter is undoubtedly the most labour and money-saving method of bedding down horses. The longest I have left a deep-litter stable (straw) was six months over winter, but I know people who have had them down for years without changing them. I have visited them regularly and have never noticed any smell, dampness, foot trouble, vermin, or other disadvantages or problems. It is most noticeable that when you walk into a box or shelter it is just like stepping on to an interior-sprung mattress, springy and firm at the same time, and the horses are always quite happy on them. . . . The secret of success in deep litter is to be meticulous about removing droppings. . . . With long established beds, you eventually reach the stage where you are hardly adding any fresh material at all, so the bed seems to stop getting higher yet remains firm, clean and warm.

This arrangement is depicted in Fig. 4b, and the small amount of labor involved is quantified in the section *Manpower Studies* in the chapter *Manure handling and disposal.*

Yearlong Sanitary Bedding with Manure Gutters (Fig. 4a). There is yet another method of keeping large animals on bedding while obviating the need to change soiled bedding at less than annual intervals. The animals are kept in stalls too small for them to turn around in, forcing them to urinate and defecate into a continuous gutter which runs behind and slightly below them (Fig. 4a). Very little excreta lands on the bedding, and very little bedding gets into the gutter (Overcash et al. 1983, p. 80). It is easy to shovel or scrape out the gutter, as is shown in the chapter *Manure handling.* Alternatively, the gutter could serve as an opening of a subjacent manure pit, where, as in the cases of the sloped floor (Fig. 1) and slatted floor (Fig. 2), the excreta could either accumulate for a year, or be continuously destroyed by vermicomposting.

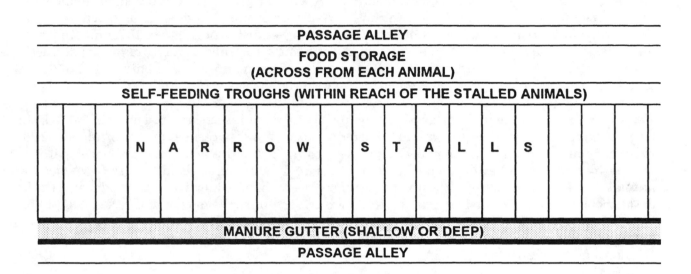

Figure 4a. Large Animals in Stalls with Attached Manure Gutter.

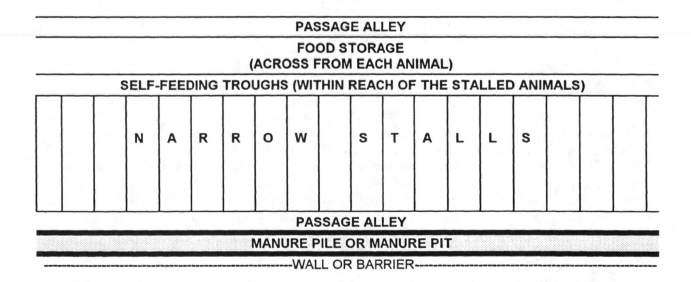

Figure 4b. Large Animals in Stalls with Manual Removal of Excreta.

Some of the aforementioned arrangements would have been even more workable if the animals had previously been captive before the Flood, and had been trained to control their body functions. For instance, it is possible to train animals to urinate, either spontaneously or on command, into buckets. This has been done, for example, in the case of horses (McBane 1993, p. 67) and various large captive wild animals (Kiley-Worthington 1990, p. 210). The urine in the animal enclosures could then simply have been piped overboard the Ark, or, as previously discussed, been allowed to be absorbed by bedding of sufficient thickness. As for defecation, large animals (such as hogs in Scandinavian-type hog buildings: Robinson 1961, p. 50; see also Wolf 1965, p. 107; and Mentzer et al. 1969, p. 389) have been trained to defecate in a dunging area, which involves only a small fraction of the total area of the group pen (Fig. 3). Since most of the manure is concentrated in one small area of the pen, the labor involved in picking up the droppings is greatly reduced.

Vermin Control. Attention is now focused on the control of insects and rodents on the Ark. Let us first consider the spread of manure-borne pathogens and parasites, of which Moore (1983) imagines must have been a considerable problem on the Ark. First of all, manure-borne parasites and pathogens would have become a potential hazard *only* if animals come in *direct contact* with animal excreta, as occurs when animal excreta is directly handled by livestock producers (Decker and Steele 1966, p. 18), or is spread on the fields as fertilizer (Downey and Moore 1980, p. 653). Such freely exposed manure could become a source of disease if, for example, the animal excreta laden with pathogens or parasites contaminates sources of drinking water, such as wells or rivers (Decker and Steele 1966, p. 19).

Obviously, the situation on the Ark was completely different from the examples given above. If animal excreta had been allowed to accumulate on the Ark in the first place, it enjoyed no further contact with the other animals, nor with the eight people, once it fell into pits below the animals (as shown in Fig. 2). There was therefore no way for parasites or pathogens to spread from creature to creature on the Ark, at least by way of excreta. In fact, one of the advantages of intensive livestock housing is the breaking of parasites' life cycles through the use of slotted floors (Curtis 1983, p. 239). Likewise, the life cycles of parasites of wild vertebrates are broken when the animals are kept in small cages or enclosures (Keeling 1984, p. 3).

Manure-borne parasites and pathogens can also be spread through airborne animal waste (in the form of dust: Decker and Steele 1966, p. 18). But since any animal excreta on the Ark probably never dried completely (due to the high humidity of the air), it probably never had the opportunity to become a significant potential hazard in terms of airborne particles.

I now consider insect pests. It is questionable to what extent flies would have become a potential problem on the Ark. Large accumulations of relatively dried-out pigeon manure do not attract insects (Levi 1957, p. 443), and neither does dried-out poultry manure (Adams 1971, p. 26; Arends 1988, p. 34-5). Let us now consider the probable fact that the air on the Ark was too humid to allow the drying out of excreta to a sufficient degree to inhibit insect proliferation. Flies would have been a potential problem only if the temperature around the manure was relatively warm (over 65 F: Robinson 1961, p. 20). In such a case, as shown below, biological control could have been readily employed.

Biological Pest Control. The simplest way to control insects on the Ark must have been biological control, a method used since antiquity. Since most land vertebrates are at least facultatively insectivorous, they control insect populations by eating any insects that come within their reach. In China, ducks have long been used to control insect pests (Wittwer et al. 1987, p. 333), and still are today in South America (NRC 1991, p. 131).

Of course, if manure was frequently dumped overboard, as discussed later in this work, any putative problems with insects would have been virtually eliminated. It need not have even been done daily. Removal of manure, during the fly breeding season, needs to be done only once every four to five days to break the flies' life cycle (Robinson 1961, p. 20).

The large supply of stored food on the Ark, along with any scenario which allows the accumulation of manure, could potentially have caused problems with rodents. A small colony of cats allowed to roam all over the Ark could have held this problem in check, as has been successfully done when manure was allowed to accumulate in poultry houses (Hartman 1970, p. 264). Dogs have also been used for this purpose (Hopkins 1913, p. 185). Mongooses have also long been used for rodent pest control in warehouses, and are said to be the best animal for rodent control (Keeling 1984, p. 10).

Decomposing Excreta: Odors and Hazardous Gases

If the excreta on the Ark had been removed frequently (as will be discussed in a later chapter *Manure handling and disposal*), all discussions of manure gases become moot. Indeed, manure odors in animal housing are slight if the manure is promptly removed (Ludington, Sobel, and Gormel 1971, p. 780). In this section, I address the alleged hazards from the gases emanating from the decomposing animal excreta, having stipulated that the manure on the Ark was never dumped overboard, and had not been destroyed on board through vermicomposting.

Let us first consider manure odors. Animal handlers frequently encounter the stench of combined animal urine, feces, vomit, and putrefied flesh, and soon become desensitized to it (Domalain 1977, p. 26). So do workers in animal housing, such as the previously-discussed poultry houses with their several years' worth of *in situ* manure accumulation. In addition, experimental evidence (Ludington, Sobel, and Hashimoto 1971, p. 858) indicates that the human nose can become relatively insensitive to even strong odors from manure gases (e.g., ammonia) in as short a time as a few days. Of course, humans in premodern times were accustomed to the constant presence of malodors, as livestock were generally not housed separately from human quarters. One example of this arrangement is the longhouse of ancient, medieval, and early modern Europe (Trow-Smith 1957). As for possible health problems in Noah's family, experience with workers in intensive livestock housing (Donham 1987, p. 90) indicates that, if problems such as bronchitis develop, they reverse themselves within a few months of removal from the situation.

The offensiveness of manure odor is not linearly proportional to the quantity of manure accumulated. The experiments of Ludington, Sobel, and Gormel (1971, p. 773) on experimental poultry enclosures have demonstrated that odor from six weeks of accumulated excreta is not significantly more offensive than the odor from two weeks of excreta accumulating under the same conditions, even when the human nose is not allowed to become desensitized to the odors. Further evidence for the non-linearity of odors from progressively greater accumulations of manure is provided by the studies of Anderson et al. (1987, p. 242). They modelled the accumulation of pig manure in a pit over a six-month period. The mass of pigs was held constant (on the Ark, by contrast, the situation was even more favorable, because the mass of the animals started relatively small, and gradually increased as the juvenile animals grew). Despite the fact that manure was added daily (in basically a linear manner as a function of time), the rate of degradation of volatile solids in the manure pit did not increase linearly with time, but levelled off asymptotically. I extrapolated their curve from six months to a full year. As a result, the degradation of volatile solids in the manure pit at the end of one year is only twice that seen after 80 days, and four times that seen after thirty days, all in spite of the fact that the total quantity of accumulated manure is greater by severalfold.

Furthermore, excreta malodors on the Ark must have been much less intense than those in modern factory farms, because the manure accumulation on the Ark did not get diluted as it does on the factory farm (for purposes of slurry removal by pipe). Note that solid manure gives off significantly less odor than does the same volume of liquid manure (Ludington, Sobel, and Gormel 1971; Ludington, Sobel, and Hashimoto 1971, p. 858; Ostrander 1971, p. 529). In fact, experiments on the odor strength of animal manures have demonstrated that even modest reductions in the moisture content of manure cause a significant reduction in the offensiveness of manure odors (Sobel 1969, p. 349).

Such reductions of manure moisture content (and also the humidity levels in the animal housing) are facilitated by the placing of absorbent substances (gravel, sand, etc., Cheeke et al. 1987, p. 60) at the bottoms of the manure pits (Fig 2). The value of porous substances in the amelioration of animal-waste odors through the partial drying of animal excreta has also been demonstrated experimentally (Ludington, Sobel, and Gormel 1971, p. 771). If, as discussed earlier, the liquid fraction of the large animals' excreta was allowed to drain overboard the Ark, this would have *ipso facto* have made the remaining manure drier and hence reduced its odor strength appreciably (O'Neill and Phillips 1991, p. 3). Of course, the greater the ventilation rate of the Ark, the less the manure odor must have been. This is not only due to the prompt dissipation of the odorous volatile compounds being constantly emanated, but also because good ventilation facilitates the drying-out of solid manure which, as we have seen, in and of itself greatly reduces its odor.

Explosive Manure Gases. I now discuss manure gases as an alleged threat to the safety of the occupants of the Ark. In the first place, the gases would have only been a potential problem depending on the manner of manure decomposition. If bedding had been used on the Ark (as previously suggested for the larger animals), the fermentation of the manure would have been aerobic (Duley 1919, p. 14), minimizing any potential problems with severe manure odors and noxious gasses. The latter are primarily the consequences of anaerobic manure fermentation (Johnson 1991, p. 144-5).

Moore (1983, p. 31) fantasizes the Ark being blown to smithereens by a methane explosion. In reality, methane from decomposing manure is very unlikely to have been a hazard on the Ark for several reasons. First of all, if methane were hypothetically to result in a devastating explosion on the Ark, it would not only have to be present in sufficient concentration, but also in the form of a massive release affecting a large fraction of the Ark's voluminous interior. By contrast, small amounts of methane may ignite without affecting a large area (Desy et al. 1973, p. 66), provided, of course, that any self-sustaining fire resulting from ignited methane can be put out.

However, all this discussion is rather academic, because it is very unlikely that methane could ever have accumulated to sufficient concentration to have been even a localized potential hazard on the Ark. To begin with, methane is generated by decomposing manure, in significant quantities, only at temperatures of 32-38 C (Muehling 1969, p. 71; Taiganides and White 1969, p. 359). (If such high temperatures ever came to be on the Ark, hazards of methane would have been the least of the crews' worries.) Furthermore, methane from decomposing manure is a much greater potential hazard in situations where the manure has been diluted by water to form a free-flowing slurry (as mentioned, in many intensive livestock units, but unlike the Ark). Experiments have demonstrated that methane is given off, from old *solid* manure, only at barely detectable levels (usually in the few parts-per-million range: Ludington et al. 1971, p. 856).

Now let us suppose, just for the sake of argument, that methane *was* generated in large quantities from the manure on the Ark. Since methane is lighter than air, it tends to collect near the ceiling (Hugh and Ridlen 1972, p. 295). It seldom becomes a hazard unless it builds up in unventilated *enclosed* spaces (e.g., coal mines). In relation to animal housing, methane explosions are *very rare*. What few times they have occurred, it was under the conditions of *closed* manure storage pits (Muehling 1969, p. 72). Under normative conditions of animal housing (which would have been applicable to the Ark), methane is almost always far below the 5% minimum concentration required for an explosion (Conrad and Mayrose 1971, p. 812). This is because only very low rates of ventilation are sufficient to keep the methane concentrations in animal houses at only trace-quantity levels (Anon. 1968a, p. 36L; Muehling 1969, p. 72). In fact, my calculated rate of ventilation of the Ark (five Ark air changes per hour; Table 7) is much greater than the quoted ventilation rates (Anderson et al. 1987, p. 247) necessary to keep methane levels, from accumulated manure, at *2–3 orders of magnitude below* that required to potentially cause an explosion.

Toxic Manure Gases. I now focus on ammonia and hydrogen sulphide—the main two most hazardous gases emitted by decomposing animal excreta. Very little ammonia emanates from

Table 7. Ventilation Requirements of the Ark (at 15-25 C)				
		HOURLY AIR TURNOVER RATES (CUBIC METERS)		
BODY MASS (Log G.)	**ANIMALS: TOTALS/ ENDOTHERMIC EQUIVALENTS**	**PER ANIMAL**	**DATA SOURCE**	**PER MASS-CATEGORY TOTALS**
5-6 (JUV)	1188/1008	50	Watts 1982, p. 151	50,400
4-5 (JUV)	1928/1658	23	Watts 1982, p. 151	38,000
6-7 (JUV)	516/379	200	Esmay 1977, p. 60	75,800
3-4	2352/1969	20.4	Besch 1985, p. 304	40,200
7-8 (JUV)	106/0	-	(NEGLIGIBLE)	
2-3	3238/2599	1.96	Besch 1985, p. 304	5,100
1-2	4686/3847	0.25	Besch 1985, p. 304	962
0-1	1738/1096	0.25	Besch 1985, p. 304	274
TOTAL HOURLY AIR TURNOVER ON ARK (CUBIC METERS): 210,000 (EQUALS FIVE AIR CHANGES OF THE ARK PER HOUR)				

decomposing manure: most of it is from the decomposition of urine (Anderson et al. 1987, p. 249; Kellems et al. 1979, pp. 440-1), particularly relatively fresh urine (Kellems et al. 1979, p. 441). Because of this, the quantity of ammonia released bears little relationship to the quantity of animal waste stored, and, therefore, accumulating manure on the Ark would have had little effect on levels of airborne ammonia. Hartung and Phillips (1994, p. 182) have shown that six months accumulated swine manure gives off only 1.5–3.0 times as much ammonia as does a swine-housing floor that is constantly washed. Obviously, this level of ammonia is tolerated in animal housing with normal ventilation.

I now consider hydrogen sulfide. Earlier beliefs about this heavier-than-air gas accumulating to potentially toxic concentrations in the lower levels of animal housing have been discounted by experiments (Nordstrom and McQuitty 1976, p. 10). As has been already discussed in relation to methane, measurements of the air in animal housing has demonstrated that these noxious gases are normally far below harmful levels at even modest rates of ventilation (Anderson et al. 1987, p. 250; Conrad and Mayrose 1971, p. 812). In fact, it is the rate of respiratory carbon-dioxide removal that *determines* the minimal ventilation rate of animal houses, even in situations where continuously-accumulating excreta is present (Anderson et al. 1987, p. 249). In other words, take care of the breathing needs of the animals (Table 7), and any putative problems with methane, hydrogen sulphide, and ammonia are automatically taken care of. Furthermore, the concentration of gases as methane, hydrogen sulphide, etc., in animal houses with accumulating manure is much more sensitive to the rate of ventilation than it is to the quantity of accumulated manure (Anderson et al. 1987, pp. 246-9).

The Near-Inertness of Undiluted Old Excreta. I now discuss the relatively few cases where manure gases *have* caused serious accidents (that is, serious or fatal poisoning of workers and/or animals) in animal houses. Countless authors (Barber 1974, p. 6; Baxter 1984b, p. 20-2; Johnson and Ridlen 1972, p. 295; Lawson and McAllister 1966, p. 274; Muehling 1969, p. 72-3; Nordstrom and McQuitty 1976, p. 7; Taiganides and White 1969, p. 361) have pointed out that *all* these instances have resulted when *diluted* manure had been *pumped out*. These cases are all obviously of a rare and accidental nature, and are not at all comparable to the conditions on the Ark. Indeed, an accumulation of old, solid manure gives off comparatively little gas and odor unless mechanically poked, shovelled, or stirred. This is true, for instance, with large accumulations of poultry manure (Adams 1971, p. 26) and rabbit manure (Cheeke et al. 1987, p. 462). If manure, without bedding, had been allowed to accumulate in large quantities on the Ark (as in a manure pit, e.g., Fig. 2), there would have been no reason to handle it, so it would have given off only low quantities of gases from decomposition. Any agitation of the manure would have been only of a continuous and low-level nature (i. e., from the moving of the Ark in the water). Since the Ark would not have any further use after the Flood, there would have been no reason to remove the manure at that time. Thus, unlike the situation in modern intensive livestock units, there would have been no large-scale agitation of accumulated animal excreta, and therefore no opportunity for any potentially-dangerous one-time massive release of toxic gases.

On-Site Disposal of Manure Through Vermicomposting

There is a very simple procedure for disposing of the manure on the Ark which requires almost zero manpower, involves virtually no handling of animal waste, and virtually eliminates any potential problems with odors, noxious gasses, and vermin. It involves the use of earthworms as natural biologic agents for the immediate biodegradation of manure under each animal cage or slotted stall (Minnich 1977, p. 208-9; Portsmouth 1962, p. 84: Templeton 1968, p. 110; Shields 1974, p. 28; Sicwaten and Stahl 1982, p. 54).

Although different species of earthworms vary in their ability to biodegrade animal manure, there is little difference between different earthworm species once earthworm biomass is equalized (Holter 1983, p. 56). It is thus clear that the antediluvians need not have had a detailed knowledge of earthworm biology in order to have successfully employed them for vermicomposting. We know that composting dates back to antiquity (Howes 1966, p. 69). It should also be pointed out that, unlike the case with some other types of composting, large amounts of heat are not generated during vermicomposting (Minnich 1977, p. 189).

The use of earthworms under rabbit hutches has long been employed to destroy the manure, thus eliminating the need for cleaning the hutches (Minnich 1977, p. 208). Earthworms have also been used to destroy large quantities of manure produced by larger animals (Barrett 1947) such as chickens, pigs, sheep, horses, and dairy cows (Fosgate and Babb 1972). Large volumes of space under the animals are unnecessary for the earthworms to be effective. Only 30 cm deep space under the animals, at least the small-to-medium ones (Templeton 1968, p. 110), is sufficient to accommodate the manure that falls into them. This applies in the case of tiered cages. Apropos to single-level animal caging, Sicwaten and Stahl (1982, p. 87) recommend earthworm-infested pits only 1.5 cm thick under single rabbit hutches. For larger animals, a vermicomposting depth of 60 cm is sufficient (Barrett 1947, p. 70). Clearly, had vermicomposting been used on the Ark, the manure pits needed (e.g., Fig. 2) could have been quite shallow.

The vermicomposting of manure is an almost completely self-sustaining operation. Labor requirements are minimal, consisting of keeping the pits moist (which may have been unnecessary on the Ark) and forking-over the manure contents every few weeks (Shields 1974, p. 29). In addition, the earthworm populations may have to be periodically thinned out (Fosgate and Babb 1972, p. 871). If vermicomposting had indeed been employed on the Ark, the excess earthworms would have found an ideal use as live food for animals. This matter is further discussed in the section *Feeding Challenges I: . . . Live-Food Eaters*, under the chapter *Insectivores*. Although most works on vermicomposting recommend that the worm beds be completely changed every several months, the same worm beds have been successfully used for a year with continuously-added fresh manure (Fosgate and Babb 1972, p. 870-1). Note that this corresponds to the conditions on the Ark.

Finally, earthworms are not the only creatures that Noah could have employed for the biological destruction of excreta on the Ark. For instance, mealworms could have achieved the same results in at least some types of animal manure (Hartman 1970), as could dermestid beetles. Thus, in Bracken Cave, Texas (USA), bats gather in such prodigious quantities that their aggregate biomass is about 271 tons (which compares to the 241 endothermic-equivalent maximal Ark biomass). All of the manure produced by these 20 million bats causes dermestid beetles to multiply to astronomical numbers (Tuttle 1994, p. 10) in the cave, and the same could have been the case in the Ark's manure pits. In addition, the manure-devouring creatures could have been recycled as a live-food source for many of the Ark animals.

Chapter 5

Heating, Ventilation, and Illumination of the Ark

Heating and Ventilation. The topics of heating and ventilation go together, as the ventilation requirements of the Ark are closely related to the need to dissipate excess body heat on the Ark. The animals' specific temperature needs are discussed in the chapter *Animals from Different Climates.* . . .

Morton (1995, pp. 70-1, 74) has used the Stefan-Boltzman constant to calculate the heat transfer from the Ark, arriving at the conclusion that the Ark interior would have to be intolerably hot before the animal-heat buildup could become dissipated. Morton's argument is absurd in the extreme, as it falsely assumes that heat transfer in such a situation occurs primarily through radiation. In actuality, as anyone with even the most elementary familiarity with building ventilation knows, heat is dissipated through convection. As demonstrated below, the convective transfer of heat from the animals to the outside is more than sufficient to have kept the Ark interior at a comfortable temperature.

Let us now address the false arguments about the ventilation of the Ark from those critics who at least appear to understand the convective nature of animal-house ventilation. Moore (1983, p. 30) and his echo, Plimer (1994, p. 128), fantasizes that the entire Ark had to be ventilated by one tiny cubit-square window! Against such nonsense, the Jewish scholar Ben-Uri, after several years of studying the Hebrew, has affirmed the fact that the Ark window was actually a series of ventilation slots (Friedler 1967, p. 5). Having conceded that the Ark window could be a row of windows, Moore (1983, p. 30) then falsely charges that the Ark design for ventilation (Genesis 6:16) was a very poor one. In actuality, the continuous slot or window running the length or perimeter of the animal house (as shown in the upper corners in Figure 5), under the eaves, is perhaps the *best* design for the ventilation of animal housing (Anon. 1983, p. 32; Esmay 1977, p. 62). Such long, under-eave slots are widely used in permanent animal dwellings as diverse as rabbitries (Portsmouth 1962, p. 35) and intensive swine buildings (Muehling and Jedele 1964, p. 141). In these situations, an adjustable baffle is used to regulate the size of the opening as needed.

Moore's (1983, p. 30) fallacious argument about the inadequacy of the slotted window probably stems from a popular misconception about the necessary relative positions of the inlet and outlet of animal houses. The intuitively-obvious suggestion is that they must be at different levels, or else the air circulation will be inadequate. In reality, when the inlet and outlet are at the same level of the animal housing, the incoming air does not, as many imagine, just make a beeline for the outlet

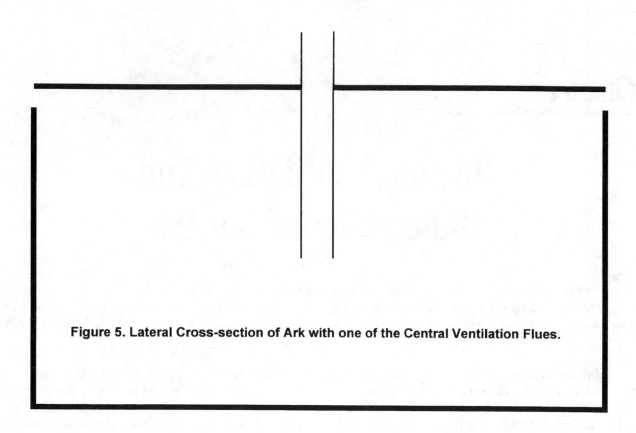

Figure 5. Lateral Cross-section of Ark with one of the Central Ventilation Flues.

and avoid mixing with the building's fetid air (Hall 1970, p. 74). Long ago, Walsh (1869, p. 168) demonstrated the fallacy of Moore's type of thinking about ventilation, and showed that an inlet and outlet, both placed at the ceiling level, are entirely adequate for the proper mixing of stable air. In fact, the entry of air near the ceiling is good because it allows the air to diffuse through the stable (or, in this case, Ark) air and get warmed before it reaches the animals (Walsh 1869, p. 168: Riley 1929, p. 126).

Air Circulation Inside the Ark. There is no need for concern about adequate movement of air inside the Ark itself. Fears about stable air stagnating were refuted long ago by smoke-release studies (Goodman 1940, p. 302) which demonstrated that air in animal houses is in constant circulation and mixing due to the interaction of animal body heat with the cooler wall surfaces. However, if, for the sake of argument, the ventilation of the Ark ever became inadequate, animal-driven fans could have been employed by the crew. One example of such an ancient rotary fan is the winnowing fan of ancient China (Temple 1986, p. 23-4).

I now compare the size of the continuous Ark window with that of modern naturally-ventilated animal houses. It is interesting to note that the height of the continuous slotted window in the piggery described by Muehling and Jedele (1964, p. 141) is 61 cm, which is not much larger than the continuous slotted cubit-tall window of the Ark (Genesis 6:16). As for sheep housing, the recommended ratio of inlet size per unit length of animal housing (Maton et al. 1985, p. 418-9) prescribes a continuous slot of 34.5 cm (compared to the Biblical 45.8 cm) for an Ark-sized animal house. In a study of variously-sized slot windows in dairy barns, Stowell and Bickert (1993) have found that the best ventilation results from a large continuous window of 2.5 meters height. However, considerably smaller windows have also been proved effective in his study, except on very hot days. When we consider the temperature-moderating effects of water, the much greater wind speeds outside the Ark (than outside midwest US barns), and the low stocking rates of animals on the Ark, a ventilation window of one cubit (45.8 cm) is very reasonable, if not ideal. The engineering wisdom of a continuous slot-window extends to the geometry of the slotted window itself. Walton and Sprague (1951, p. 205) have demonstrated that, per equal area of inlets, a slotted window allows for a greater rate of air flow than does an L-shaped slot, a T-shaped slot, or a series of 5 cm-diameter holes.

Objectives of Ventilation. As noted earlier, the chief purpose of ventilating animal housing is not, as one might suppose, the removal of malodors and gases, or even the dissipation of exhaled carbon dioxide and replenishment of oxygen. It is primarily for the dissipation of animal body heat, whether it is sensible or insensible (i. e., in the form of water vapor). Indeed, Curtis 1983, p. 269) has calculated that, in the event of a hermetically-sealed intensive poultry unit, the air itself would be breathable for twenty-two hrs, but the hens would have be killed by their own collective accumulation of body heat in a small fraction of that time. Applying his calculations to the *maximal* heat-producing biomass on the Ark (241 tons, just before disembarkation, as shown below), the Ark would, if hermetically sealed, have sufficient air to sustain 13 hours of respiration by its occupants.

Morton (1995, p. 71, 74) has performed a similar calculation and argued for the depletion of all the oxygen in the Ark. Of course, in tacitly assuming a hermetically-sealed Ark, and its only solution a "modern and extremely efficient ventilation system," he appears to show nothing less than a reckless disregard for the facts. Does this reflect sloppy thinking, or is it an intentional effort to deceive the unsuspecting reader?

Quantifying Total Ark-Animal Body Heat. In order to calculate the body heat produced by the 16,000 animals, we first need to differentiate between the animals in terms of their relative importance as generators of body heat. Thermal physiology is the most important variable. For this reason, I allowed one gram of bird and mammal to be counted as a one-gram unit of heat-producing biomass. By contrast, one gram of non-sauropod dinosaur and therapsid was counted as half a gram of heat-producing biomass, and one gram of reptile was counted as zero grams of heat-producing biomass. The total body heat production on the Ark by the many small endotherms, as well as all ectotherms, was dwarfed by that produced by the relatively few large endotherms (compare Kaplan 1974, p. 371, with Besch 1991, p. 159). Since the large animals were continuously growing during the Flood, the required rates of ventilation were correspondingly increasing. Obviously, they peaked just before the disembarkation of the Ark (when the biomass—assuming no mortality on the Ark—had risen to 411 megagrams). Of this total biomass, the total heat-producing biomass on the Ark totaled 241 tons, again a maximal value. The values I quote for the ventilation of the Ark (Table 7) are all based on these *maximum* ventilation requirements.

It should be emphasized that the rate of animal-heat buildup on the Ark is much less than that of most contemporary animal housing, even non-intensive housing. This can be verified by contrasting the animal housing density, expressed in units of animal biomass per cubic meter, between the Ark and modern animal housing (for details, see *Implications of Animal Crowding*).

Ventilation of the Ark under Different Ambient Conditions. Under summerlike temperatures, the dissipation of body heat is *the* critical factor in the ventilation of animal housing. Consider the thermal implications of the Ark floating on floodwater. Owing to the large thermal inertia of water, and the absence of large exposed continental areas (with their attendant temperature extremes) during most of the Flood, air and water temperature excursions outside the Ark were probably well-buffered. This must have led to almost continuous moderate temperatures outside the Ark. I have calculated the rates of ventilation required on the Ark (and have explained them below) under moderate summertime conditions (Table 7). The calculated rate, five air changes of the Ark per hour, is comparable to that of many large public buildings (Porges 1982, p. 168).

The ventilation requirements of animal houses are quite different during summer and winter. Once again, the buffering effect of water is likely to have prevented subfreezing external temperatures. This must have even been the case even if sunlight had been blocked by volcanic dust, which would have caused severe freezes over land areas. However, let us consider the effects of wintry conditions outside the Ark (that is, outdoor temperatures just above freezing). In such a situation, there would have been no need to heat the Ark, as animals' body heat would have done so. Indeed, animal body heat often serves as the sole source of heat in animal shelters during wintertime (Esmay 1977, p. 57). One 454-kg animal generates enough body heat to keep 16.8 cubic meters of air warm in winter (Fairbanks and Goodman 1926, p. 4), under typical conditions encountered during winter in ventilated barns. At this rate, over one-third of the air volume of the Ark could been kept acceptably warm through the animals' body heat. By reducing ventilation rates further by closing most of the continuous-slot window, the entire volume of the Ark could have been kept warm solely by the animals' body heat.

During rainy or foggy periods, the relative humidity outdoors commonly reaches 100% (Parker 1953, p. 690). The relative humidity on the Ark should not have been allowed to much exceed 70%, based on the requirements of cattle housing (Jedele 1967, p. 621), though different animals have different requirements. For instance, poultry can readily tolerate a relative humidity of 80%, with 90% for brief periods (Parker 1953, p. 690). Under wintertime conditions, ventilation is necessary to dissipate the moisture exhaled by the animals in order to prevent the condensation of water on the Ark walls. Based on calculations involving the wintertime moisture production by confined cattle (Hall 1970, p. 32), poultry (Parker 1953, p. 690), and pigs (Sainsbury and Sainsbury 1979, p. 171), I estimate that the Ark animals generated between six and twelve tons of airborne moisture per day. This large range includes not only the uncertainties of extrapolation of one kind of animal to a large variety of animals, but also uncertainties in the amounts of moisture present in floor litter, etc. In conclusion, a ventilation rate about half that of the summer rate (quoted in Table 7) was sufficient (based on Sainsbury and Sainsbury 1979, p. 171) to dissipate the maximal twelve tons of airborne moisture, under common wintertime conditions.

Overall Ventilation Rates on the Ark (Table 7). For commonly-encountered temperatures, it is sufficient, for practical purposes, to approximate the air turnover per hour for an animal of given size. One can then approximate a value for the overall ventilation rate of the animal housing by multiplying this rate times the total number of animals in the housing. On the Ark there were, of course, variously-sized animals, each requiring its own set of calculations.

Thus, referring to Table 7, I now show, as an example, how I arrived at the quoted values for the 100kg-1 ton category. One endothermic juvenile of a 100 kg-1 ton animal requires an hourly air turnover rate of 50 cubic meters per hour (based on calves of assumed 200 kg body mass: Watts 1982, p. 151). There are 1188 animals on the Ark which are the juveniles of 100 kg-1 ton animals. These 1188 animals are 1008 heat-producing units (that is, following the earlier-discussed methodology for computing heat-equivalent biomass, we have the 896 mammals and birds weighed as one unit each, the 224 therapsids and dinosaurs weighed as a half-unit each, the 62 reptiles weighed as zero units each).

I neglected the body-heat production of the animals in the 10-100 ton category (Table 7) for the following reason. Medium to large sauropod dinosaurs were the sole occupants of this category, and, being ectothermic (Spotila et al. 1991), their body-heat production was relatively small compared to that of the many medium-sized mammals. As was the case with all other ectotherms, they were neglected as sources of appreciable body heat.

What Drove the Ventilation of the Ark? For the quoted rate of five Ark air changes per hour (Table 7), external wind was more than adequate to effect the required turnover of air in the Ark. At a wind velocity of merely 5 km/hr (calm), an opening of 0.093 square meters is sufficient to admit 420 cubic meters of fresh air an hour (Gay 1924, p. 255). This changes to only 0.0186 square meters at a wind velocity of 20.9 km/hr (light breeze), and 0.0116 square meters at 37 km/hr (moderate breeze). To put these figures in perspective, we need to remember that the area of the entire Ark window was 146 square meters, and the area of the window of only the short side of the Ark facing the oncoming wind was 10.5 square meters. The total inlet areas for the three different wind velocities, quoted above, are 46.7, 18.7, and 9.33 square meters, respectively. It is obvious that only a small fraction of the Ark window needs to be open for adequate ventilation, even at quite low wind velocities.

To investigate this point further, I have determined the minimum wind speed necessary to adequately ventilate the Ark. In this calculation, I have assumed that the Ark was continuously oriented with its long axis approximately collinear with the direction of the wind. I then performed calculations based on the formula in Stowell and Bickert (1993, p. 395) for windows set at different angles to the prevailing wind. The results of my calculations are as follows (in minimum km/hr of wind): 33.5, 13.5. and 9.6. The largest value assumes that the short side of the Ark is perpendicular to the incoming wind, and any wind entering the long-walled Ark windows is negligible. The second value assumes that the short-side windows are closed, and the ventilation is solely from side-glancing wind going past the long sides of the Ark, at an opening effectiveness of 0.25. The last value is for an ideal situation where both the short-side and long-side Ark windows are used simultaneously for ventilation, and the Ark is oriented at an angle to the wind that causes the windows to have opening effectiveness values of 0.6 and 0.25 respectively. In light of the stormy conditions at the start of the Flood, and the continuous wind which was drying the earth afterward (Genesis 8:1), it is certain that there was more than enough wind available for the ventilation of the Ark.

Ventilation Flues in the Ark? I now consider a somewhat different Ark design for ventilation, one which goes beyond Scripture but does not in any way contradict it. I consider the following. As sketched in Fig. 5, the window area of the Ark (Genesis 6:16) served as an air inlet, whereas the outlets were a series of chimney-like flues that went deeply into the Ark and exited above the longitudinal center of the Ark roof. The flues draw the air out of the ark because of the rising air generated by animal body heat, and because of the wind outside. In fact, this system of ventilation works best in the presence of a strong wind (Hopkins 1913, p. 57), which, as noted in the previous paragraph, was certainly plentiful during the Flood. Based on a rate of one flue every 61 meters length of animal housing (Goodman 1940, p. 301), the Ark probably had at least two such flues. Using the table in Riley (1929, p. 127), it can be estimated that the maximal 241-ton Ark heat-producing biomass, at assumed flue heights of 15.25 meters, required a total flue intake area of 9.26 square meters.

Monitoring Changing Ventilation Requirements. How was the crew of the Ark able to decide how much ventilation was needed at a particular time? In the absence of modern equipment that monitors temperature, humidity, etc., Noah probably relied on the needs of the humans. Thus, if the ventilation rate was adequate for human comfort, it was automatically also adequate for the animals (Baxter 1984a, p. 359). If necessary, Noah could also utilize behavioral clues provided by the animals. For instance, when animals are too cold, they huddle together. When birds pant or hold their wings away from their bodies, they are too hot (Ensminger 1980, p. 60-1). If walls and ceiling become wet, the humidity is too great. The crew on the Ark must have observed the animals and then adjusted the window openings in the light of changing ventilation needs. After the Ark landed, extra ventilation may have been necessary, particularly if the winds died down. If this was the case, it could have been easily achieved (See the chapter *Ark landing . . .*) by means of the opening of the Ark roof (Genesis 8:13).

Illumination within the Ark. The window around the perimeter of the Ark allowed natural daylight to illuminate the Ark. Of course, the brightness of the sky probably varied greatly, even under overcast conditions (which, presumably, was the case throughout the Flood). In the mid-latitudes, an overcast sky can give an illumination at the surface of anywhere from a few hundred footcandles to over 4000 footcandles, depending upon time of day, season of the year, and, of course, the depth of cloud cover (IES 1950, p. 4). However, for purposes of this work, I will be conservative and use the illumination provided by a "standard sky" (500 footcandles: Hopkinson et al. 1966, p. 19).

Let us consider what levels of interior light were necessary on the Ark. Obviously, the high levels of interior illumination experienced in modern classrooms and factories are unnecessary. It is not easy to provide a definite value for the light requirements of animals, since the optimal intensity of light for laboratory animals is not well understood (Besch 1985, p. 308; ILAR 1978, p. 26). Many lab animals are kept at low levels of illumination—on the order of 18-37 footcandles (Brainard 1989, p. 70), and a considerable number of animals can be kept in near total darkness (see below). For this reason, the minimal level of illumination within the Ark was probably dictated primarily by human needs. Thus, an illumination of twenty footcandles is sufficient for public areas with dark surroundings (Bryan et al. 1981, p. 4-21). Areas of rough-seeing tasks require only five footcandles (IES 1950, p. 20), and the same number is adequate for open corridors and store rooms (IES 1950, p. 10). Print can be read easily at an illumination down to 1 footcandle (Hopkinson et al. 1966, p. 398).

The window around the Ark had a total area of 144 square meters, which comes out to 4.6% of the Ark floor area. This compares favorable with the recommended ratio of window area to floor area for the natural illumination of stanchion barns for cows (6.7%: Maton et al. 1985, p. 101) as well as intensive confinement facilities for sheep (3–5%: Kruesi 1985, p. 18). The fact that the Ark window occurs at the top (Fig. 5) is highly advantageous in terms of the illumination of the interior. When there is an overcast sky, the higher the window the brighter is the sky which is seen through it (Hopkinson et al. 1966, p. 434). This fact is commonly employed in modern engineering (IES 1950, p. 14). Under this condition, the width of the room should be no more than twice that of the height of the window above the floor (Hopkinson et al. 1966, p. 435; IES 1950, p. 14). This stipulation is more than satisfied by the Ark design (13.7m height and 23m width), even without considering the illumination provided by the opposite window.

There are many formulae for calculating the interior illumination of rooms, but these are of limited relevance with regards to the Ark, because they generally assume mostly empty space surrounding the windows (e.g., classrooms, gymnasiums, etc.). For a realistic calculation of the illumination within the Ark, we need to use a method which accounts for varying amounts of obstruction of the ceiling-level window. The fenestra method (Randall and Martin 1930) is suitable for our purposes. For illustrative purposes, I consider the lowermost deck of the Ark, specifically the central point of it. This point is equidistant from all the windows around the Ark, and, being the furthest possible distance from them, is the most difficult to illuminate by natural daylight. I have converted the data in Table II of Randall and Martin (1930, p. 268) graphically to allow for a one-cubit slot opening that has no glass. As a starting assumption only, I begin with a relatively unobstructed view which permits 61 m (out of the 137 m Ark length) of the slot-window to be visible below. The central point on the lowermost deck of the Ark is thus 30 cubits below the plane of the window opening, and is twenty-five cubits from the plane of the window. Under these conditions, 3.75% of the illumination provided by the sky reaches the floor at that point. Based on the aforementioned conservative 500 footcandle "standard sky," this amounts to nineteen footcandles of illumination, which is well within the previously-discussed permissible range for animal housing.

In order to make the calculations more realistic, however, I now allow for a much more obstructed view of the window from a vantage point deep within the Ark. Considerably less than 61 m of the Ark window can be seen from the point in the central part of the lowermost deck of the Ark. If only 24.4 m of the window is in the line-of-sight, the originally-quoted 19-footcandle value must be reduced to 13.3 footcandles. At 12. 2 m, the value drops to 7.6 footcandles, whereas at 6.1 m, the value is still 4.2 footcandles). As noted earlier, this lowest value for interior Ark illumination is still comparable to the recommended level of illumination for areas of rough-seeing tasks. In all these calculations, I have been conservative. For instance, I have assumed that each deck in the interior of the Ark is illuminated only by one window. When illumination is combined from four windows (as is the case for the perimetric Ark window), the illumination is the sum of that coming from each window at any point (IES 1950, p. 12). This means that, if the lowest decks were in the line-of-sight of two opposite windows, the previously-quoted levels of illumination could be doubled.

There is another factor, not considered in my calculations, which would have significantly increased the illumination of the interior of the Ark above the values I have figured. This is the fact that the water surrounding the Ark must have reflected both skylight and sunlight into its interior (Bryan et al. 1981, p. 5-51). Owing to lack of readily-available information, I have not pursued this further. Nevertheless, with or without these additional factors, it is clear that levels of illumination comparable to that of modern laboratory animal housing could have reached even the lowermost decks of the Ark, provided that at least a few tens of meters of the window was in direct view of the floor.

The Advantages of Darkness. However, daylight probably did not reach all of the innermost recesses of the Ark because of some of the Ark interior had been highly obstructed. Some form of artificial illumination could have been provided there (see below). However, the darkness that did exist could not only have been tolerated, but actively exploited. Near-total darkness would have been advantageous for several purposes, such as the mass-raising of hydroponic greens (see chapter *The Preservation . . .*). In addition, many animals (e.g., various livestock; Mason and Singer 1990; p. 36; Maton et al. 1985, p. 301, 319) are quieted by darkness, and potentially aggressive encounters between animals are reduced under such conditions. Various burrowing animals, when denied a soil surface to burrow in, adapt well to captivity when caged in darkness (Batten 1976, pp. 141-2). In addition, nocturnal animals, such as certain lizards (Cogger 1992, Introduction), can be housed in poorly-lit areas. However, this is not always necessary, as many captive nocturnal animals (e.g., pacas: NRC 1991, p. 197, 268) switch to a daylight cycle when in captivity.

Artificial Lighting Within the Ark. Besides obvious sources of light involving open flame (candles, oil-lamps, torches), there are alternative sources of illumination which could have been used on the Ark in order to eliminate any putative hazards from fire. In the absence of electrical illumination, biological sources of light are probably the best non-electrical and non-fire sources of illumination that have been used. Consider fireflies. They have been collected in the Far East since antiquity (Needham 1962, p. 76). Even in fairly recent times, Chinese and Japanese who could not afford to buy fuel for oil lamps, or candles, would gather fireflies into a bag to make a lantern by which to read (Joya 1912; Needham 1962, p. 76). Fireflies could have been raised on the Ark for purposes of illumination, and would have generated light that, unlike that of either a torch or a modern electric light bulb, is bright but not glaring (Joya 1912, p. 72). There are many other sources of bioluminescence that could have been utilized. For example, during World War II, the Japanese raised luminous bacteria for purposes of illumination during air-raid blackouts (Haneda 1955, p. 338), and the same might have been done on the Ark.

I now consider non-biological sources of flameless illumination. There are many references to "luminous gems" in ancient literature, along with an apocryphal account of luminous pearls being used on the Ark (von Wellnitz 1979, p. 45). If accurate, these descriptions may refer to some fluorspars which light upon being scratched, or else to phosphors (Needham 1962, p. 76). However, owing to the difficulty of evaluating this matter, I cannot consider it further.

Part II

Alleged Difficulties Regarding the Ark and its Cargo

Chapter 6

Some Factors in the Construction of the Ark

Wooden Vessels of Ark Size: Were They Possible?

A comprehensive study of the engineering of Noah's Ark, as a vessel, is beyond the scope of this work. However, Moore's (1983) and Plimer's (1994) remarks about the Ark are so egregious that they cannot go unanswered. For instance, Plimer (1994, p. 94) has tried to relegate the Ark to a Sumerian-type reed-raft, not a multi-deck vessel. However, a detailed study of the original Hebrew by the Jewish scholar Ben-Uri (Friedler 1967, p. 5) has affirmed the fact that the interior of the Ark consisted of three stories.

Which is Overloaded: the Ark, or Infidels' Imaginations? Armed with his transparently unreasonable figures for the Ark contents, Moore (1983, p. 16) has asserted that the Ark was so overloaded that it would have "sunk like a brick." Not to be outdone, Plimer (1994, p. 108) has embellished Moore's farce by claiming that the drinking water aboard alone would have sunk the Ark. His fantastic claim of "millions of megaliters" of daily drinking water on the Ark (Plimer 1994, p. 126) is off by only about eight orders of magnitude. The actual figure is 4.07 million liters for the *entire* voyage (Table 6).

These Ark critics' follies aside, let us take a look at reality. Table 8 shows the actual mass of the Ark and its contents. The values quoted are only slightly larger than some earlier rough estimates (e. g., Collins 1977). The calculations recognize an Ark draft of fifteen cubits, as there is no doubt from the original Hebrew that Genesis 7:20 refers to the draft of the Ark being 15 cubits (and *not* the mountains being covered by only fifteen cubits of water: Akridge 1981, p. 212). An empty Ark mass of 4,000 tons is estimated independently by Collins (1977) and Hong et al. (1994). The Jewish scholar Ben-Uri has suggested a figure of about 6,000 tons, along with a cargo capacity of 15,000 tons (Friedler 1967, p. 5).

It is obvious that, far from being overloaded, there is plenty of *extra* space on the Ark beyond that which has been accounted for in this study. As discussed in the early part of this work, this amounts to a surplus of 6,000 tons of cargo (Table 8), allowing the accomodation of many unknown extinct animals on the Ark, and also the birth of new animals during the Flood (if this had taken place). Of course, the extra space also allows for cross-beams within the Ark although, if the Ark had been rhomboidal in shape, little cross-bracing would have been necessary (Friedler 1967, p. 5).

Table 8. INVENTORY OF THE CONTENTS OF THE ARK BY MASS		
	TONS	**DERIVATION**
EMPTY ARK	4,000	**Based on a marine-engineering study (Hong et. al. 1994)**
BIOMASS AT START OF FLOOD	111	**See chapter *Large animals as juveniles...***
BIOMASS AT END OF FLOOD	411	**See chapter *Large animals as juveniles...***
FOOD AT START OF FLOOD	2,500	**See chapter *Quantities of Water and Provender Required***
WATER AT START OF FLOOD	4,070	**See Table 6**
TOTALS	11,000	**ASSUMES NO MORTALITY ON THE ARK, WHILE ADDING ALL THE HIGHEST VALUES FOR ARK CONTENTS**
SPARE MASS ON THE ARK	6,000	**BASED ON A DRAFT OF 15 CUBITS (Genesis 7:20), RESULTING IN A CARGO MASS OF 17,000 TONS (Hong et. al. 1994)**

The "Primitiveness" of Ancient Shipbuilding. In common with 19th-century rationalists, Moore (1983, p. 2) scoffs at the notion of the ancient peoples having been capable of such a large-scale enterprise as the Ark account requires. There appears to be a tacit assumption that peoples of that time were little more than savages. In actuality, archeological discoveries keep proving the exact opposite. The ancients were capable of large-scale enterprises, some of which rival those of modern times. For instance, the olive industry in Israel just before the time of Abraham was described as a true mass-production industry (Heltzer and Eitam 1987, p. vi), with an output that amounted to a significant fraction of today's Israeli olive production. As for engineering, we know that the ancients in the Middle East built complex structures, at least some of which were based on architectural drawings (Wright 1985, p. 464).

Moore's (1983, pp. 2-3) conception of ancient shipbuilding is likewise very naive and outdated. He is obsessed with dugouts. In actuality, certain shipbuilding cultures (e. g., the Chinese: Worcester 1966, p. 1) never used dugouts. He also erroneously supposes that the archeological record keeps turning up only small vessels. Even if he were correct, he would be confusing absence of evidence with evidence for absence. By contrast, Jett (1971, p. 8) notes the low probability of watercraft being preserved in the archeological record, and warns against viewing the absence of a certain type of ship in the record as necessarily significant. Furthermore, Jett (1971, p. 12) points out that it is difficult to obtain a clear picture of the navigational abilities of ancient peoples based on the scant evidence which has survived to this day.

Moore (1983, p. 2) supposes that shipbuilding developed one little bit at a time. This notion is an assumption (Meijer 1986, p. 1), and is admitted to be a simplistic one at that (Needham 1971, p. 389). He also tacitly assumes that technology incrementally evolved, at about the same time in each culture, and in a steadily progressive direction towards ever-larger and ever more-sophisticated watercraft. In actuality, cultures with relatively advanced technologies commonly coexist with nearby cultures that are relatively primitive (Alexander 1969, p. 124), so cultures knowing only how to build small vessels do not mitigate in the slightest against the existence of an earlier (or even contemporary) culture knowing how to build an Ark-sized vessel. What we do know of the history of shipbuilding technology clearly shows that technological progress most definitely does not show a simple linear advancement with time. For instance, the Chinese invented various engineering features in wooden vessels at least 500 years before the Europeans did (Levathes 1994, pp. 81-2). As for woodworking in general, the Chinese of 5,000 years ago (by conventional dating) already used "rather advanced joinery" (Chang 1986, p. 209) in the construction of wooden structures near rivers.

Nor does ship size necessarily increase with time in a given culture, much less with the human race as a whole. For instance, the sea-going junks of China at the time of Marco Polo are believed to have been significantly larger than those which the Chinese built centuries later (Worcester 1947, p. 27), and, for that matter, larger than Europeans built until many centuries later. Also, it is abundantly clear that technologies can arise independently, as evidenced by apparently independent sophisticated shipbuilding inventions amongst various ancient peoples (Johnstone 1980, p. 193; Needham 1971, p. 389).

Moore (1983, p. 3) naively wonders why, if the ancients knew how to build an Ark, they soon apparently forgot how to build such large vessels, and supposedly reverted to use of only small boats. For his information, it is recognized that complex technologies *can* be forgotten (Jett 1971, p. 49), or fail to transfer to other cultures. In fact, the forgetting of previous inventions is a *hallmark* of the entire history of human invention (Temple 1995, p. 419).

At the same time, we need to remember that the Ark need not have been a particularly complex structure. The Jewish scholar Ben-Uri (Friedler 1967) has suggested that the Ark was built from a series of triangular templates, each of which had been of the same size and shape. This must have enabled Noah to use virtual mass-production methods in the construction of the Ark. It should be added that this combination of "prefab" components into an Ark has been determined to be seaworthy (Friedler 1967, p. 5).

We need to put ancient archeological evidence in perspective by noting that the record of the earliest ships is very skimpy (Worcester 1966, p. 1). It is acknowledged that we are still in the early stages of the study of the history of boat structures (Greenhill 1976, p. 22). We can only know when a certain state of shipbuilding technology is first *mentioned* in writings or drawings (or as tangible archeological evidence), but this certainly does not tell us how far back this technology goes (Donnelly 1930, p. 4). For instance, the earliest representations of vessels date from 3000 BC (Meijer 1986, p. 1), and there is, of course, no basis (much less guarantee) that this represents the most advanced shipbuilding capabilities of that time. Imagine some future archeologists discovering the remains of rowboats and canoes, and then using these to try to draw firm conclusions about the upper limits of shipbuilding technology in 20th-century America!

Bronze-Age "Savages" Limited to Dugouts? Although the archeological evidence dating from the millennium or so after the Flood is meager, what little is available provides a decisive blow against the caricature of the Bronze Age peoples as little more than savages with their tiny boats.

Consider the astonishingly sophisticated maritime technology existing in India in the period 1500–3000BC:

> Lothal had an artificial dock for berthing ships—a trapezoid basin measuring about 214mx36m with an inlet and spill-way as well as a water-locking device. Regarded as the largest maritime structure ever built by any Bronze Age community, the dock—together with the warehouse built on a 4m high platform with facilities for loading and unloading—is indicative of the engineering as well as the overseas commercial activities of the time (Subbarayappa 1982, p. 177).

The oldest actual shipwrecks date only from about 1550–1200 BC (Wachsmann 1990, p. 73). The notion that peoples of even that time were incapable of building anything larger than small boats is overthrown by this evidence, which indicates that ships capable of carrying at least 450 tons of grain were in *widespread* use (Wachsmann 1990, p. 73). While this is over an order of magnitude smaller than the Ark's cargo (Table 8), it is still an engineering feat far beyond that of throwing together a small vessel. Moreover, Plimer's (1994, p. 94) claim that the ancient Hebrews were "only pastoralists" who were "afraid of the sea" is absurd in the extreme. For Plimer's information, Wachsmann's (1990) research indicates that, not only were the ancient Hebrews able seafarers, but may have circumnavigated Africa over 2,500 years before Vasco da Gama did.

Ark Length an Impossibility? Let us now consider the oft-repeated argument (e.g., Moore 1983, p. 4) that a functioning wooden vessel of Ark size (137 meters long: Genesis 6:15) is an engineering impossibility. It *is*, in fact, theoretically possible to build a seaworthy vessel of such great length out of wood, as is pointed out by Mills (1960, p. 147). Furthermore, the very design of the Ark (long and shallow with flat bottom: Jackson 1927, p. 116) mitigates potential problems with sagging. Furthermore, no one said that planks had to be used in Ark construction. Werff (1980), a member of a Dutch shipbuilding family, suggests that putative problems with ship bending could be overcome by building the lower deck out of logs, four layers deep, instead of planks. If, as some commentators suggested, the gopher wood used to construct the Ark (Genesis 6:14) had been a much-hardened wood, problems with sagging were even more unlikely.

There is evidence that ships approaching Ark length have in fact existed in ancient times. The ancient Greeks had a ship named *Syracusia* (or *Alexandris*) whose cargo is described by a writer named Moschion (Casson 1971, p. 185) as carrying around 4,000 tons of cargo. Most of the details of the ship described by Moschion have been corroborated, and Casson (1971, p. 185) acknowledges that Moschion's account cannot any longer be dismissed as mythology. However, Casson (1971, p. 186) cannot bring himself to acknowledge the validity of the ship's cargo capacity because of his admitted preconception that ships of that size did not exist prior to the 19th century.

The pre-modern Chinese also built giant wooden ships. The 15th-century sea-going junks of the ambassador Cheng Ho approached the size of the Ark (Mills 1960, p. 147; McWhirter 1985, pp. 284-5), and some 8th century (AD) vessels, intended for use in lakes, were even larger (Mills 1960, p. 147). Again, these figures have been disputed because of preconceptions against their validity, but there is independent corroboration from archaeological evidence (a huge rudder) that Cheng Ho's junks were in the size range claimed (Needham 1971, pp. 481-2). Other scholars (Levathes 1994, p. 80) are prepared to accept somewhat smaller figures for the size of these ships which nevertheless keep them within the general size range of the Ark.

The Engineering and Infrastructure of the Ark

The Pitch Which Sealed the Ark. In spite the fact that it was shown long ago (e. g., H. Morris 1976, pp. 181-2) that the covering of the Ark (Genesis 6:14) need not have been a petroleum derivative, compromising evangelicals (e.g., Young 1977, pp. 211-2; Youngblood 1980, p. 131) and anti- creationists (Moore 1983, p. 4; Plimer 1994, p. 108)) never tire from repeating the old chestnut about there being no petroleum before the Flood. Even if, for the sake of argument, the covering of the Ark *must necessarily* have been a petroleum derivative, it certainly does not follow that this presents any problem. Gold (1987) has presented an intriguing theory that oil is abiogenic, and comes from the earth's mantle. The evidence of biologic activity in oil can be explained as a later contaminant (Gold 1992). Even if his theory is incorrect with respect to the majority of the earth's petroleum deposits, some petroleum still must have originated abiotically from the mantle, as demonstrated by a wide variety of evidences (Gold 1987, pp.10-11; Sugisaki and Mimura 1994). It is thus obvious that some petroleum *did* exist before the Flood, and was available for the sealing of the Ark, if it was necessary.

Did the Ark Deteriorate? Not content with simply burlesquing the Ark construction itself, Moore (1983, p. 32) multiplies his fantasies when he asserts that the Ark would have needed constant repair. He uses a completely inappropriate analogy when he ascribes the problems of 19th century ships to the Ark. As is, many 19th-century ships were poorly built (Y 1842), and well-constructed wooden ships have needed repairs at much greater intervals than just one year. For instance, some ships built of teak went without significant repairs for at least 35 years of continuous use (Barbour 1870, p. 272). As for the infrastructure, bearing in mind that the Ark only had to function for a year, we should note that: 1) even urine-soaked wooden floors can last eight to ten years (Kruesi 1985, p. 21), with urine-soaked slats lasting two to three years (Baxter 1984a, p. 271). Furthermore, certain woods (such as the African Teak: Shikaputo 1986, p. 353) are very resistant to moisture, and could have been used as part of the Ark construction.

Moore (1983, p. 32) also imagines that wooden ships must leak, and so the Ark certainly took in water. In reality, leaks in wooden ships are not inevitable, and can be eliminated by various methods of construction, for periods of time considerably in excess of one year (Y. 1842, p. 322). In fact, the leakages in 19th-century ships were caused by defective construction and/or engineering (Y. 1842, p. 321), not some mythical inevitability of leaks in wooden ships.

Ramifications of Ark Wood Construction. The identity of the gopher wood used to construct the Ark (Genesis 6:14) remains a mystery (Wright 1985, p. 367), although some commentators have suggested that "gopher" is not a type of tree, but a process which makes wood very hard. But what kind of wood was the Ark made of? Indian teak has been found by archeologists in ancient Babylon (3000 BC: Edwardes 1923, p. 165), so it had been known to the peoples immediately after the Flood and—by implication—also to the antediluvians. Because of its strength and durability, teak is probably the best wood of all for the construction of ships (Barbour 1870; Edwardes 1923). Teak structures have resisted deterioration for thousands of years (Edwardes 1923, p. 166), and the possible survival of the Ark in Ararat to this day may be due to this fact. Moreover, the Chinese practice a method of burying teak underground in order to make it even harder (Hughes 1989, p. 166), and Noah may have also employed this technique. Some trees presently confined to India are half-again stronger than teak (Sekkar and Gulati 1988, p. 8). Other woods, such as locust, mahogany, and tonquin, are also very strong (Barlow 1832; Haswell 1860), and could have been used to build the Ark.

No doubt the construction of the Ark must have required very skillful wood workmanship. An example of such pre-modern workmanship is provided by the construction of the Chinese pagodas. One of these is 67 meters tall, with construction so sturdy (i.e., internal network of struts), that these wooden structures have withstood 1000 years of Mongolian sandstorms and snowstorms (CAS 1983, pp. 471-7). The much more ancient uses of sophisticated wood joinery by the Chinese (Chang 1986, p. 209) bears repeating. Microscopic-level wood workmanship is also no recent child of the Industrial Revolution. For instance, the Innuit peoples carved statues out of ivory down to microscopic-level detail (Levi-Strauss 1966, p. 64).

Did Shipworms Perforate the Ark? Moore (1983, p. 32) surmises that they did, but the evidence shows otherwise. Indeed, if shipworms (that is, wood-burrowing organisms) were a universal problem, the transoceanic voyages of centuries ago (Columbus, Magellan, etc.) would have been impossible. Their wooden ships would have been perforated and sunk long before reaching their destinations. Shipworms are primarily a coastal phenomenon, and are uncommon in the open ocean (Whitaker and Carter 1954, p. 699), tending to be localized in the open ocean when they do occur (Edgar 1987, p. 599). Furthermore, shipworms (notably the notorious *Teredo*) do not occur everywhere even in coastal regions, but tend to be localized geographically (Ricketts 1968, p. 359). Finally, most genera of shipworms do not typically burrow more than 1.3 cm deep into the wood (Srinivasan 1955, p. 342).

Most probably, the Ark was buoyed to open waters, denying shipworms access to it. The factor of time is also of significance. Whereas wooden structures may be attacked within months of emplacement in waters heavily infested with shipworms, it usually takes from a few to several years for complete perforation (Clegg 1852, p. 39), which is far in excess of the time the Ark was in water (1 year). However, if shipworms *were* an anticipated problem in the antediluvian seas, one or more steps could have been taken to thwart them. For instance, creosote treatment greatly retards penetration of wood by shipworms (Clegg 1852, p. 39), as does coal tar (Merrien 1954, p. 273). The pitch covering the Ark probably did the same (Werff 1980, p. 167). Furthermore, if the teak had been hardened by a Chinese method of burial in damp soil, it would have been virtually impervious to insects and probably borers (Hughes 1989, p. 166), at least for a duration of one year. If all this had somehow still been insufficient, the Ark hull could have been covered with thin metal plating. This has been practiced by Chinese shipbuilders for thousands of years (Needham 1971, pp. 664-5) to protect ships' hulls from shipworms.

The Ark Hit by Lightning? Moore (1983, p. 24) falsely reasons that, since the tallest objects on land commonly attract lightning bolts, objects in large bodies of water do the same. Were he correct, pre-modern navigation in wooden ships would have been impossible. As soon as the ships of Columbus or Magellan encountered a thunderstorm, they, being the tallest objects in the water, would have been destroyed by lightning strokes. We must also remember that, unlike the sailing ships of yore, the Ark did not have tall proturbances such as rigging and masting that could potentially attract lightning strokes.

Moreover, lightning even on land is very rare where there is damp air combined with low temperatures, but exceedingly common when there is a combination of moist air and sun-heated surfaces (Newcott 1993, p. 91). It is especially prevalent in the tropics over continental areas (Uman 1992, p. 7). In contrast to land, there is relatively little thunderstorm activity above the central oceanic regions, as evidenced by the number of thunderstorm days per year (Uman 1992, p. 7) as well as lightning flash frequencies seen by satellites (Orville and Spencer 1979, p. 940). The same may have been true when the earth had been a shoreless ocean during the Flood.

The Ark Destroyed by Waves? Moore (1983, p. 24) has boldly asserted, without presenting a shred of evidence, that the floodwaters would certainly have been too violent for any vessel to have survived them, and so the Ark could only have survived by constant Divine miraculous intervention. On the one hand, there is no doubt that the Flood was violent, if only because the English translation tends to understate the Hebrew descriptions of the Flood's extreme force (Akridge 1981). However, the certainty of the Ark's destruction in the absence of Divine intervention does not follow from this. Only sophisticated modelling of the Flood waves and currents, not baseless speculation a la Moore (1983), can answer this question. Only then can we have an *idea* what *degree* of Divine protection (ranging from entirely miraculous to "only" providential; see below) would have been necessary to have preserved the Ark from destruction.

Let us begin by discussing tsunamis. Moore (1983, p. 23), grudgingly acknowledging that tsunamis in deep water are barely even visible, let alone harmful. It should be added that even catastrophically-large tsunamis, such as those projected from small-asteroid impacts into the ocean, largely confine their damage to coastal areas as a result of runup (Yabushita and Hatta 1994). Not to be denied, however, Moore (1983, p. 23) says, without a shred of basis, that the Ark would have been destroyed at the time of its launch by encroaching waves. In actuality, we have no idea under what conditions the Ark was buoyed up by the floodwaters. Moreover, if the antediluvian terrain had been relatively gentle (i.e., a much more shallow beach slope than is usually seen today at oceanic shores), tsunamis even at the start of the Flood would have had a relatively small effect, since their energy would have been largely dissipated by the time they got close to shore (Yeh et al. 1994, p. 354). Of course, the fate of the Ark during the earliest stages of the Flood need not have been at the mercy of the elements. As noted earlier, the peoples of ancient India had sophisticated ship-launching berths, including ones with water-locking devices (Subbarayappa 1982, p. 177). If the same had been true of the antediluvian peoples, the Ark could have been launched at a time of favorable wave intensity.

There is some suggestive evidence that the Floodwaters need not have been extremely violent in terms of the generation of tsunamis. Gold (1987, p. 49, 77) has suggested that the intensity of a tsunami bears little relationship to the amount of displacement of land during the earthquake, but is instead closely related to the amount of upper-mantle gasses released during the earthquake. If he is correct, it may mean that the tsunamis during the Flood may have, contrary to all intuitively-held beliefs, been *less* violent than those encountered in recent times from "normal" earthquakes. This would have occurred if, despite the large horizontal and vertical movement of crust during the Flood, the reservoir of upper-mantle gas had been low (or even depleted), so only small amounts of gas had been released and thus only comparatively small tsunamis had been generated.

Another factor to consider is the constructive and destructive interference of large waves on a flooded planet. This could have occurred in regions that were approximately equidistant from the submerged continents, as well as other foci of intensive tectonic action. This type of destructive interference has also been shown to apply to large wind-driven waves (Cornish 1934, p. 48). Had there been regions of destructive interference of waves on the shoreless ocean, the Ark would have been safe whenever it was present in these nodal regions. The Divine intervention for the preservation of the Ark, under such circumstances, could then have been limited to having angels keep the Ark from straying away from these regions of low-intensity waves.

Let us now shift our discussion to wind-generated waves. Moore (1983, p. 24) insists (again without a shred of supporting evidence) that giant wind-driven waves must have destroyed the Ark. To begin with, the engineering of the Ark made it very resistant to wind driven waves. A major problem for conventional wooden vessels during severe storms at sea had been their tall masting and rigging, which provided a large moment-arm for wind to catch and move relative to the water. By contrast, wooden vessels which have very little surface area sticking above water (certainly true of the Ark) provide very little moment-arm for the wind and waves to catch (Merrien 1954, pp. 11-12). In fact, Collins (1977, p. 86) has shown that the Ark could survive three times hurricane-force winds without danger of being capsized.

It is worth noting that the Ark was capable of surviving waves of at least thirty meters height (Hong et al. 1994, p. 36). Yet it is by no means a foregone conclusion that the Ark would have been overturned if the waves had been far larger than 30 m in height. Small boats have successfully negotiated oceans under very stormy conditions, and have rarely been overturned by waves in spite of the fact that the waves dwarfed them in size (Merrien 1954, p. 21).

As is the case with tsunamis, deep water is safer than coastal water in the case of wind-driven waves (Merrien 1954, p. 10-11). After all, it is during the approach to shallow water that large wind-driven waves experience steepening, causing the crests to overtake the troughs with resulting breaking of the waves (Jelley 1989, p. 151). Even large wind-driven waves have relatively little energy, and this energy declines rapidly with depth (Yeh et al. 1994). When the fetch of the wind-driven waves is virtually unlimited (as occurs today in the southern ocean: Cornish 1934, p. 30), the wind-driven waves have great wave-length and great crest-length, but not excessive height (Cornish 1934, p. 30). In this respect, the wind-driven waves become more tsunami-like, possessing long wavelengths (Jelley 1989). During most of the Flood the wind-driven waves, of course, had unlimited fetch on the shoreless ocean.

There are many factors which must have greatly mitigated the heights of wind-driven waves during the Flood, and it is essential that we contrast extant meteorology with that during the Flood. In the present world, waves reaching tens of meters in height on the modern ocean are relatively rare, and occur during hurricanes, typhoons, etc. (Russell 1953, p. 32). By contrast, these vast and powerful storms probably could not form during the Flood, because the latitudinal differences in temperature were probably insufficient to support them owing to the equitable antediluvian climate. Also, hurricanes require a calm atmosphere to form, and are inhibited or suppressed by wind shear (Emanuel et al. 1995, p. 13, 759). Owing to the undoubtedly windy conditions during the Flood, it is more than possible that few or no hurricanes could develop during most of the Flood. Moreover, monsoons could not form during the Flood because the large continental-oceanic temperature contrasts needed to generate them were nonexistent due to the submergence of all land masses.

Let us now consider "ordinary" storms at sea. Even with winds of high velocity, it takes some time for large wind waves to develop. For instance, it would take a wind of Beaufort (9) strength nearly forty-eight hours to generate waves ten meters high (Jelley 1989, p. 149), even with virtually unlimited fetch. If there were very many storms on the floodwater at the same time, they would have short-circuited each other, preventing a long period of strong unidirectional wind with resulting waves of giant size. Indeed, when there is a succession of storms at sea, the waves tend not to grow to great heights before they are knocked down by the opposing winds (Russell 1953, p. 57) of adjacent storms. Note that this is very different from the modern hurricane, where strong unidirectional winds blow for many tens of hours, generating giant wind-waves.

The velocity of the wind is, of course, another variable in the size of the waves generated. Wind velocity is determined by the spacing of the isobars (Russell 1953, p. 56), which is closely related to the power of the storm. We do not know, of course, the intensities nor durations of the storms on the floodwaters, much less their geographic distribution. Research is obviously needed to elucidate the meteorological conditions during the Flood, which in all probability were entirely different from anything experienced at present.

Still another major variable in terms of the size of wind-driven waves is the tensile strength of the water itself. Petroleum, mineral oils, and organic material can calm the roughest water by greatly reducing the grip of the wind upon it (Jelley 1989, p. 152). If the Ark had been in a region of floodwater covered by oil or organic slicks, winds would have great difficulty whipping-up waves to great heights, even if all the other aforementioned unlikely conditions had been met.

It is obvious that the need for constant miraculous Divine intervention to preserve the Ark in the floodwater (Moore 1983) does not rest on any evidence. Of course, we must also remember that Scripture does not inform us what God did specifically to "remember" Noah (Genesis 8:1), but we can consider a *range* of possibilities. The Divine protection could have been entirely providential, and little different from what happens today when we pray for a safe voyage. At the other extreme, the protection could have been entirely miraculous, such as a permanent cordon or bubble of angels that surrounded the Ark and continuously deflected dangerous waves away from the Ark, or created a zone of perpetual calm around the Ark—the way He did millennia later with seas at the time of Jonah (Jonah 1:15) and then again during the earthly ministry of our Lord (Matthew 8:26). Bypassing these extremes, note that the Divine protection of the Ark may have been intermediate in character (for instance, angels *occasionally* coming to nudge the Ark away from the more violent regions of floodwater, or, as mentioned earlier, simply keeping the Ark confined to the aforementioned postulated regions of low-intensity waves). Again, only modelling the intensity of the waves can shed light on the question of how much if any miraculous assistance was necessary to enable the Ark to survive the Flood.

Chapter 7

The Gathering of Animals Suitable for Year-Long Captivity

The Ancients' Abilities in Husbandry

Owing to the complete destruction of the antediluvian civilization, we are necessarily ignorant of the technical know-how of the antediluvians, and it is even hard to determine what the post-Diluvian ancients were capable of in terms of husbandry. We do not have a good archaeological record of the origins of husbandry (Johnson 1991, p. 6), and the data that we do have tend to be skimpy. For instance, accounts of ancient reptile-keeping provide very few details about how the animals' needs were met in captivity (Bodson 1984, p. 16). It is also recognized that many facts about, for example, animal nutrition must have been repeatedly discovered, lost, and then re-discovered because of the absence of written records (Loosli 1991, p. 26).

To *get* an idea of the *minimal* technical know-how of Noah and his family, we can compare some of the animal-care know-how of nonscientifically-trained peoples today (and of the relatively recent past). Although only a relatively small number of animals have been domesticated, a very large variety of wild animals have been tamed by various peoples (Budiansky 1992, pp. 22-3). Probably every type of animal has been tamed at some time or another (Mathews 1971, p. 11), a fact confirmed by Scripture (James 3:7).

When citing some real or imagined animal need, Moore (1983, p. 28) sarcastically asks, "Did Noah know this?" For his information, knowledge of animals and their care is hardly limited to 20th century veterinarians or zookeepers. For instance, the 16th-century Aztecs had an extensive aviary, and knew in detail the specialized diets of the birds (Prescott 1855, p. 117), as well as their diseases (Alison 1978, p. 222). In fact, the aviaries of Montezuma are said to be superior to many *modern* ones (Cherfas 1984, p. 17; Fisher 1967, p. 43). The Aztecs also knew a great deal about captive reptiles' needs (Prescott 1855, p. 118). Of course, information about ancient zoos is very scanty (Cherfas 1984, p. 17), so we can only underestimate Noah's husbandry skills.

Moreover, many examples could be cited which demonstrate the fact that contemporary peoples without formal scientific training know a great deal about plants and animals in terms of practical information (see Levi-Strauss 1966, pp. 4-11). For instance, the pygmies of the Philippines not only can list a phenomenal number of plants, birds, animals and insects, but also have a knowledge of the habits and behavior of each (Levi-Strauss 1966, p. 4). The Penobscot Indians of the US northeast know more about the habits and character of the moose than do the zoological experts (Speck 1923,

p. 273). Uneducated Chinese are said to be superior to western biologists in discerning the gender of pandas (Catton 1990, p. 95). The American Indians of the US Southwest know a great deal about reptiles, far in excess of their practical needs (Speck 1923). Likewise, Aristotle knew basic facts about reptiles (Bodson 1984, p. 19). The ancient Israelites, though of course living long after the Flood, had a very high rate of literacy, and were well aware of the ecological relationships among different animals (see Huttermann 1991). All of the foregoing facts indicate that it was certainly within the know-how of the ancient peoples to have accomplished what was necessary to take care of the animals on the Ark.

Contrasting Obligatory and Optional Animal Needs. Moore (1983) raises various "problems" about the needs of animals in captivity, completely failing to distinguish provisions for animal comfort versus provisions absolutely necessary to sustain animal life. For instance, his quote of Hediger (1968, p. 17), about the need to provide "a thousand and one small insignificant attentions," for animal care, is clearly out of context. Hediger is discussing animal well-being and comfort, *not physical survival*! Indeed, in the vast majority of cases, animal enclosures do not need to replicate the animal's natural environment, even in a zoo situation (Maier and Page 1990, p. 23). Thus, the claim that squirrels require trees to climb on, to survive in captivity (Moore 1983, p. 29) and that, just for embellishment, these must be live trees (Plimer 1994, p. 110), is absurd in the extreme.

Batten (1976, p. 47) claims that some zoos only prove that tropical animals can survive a great deal of abuse and discomfort. In fact, many wild animals can survive for prolonged periods of time under the most atrocious conditions, even crated for months while wallowing in their excreta and in uneaten food (Domalain 1977, p. 119). Of course, I am not at all suggesting that the Ark was like this, but merely pointing out that wild animals are not as fragile as Moore (1983) portrays them.

Large-Scale Ancient Animal-Keeping. Moore (1983, p. 19, 32) once again displays his ignorance when he asserts that an ancient personage like Noah could not possibly have gathered and cared for so many animals. For his information, many ancient individuals of renown possessed menageries with *tens of thousands of animals* (for histories of large-scale ancient animal keeping, see Bodson 1984; Fisher 1967, pp. 23-43). As an example of an ancient personage who had an animal collection comparable to the one that Noah needed to have (Fig. 6), consider the Roman Emperor Trajan. He had 11,000 wild and domestic animals in his collection (Mullan and Marvin 1987, p. 95). In later Biblical times, Solomon had many animals, including 4,000 stalls for horses (2 Chronicles 9:25). Of course, prior to the Flood, Noah need not have gathered and cared for the 16,000 animals himself, but could have used hired help or the labor of servants, just as the emperors did to stock their menageries. Even today, it is common to hire natives to collect various desired animals (Delacour 1951, p. 159).

Large-Scale Ancient Animal Housing and Transport. There were even some ancient analogs to the Ark itself (i. e., animal housing stocked with thousands of animals). For instance, the ancient Romans built aviaries where several thousand diverse wild birds could be housed, fed, and watered (Varro 36 B.C., p. 265, 282). They also had special aviaries, called *columbaria*, for thousands of pigeons (Levi 1957, p. 506). As for animal transport, we now realize that the ancients managed and transported vast numbers of animals on a *regular* basis. For instance, a Sumerian tablet indicates that, in one year alone, a total of nearly 400,000 cattle and sheep had been received from foreign vassals (Bostock 1993, p. 9).

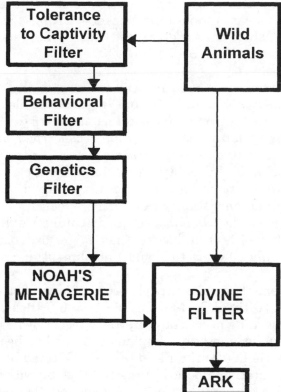

Figure 6. The Selection of Animals for the Ark.

Ark Animals from Antediluvian Menageries

Obtaining Animals for the Ark. How did the animals get on the Ark itself? Scripture indicates that God told Noah to gather the animals for the Ark (Genesis 6:19; 7:2), as well as the fact that God commandeered the animals to come into the Ark after Noah went inside (Genesis 6:20; 7:9; 7:15). Some commentators understand these Scriptures as indicative of the fact that Noah was to get the credit for getting animals on the Ark even though God is the One who did it. Or perhaps Noah saw the impossibility of God's command for him to get the animals for the Ark, and so he let God do it. I, by contrast, accept these Scriptures in their most literal sense, which means that *both* Noah and God were directly involved in the gathering of animals for the Ark. This is depicted in a flow-chart (Fig. 6). First Noah gathered the animals into a menagerie in anticipation of the Flood, and then God miraculously commandeered the animals, forcing them to leave their menagerie enclosures and go to the Ark after Noah. Of course, He also probably commandeered some wild animals as well (Fig. 6). These selections of animals, first by Noah and then by God, served as an important series of filters (see Fig. 6) for the selection of the best individual animals for the Ark (much more about this later). Yet even if Scripture (Genesis 6:19; 7:2) does not actually mean that Noah had to gather animals beforehand, he still could, of course, have possessed a large menagerie, as did many other ancient personages.

In considering the Divine commandeering of animals into the Ark, let us keep in mind that there are many times that God has subsequently performed this miracle of controlling animals' behaviors, albeit in different contexts. For instance, God caused: the locusts to devour Egypt's crops (Exodus 10:13-15), Balaam's ass to speak (Numbers 22:28), the fish to swallow Jonah and then disgorge him in the appointed place and time (Jonah 1:17), the larva to eat Jonah's plant (Jonah

4:7), a lion to kill a disobedient prophet (1 Kings 13:24), the lions to be thwarted from harming Daniel (Daniel 6:22), bears to maul the mockers (2 Kings 2:24), the ravens to bring food to Elijah (1 Kings 17:6), the fish to enter Peter's net (Luke 5:4-9), and the demons to enter the swine and run them to their doom (Mark 5:12-13).

Migration of Animals. Let us consider first how all the different kinds of animals got to the general region of the Ark. Moore (1983, p. 17) rejects the idea that animals could have migrated to the Ark region because only one type of animal migrates to Mesopotamia. The egregious fallacy of his reasoning, as far as naturalistic migration is concerned, is his implicit premise that animals in antediluvian times migrated exactly the same way as they do today, and that the Ark originated in present-day Mesopotamia. In reality, we do not know the geographic point of origin of the Ark in the antediluvian world, much less the migratory patterns of the animals of that time. Moore's argument about animal migrations is all the more foolish when we realize that migratory paths of animals are far from static, even on a subcontinental scale. Recent evidence (Berthold et al. 1992; Berthold and Pulido 1994) indicates that migratory paths of birds can change, through microevolution, in only 30 years time and 1,500 km distance.

After raising some transparently absurd problems of snails and earthworms (animals *not* on the Ark) migrating to the Ark, Morton (1995, p. 69) then dusts off the old chestnut about the slow-moving sloth needing practically forever to reach the Ark from South America. To begin with, we do not know how far apart the sloth and the Ark had been in antediluvian times. Secondly, if Noah had a menagerie before the Flood (Fig. 6), he could have gathered a sloth far in advance of the Flood, and the putative inaction of the sloth, along with its supposed great distance from the Ark, would have been rendered irrelevant. It is not at all difficult to visualize an ancient personage gathering animals from thousands of kilometers in every direction. The ancient Chinese emperor Chi Hang-ti not only had a huge menagerie, but possessed a botanical collection comprising 3,000 types of trees and plants *from all parts of his empire* (Mullan and Marvin 1987).

Thirdly, we badly need accurate information on the physiology of sloths. Up to now, I have tacitly accepted, for the sake of argument, that sloths actually migrate extremely slowly. In actuality, we still know relatively little about these cryptic creatures (Greene 1989, p. 371), least of all how rapidly they can migrate under the right conditions. Greene (1989) has debunked many old myths about these animals, and showed that they are not nearly as primitive and inactive as previously thought.

Animal Transport "Difficulties." Moore (1983, p. 25) once again is unrealistic when he belabors the panic which wild animals often experience when transported. For his information, whatever the realities of animal panic, the transport of even large and dangerous animals has been proven to be within the capabilities of ancient man. For instance, Fisher (1967, p. 32) marvels at the ancient Greeks for being able to transport rhinos from Africa. Similarly, Bodson (1984, p. 20) calls it a "remarkable performance" in that the ancient Romans were capable of capturing crocodiles in the Nile marshes and transporting them to Rome.

Much of the difficulty in capturing wild animals stems from animals' fear of humans, but at least part of this fear is caused by human predation. For instance, sea otters showed no fear of humans until they were hunted (Davis 1968, p. 12). The same holds true for Chinese pheasants (Delacour 1951, p. 187), and entire populations of black rhinoceros (Schenkel and Schenkel-Hulliger 1969, p. 22). Therefore, if Noah had to gather wild animals for his menagerie, his task would have been made easier if he had access to wild animals that had never experienced humans as predators.

However, this is probably a moot issue, as Noah's menagerie probably consisted largely or entirely of captive-born wild (and, of course, domesticated) animals.

Managing Animals Without Force. Consider the implications of Noah having a menagerie (Fig. 6), thus knowing his animals well before the Flood:

> In addition, mutual levels of confidence with each other can build up to a point where the animal has confidence in his handler and will therefore go places and do things with him that he would otherwise be frightened to do (Kiley-Worthington 1990, p. 106).

The use of physical force to manage animals (chains, whips, tranquillizer guns—had they existed then, etc.), would have been unnecessary had the future Ark animals learned to be led or moved without trauma, as is routinely done with circus animals (Kiley-Worthington 1990, p. 109). In fact, zoo managements often have to hire circus people when they have problems handling or transporting their animals (Kiley-Worthington, p. 136). It should be added that this human-animal relationship is not limited to husbandry successes with mammals and birds. For instance, various ancient peoples were able to handle even venomous snakes by developing rapport with them (see Bodson 1984, pp. 16-19 for review).

If Noah had raised animals, for his antediluvian menagerie (Fig. 6), from infancy, the handling of the animals would have been much easier. Certainly, wild animals raised from youth are tractable (Batten 1976, p. 157). Gordon (1991, p. 234) claims that there are no known cases of *captive*-bred ungulates dying from the stresses of transport. In addition, animals are easier to handle if they have been raised in cages (Ellis 1985, pp. 125-6). Various other practical problems can also be avoided. For instance, tamed skunks, even if not descented, will not spray anyone (Crandall 1964, pp. 735-6), even when crossing the ocean in a ship (Bartlett 1899, p. 157).

Success in Captivity: Microevolutionary Differences. Wild animals vary greatly in their suitability to captivity, but most of these differences occur within the created kind: (i. e., within the family, genus, and even species). The trans-generic sensitivity to captivity shows up in Mitchell's (1911) compilation of the average and maximum durations of which captive wild birds and mammals have survived in captivity. The durations vary greatly according to species. Much the same can be seen in a similar inventory of reptiles in captivity (Slavens 1988).

Different genera of bats of the Family Vespertilionidae react very differently to captivity—ranging from easy adapters to "fragile" ones (Barnard 1991, p. 7). In fact, bats as a whole vary in their adaptability to captivity; both as species and as individuals (Barbour and Davis 1969, p. 245). This is also supported by a comprehensive database of suitability of bats to captivity (Wilson 1988, pp. 250-2). The fact of microevolutionary differences in animal "nervousness" is not confined to mammals. Among birds, different tribes in the parrot family vary greatly in their ease of adjustment to captivity (Fisher 1967, p. 76), and the same can be said for pheasants (Delacour 1951, p. 76, 284). Among lizards, different species of *Agama* differ in their stress reactions to crowding (Langerwerf 1984, p. 173).

It has been experimentally demonstrated that animal nervousness is largely hereditary in origin, and subject to major changes with selective breeding in creatures as diverse as foxes (Belyaev 1979, p. 301) and mice (Powledge 1993, p. 362). Since these are clearly only microevolutionary differences, they must be largely post-Flood in origin. In all probability, all the animals which Noah dealt with were relatively easy to handle and keep in captivity. However, I will consider, in the ensuing chapter, how any problems with "difficult" animals could have been overcome even if such had not been the case.

The Screening of Desirable Animals for the Ark. If, as suggested, Noah kept animals in captivity (or had someone else do it for him), this would have the advantage of allowing him to weed out the animals that were either weak or not temperamentally suited for captivity. This is shown as the tolerance-to-captivity and the behavioral filters in Fig. 6. By the time God initiated the Flood, He could have picked and commandeered only the hardiest and best-suited animals into the Ark. His final say as to which animals actually boarded the Ark is depicted as the Divine filter (Fig. 6).

For captive animals that are difficult to keep alive, it is imperative to find that rare individual that *will* do well in captivity. Such has been the case with the Mandarin Ratsnake (Gillingham 1989, p. 87), the platypus (Burrell 1927, pp. 216-7), and several other animals (e.g., the three-toed sloth) discussed later in this work. Many other wild animals (e.g., rhinos: Player 1967, p. 144) vary as individuals in terms of their acceptance of captivity. This individual variation can even be seen in the physiological response to stressors in reputedly-nervous animals such as the giraffe (Wienker 1986, p. 371) and the impala (Knox et al. 1992, p. 5).

Moreover, the tolerance-to-captivity filter (Fig. 6) begins as a passive process, in that there is weeding out of individual animals, not well suited to captivity, due to the deaths of weak individual animals. This must also have taken place in Noah's menagerie, enabling him to replace the animals that had died, and ending up with a stock of animals quite resistant to the stresses of captivity by the time the Ark was to be boarded. Indeed, a wide variety of studies have demonstrated an asymptotic decline in the death rate of captive wild-animal individuals as their time in captivity increases from days to months to years. This has, for instance, been seen with captive bats (Rasweiller 1973, p. 395; 1977, p. 532, 564), reptiles (Cowan 1980, p. 191), and with various birds and mammals. The latter is evidenced by the usually small difference between mean and maximum durations of survival in captivity (Eisenberg 1981, pp. 472-5; Mitchell 1911, pp. 486, 541-3).

Habituation of Animals to the Stresses of the Ark Voyage. Moore (1983, p. 25) belabors the terror of wild animals in transit, and then imagines that this would have been applicable to the animals on the Ark. Apart from the factors already discussed, Moore completely ignores the effects of habituation:

> In fact, most animals will usually become accustomed to strange or inappropriate physical conditions over time (provided that those conditions are kept constant) (Martin 1975, p. 159).

For instance, dangerous panic reactions from elephants exposed to loud noises can be avoided by allowing the animals to get used to them (Kiley-Worthington 1990, p. 121). Likewise, pigeons soon become habituated to the reports of rifles, as well as to bomb explosions (Levi 1957, p. 373). Experiments with hogs placed into continuously-shaking crates demonstrates that their nervous reactions wear off after the first few hours of such treatment (Curtis 1983, p. 223). This process of habituation is also true of more "delicate" animals. For instance, flamingos come to ignore nearby train and airplane traffic (Allen 1956, pp. 214-215), whereas cranes become desensitized to nearby humans and motor vehicles (Roberts and Landfried 1987, p. 143). Giraffes, well known for their nervousness in captivity, can be conditioned to accept their enclosures calmly without the need of sedatives (Wienker 1986. p. 374).

It is interesting to note that the animals were on the Ark a full week before the Flood began (Genesis 7:4,10). This was probably to accustom the animals to the Ark itself. George (1982, p. 71) recommends that cuscuses be kept in the box they are to be transported in for a week or two before departure. Rhinos are held in bomas and are fed in travelling crates for two weeks prior to travel (Merz 1991, p. 27). This is to accustom them to their new surroundings, as well as close confinement, before they are subject to the additional stresses of transport. Not surprisingly, the rhinos become much easier to handle and are much less stressed by their journeys (Merz 1991, p. 27).

Once the Ark began moving in water, the animals must have become habituated to the movement itself. Thus, livestock that are transported by ship will only suffer from seasickness for one or two days and then their behavior will return to normal (Platte 1982, p. 183). Other animals (e.g., rhinos: Player 1967, p. 145) are undisturbed by bad weather at sea.

Boarding the Ark Itself. Armed with a straw man—the absurdly bloated numbers of animals on the Ark—detractors of the Biblical account make another unwarranted charge: there would not be enough time for the animals to enter the Ark in the allotted time (Genesis 7:13-16): whether one day (Moore 1983, p. 21) or even one week (Morton 1995, p. 68). Let us assume that the larger animals (i. e., those 100 kg when adults) entered the Ark no faster than do animals of comparable size when killed in and processed in slaughterhouses (i. e., 1000 hogs per hour: Clifton 1991, p. 41). Smaller animals, of course, must have boarded the Ark at a rate of several times that of the larger ones. It is easy to see that the 16,000 animals could have boarded the Ark in, at most, five hours. Of course, this assumes single-file entry, but there is no reason why several lines of animals could not have entered the Ark simultaneously, especially the many small to medium animals. Scripture, of course, does not inform us about the width of the Ark door.

Morton (1995, p. 68) raises another contrived problem when he asserts that Noah must have exerted himself to a herculean extent in order to cage even a smaller number of animals. Morton proposes, without a shred of supporting evidence, that Noah had to escort each animal, *one at a time*, from the outside of the Ark, up the ramps, to the appropriate enclosure within. Against such nonsense, we note that, when God commandeered the animals into the Ark (Genesis 6:20; 7:9; 7:15), He could have had them move up the ramps en masse (again, like cows to slaughter). Let us assume that the Ark crew had been involved in the caging procedure itself. Each animal (or group of animals) need only have been called and pulled into the proper enclosure, followed by the locking of each enclosure door. This need have taken only a few seconds average per animal, and have required only a light to moderate amount of physical exertion.

The Sexing of Monomorphic Animals

Since many animals do not show visible differences between males and females, Moore (1983, p. 19) imagines that Noah would have no way of knowing if he has an opposite-sex pair of animals on the Ark in every case. Of course, since God commandeered the animals into the Ark (Fig. 6), He certainly knew their gender and whether or not they were compatible and fertile, but that is not the point. I show that Noah himself could have determined the gender of monomorphic animals.

First of all, it is important to know that many if not most monomorphic animals actually reveal subtle differences between the genders once they are closely observed. For instance, non-scientifically trained Chinese hunters can distinguish between male and female pandas by relatively small differences in morphology and/or behavior (Catton 1990, p. 95). Among many "monomorphic" birds, there turn out to be subtle differences in body plumage, especially during the time of mating (Goodwin 1984, p. 49: Smith 1983, p. 30), which can be reliably used to distinguish male from female. In other such birds, there are slight but noticeable differences in the genital region during the mating season (Mason 1938, p. 47; Vriends 1985, p. 151). Furthermore, many monomorphic birds give away their gender by their behavior (Smith 1983, p. 31). The most reliable way to sex monomorphic animals is to put several of them together and then observe which ones will pair off and mate (Alderton 1986, pp. 62-3; Thompson 1983, p. 195). This pairbonding assures not only that the individuals are of opposite sexes, but that they are behaviorally compatible. If Noah had a menagerie before the Flood, he could have employed the behavioral filter (Fig. 6) by experimenting with pairbonding in order to verify the gender and compatibility of pairs of animals for the Ark. He could have also observed which pairs gave rise to offspring so that he could be certain which pairs were fertile.

However, all the foregoing discussion assumes that sexual monomorphism existed at the time of the Flood. It is possible that sexual monomorphism has arisen, through microevolution, only since the Flood. Evidence for this includes the presence of monomorphic species of parrots within the same genus as slightly dimorphic ones (Smith 1983, p. 30).

Large Animals as Juveniles: The Implications

This section discusses in detail the growth, feeding, and alleged difficulties of taking animals on the Ark as juveniles. On the Ark, only animals larger than 10 kg were represented as juveniles, because the young of smaller animals would have been near or at adult size by the time of their disembarkation from the Ark (Calder 1984), and their food intake would have been comparable to that of the adult.

There are various advantages in using juveniles besides the greatly reduced feeding/watering and waste-disposal requirements. Juveniles tend to be much more tractable than adults, as can be seen from rhinos (Gleeson 1933, p. 171), the platypus (Burrell 1927, p. 217), and many other creatures. Perhaps only one in ten raccoons, raised by humans since infancy, remain docile after reaching puberty (Mathews 1971, p. 73).

Juvenile Mortality Problems? Moore (1983, p. 11) has objected to the taking of juveniles on the Ark for several reasons. His remark about the unweaned kitten on the Ark is too juvenile (pardon the pun) to merit a response. He also supposes that the high death rates of young animals would have vitiated their use on the Ark. There are several fallacies of his argument. In the first place, the juveniles of many large animals (which, of course, would be the only animals represented as juveniles on the Ark) have a low overall death rate (for tabulation, see Promislow and Harvey 1990). Secondly, the high rates of juvenile mortality seen in wild animal populations are primarily due to exogenous factors (e. g., starvation, predation) which would not have been experienced by captive animals. The mortality rate of properly cared-for captive wild animal juveniles is small. For instance, a survey of the juvenile deaths among 112 births of a variety of captive wild ungulates (Ralls et al. 1979, p. 1102) indicates only twenty-three deaths in the first six months after birth. While this does not equal the full year of captivity on the Ark, the additional deaths from six months to one year must be inconsequential (see below). Moreover, Ralls' total also includes premature births and stillbirths which, of course, would not have been taken on the Ark.

Moreover, it is the *timing* of most juvenile deaths that is paramount. The relatively small endogenous juvenile mortality rate that does occur in captive animals displays a very steep asymptotic decline in only the first few days to weeks of life. For instance, in a study of the births among noninbred parents of the Speke's gazelle, Templeton and Read (1983, p. 246) found that, of the thirty-three deaths among juveniles that took place within the first year after birth, twenty-four of these occurred within the first thirty days. Among captive pandas, relatively few juveniles die after the first eight days postpartum (Jinchu 1990, p. 325).

The very rapid decline in the death rate of very young animals has long been known for a wide variety of animals (e.g., Mitchell 1911, p. 427), including young primates (Kirkwood and Stathatos 1992, p. 1), and is characteristic of mammals in general (Loudon 1985, p. 185). The same holds true for domesticated animals. For instance, lambs are well-known for their high postpartum mortality rates, yet 73% of lamb deaths that will occur in the first forty-five days after birth will take place in only the first 5 days (Safford and Hoversland 1960, p. 272). The same high juvenile mortality, in the first few days of life, is characteristic of ibex (Geist 1971, pp. 284-5), as well as many farm animals such as calves and piglets (Curtis 1983, pp. 111-112).

Keeping all this in mind, the solution to the "problem" of juvenile mortality is obvious. Noah could have kept only juveniles at least a few weeks old in his menagerie (Fig. 6). Those neonates that had been born with developmental defects would have been already weeded out by death in the first few days or weeks of postpartum life. In addition, Noah could have examined these few week-old juveniles to judge which were the strongest, and retained only those to be later taken by God into the Ark. Of course, when God actually commandeered the animals into the Ark (Genesis 6:20, etc.), He could have chosen those particular juvenile animals which He foreknew were healthy, thus once again exercising the Divine filter (Fig. 6).

Juveniles' Deaths on the Ark in Perspective. At the same time, it must be realized that, barring Divine miraculous intervention, it is unavoidable that a certain small fraction of the animals must have died on the Ark, irrespective of their age. Plimer (1994, p. 124) says that the Ark would have been a failure if only one animal aboard died. His bold claim is an egregious assumption, as nowhere does the Bible state that *all* the animals taken on the Ark were still alive at the time of their disembarkation a year later! The fossil record demonstrates that it was not His will for all the animals that He had originally created to have survived the Flood, at least on a long-term basis. Earlier in this work, I had answered Morton's (1995) argument about animals on the Ark being there in vain if their fate had been eventual extinction.

It is difficult to quantify the possible death rate on the Ark. Experience with early twentieth century zoos suggests a 10–20% annual mortality rate (Ratcliffe 1956, p. 11). This range is far too high for the Ark, as it is applicable to animals that have had little previous experience in captivity. If, as discussed earlier, Noah had a menagerie before the Flood, most of the weaker animals must have already died off before the time came to board the Ark, having passed through all the filters shown in Fig. 6. This would have guaranteed a very low mortality rate of animals on the Ark.

Quantifiable Advantages of Juveniles: Animal Biomass on the Ark. The juvenile of large animals were, of course, gaining weight as they grew, so the overall biomass on the Ark increased greatly as the Flood year went on. The minimal biomass on the Ark is the aggregate mass of the animals just after they had boarded the Ark. It comes out to approximately 111 megagrams, or metric tons (Table 8). To arrive at this number, I have considered the masses of the largest extant land animals a few weeks after birth. Based on the neonate masses of medium to large mammals (Saether and Gordon 1994, p. 267), and allowing for the aforementioned few-weeks growth, I used a value of 100 kg for a few-week old juvenile of a 1–10 ton adult, 30 kg for the same of a 100 kg-1 ton adult, and 5 kg for the few week-old juvenile of a 10–100 kg adult. For a few week-old sauropod hatchling (eventual mass of 10–100 tons), I have assumed a mass (see below) of 10–20 kg (Lockley

1994, p. 359). For juveniles of smaller dinosaurs, I have assumed growth rates comparable to that of mammals, reflecting their probable thermal physiology.

In order to arrive at the *maximal* biomass on the Ark, (i.e., 411 metric tons at the time of disembarkation, shown in Table 8; having assuming zero mortality on the Ark), I used the following procedure. I took the yearling masses quoted in the ensuing paragraph and multiplied them by the number of animals of the given body-mass category. For smaller animals which, of course, had been adults on the Ark all along, I multiplied the number of animals of each respective body-mass category by the arithmetic mean of each category.

Quantifiable Advantages of Juveniles: Housing. In order to calculate the savings of floor space caused by the taking of juveniles instead of adults of large animals, we need to contrast their respective housing requirements. Since the floor-space calculations are very sensitive to the space required by the relatively few large animals (see Table 3), and the large animals were continuously growing, we need to know the maximum size of each juvenile (i. e., at the end of the 371-day Ark period). This has been determined by utilizing the juveniles' sizes just a few weeks past yearling age. The data for yearling masses of various medium to large mammals was obtained for the rhinoceros (Hagenbeck 1966, p. 86), elephant (Sikes 1971, p. 128), and a few other animals. These approximate body masses are: 10 kg (for an average 32 kg animal of 10–100 kg adults), 100 kg (for an average (316 kg) animal of 100 kg-1 ton adults), 300 kg (for an average (3.16 ton) animal of 1–10 ton adults), and 1 ton (for yearlings of average 31.6 ton sauropod of the 10–100 tons category. The floor-space requirements for juveniles of large animals (Table 3), discussed toward the beginning of this work, is based on these data.

Quantifiable Advantages of Juveniles: Feeding/Watering. Since the regressions of food and water consumption (Nagy 1987; Calder 1984) are applicable to adult animals, I have generated a conversion factor, which I call JF (Juvenile Factor), and used it, as shown in Tables 4 and 6, to convert the adult intake to juvenile animal intake. However, we must note that the Juvenile Factors (JF) I quote below (and use in Tables 4 and 6) are not the lowest values that could have been applicable to the animals in question. Growing animals can be fed reduced rations for a year and then be allowed to catch up at a later time (Acker 1983, p. 139). In our case, of course, the catch-up could have occurred after their release from the Ark. My calculations of the JF are thus conservative, as I have not allowed for any such deliberate reduction in the feeding of young animals.

I now demonstrate the calculation of the JF for medium to large mammals (spanning the range of 10 kg all the way to 10 tons). This calculation is paramount, owing to the fact that it was mammals of this size which accounted for the largest share of food/water consumption, and waste production, on the Ark. As the large mammals were growing continuously on the Ark, their body masses increased nonlinearly. At the same time, the metabolic requirements per unit body mass either decreased during growth, or followed a more complex pattern of increase followed by decrease (Kirkwood 1991, p. S32). For purposes of this study, I have evaluated the actual food requirements of several medium to large mammals during their growth over a 371-day period. Using the sources of data below, I graphed the progressively-increasing food requirements of the growing animals. I then counted the squares under each food-consumption curve, and expressed this total as a fraction of the squares occurring under the food-intake horizontal curve of the respective adult for the same 371-day period.

The results are as follows, beginning with the 10–100 kg body weight category. Based on the energy requirement and growth curves of the juveniles of large dogs (Lewis et al. 1987, p. 1-6; Church 1991, p. 450), growth curves plus food intake of growing pigs (Brody 1945, p. 492; Ensminger 1991) and the same for growing deer (French et al. 1956), I have arrived at 0.45 as the JF (Juvenile Factor) for juveniles of 10–100 kg adults. With regards to the 100 kg–1 ton adult mammals, I have evaluated growth curves and food intake of growing horses (Willoughby 1975, p. 53, 142-5; Pelliner 1992, p. 148) and calves (Brody 1945, p. 492; Acker 1983, p. 79; Ensminger 1991) as well as general figures for the upper limits of food intake of young lions (Schaller 1972, p. 278). From this, I arrive at a value of 0.34 as the JF for juveniles of 100 kg–1 ton adults. As for the 1–10 adult mammal body-weight category, I have relied on growth curves and food intake of young elephants (Laws et al. 1975, p. 169; Reuther 1969, p. 172; Sikes 1971, p. 97; Sukumar 1989, p. 56, 125). From these data, I have concluded that the JF of a 3.16 ton adult comes out to 0.05. As for heavier animals, there are no known land mammals that much exceed ten tons adult weight. The largest known land mammal, the extinct rhinoceros *Indrichotherium* (formerly *Baluchitherium*), once believed to have reached 20–30 tons, is now thought to have averaged only eleven tons (Fortelius 1993).

The Juveniles of Therapsids and Dinosaurs. The 10–100 ton category consists entirely of the medium-to-large sauropod dinosaurs, which I consider first. Based on evidence from dinosaurs whose nests have been found, and on various physiological constraints, each sauropod hatchling must have been small, as it was only one out of a clutch of many eggs (Janis and Carrano 1992, p. 210). As noted earlier, the sauropods must have been ectothermic or nearly so (Spotila et al. 1991). For these reasons, growth curves and calculated juveniles' food intake for sauropods have been based on extrapolations of the same for modern large reptiles, beginning with very small hatchlings.

In order to arrive at values for the Juvenile Factors of non-sauropod dinosaurs, and of therapsids, we must first take into account their respective thermal physiologies. Long considered to be little more than oversized lizards, dinosaurs came to be considered possibly endothermic because of a wide variety of evidences cited in the 1970's and 1980's. It is now recognized that most of these alleged evidences are inconclusive (Barrick and Showers 1994, p. 222; Chinsamy 1993, p. 107; Ruben 1995, p. 89), and that different dinosaurs probably employed a variety of strategies for thermoregulation. It is currently believed that dinosaurs below sauropod size may have been either endothermic or ectothermic (Spotila et al. 1991), with the proven ability of at least some of them to forage (for altricial young in nests) being indicative of at least a partial endothermy (Lambert 1991). Very probably they had a thermal physiology between that observed in modern birds and mammals on one hand, and modern reptiles on the other (Barrick and Showers 1994). The same type of transitional thermal physiology was probably operative in therapsids (Hillenius 1994).

In order to make these findings applicable to the JF (Juvenile Factor) calculations regarding the therapsids and dinosaurs, I have calculated food-consumption rates for both therapsids and non-sauropod dinosaurs by assuming that their metabolic rates averaged 50% of that of mammals of identical size. (If, however, most dinosaurs were ectothermic as are modern reptiles, their metabolic rates would have only been 14% of that of comparably-sized mammals: Farlow 1976). The growth rates of the very young of large therapsids and large non-sauropod dinosaurs were probably intermediate between those expected for modern reptiles and modern mammals (Chinsamy and Dodson 1995, p. 180). However, I have made our challenge more difficult by assuming that these rates were comparable to that seen in equivalent-sized mammals. For this reason, I have used the same Juvenile Factors for these creatures as I have for the young of large mammals elsewhere in this work. As for sauropod dinosaurs, the calculation of their growth rates and yearling sizes presents a problem, as they have no extant analogs. Simple extrapolations of known reptilian, avian, or mammalian growth rates to a 10–100 ton adult size result in biologically unrealistic values. For instance, projecting reptilian rates (applicable to their relatively linear period of growth) suggests a yearling-sauropod body mass of only a few hundred kg., which would require an unrealistically-long century (or more) to reach maturity (Case 1978, p. 323). However, more recent estimates of juvenile reptilian growth rate (Ruben 1995, pp. 87-8) shows its great variability, with growth velocities sometimes comparable to that of some young placental mammals.Yet, the scaling of mammalian growth rates to sauropod size (Zullinger et al. 1984, pp. 625-7) results in absurdly high juvenile growth rates which would be physically impossible for an ectotherm to sustain.

As is the case with other dinosaurs, the young of the large sauropods probably grew at rates intermediate between that of endotherms and ectotherms (Chinsamy and Dodson 1995, p. 180), but were closer to the latter, since sauropods themselves were ectotherms. For this reason, I have taken only the lower range of K-values (i.e., daily rate of increase) for large mammals (Zullinger et al. 1984, p. 625) and extrapolated them to sauropod size. Using them to solve the von Bertanfly growth equations, I arrive at an estimate of about one to three tons as the mass of a yearling sauropod. The lower value is applicable to an average sauropod of about thirty tons adult mass (Peczkis 1995), whereas the larger one is for a giant sauropod (70–100 tons adult mass). The 1–3 ton value is consistent with the sizes of actual skeletons of sauropods reckoned to be yearlings at the time of death (Lockley 1994, pp. 358-9), when converted to body mass according to the pelvic-scaling method of Colbert (1962). However, the upper range of the 1–3 ton value may be excessive, as sauropod growth on the Ark may have been retarded by relatively low temperatures and/or reduced food rations (as has been experimentally done with small ectotherms: Sinervo and Adolph 1994, and citations therein). Therefore, for our purposes, I have adopted a value of one ton to represent the yearling mass of every sauropod on the Ark.

Quantifiable Advantages of Juveniles: Excreta Generated. When calculating manure and urine production, I have relied on the same scaling factors for manure production as I have for the food intake (which, of course, follows from the fact that manure is the undigested fraction of the food, whose intake has already been calculated (Table 4), and is elaborated below). Urinary water loss closely parallels metabolism (Edwards 1975, p. 65), at least in mammals, so no additional factor is necessary to account for the urine production of juveniles. Of course, as discussed much earlier, the amount of urine produced is dwarfed by the moisture present in manure, so a separate calculation of urine production is unnecessary.

Dwarf Races to Represent Large Animals on the Ark. Up to now, I have considered the taking of juveniles as the only method for reducing the size and corresponding needs of large animals on the Ark. There is another method available, in addition or instead of, the juvenile-animal option. It follows from the fact that most medium to large animals have dwarf counterparts. For instance, there are dwarf races of elephants, hippos, deer, etc. (Davis 1987, p. 118-124). These pygmy races are as much as an 1.5 orders of magnitude lighter, as adults, than the corresponding full-size versions (e.g., dwarf elephants: Roth 1990, p. 161). It is commonly supposed that these dwarf races only occur on islands. This is far from the case. Dwarf varieties of cattle, goats, sheep, horses, and pigs occur in many areas of equatorial Africa (Epstein 1971, pp. 230-1), and dwarf races of wild hogs also exist in India (Tessier-Yandel 1971).

The taking of dwarf races of large animals on the Ark would have been practical if the full-sized animals could be bred back from the dwarf varieties. What we need is detailed genetic studies to show to what extent, and under what circumstances, full-sized elephants, etc., can be bred back from single-pair dwarfed representatives.

No such caveat would, of course, be required for animals which are extinct today. For instance, sauropod dinosaurs could all been represented on the Ark as dwarf variants, or even as juveniles of sauropod dwarfs. If controversial reports of live dinosaurs in central Africa have any merit at all, they are most likely, of course, to be dwarf sauropods rather than full-sized versions.

The microevolution of dwarf races from full-sized stocks can occur in nature in only a few thousand years (Lister 1989), and probably the reverse is also true. The use of dwarf representatives of large animals on the Ark clearly merits further research.

Early post-Flood Egypt: dwarf adult elephant (Rosen 1994), or ancient artistic-cultural convention (White1994)?   Line drawing modified after Egyptian artist's painting.

Chapter 8

Manpower Studies: Eight People Care for 16,000 Animals

Feeding and Watering

One of the most often-repeated charges against the veracity of the Ark is the one that the eight people could not possibly have cared for the many thousands of animals on the Ark (e.g., Youngblood 1980, p. 131). Countless believers have been wrongly intimidated by this fallacious argument, and have never seriously considered how long it *does* take to take care of animals in an emergency situation. This section shows that, based on *actual* manpower studies (and with no miraculous assistance nor animal dormancy), eight people could definitely have taken care of tens of thousands of animals.

Moore (1983, 32) has embellished the hoary "eight-people-far-too-few" argument by noting that, in a zoo situation, one person can only care for twenty-three animals. His comparison of the Ark and zoos is patently misleading for a number of reasons. First of all, zoos conspicuously lack even the most rudimentary labor saving devices (Markowitz 1982, p. 18, 160) as, for that matter, do circuses (Kiley-Worthington 1990, p. 212). More important, the one-on-one care of animals in the zoo is very different from the care en masse, for strictly emergency survival, of large numbers of animals. Indeed, even under normative conditions, one person can care for thousands of animals, as extensively documented below.

Time to Care for an Animal: Modern Examples. Consider, even in non-emergencies, the different amounts of time spent in the care of a horse under different conditions. The care of just one race horse requires much of the workday of one stable lad, with one hour devoted just to the morning routine (Hayes 1969, p. 330). The American farm horse in the early 20th century, by contrast, required an average of only seventeen minutes of total labor daily (Cooper 1917, p. 8). Today's horses need undoubtedly less, as modern stables have labor-saving features, including things as basic as chute feeders (e.g., Brown and Powell-Smith 1984, p. 143). Deer, used in experiments and cared for under non-mechanized conditions, require five minutes per deer per day (Wood et al. 1961, p. 295). Of course, the deer are subject to time-consuming experimental procedures which, of course, had no parallel on the Ark. Under emergency situations, the time per deer would be a small fraction of five minutes per animal per day.

A second major factor in the time required for animal care has to do with labor-saving devices and practices. In the modern laboratory animal situation, we have one person caring for over 5,900 animals (mice, rats, rabbits) using semi-automated caging systems (Hickey 1973, p. 32). In the case of factory farming, we have one man to 3,840 pigs (Maton et al. 1985, p. 304), one worker per 5,000 cattle in mechanized feedlots (Miller and Hodges 1970, p. 57; see also Owen 1983, p. 101), and one stockman to 30,000 laying hens (Johnson 1991, p. 24) or even 50,000 ones (Maton et al. 1985, p. 363). Of course, I am *not* suggesting that late Twentieth Century levels of mechanized animal care were available to the antediluvians. But, then again, they need not have been—far from it. Note that the 2,000 animals per person on the Ark, the vast majority of which are smaller than hens, require but a small fraction of the labor efficiency of the modern factory farm and its many *tens of thousands of animals per person*. At the same time, it should be noted that labor-saving is not an exclusive provenance of modern times. For instance, some assembly-style techniques had been employed in fourteenth century France (Gimpel 1976), and there is no reason why rudimentary labor-saving techniques should have been unknown to the antediluvians.

Time to Care for an Animal under Rustic Conditions.
Let us therefore consider the actual labor requirements, when caring for animals, when one has nothing more sophisticated than a shovel, bucket, wheelbarrow, etc. Under such non-mechanized conditions, one person can raise and care for a few hundred to several hundred rabbits (Portsmouth 1962, p. 98; Casady 1971, p. 66-7; Cheeke et al. 1987, p. 50), 842 pigs (Maton et al. 1985, p. 304), 500 steers (Hervey 1953, p. 106), 2,000 pigeons (Levi 1957, p. 552), 1,000 guinea pigs (NRC 1991, p. 248), and 2,000 to 9,000 laying hens (Parks 1950, p. 23; Maton et al. 1985, p. 356). Of course, the above-cited examples are not strictly comparable to the Ark situation because they include chores (such as breeding of rabbits, changing the bedding of guinea pigs, and daily collection of the eggs laid by the hens) which were not done on the Ark, at least not on a large-scale basis. Note, furthermore, that the efficient use of labor when caring for numerous animals is not limited to domesticated farm livestock. Consider some situations involving captive wild animals. One person can care for: 250-333 ostriches (Bertram 1984, p. 29), over 900 lizards (Langerwerf 1980, p. 37), and 1,000 ducks (van Arsdall 1980, p. 36). The latter case involves duck production in China, which is all the more interesting because there is a surplus of manual labor with concomitant disincentive for labor-saving practices.

Ancient Labor-Saving Animal-Care Practices.
Details about animal care in pre-industrial times appear to be very scanty (Loosli 1991, p. 26). However, we do have a few examples which clearly demonstrate that Noah could easily have been familiar with mass-feeding practices. For instance, a French visitor to 14th century China noted that one monk could feed 3,000 monkeys, in a pagoda garden, once they had been trained to respond to a bell (Bostock 1993, p. 18). The ancient Romans knew about mass feeding and watering of both domestic and wild birds, using feeding and drinking gutters that were filled with water from pipes (Varro 36 B.C., p. 265, 273, 293, 310). Food for pigeons was also provided en masse through troughs that were filled by pipes from the outside of the pigeon housing itself (Varro 36 B.C., p. 284).

Quantifying the Time Spent on Animal-Care Chores on the Ark.
The most relevant labor studies to the Ark situation are those which give specific time allowances, *under non-mechanized conditions*, for the feeding, watering, and waste disposal for large numbers of animals. I have examined many such studies and summarized many of them in Tables 9 and 10. (The labor involved in waste management (Table 11) is discussed in the ensuing chapter.) In order to facilitate comparison of one study with another, I have standardized all the studies by expressing them in terms of seconds per animal per day. I assume a ten-hour day and six-day workweek even though some work could have been done on the Sabbath, as God permits work on the Sabbath for animal-care emergencies (Luke 14:5), and even routine animal-care chores (Luke 13:15).

NO.	ANIMAL	DESCRIPTION	SEC/ANIMAL/DAY	REFERENCE
		Table 9. Labor-Requirement Studies on the Feeding of Animals		
1	Cows	Self-feeder pen-type barns vs stanchion barns	12-24 vs 24-48	Brown et. al. (1950)
2	Cows	Nearby ground-stored feeds: hay vs silage vs grain	18 vs 24 vs 30	Byers (1952)
3	Cows	Self-fed vs hand-fed hay	12 vs 18-181	Byers (1952)
4	Cows	Self-feeder silo	10.3	Anon (1954)
5	Cows	Overhead chute or nearby grain	12	Byers (1952)
6	Cows	Grain from feed cart	30	Byers (1952)
7	Cows	Grain from feed cart	16.4	Carter (1943)
8	Cows	Feed from pail or scoops from cart	6-42	Smith et. al. (1947)
9	Cows	Hand-tossed bales	17.3	Schneider (1955)
10	Cows	Hand vs tractor silage feeding	113 vs 11	Anon (1961)
11	Cows	Self-fed wafered hay	1.73	Dobie et. al. (1964)
12	Pigs	From moving feed-car	1.44	Anon (1921)
13	Pigs	From manually-filled hoppers	0.53	Maton et. al. (1985), p. 355
14	Pigs	Hand-feeding	12	Mentzer et. al. (1969)
15	Pigs	Hand-feeding	2.17	Daniel et. al. (1967)
16	Hens	Hand-feeding	0.228-1.13	Hurd & Bierly (1947)
17	Hens	Overhead chute vs hand-feeding	0.134 vs <1.0	Bressler (1950)
18	Pigeons	From self-feeder	(0.00156 X refill time)	Levi (1957)

	Table 10. Labor-Requirement Studies on the Watering of Animals			
NO.	**ANIMAL**	**DESCRIPTION**	**SEC/ANIMAL/DAY**	**REFERENCE**
1	Hogs	Large field drinking tanks filled from barrels on tank wagon	9.4	Oberholtzer & Hardin (1945)
2	Hogs	Large field drinking tanks filled from pipes	3.6	Oberholtzer & Hardin (1945)
3	Hens	Drinking troughs filled manually, using buckets	1.93-2.66	Bressler (1950)
4	Hens	Drinking troughs filled by pipes	1.2-1.8	Kennard & Chamberlin (1938)
5	Hens	Self-filling drinking fountains	0.315-0.568	Bressler (1950)
6	Hens	Water piped into drinking fountains	0.036-2.08	Hurd & Bierly (1947)
7	Pigeons	Drinking/bathing pans filled from pipes	0.22	Levi (1957)
8	Hens	Cleaning water troughs	0.23	Maton et. al. (1985), p. 355

One of the most important factors in the efficient use of labor in the care of many animals is a judicious configuration of the animal housing and supplies. Obviously, animal enclosures themselves must be easily accessible through an aisle (Levi 1957, p. 516).

Labor-Saving Interior Configuration of the Ark. Much time is wasted during animal feeding chores through unnecessary walking around, as demonstrated by time-travel studies in barns (Cleaver 1952) and poultry houses (Bressler 1950). Some commentators have suggested that animals on the Ark and the fodder were located on separate floors. If this had actually been the case, (with the food carried or rolled on a cart) it would have added up to a very inefficient arrangement. By contrast, the most efficient labor-saving arrangement is for the food to be stored proximate to the animals, either in overhead bins or nearby (Atkeson and Beresford 1935, p. 149; Cleaver 1952, p. 139). For instance, in a study by Cleaver (1952, p. 142), hay never had to be carried more than 4 meters to the cows, and most of it had to be carried less than two meters. If food is to stored overhead, it must be readily accessible so that it can be quickly thrown down to the animals. In such a situation, grain stored overhead takes about the same time to feed to cows when stored directly overhead as it does when stored immediately lateral to them (Study #5, Table 9). In a poultry-feeding situation (Study #17, Table 9), only 0.134 second/hen/day feeding time was necessary when feedstuffs were arranged in such a configuration that they could be thrown down chutes, to the hens below, from storage bins above.

The labor-saving value of the judicious configuration of animals and provender has also been demonstrated in study #7 (Table 9). Repeated trips to carry fodder to cows were eliminated, and so the time to feed one cow fell to less than seventeen seconds per day. Likewise, it has been shown (Study #1, Table 9) that pen-type barns utilize labor more efficiently than do stanchion barns. One reason for this is, again, the fact that fodder is stored closer to the animals in a pen-type barn. Consider also the feeding of hay. The time required for this chore declines from 181 seconds/cow/day to only eighteen seconds/cow/day (Study # 3, Table 9) when hay is stored nearby instead of being carried from a storage area. As for time-travel studies involving the non-mechanized feeding of poultry (Study # 16, Table 9), the time quoted (less than one second per hen per day) is applicable to food and animal layout conditions where feed is stored close to the hens. Finally, it should be emphasized that, in my pictorial depictions of the Ark interior (Figs. 3 and 4), the food (and water) are *always* stored close to the animals.

Self-Feeding Devices. Up to this point, I have considered the daily feeding of animals. In actuality, most animals, especially the time-consuming larger ones, do not have to have fresh food daily. This fact could have been exploited to effect a further reduction of feeding time. For this reason, I consider the use of self feeders. Their use is included in Figures 3 and 4.

Self-feeders are hardly new. For instance, in the 19th century, self-feeders for pigs resembled the hoppers of mills (Baxter 1984a, p. 17), where dried food went down pipes into the small feeding troughs of individual pigsties. However, probably the first "self-feeder" was simply the dumping of food, in quantity, for animals in the field or paddock to eat over several days. As for specific designs of modern self feeders, the interested reader is referred to Carter and Carroll (1943) regarding hog self-feeders, O'Brien (1953, p. 40) for large cattle self-feeders, and an anonymous author (1967, p. 16) for pigeon feeders. In addition, Moreng and Evans (1985, p. 165-7) and Anderson et al. (1964, p. 307) describe simple self-feeders for chickens and turkeys. These very much resemble the common outdoor bird-feeders. Self-feeders could also have been built into the floor in the form of bunkers or trenches filled with food (Lindley 1978, p. 139). These could have been filled before the Flood and then uncovered for animal self-feedings at appropriate times.

The time savings resulting from the use of self-feeders accrue for two reasons. First of all, the filling of an animal feeder for, say ten days, takes much less than ten times the time it takes to fill an animal feeder for only one day. The time expended walking from animal enclosure to animal enclosure is greatly minimized because each trip to a group of animals suffices for several days instead of just one. The quantification of labor required when using a self feeder is as follows: The total labor involved in feeding is divided by the number of days and animals. For instance, if it takes ten minutes to fill a self-feeder that feeds 100 animals for ten days, this comes out to 0.6 second/animal/day feeding labor. In Table 9, Studies number 1, 3, 4, 11, and 18 clearly demonstrate the small amounts of time required to feed animals when self-feeders are put to use.

In an later section of this work, *The Colossal Bulk of Hay. . .* , I will discuss, in detail, the possible compression of hay into pellets or wafers. At that point, I will approach it as a space-saving procedure. Now, however, I demonstrate its utility as a major labor-saving feature. As exemplified by a study of the feeding of compressed feeds to cows (#11, Table 9), less than two seconds per cow-sized animal per day (assuming ten-hour days, six-day workweeks, and fifty-two-week work year) were needed when self-feeding was combined with the use of previously-wafered hay.

There have been a number of problems alleged in the use of self-feeders, but most of these are without merit (Esmay and Brooker 1953, p. 623). Other problems (e.g., food wastage) are relatively unimportant. Thus, food wastage may be uneconomical to a farmer but is quite tolerable in an emergency situation (i.e., the Flood).

Labor for Providing Potable Water to the Animals. As with animal feeding, much time is wasted when there is a lot of unnecessary walking around, and extremely so when each worker has to fill one drinking bowl or dish at a time for every animal. Once again, the configuration of the animal housing plays a major role in eliminating such inefficient use of labor. For instance, study #6 in Table 10 summarizes the labor requirements for watering poultry on eight different farms. The lowest quoted value applies to a poultry farm whose building is atypical for poultry housing, but similar to the Ark: a multi-story building with large drinking pens and little need for workers to walk long distances to fill them. Referring to Figures 3 and 4, the drinking troughs could have been placed adjacent to, or just above, the self-feeding troughs (see also cover art).

The most efficient method of watering animals is to eliminate entirely the manual carrying of water by having it piped into troughs, with the animals themselves trained to turn on the water when needed (Moreng and Avens 1985, p. 166). Of course, I am not suggesting that such extreme levels of automation existed on the Ark, but then again they were unnecessary. Plimer (1994, p. 126) makes the farcical claim that the Ark crew must have been limited to the use of buckets to move water within the Ark. For his information, the history of plumbing goes back to early antiquity. The ancient Minoans and Egyptians had extensive plumbing (Panati 1987, p. 200; Needham and Ling 1965, p. 129). The ancient Chinese were capable of transferring water long distances through hollowed-out bamboo pipes whose ends had been sealed with tung-oil and lime (Needham and Ling 1965, p. 129), as well as using ceramic pipes for drainage (Chang 1986, p. 267, 311). Even if the antediluvian technical know-how was no more sophisticated than this, it is easy to see how even a rudimentary plumbing system must have greatly expedited all the animal-watering chores on the Ark. In fact, there is an apocryphal account of pipes being used to move water within the Ark (von Wellnitz 1979, p. 45).

Let us consider the labor savings which accrue when water is piped in to animals instead of having to be carried to fill the drinking pens. The time required to manually water large animals drops to nearly a third when water is piped in (contrast studies #1 and #2, Table 10). For smaller animals, the difference between manual watering and piping-in water can be even more dramatic (compare study #3 with #4-7). Of course, further labor savings occur when animals are only periodically watered to avoid slime buildup in the drinking/feeding troughs (Kimbark 1968, p. 255).

Manure Handling and Disposal

Earlier in this work, I considered waste management in its simplest form, which involved simply allowing the excreta to accumulate on the Ark within thick animal bedding (Fig. 3) or in deep pits (Fig. 1, 2, and 4), with or without subsequent destruction by vermicomposting in the case of deep-pit storage. These procedures, if actually used on the Ark, consumed very little time (usually only a fraction of a second per animal per day: Cases 11 and 12, Table 11). In this section, I assume the active handling of animal excreta by the crew, up to and including its being dumped overboard. We are left with a range of procedures for animal-waste handling which span the no-removal of waste (discussed earlier) to its daily removal, thus requiring a progressively larger investment of labor. In general, the amount of time needed to clean up the waste of an animal is as dependent on labor efficiency as it is on animal size. Note, for example, from Table 11, that the time to clean up after a rabbit (Case 5) is not always less than the time to clean up after a cow.

| \multicolumn{5}{c}{Table 11. Labor-Requirement Studies on Animal-Waste Disposal} |

NO.	ANIMAL	DESCRIPTION	SEC/ANIMAL/DAY	REFERENCE
1	Cows, Horses	Clean stalls using shovel & wheelbarrow	38.9 vs 138	Carter (1943)
2	Cows	Clean stalls using shovel & wheelbarrow	10-90	Smith et. al. (1947)
3	Cows	Clean stalls and change bedding	28.6-35.1	Porterfield et. al. (1957)
4	Cows	Remove manure with vs without change of bedding	3.48-6.24 vs 20-29	Witzel et. al. (1967)
5	Rabbits	Manual removal	7.2	Hickey (1978)
6	Pigs	Solid pen floors scraped manually	0.74	Robinson (1961)
7	Pigs	Slotted floors	1.8-3.0	Kadlec et. al. (1966)
8	Pigs	Bedded vs slotted floors	16 vs 2	Conrad & Mayrose (1971)
9	Pigs	Sloped floor (self-cleaning floor)	0.2	Eftink & Searle (1973)
10	Hens, Pigeons	Accumulation of manure in subjacent pits	<1	Adams (1971) Kimbark (1968) Levi (1957)
11	Various animals	Vermicomposting of manure in subjacent pits	<1	Fosgate & Babb (1972) Shields (1974)
\multicolumn{5}{c}{RATES OF MANURE DISPOSAL PER ACCUMULATED MASS:}
12	Pigs	Manual shovelling-away of manure	1 ton per man-hour	Schulz (1960)
13	Hens	Manual shovelling-away vs tractor removal of manure	0.9-2.46 tons vs 21.3 tons per man-hour	Toleman (1967)
\multicolumn{5}{c}{RATE OF MANURE DISPOSAL PER SOILED FLOOR AREA:}
14	Pigs	Solid pen floors scraped manually	3.2-8.4 seconds per square meter of pen area	Robinson (1961)

Proximate Removal of Droppings. The simplest step up from having large animals just trample their excreta into a thick bed (as in Fig. 3) is to remove the droppings daily, and just toss them into a gutter which runs parallel to, but completely outside of, the individual animal stalls. This is depicted, in plan view, in Fig. 4b. Labor is not expended to dispose of the manure, only to remove it from the animal enclosure itself in order to prevent further possible contact with the bedded animals. The labor time required for a cow-sized animal is less than seven seconds per animal per day (Case 4, Table 11). Of course, since this procedure does not dispose of the manure itself, it must be allowed to accumulate on the Ark or be destroyed by vermicomposting.

Time Required to Handle Excreta—per Animal. Up to now, I have considered waste-management practices in which the manure, or some form of it (i.e., vermicomposted mulch), never physically left the Ark. I now consider situations where the excreta is actively handled and disposed of overboard. Consider, first of all, extensions of the previously-discussed methods. In each case, the original tossing or flowing of manure can be followed by disposal of it. As a result, the labor time rises to a total of about half a minute per animal per day (Cases 3 and 4, Table 11). This total also includes adding a little supplementary bedding to the stalls in the case of the manure being tossed out of the stall.

Now, let us suppose that the manure thrown into the channel slopes and drains out of the Ark itself through an outfall (see Turnbull 1967, p. 34, for details). Assuming that the excreta remaining in the channel needs to be cleaned out only occasionally, and with an efficient use of labor, the labor expended can be as little as a fraction of a second per animal per day (e. g., Case 9, Table 11). It should be noted that an outfall should have been well within the technical capabilities of the antediluvians, as sewer outfalls have been discovered at Skara Brae (present-day Scotland)(James and Thorpe 1994, p. 359) conventionally dated to the third millennium BC—which is not long after the Flood.

Let us now focus on the labor expended in the case of the slatted floor (Fig. 2). The labor time varies inversely with the amount of bedding used (Cases 7 and 8, Table 11). As can be seen, it can take only a small fraction of the labor needed to clean a stall in which the excreta accumulates. However, let us now suppose that there were no sloped floors (Fig. 1), no slatted ones (Fig. 2), no manure gutter (Fig. 4a), and no short-distance tossing of animal manure (Fig. 4b). Under such circumstances, each stall would have to be laboriously cleaned out. For a cow or horse stall, this would take prohibitively long (Case 1, Table 11), especially if the collected excreta has to be pushed a great distance in the wheelbarrow before being dumped overboard. However, the amount of time for this chore varies greatly (see Case 2 in Table 11), depending upon such factors as the type of tool used (scraper vs. shovel) and the slope of the incline on which the manure-loaded wheelbarrow had been pushed.

Time Required to Handle Excreta—per Ton. Manual animal waste removal can be expressed, instead of on a per-animal basis, in terms of man-hours per ton (Cases 12 and 13, Table 11). At the previously-quoted daily animal-waste production of 12 tons, only 4.9 to 13 man-hours of labor (out of the 80 available daily) would have been necessary to shovel up the waste and dump it overboard. The corresponding range of values, converted to a per-animal basis, is 8.8 to 24 seconds/animal/day.

Time Required to Handle Excreta—per Pen Area. Still another approach for calculating the time required for animal-waste disposal chores calls for figuring the time needed to clean a given area of soiled floor in the animal enclosure. For our purposes, we are considering the removal of excreta from the floor and the pushing of it into a storage channel (in the case of the Ark, an outfall channel). This chore is accomplished by means of a hand-held scraper (the blade of which is at least

10-15 cm deep and 41-61 cm wide: Robinson 1961). It does not matter if the excreta is relatively dry, or if it is soupy in texture. The amount of labor needed to clean a unit area of soiled animal-pen floor is shown in Table 11 (Case 14). The lower quoted value applies to daily removal of animal waste, whereas the larger value applies to its removal only once every three to four days.

The most obvious application of this method would have occurred had the large group pen (Fig. 3) possessed a solid floor instead of a deep litter bed. In the case of the subjacent manure pit (Fig. 2), the task would involve the scraping of the excreta off the continuous floor of the pit into a channel, and then allowing the channel to empty the animal waste overboard. Assuming that the animal enclosures were not tiered, the excreta-holding pits subjacent to the animals on each Ark floor would have had a total area corresponding to that of the animal enclosures themselves, or 46.8% of the area of the three Ark floors (Table 3). At this rate (4424 square meters), and the time needed to scrape the manure off one square meter of flooring (Case 14 in Table 11), between 3.9 and 10.3 man-hours of work daily (out of the eighty available daily) would have been necessary for Ark waste management under these conditions. Converting to a per-animal basis, this comes out to a range of 7.1 to 19 seconds per animal per day. Note that this range of time consumed is not very different from the one quoted earlier (4.9 to 13 man-hours, or 8.8 to 24 seconds per animal per day), based on the tonnage of daily excreta removed daily.

Animal Labor to Remove Excreta. Thus far, I have assumed that the eight human occupants of the Ark were the sole source of labor on the Ark, and neglected draft animals. A variety of beasts of burden could have been used on the Ark. For instance, llamas have been used in circuses to pull small muck carts around during waste cleanup (Kiley-Worthington 1990, p. 210). Beasts of burden have been used since early antiquity as a source of labor, such as the pumping of water (Stewart 1928, p. 349), and could easily have been used on the Ark to, for example, facilitate the removal and disposal of animal excreta.

If horse labor had been employed, allowing the use of much larger plows and much faster scraping-away of the excreta deposits, the man-hours required for this chore would have been greatly reduced. One horse can do ten MJ of power per six hours of work compared with only 4 MJ for a man (Inns 1980, p. 6). It is difficult to quantify horse labor because, in many parts of the world, horse labor is rarely used in this way any more, leading to the relative unavailability of such information. However, we know that a mechanical tractor can do the job of bulk manure removal ten to twenty times faster than human labor (Case 13, Table 11). The efficiency of horse labor falls somewhere in between that of human labor and that of the mechanical tractor.

Horse labor is much more readily quantified if the manure of the large animals fell into a continuous gutter in back of them (Fig. 4a). A three-horsepower electric motor can remove three tons of manure per hour out of such a gutter (Velebil 1977, p. 158). At this rate, it would have taken twelve horsepower-hours for the daily removal of excreta from the Ark.

Other Possible Technologies. In addition to the use of animal labor, a variety of other simple technologies would have greatly reduced the investment of labor which I have quoted (Table 11) for the frequent removal of animal excreta. For instance, the use of manure wagons mounted on trolleys (for photo, see Hopkins 1913, pp. 60-1) is much more efficient than the use of push-carts or wheelbarrows. Many animal houses use large augurs for the expulsion of manure from pits or gutters (Jones 1969). In the absence of electricity, animal labor could have been used to turn the augurs. The earliest reference to the use of augurs for the cleaning of the bilges of ships is probably ancient Greece (Needham 1971, p. 666). The ancient Chinese employed the chain-pump, whereby human (or animal) labor was used to rotate a series of paddles or buckets for the relatively rapid transfer of loose materials to different levels. On the Ark, this would have greatly facilitated the dumping of excreta overboard. I am not aware of any studies on the labor efficiencies of these simple technologies. Yet with or without them, it is evident that the endlessly-repeated arguments (e.g., Teeple 1978, p. 71; Plimer 1994, p. 128; Morton 1995, p. 70) about the impossible sanitation problem on the Ark cannot stand up to critical examination.

Allocations of the Eighty Man-Hours of Daily Labor

Most of the studies of labor-time needed for basic care of animals (Tables 9, 10, and 11) have been based on domesticated animals. However, the use of bulk feeding has also been successful for a wide variety of captive wild animals, and this has resulted in great savings of time in their feeding (Ratcliffe 1956, p. 8). There were, of course, many other chores on the Ark besides the feeding, watering, and waste management of the animals. However, these three are by far the most essential in an emergency situation, and the vast majority of animals can physically survive for a year with only these three basic needs met. Since it is all but impossible to quantify the labor time required for all of the auxiliary tasks on the Ark, I will instead set aside forty man-hours daily to these auxiliary tasks. This means that the paramount chores of feeding, watering, and waste disposal must be achieved daily within the remaining forty man-hours.

We are now in a position to evaluate the total amounts of animal-care labor required on the Ark. Again, I assume that eighty man-hours were available daily (ten-hour workdays for the eight-person Ark crew). If only forty man-hours were allotted to each person on the Ark on a daily basis for these paramount chores, it means that each human on the Ark could have spent only 7.2 seconds per animal per day. However, this is only an overall average which obscures the real story. Since the labor required to care for small animals is so much smaller than the same for the large animals, we need to have separate computations for the labor-time required for the large (100 kg when adult) and small (<100 kg when adult) animals. Note that, as seen in Table 1 and discussed earlier, less than 12% of the animals are large. This means that the calculations are very sensitive to the time required for the basic care of the small animals which, for the most part, need very little time. The sensitivity of the calculations can be vividly demonstrated by setting the time to care for one set of animals (larger or smaller, one group at a time) at zero. If the time needed to care for the large animals were reduced to zero, the time left for each small animal would have been nearly the same as the overall quoted average of 7.2 seconds (it would actually be nearly ten seconds per animal per day). By contrast, if the time required to care for the smaller animals could be reduced to zero, the time left for each of the larger animals would increase greatly, to 1 minute and 2.6 seconds per person per animal per day.

Of course, the labor can never fall to zero, but it can approach it. If the time required to care for each of the small animals is very small, the labor time available for the large animals is almost as great as cited in the previous paragraph. For instance, if each of the small animals needs only one second of care per animal per day, fully 54.9 seconds per animal per day are available for each one of the larger animals. Other combinations of time, expressed as ordered pairs (wherein the first number refers to the time expended for smaller animals and the second one to the same for the larger animals) are: (0.5, 58.8), (1.5, 51.5), (2.0, 47.2), (3.0, 39.5), (4.0, 31.8) and (5, 24.1). Each one of these ordered pairs satisfies the overall average of 7.2 seconds per animal per person per day. One can readily see the relatively large amounts of time available per large animal if only the time spent per small animal is held down to a few seconds per animal per day (a feat easily accomplished, as many of the entries in Tables 9, 10, and 11 clearly show).

One needs only to take a cursory look at Tables 9, 10, and 11 in order to see that *very many* different combinations of procedures chosen from those tables would have satisfied the daily 7.2 second/animal/caretaker maximal time allotment. Hence, not only was it possible for the humans to have cared for all the animals on the Ark, but also there was a great deal of flexibility in the types of animal-care procedures that could have been used on the Ark and still have been compatible with the eight people having cared for the nearly 16,000 animals. There is also plenty of time left over for less essential chores, as discussed below.

Animal-Exercise Chores. Let us suppose the larger animals were removed from their enclosures for exercise (see next chapter for details). Consider the handling of medium to large animals without modern equipment. It takes less than eight man-hours to move and weigh 107 deer-size animals (Wood et al. 1961, p. 299). Simply removing and then re-caging these animals would, of course, have taken only a small fraction of that time, probably at most one to two man-hours per the 107 animals. Let us apply this figure for the periodic release of animals within the Ark for exercise. There were 1810 animals of greater than 100 kg mass (when adult) on the Ark (Table 1). Releasing these animals from their respective enclosures, allowing them to run around on a track, alley, or exercise ring in the Ark, and then recaging them would, at the above-quoted rates, have required between seventeen and thirty-four man-hours of work. This assumes a daily routine for exercise. Had animals been allowed to exercise only every other day, the labor required would, of course, been halved (i.e., 8.5 to 17 man-hours). Of course, the time would have been even lower if the animals could be moved en masse by voice commands, as is done to routinely shift deer between yards (Monfort et al. 1993, p. 45). Noah may have previously trained the animals to respond to voice commands while they were in his menagerie (Fig. 6).

Miscellaneous Auxiliary Chores. Now let us consider some other daily routines: basic medical care for cow-sized animals, basic maintenance of the enclosures, and cleaning the large animal-pen drinkers. This takes approximately six man-hours per 1000 cows (Kelly et al. 1953, p. 604-5). For the 1810 large animals on the Ark, this, of course, would have taken less than eleven man-hours. Very little labor would have been necessary for the smaller animals, as evidenced by the vast numbers of small animals feasibly cared for by one person, and discussed earlier.

I have already discussed the use of beasts of burden for tasks such as pulling manure scrapers and hauling manure-filled carts. Yet the possible use of animal labor is not limited to that of brute force, as various trained animals could have been used to assist the eight humans on the Ark. The utilization of suitable animals for vermin control has already been discussed. Dogs have been used to herd large animals in circuses (Kiley-Worthington 1990, p. 210), and could have done the same on the Ark if animals were occasionally allowed to walk around for exercise. Of course, dogs could have performed a variety of functions, such as watching out for sick or injured animals and then leading the human caretakers to these animals in need. This would have obviating the time-consuming task of eight people having to inspect the 16,000 animals daily, and allowed the eight persons to be quickly apprised of any Ark animals in dire need.

In conclusion, it is evident that the eight humans on the Ark *could* have cared for all the animals on the Ark. In fact, as shown earlier, the most critical tasks in the caring for the animals could have been accomplished with still half a workday to spare. Moreover, I have ignored the existence of animal dormancy because its effects are difficult to quantify. This would certainly have significantly reduced the manpower further, as is discussed in detail under *Dormancy of Animals.* . . .

Chapter 9

Basic Living Conditions on the Ark

Implications of Animal Crowding

Earlier, I had used contemporary laboratory housing standards, as well as those of intensive livestock units, to figure out the floor space for the animals on the Ark (Table 3). I now elaborate this by pointing out that this degree of crowding is hardly limited to those situations. For instance, penned pigs on conventional hog farms are not stocked at a rate (Wolf 1965, p. 107) much greater than that of some factory farms. Among wild animals, those in circuses are often housed in small beast wagons (Kiley-Worthington 1990, p. 28), where their only opportunity for exercise is a few minutes per day during performances (or none at all during the off-season). It is now recognized that, for various animals, larger cages are not necessarily better than small ones (Bantin and Sanders 1989). In this section, I take a more detailed look at different animal needs in terms of crowding. The provision of exercise for the animals is also detailed.

Crowding in Three Dimensions. The values I have quoted for animal crowding (Table 3) are relative to floor area (i.e., in two dimensions). Let us now consider the implications of the 16,000 animals on the Ark in terms of the heat-producing biomass per unit of Ark volume. As discussed under *Ventilation*, we have a maximum (i.e., at disembarkation) heat-producing biomass of 241 tons, and this is housed in the Ark which has a volume of 43,200 cubic meters. This comes out to 5.58 kg heat-producing biomass per cubic meter of Ark volume. This rate can be put in perspective by noting that it is only twice that of common, non-intensive poultry housing (2.75 kg/cubic meter: Parker 1953, p. 691). For horse stables, the recommended stocking density is 16.2 kg of animal mass per cubic meter of air volume (Gay 1924, p. 255), which is nearly three times that of the Ark. As for cows in conventional barns, quoted stocking rates (Stowell and Bickert 1993, p. 396) are between two and five times that of the Ark. The differences in stocking density of the Ark and factory farm buildings is even more striking. In the most modern intensive poultry units, the stocking density is commonly over 16 kg per cubic meter (Wathes 1981, p. 403). Some piggeries have a stocking rate of over 37 kg of animal per cubic meter of animal housing (Maton et al. 1985, p. 308; Wathes 1981, p. 402).

Finally, it is noted that the figures I quote come nowhere near the upper biologically tenable limit of crowding. For instance, in the German concentration camp at Auschwitz, human inmates were crowded into former horse stables at a rate of one person per 0.28 square meter, and, in terms of volume, at a rate of over 90 kg per cubic meter (CCIGC 1982, p. 61), with variable degree of survival.

Space Requirements of Large Animals. As noted earlier, the smallness of the Ark enclosures forced the large animals to trample their waste through the slatted floor (Fig. 2), or to eliminate into a gutter (Fig. 4a). Claims that captive animals require large areas of housing in order to survive (Moore 1983, p. 16) are largely untrue. I have already demonstrated the success of long-term domestic and wild-animal housing under laboratory conditions. Also factory farming, with all its attendant severe crowding of animals, has not been limited in success to domestic livestock. It has also been employed with a wide variety of wild animals (Maton et al. 1985, p. 455-7); Johnson 1991, p. 47). In discussing various captive wild animals, Keeling (1984, p. 3) points out that large animal enclosures (as commonly seen in modern zoos) do *not* invariably lead to long-term animal survivorship:

> It is a well-known, but in these days of spacious paddocks and enclosures, often hushed-up fact that animals often do much better in small cages than in the other types which are largely sops to popular demand. . . .

There are contemporary zoos, mainly in the Third World, which still house animals under very crowded "barbaric" conditions. (Mullan and Marvin 1987, p. 84). For instance, adult tigers are sometimes housed in cages with floor areas of only 0.558 square meters (Mullan and Marvin 1987, p. 17).

The smallness of the animals enclosures on the Ark actually had several positive consequences, including the limiting of the animals' motions. Moore (1983, pp. 24-5) is rather melodramatic in his wild imagination about how the animals on the Ark would be reduced to a pulp because of the Ark's motion and the animals' panic. Of course, there are various simple procedures for reducing potential injury to animals in transit. For instance, birds can be pinioned to reduce their dashing into netting when panicked (Delacour 1951, p. 187). However, it is the smallness of the animal enclosures on the Ark (Table 3) which, in addition to the previously-discussed habituation of animals to stress, must have been the main factor protecting the animals from injury:

> The reason for a narrow crate is that, unable to turn around or lie down, the occupant will of necessity remain quiet and therefore will not come to any harm before it arrives at the other end. A crate that was large enough to allow movement would result in the animal wandering about the whole time in an enclosed space and making constant attempt to escape. After a few hours it would have any number of abrasions and cuts and broken horns or teeth (Nichol 1987, p. 102).

This, of course, also applies to animals in long-term confinement. Monfort et al. (1993, p. 45) point out that nervous zoo animals such as deer can be more safely manipulated when confined in small barn-type enclosures instead of large areas.

Animals Requiring Spacious Enclosures. The values which I have quoted for animals in Table 3 can be considered as averages, with some animals requiring more space, and others less. It must also be remembered that my calculations are very insensitive to the floor area allotments of the many small animals. For instance, if I were to arbitrarily *double* the allotted floor area (Table 3) for every one of the nearly 10,000 animals on the Ark which is under one kg in mass, the total Ark floor area required for animal housing would rise only a trifle—from 46.8% (Table 3) to 48.8%.

Another important factor to consider is the fact that the total floor area used for animal housing (Table 3) assumes no tiering of enclosures. This fact is reflected in Figs. 1–4. While, as discussed in terms of labor efficiency, the overhead space is usually utilized to store food and water above the animals, some of it also can be used for animals which require spacious (especially taller) enclosures. For instance, arboreal reptiles and mammals do not need particularly large floor areas for cages, so long as the cage has an appreciable height (Mason et al. 1991).

As for birds, the length of the cage is more important than the width in most cases (Harrison 1972, p. 50), especially for hummingbirds (Mobbs 1982, p. 5). For birds in general, volume of the cage is more important than cage floor area. For instance, finch-sized birds require 0.7 cubic meter per individual (Harrison 1972, p. 49). However, this is true of breeding birds, and smaller volumes have otherwise proven successful. At the quoted volume of 0.7 cubic meters per finch-sized bird, a .233 square meter floor space would have sufficed if the cage is three meters tall. This standard for bird enclosures should not, of course, be seen as an absolute. For instance, the Chinese regularly house their birds in cages much too small by European standards (Morrison 1947, p. 1; Roberts 1973, p. 130). Of course, many birds do not, by anyone's reckoning, require spacious enclosures. For instance, the domestic chickens have, under experimental conditions (Fraser 1989, p. 96), chosen cage sizes significantly smaller than the values I allot for birds of their size (Table 3). Quail have also been successfully housed in much smaller enclosures than those I quote in Table 3 (Beebe and Webster 1964, p. 312; NRC 1991, p. 148).

Primates are a major group of animals reputed to need spacious enclosures. However, standards for the laboratory caging of primates are ill-defined and contradictory (Bantin and Sanders 1989, p. 49). Some of the standards for cage size for captive primates (NAS 1973, p. 20) are not much greater, in terms of floor area, than those I quote (Table 3) for other animals of comparable body mass. As is the case with birds, volume of the cage is more important than floor area in the case of arboreal monkeys (Bantin and Sanders 1989, p. 49). In experiments on crowding, baboons increasingly exhibited various behavioral problems, but they did not die from the crowding (Elton 1979). As for primate social behavior, we now realize that, contrary to earlier ideas, primate aggression cannot be simply defined in terms of reduced living space (deWaal 1989). Of course, in most of these experiments, primates had been housed in a group, whereas they were probably housed singly on the Ark. Antagonistic behaviors among crowded primates can be drastically reduced simply by placing visual barriers between them (Wiepkema 1985, p. 238).

Up to now, I have considered animals which may require greater floor spaces than I have allotted for them (Table 3). These must be kept in perspective, as there are also many animals that can be kept in enclosures appreciably smaller than those I have quoted. For instance, rabbits of 2.7 kg mass have been housed at a density of one every 0.023 square meters (Johnson 1991, p. 45). Various rodents have successfully survived, for long periods of time, in very small enclosures (Armario et al. 1984; Ernst and Weiss 1984). In fact, laboratory rodents are commonly stocked, at rates of floor space per individual, much less than the values I have quoted in Table 3 (Poiley 1974, p. 39). Many reptiles take well to extreme crowding. For instance, lacertid lizards can be stocked at densities on the order of 100 per square meter of cage floor (Langerwerf 1984, p. 173), and green iguanas raised intensively also tolerate severe crowding (NRC 1991, p. 352). Nor is this capability limited to small reptiles. A pair of snakes, each of which is 1–1.5 meters long, can be housed in a cage with a floor area of only 0.25 square meters (Mattison 1987, p. 247).

Providing Exercise for the Animals on the Ark. The smaller animals on the Ark, for the most part, need not have been ever released from their cages during the Ark stay, as they probably got sufficient amounts of exercise in their enclosures. For the larger animals, periodic exercise was probably necessary, although many animals (as evidenced by the experience of Nineteenth-Century zoos, as well as modern laboratories, circuses (Kiley-Worthington 1990, p. 28), and certainly factory farms), were or are enclosed with little opportunity for exercise for long periods of time. Yet they survive.

I have already discussed the human labor involved for the exercise of the animals in the previous chapter, and now I provide some details on its implementation. One way that exercise could have been provided on the Ark for the large animals was through the use of a circular room with devices for animals to climb on (for a sketch of this, see Kiley-Worthington 1990, p. 30). In this scheme, animal enclosures are connected to this ring, and groups of animals can be periodically released from their enclosures for exercise. Alternatively, a running track could have been provided on the Ark so that large groups of animals could be allowed to run around for exercise.

The Animals' Immediate Housing Environment

In this section, I focus on the animals in the context of their enclosures, demonstrating that most animals can live in very unnatural conditions. They could clearly have survived for a year on the Ark without esoteric provisions or excessive additional investment in human labor. In terms of specifics, I evaluate various animal-care issues raised by Moore (1983): "problems" of horn, hoof, beak, and talon damage, and the alleged need of bathing and burrowing facilities for certain captive animals.

Caging Materials. On the Ark, netting may have been used to separate bird enclosures, as had been done in the aviaries of the ancient Romans (Roberts 1973, p. 15). Lightweight materials such as bamboo would also have sufficed for the smaller animals (Morrison 1947, p. 1). This, of course, would also have facilitated the interior illumination of the Ark as well as the flow of air for ventilation, and have contributed to the lightening of the Ark infrastructure. Where necessary, strong wooden cages could have been built, as the ancient Assyrians did for their captive lions (Bostock 1993, p. 10). Tin-covered wooden cages (Faivre 1973, p. 44) could have been built for gnawers (e.g., rodents), although this is unnecessary, as hard wood is sufficiently gnaw-proof (Neubuser 1968, p. 167).

Bird Extremities. There is no doubt that the birds on the Ark did not get anywhere near the individualized attention that they get in well-run zoos, but most of them could have survived without such treatment. Captive eagles' talons and beaks normally go a year without trimming (Street 1956, p. 96). Even if neglected, they cause discomfort (Batten 1976, p. 84), not death. In fact, the bills and claws of captive birds are commonly neglected by their owners (England 1974, p. 188).

Moore (1983, p. 30) has emphasized the difficulties of transporting wading birds without injury to their long, fragile legs. He mentioned constricting devices (which, of course, would have been impractical for a whole year). In actuality, there is no general agreement on the best way to transport flamingos, and some workers just move them in a large, well-padded crate (Ogilvie and Ogilvie 1986, p. 110). However, most if not all of the problem stems from the ease with which flamingos panic during crate movements (Bates and Busenbark 1970, p. 480). If flamingos that were taken on the Ark had been carefully selected for their placid temperament by Noah and/or God (Fig. 6), this problem could have been avoided. In addition, the long-legged wading birds could have been maintained on a substrate of peat or sand to eliminate potential leg or foot problems (Goss-Custard et al. 1971, p. 17). A cage on the Ark, layered with fishing net, would have probably been ideal, as it resembles a "geometrix floor" used by zoos (Russell 1989, p. 195) to prevent foot problems in both long-legged and short-legged birds.

Moore (1983, p. 3) informs us that birds need perches of varying diameters in order to avoid foot problems. This "problem" is easily solved by providing the birds perches of assorted diameters (Alderton 1991, p. 337; Bendiner 1981, p. 102) so that they can choose where to alight. Perches also cause foot problems when they are perfectly smooth (Beebe and Webster 1964, p. 285). This is a problem with modern mechanically-cut perches, but not with natural branches. In fact, branches with somewhat irregular contours are ideal for birds' feet (Beebe and Webster 1964, p. 286), and also provide the requisite diversity of diameters (Dilger and Bell 1982, p. 12). However, even if, for the sake of argument, there had been inappropriate perches on the Ark, it would not have amounted to a major problem for the survival of the birds for a year. In the event that birds get claw injuries from very improper perches, the resulting lesions are not usually fatal. This has been shown, for example, by their occurrence in captive birds that have escaped and been recaptured (England 1974, p. 188)

Hoofed Animals' Extremities. Moore (1983, p. 3) emphasizes the difficulties of transporting horned animals without them getting injured. First of all, most bruises in horned animals (e.g., cattle) are the result of rough handling and improper partitioning of animal enclosures (Ensminger 1991, p. 164) which, or course, is largely preventable. In spite of this, many animals (e.g., rhinos: Merz 1991, p. 94; Player 1967, p. 145) do get their horns broken during transport. However, this is a non-issue, as it is not a serious injury. In fact, horned animals seem to suffer no distress in having their horns broken off (Merz 1991, p. 94). In addition, some captive rhinos wear away their horns by rubbing against their enclosures (Batten 1976, p. 64). Cattlemen often de-horn their cattle in order to forestall problems with horns during transport (Esmay and Brooker 1953, p. 623; Wierenga 1983, p. 172), and Noah may have done the same with his animals while they were in his menagerie (Fig. 6).

Let us now consider hoof injuries caused by flooring that is either too soft or too hard, which Moore (1983, p.3) supposes Noah could not have known about. In doing so, he forgets the ancients certainly knew about basic care of horses, for they were dependent upon them. For instance, the ancient Romans knew about proper surfaces that prevent hoof injuries in horses (Varro 36 B.C., pp. 194, 213). Yet even if, for the sake of argument, Noah had been ignorant of hoofed animals' flooring needs, it would have been of little consequence, as hoof problems are seldom fatal (see below). Indeed, the mummies of ancient captive hoofed animals commonly show overgrown hoofs (Bostock 1993, p. 8). Even modern zoos sometimes neglect excessive hoof growth in captive ungulates (Batten 1976, p. 39).

It needs to be emphasized that very rarely are hoof injuries, from unnatural floors, fatal to the animals (Gold 1983, p. 24; Kadlec et al. 1966, p. 7). In fact, moderate to severe hoof lesions, when they do occur, do not even affect the growth rate and food intake of young hoofed animals (Wright et al. 1972, p. 99). If the foot does becomes infected from the hoof lesion, it seldom becomes systemic (Newton et al. 1980, p. 15). Moreover, hoof lesions in cattle tend to disappear once the cattle are allowed on grass (Greenough et al. 1981). In like manner, any putative hoof problems among the Ark animals must have corrected themselves soon after the animals disembarked from it. Finally, hoof problems cannot simplistically be related to the surface that the animals stand on. We now realize that many factors (e.g., diet: Greenough et al. 1981) affect potential hoof problems.

It has long been known that slatted floors (Fig. 2) produce uneven pressures on the animals' hooves (though not all studies have unambiguously linked slatted floors to increased incidence of hoof problems, when contrasted with bedded surfaces: Preston and Willis 1975, p. 393). The partially-slotted/partially-solid floor, the latter on a slope, is a good compromise between maximal animal cleanliness and minimal hoof injuries (Dumelow 1993, p. 212). For smaller animals, a natural floor surface is easily provided. For instance, the incidence of sore hocks in rabbits is less in bamboo cages than in wire cages (Cheeke et al. 1987, p. 384-5).

Bathing Pools—No Necessity on the Ark. Moore (1983, p. 29) raises another non-issue when he asserts that many animals need to bathe frequently. He again fails to distinguish a need that is founded on a perception of animal well-being from one that is proven to be a matter of life and death. For most animals, lack of access to bathing water is demonstrably not life-threatening, at least for a period of one year.

Despite the fact that zoos provide bathing facilities for pachyderms, most of them can clearly go for long periods of time without bathing, even if skin problems do in fact develop. For instance, many zoos (and especially circuses) fail to provide sufficient water for elephants to bathe in (Adams 1981, p. 134), but this obviously does not have fatal consequences. It is also a little-known fact that some elephants live in the desert (Viljoen and Bothma 1990) where, of course, they rarely have access to bathing water. Some elephants in the drier regions of India spend much of their lives without ever experiencing standing water (Chadwick 1992, p. 287).

Likewise, rhinos can be led across the desert (Gleeson 1933, p. 172), and even live there permanently (Montgomery 1989, p. 233). Even in more conventional climes, they are denied bathing for months at a time because of the dry season (Schenkel and Schenkel-Hulliger 1969, pp. 16-7), without serious problems. One captive rhino, at the Copenhagen zoo, given no bathing facilities, did develop cracked and brittle skin, yet survived for two years in that condition (Voss 1968, p. 151-2). Subsequently, a shower and mud bath were provided, clearing up the skin problem. As for tapirs, we are given contradictory advice. Hediger (1968, p. 17) claims that they require bathing facilities, whereas Crandall (1964, p. 501) says that they do not.

The hippopotamus is a semi-aquatic creature, yet there is some leeway in its need to bathe. For instance, the dwarf hippopotamus in Liberia is said to eschew the river in favor of land (Beddard 1905, p. 66). As for the larger hippo, its skin does become dry and cracked, with possible life-threatening consequences, if not given access to water (Bartlett 1899, p. 78, 360). However, this does not need to be a bathing facility (see below). Brown and black bears are said to enjoy water for bathing no less than do polar bears, but this is clearly optional. They were successfully kept in Nineteenth Century zoos without bathing facilities (Peel 1903, p. 174), and the same held true for travelling menageries (Gleeson 1933, p. 70-2).

Let us now consider birds. Most of them can forego bathing, as demonstrated by the efficacy of the small Chinese bird cages which lack bathing facilities (Morrison 1947, p. 1). Pigeons can easily go a year without bathing (Levi 1984, p. 111), as can captive geese and most ducks (NRC 1991, p. 94, 110). Captive cranes are often given bathing water only during the heat of summer (Xueming and Junchang 1991, p. 81). In fact, cranes need wet conditions only if we want them to reproduce in captivity (Sauey and Brown 1977, p. 90). Although oceanic birds were probably not on the Ark, it is ironic to note that sea-birds do the best in captivity when kept in dry cages (Swennen 1977, p. 5).

The animals most requiring immersion in water are, of course, the aquatic ones—precisely the ones not on the Ark. Among mammals, the Cetacea and Sirenia are completely aquatic and independent of land, whereas the Pinnipedia have to come on land only to bear young (Bonner 1982, p. 2). Although it is doubtful if any of even the Pinnipeds were on the Ark, it is interesting to know that many seals can be kept in enclosures for prolonged periods without bathing water, provided that they are protected from excessive heat (Hubbard 1968, p. 311).

Substitutes for Bathing. For those few animals which apparently or actually cannot do without bathing water without serious problems, there are alternatives to the provision of standing pools of water. For instance, water can be applied topically to the skin of elephants (Anon. 1855, p. 154) and hippos (Foose 1982, p. 67). In fact, placing cloth or blankets on the hippo's skin and keeping it wet is a satisfactory long-term alternative to bathing (Bartlett 1899, pp. 78-9).

Finally, even if bathing facilities were provided on the Ark, they need not have been extensive, as relatively small quantities of water could have sufficed as a substitute for large bathing facilities. For the small animals, water for bathing could have been piped into bowls as an adjunct to the drinking-water supply. For instance, this has proven effective for hummingbirds, serving as a practical alternative to a large fountain spray (Riggs 1966, p. 40).

Burrowing Surfaces. Moore (1983, p. 29) surmises that provision of soil to burrow must have been absolutely necessary for the fossorial animals. In most if not all cases, this is patently untrue, at least for the duration of one year. Most, if not all, fossorial animals will not die if not allowed to burrow. In fact, some modern zoos house normally-burrowing animals on concrete floors, with darkened enclosures to reduce their frustration (Batten 1976, pp. 141-2). Among captive fossorial rodents, pacas (Ocana et al. 1988, p. 373) and gerbils (Price 1984, p. 17) have been raised without burrowing facilities. Captive woodchucks and prairie dogs can forego burrowing (Clark and Olfert 1986, p. 732). Captive armadillos need a burrowing surface only when breeding (Leslie 1970, p. 124). *Lasiorhinus*, a normally-burrowing wombat, can be kept in captivity without burrowing facilities, provided that the animal does not overheat (Gaughwin 1982, p. 144, 146). It can also be given darkened boxes as a burrow substitute. As mentioned under *Illumination*, some of the deep-interior Ark stalls were probably dark, serving this purpose as well.

Chapter 10

The Preservation of Feedstuffs on the Ark

We are informed that stored hay deteriorates rapidly (Moore 1983, p. 28). If properly cured, this is not true at all (see Sullivan 1973, p. 23). Year-old hay (the duration of the Ark voyage) is commonly fed to animals as diverse as horses (Hitchcock 1959, p. 126) and elephants (Adams 1981, p. 163). As is the case with hay, various dry feeds keep for a long time if their moisture is sufficiently low (Rickett 1984, p. 47). The know-how for preserving feedstuffs, for durations of at least three years, was known in Biblical times (Leviticus 25:21-22; Short 1938, p. 28). The ancient Romans knew how to preserve various grains for durations of up to several decades (Varro 36 B.C., pp. 110-111), as did the ancient Egyptians (Noton 1982, p. 181). The grain-storage silos in ancient Palestine show evidence of a sophisticated system for drying grain (Wright 1985, pp. 300-1).

Moore (1983, p. 20) asserts, without a shred of evidence, that Noah could not have known how to store seeds in the Ark and safeguard them from either decomposition or premature germination. Morton (1995, p. 71) has embellished Moore's argument with the totally baseless charge that the Ark must have been "anything but dry" inside. Of course, in order to preserve grain, it is necessary not only to dry it, but also to prevent moisture from seeping back into it. Even if Morton (1995) were correct about the wetness of the interior of the Ark, it need not have doomed the feedstuffs and seeds to ruin, as the materials could have been stored in water-tight containers. This is not a procedure requiring high technology. Today, the people of India can keep grain in good condition for 3–5 years in water-tight containers made of nothing more elaborate than husk and straw (Pingale and Balu 1955, pp. 88-89). Grain-based foods can also be preserved for durations comparable to the Ark voyage. For instance, some Polynesian peoples of the South Pacific know how to dry and keep breadfruit for at least a year (Peters and Wills 1956, p. 1252).

Furthermore, the successful storage of seeds is not limited to modern peoples. The ancient Romans, Greeks, Chinese, etc., all knew how to store seeds in a viable condition for many years (see Priestly 1986, p. 14), evidently without being overwhelmed with problems from moisture, pests, etc. In fact, stored seeds are very robust. For instance, a seed-viability nomograph (see Ellis and Roberts 1980, p. 21) indicates virtual 100% germination of barley seeds, over a 370-day storage period, at common temperatures (20–25C), provided that their internal moisture is less than 15–25%. Similar nomographs have been found applicable to many other kinds of seeds, with similar predictions of viability (Roberts and Ellis 1989, p. 39).

Dehydration of Meat. This has been used to preserve meats and fish since ancient times (for early post-Diluvian Egypt, see Chimits 1957, p. 211). Many uneducated Third-World peoples today know how to dry fish and meat so that they keep at least one year (Anon. 1976; FAO 1990, pp. 42-5). Some types of dry meat can last at least 3 years at moderate temperatures (Sharp 1953, p. 174). In terms of nutrition, dried meat has almost the same nutritive value as fresh meat (FAO 1990, p. 37). Of course, meat need not be a feed by itself, but can be combined with other foods and dried to make a compact, highly-nutritious mixture. The pemmican made by American Indians comes to mind (Ashbrook 1955, p. 228).

Long-Lasting Fresh Foods. Up to now, I have only considered the preservation of foods in a situation where the food has little moisture. I now show that, despite the apparent lack of refrigeration, there could have been a limited supply of fresh foods on the Ark. Indeed, there are vegetables and fruits that could have survived in a fresh state on the Ark, without refrigeration, for at least several months and up to the entire Flood year. For instance, many root crops (e.g., potato) can last at least several months if properly wrapped and kept at relatively cool temperatures (USDA 1973). Cassava tubers can keep for a whole year (Ingram and Humphries 1972, p. 135). The wax gourd (*Benincasa hispida*) deserves particular attention, as it could have served as the staple of fresh fruit on the Ark. It is an unusual vegetable in that it can keep *a whole year in a fresh state* (Morton 1971; NAS 1975, pp. 53-5) without any form of preservation.

Preserved Fresh Foods. There are various media that can preserve foods. For instance, the ancient Romans preserved berries in honey (Thorne 1986, pp. 14-15). Many foods such as berries, leaves, roots, and fresh meats can be preserved in blubber or oil, as has been done since time immemorial by the peoples of the Arctic (Eidlitz 1969, pp. 112-114).

We know that canning of foods was invented, or perhaps re-invented, in the 18th century (Cosper and Logan 1951, p. 210; Thorne 1986, p. 25). One form of early canning was the sealing of food in glass bottles and then immersing them in boiling water (Cosper and Logan 1951, p. 210). Owing to the fact that this primitive form of canning is only a simple step up from the aforementioned bottling of fruits in syrup or sugar, it is recognized that this bottling/canning of fruit may have appeared long before modern times (Thorne 1986, p. 23). It is entirely possible that the antediluvians also had this know-how, which would have been facilitated by the fact that fruits can be canned by relatively low-level technology because of the fact that their high acidity already inhibits most of the highly-dangerous and heat-resistant bacteria (Thorne 1986, p. 23).

Eggs are a versatile food that also serves as a common ingredient of animal feeds. Eggs could have been preserved in a quasi-fresh state by being soaked in brine. This procedure is known from China, and allows eggs to be preserved for up to several years (Anon. 1846, p. 284)

Re-Vitalized Dried Live Plants. There exist fascinating forms of life that can undergo almost complete dehydration and yet survive this experience. This process is called anhydrobiosis or cryptobiosis. Upon re-wetting, these dried-up and seemingly long-dead creatures become rehydrated and resume normal biological activities. Examples of anhydrobiotic plants are certain types of seaweed (Roser and Colaco 1993, p. 24) and the Resurrection Plant (*Selaginella rupestris*; Roser and Colaco 1993, p. 28; Voigt 1972, pp. 29-30). Among fungi, the Japanese *Shiitake* mushroom is an example of anhydrobiosis (Roser and Colaco 1993, p. 24). Certain insect larvae also have this property (Hinton 1951-2). On the Ark, such living things could have been taken aboard in a dehydrated state, to be rewetted and served as fresh food for the animals, whenever desired, throughout the entire Flood year. Indeed, many of these anhydrobiotic organisms can remain in a dehydrated state for years before returning to a viable state upon rewetting (Roser and Colaco 1993, p. 24).

Hydroponic Greens. Fresh vegetation on the Ark could also have been stored in the form of seeds, to sprout hydroponically as needed. To start the process, simply a slight dampening of grain or seed would have sufficed (Levi 1957, p. 466). Hydroponic greens can be raised in total darkness (Frye 1991, Vol. 1, p. 72), which would have made good use of any deep recesses of the Ark which possibly never received any natural light. Finally, hydroponic greens grow rapidly; as much as 17 cm per week (Lint and Lint 1981, p. 196).

The Suitability of Dry Vegetation. However, all the foregoing discussions needs to be kept in perspective, as dry vegetation can substitute for fresh vegetation for most mammals (e.g., see the ensuing chapter on hay). The same holds true for birds. Among granivorous birds, many (e.g., pigeons: Levi 1957, p. 500; and also finches: Black 1981, p. 45) can be switched completely to dry foods in captivity. In the instance of finches, these can be in the form of dehydrated greens (Bates and Busenbark 1970, p. 28-8). Likewise, herbivorous reptiles can be switched to dry plant matter (Frye 1991, Vol. 1, p. 90; Sokol 1967, p. 194).

Chapter 11

The Colossal Bulk of Hay Required for Large Herbivores

Detractors of the Ark account (e.g., McGowan 1984, Moore 1983, p. 28) never tire from citing the bulkiness of hay and the vast quantities of it required to be fed to large mammals. The argument about the bulkiness of hay revolves about the following three fallacious premises: 1) that the animals in question *must* have had their food intake satisfied by hay, 2) that, to the extent that large herbivores have an obligatory dietary-fiber requirement, only hay could have satisfied it, and, finally, 3) if there is any situation where hay feed is absolutely necessary in animals' diet, it must have been in its conventional low-density form.

High-Fiber Substitutes for Hay

Let us consider, first of all, the fact that many ungulates can be largely (and some even completely) switched to a grain-based diet (which, needless to say, drastically reduces the volume necessary for storing the feedstuff). As a matter of fact, this was known in Biblical times (Genesis 24:25,32; Gen. 42:27; Gen. 43:24; Judges 19:19; Isaiah 30:24). Hoofed animals used for long journeys carried "provender" (which is a concentrated grain feed: Short 1938, p.29) as a means of greatly reducing the bulk which would otherwise have resulted from pack animals being forced to transport their cumbersome rations of hay. The ancient Romans used to feed their cows a wide variety of high-fiber substitutes for hay (Varro 36 B.C., p. 190).

Many non-ruminants such as pigs can be placed on an all-grain diet, because they have no need for fibrous feeds in their diet (Shingoethe 1988, p. 449). As for ruminants, Shingoethe (1988, p. 449) recommends that no more than two-thirds of the dry-matter intake of the animals be in the form of grains. However, ruminants such as sheep and cows have been successfully raised on all-grain diets on numerous occasions (Barnes and Orskov 1982, p. 39; Niekerk 1985, p. 67), at least when they don't have to bear calves (Hart et al. 1919, p. 202).

Despite the fact that an all-grain diet often results in digestive problems such as acidic ruminitis, this is tolerable in an emergency situation, as it is seldom fatal (Church 1991, p. 267). There also appears to be individual variation among cattle in their ability to tolerate all-grain diets for long periods of time (Anon. 1968b, p. B-12). If this is the case, when God commandeered the animals into the Ark (Genesis 6:20, etc.), He could have once again used the Divine filter (Fig. 6), this time by selecting those animal individuals which He foreknew would be highly amenable to an all-grain diet. Of course, if Noah had a menagerie in anticipation of the Flood (Genesis 6:19, etc.), he could have used the behavioral filter (Fig. 6) by limiting his menagerie to those particular large herbivores which displayed the greatest tolerance to an all-grain diet regimen.

It is interesting to note that extinct ruminants appear to have been concentrate feeders to a greater extent than are extant ones (Solounias and Moelleken 1993). For this reason, the extinct ruminants may have been even more amenable to mostly-grain and all-grain diets than are the ones with which modern agriculture is familiar with.

Elephantine Exaggerations of Hay Consumption. Both Moore (1983, p. 28) and McGowan (1984, p. 56) quote fantastically large quantities of hay supposedly required daily by elephants (136 kg and 160 kg, respectively). The actual value, carefully determined by experiment, is 28–30 kg (Rees 1982, pp. 195-6). However, all this supposes that elephants must have hay, which is far from the case. During the 19th century, many zoos fed their pachyderms small amounts of wheat cakes (Peel 1903, p. 173), leaving the animals in a thin and emaciated condition. One undisclosed zoo kept an elephant alive on less than 2 kg of wheat cake daily (Peel 1903, p. 173). Of course, I am not suggesting that Noah actually fed the animals such meager rations. I only wish to emphasize the enormity of the savings of bulk when medium to large herbivores are switched, in part or in whole, from hay-based to grain-based diets. In many zoos today, grains are given as supplemental feeds to a wide variety of captive medium to large mammalian herbivores (AAZK 1988; Wallach and Boever 1983, p. 778). At other times, grain-dominated diets have been successfully fed to a variety of large wild mammalian herbivores (Ratcliffe 1956, p. 4), sometimes in pellet form (Blair 1927, p. 29).

High-Fiber Hay Alternatives. Of course, some ungulates cannot be switched to an all-grain diet without suffering potentially serious digestive problems. Consider horses. It is not recommended that high-fiber foods account for less than half of their daily dry-matter intake (Bradbury 1974, p. 48; Green 1977, p. 32). However, somewhat lesser amounts of fiber have proved to be harmless (Cunha 1991, p. 190). This daily hay ration amounts to an equivalent of at least 0.4% of horse body weight (Hintz 1983, p. 155). Such a dietary requirement probably also applies to animals such as the hippos, zebras, elephants, tapirs, rhinos, etc., because the digestive physiology of these animals closely resembles that of the domesticated horse (Wallach and Boever 1983, p. 778).

However, it does not follow that hay, for all its bulkiness, is the only way that this need can be met. In fact, there are many foods denser than hay that can satisfy an ungulate's fiber requirements. For instance, horses have been switched for periods of at least 22 months to an all-oats diet (Hintz 1983, p. 155-6), without ill effects, provided that the oats are rich in fiber. Other sources of dietary fiber for horses, in place of hay, have included beets and citrus pulp (Hintz 1983, p. 155), and they have been successfully maintained on loaves of bread made of rye and oat (Anon. 1827a, p. 207-8). Furthermore, many ungulates subsist, or once subsisted, on seed pods and nuts (Janzen and Martin 1982, pp. 19-27). In nature itself, when neither fresh nor dry browse (i. e., hay equivalent) is available, as during droughts, rhinos subsist on dried twigs for long periods of time (Merz 1991, p. 104).

To the extent that a fiber requirement has been recognized for cattle, it need not be hay, but can be a variety of high-fiber foods such as cassava chips (Moore and Cock 1985) and pineapple bran (O'Donovan et al. 1972). During World War I, the Germans fed hazelnut waste to their cattle (Anon. 1918, p. 313). It has also proven feasible to switch both domesticated and wild ungulates to foods commonly eaten by humans. For instance, cattle have been successfully raised on molasses-dominated diets (with only a small daily supplement of straw: Bird and Leng 1978). Dried-fish diets have served as a sole food source, for much of the year, for cattle, sheep, and horses

(Anon. 1827b). An elephant was maintained on a diet consisting of soup and bread (DiSilvestro 1991, p. 24), whereas the one belonging to the Seventeenth-Century French King Louis XIV subsisted for thirteen years on a diet of gruel, wine, and bread (Blunt 1976, p. 161). Work elephants in Sri Lanka have been maintained on various common foods, centered on oat-cakes and grain, instead of hay (Gleeson 1933, p. 97).

Space Saved by Hay-Replacement Diets. We now are in a position to assess, in terms of the overall volumetric storage space on the Ark, the effects of replacing most of the hay by grain or high-density sources of fiber. Let us remember that it is the larger animals, comprising less than 12% of the total animal population on the Ark, which collectively account for most of the food intake on the Ark (Table 4). As shown in Table 1, were *all* of the requisite 1990 tons of dry matter food equivalent (Table 4) on the Ark in the form of settled hay, just over half of the volume of the Ark would have been occupied by it. At the other theoretical extreme, were it possible to replace all the bulky feedstuffs on the Ark with high-density grain feeds, less than 7% of the Ark volume would have been required to store all the provender for the entire journey.

In reality, of course, the actual volume on the Ark was between those extremes, but much closer to the smaller value. For instance, suppose that an average of 80% of the putative hay ration had been replaced by hay substitutes. The requisite volume of the Ark would then have been 15.4%. At a rate of 90% replacement, it would drop to 11.1%

Methods for Greatly Increasing Hay Density

I now consider the possibility of a further reduction in bulk food volume on the Ark, in addition to the partial or total replacement of hay. This reduction could have taken place if whatever hay had been taken on the Ark had been compressed or wafered. In the section *Manpower Studies . . . Feeding and Watering*, I had quantified the labor savings when self-fed wafered hay is used (Table 9, Case 11).

During World War II, both the German and Russian armies fed rations of pelleted hay to their military horses (Earle 1950, pp. 255-6). Horses routinely eat such rations (Cunha 1991, p. 260; Hintz and Loy 1966), and so do other draft animals (Hintz et al. 1973). Pelleted feeds have also been fed the rhinoceros (Salvadori and Florio 1978, p. 100; Merz 1991, p. 100) and many other captive wild ungulates (Ratcliffe 1956, p. 4; Wackernagel 1968, p. 5; Wallach and Boever 1983, p. 778). Wild ruminants have also done well on pelleted diets (Hintz et al. 1976).

The use of pelleted diets on the Ark is predicated on the fact of the antediluvians having the know-how to compress substances. Let us consider the pessimistic possibility that the technology of the antediluvians had been no greater than that of the peoples of later Biblical times. We know that, in ancient Israel, mechanical presses were in use to compress olive pulp to extract its oil (Eitam 1987, p. 42). The presses need only have been capable of exerting a small fraction of the pressure of modern hay-compressing equipment, since even a modest amount of pressure applied for a fairly long time will reduce the density of hay considerably, particularly if sufficient moisture in the hay is available (Butler and McColly 1959). Indeed, pellet density scales linearly with the logarithm of the pressure applied (Butler and McColly 1959, p. 443), meaning that increasing multiples of pressure have a progressively smaller effect in increasing the density of compressed hay.

In terms of specific numbers, let us note that modern hay-compressing machinery exerts a pressure up to 300 kg per square centimeter (Bruhn 1959, p. 206), whereas pressures of only 14 kg per square centimeter have proved sufficient for the making of adequately compressed hay pellets (Earle 1950, p. 258), provided that the correct combinations of temperature and moisture are met. In contrast to some modern compressed-hay briquets which have densities of as much as 1.25 (Earle 1950, p. 259), I will pessimistically assume that the antediluvian technical know-how was capable of merely doubling the density of stacked hay; that is, from 0.09 (Table 5) to 0.18. Let us consider the implications of this slight compression of hay in conjunction with the grain-based replacement of hay discussed in the previous chapter. We had showed that replacement of hay by the dense grain-based feeds, at rates of 80% to 90% of original hay ration, would have resulted in a total Ark storage space, for provender, of 15.4% down to 11.1%. The mere doubling of hay density would have been functionally equivalent to changing an 80% replacement rate to a 90% replacement rate, or a 90% replacement rate to a 95% replacement rate. The corresponding range of Ark volume needed for provender storage would then have fallen to a range of 11.1% down to 8.9%.

In conclusion, it is evident that the oft-repeated argument about the bulkiness of hay on the Ark has no merit. It is also worthwhile to add that other types of food can have their bulk greatly reduced by simple procedures. For instance, the drying of fresh fruits and vegetables not only reduces their mass by 75% to 95% (Caldwell 1918, p. 61; Cruess et al. 1942, p. 8), but also greatly reduces their bulk, particularly if the product is somewhat compressed (Cruess et al. 1942, p. 8). This is certainly no child of modern technology. For instance, certain American Indians taught the US Army how to preserve feedstuffs by drying. So skilled were the Indians in this that they could take the volume of powdered potatoes equivalent to a shoebox and make 100 meals for humans (Levi-Strauss 1966, p. 43).

Chapter 12

Feeding Challenges I: Animals that Eat Fresh or Live Food

Carnivores and Piscivores

A variety of commentators have suggested that carnivory among humans did not begin until after the Flood. Jewish tradition about Noah also supports this viewpoint (Ginzberg 1909, 1988, p. 333). Some have gone further and suggested that no creature was carnivorous until after the Flood. If this is correct, then this chapter is superfluous. However, I assume, for purposes of this study, the existence of carnivory among the same animals in which it occurs today, along with extinct animals whose dental anatomy resembles that of modern-day carnivores.

Which Animals on the Ark were Carnivorous? Table 12 provides a list of these animals. Among modern squamate reptiles, all snakes are carnivorous. However, due to the fact that there is an erroneous belief (Moore 1983, p. 28) that snakes will only eat live prey, discussion about them is deferred until the chapter *Insectivores and Live-Food Eaters*. As for lizards, practically all those under 50–100 grams, and most lizards between 100–300 grams (Pough 1973, p. 841) are insectivorous and/or carnivorous. However, owing to their usual small size, and ectothermy, their dietary intake of meat is very meager. Indeed, it was the carnivorous mammals, dinosaurs, and therapsids which were the most important meat eaters on the Ark (Table 12), dwarfing by a large factor the cumulative meat intake of all the remaining carnivorous reptiles and birds of prey.

Quantity of Meat Required as Food. Moore (1983, p. 27) chortled at the (imagined) impossibility of supplying the carnivores on the Ark with sufficient meat. The joke is on him, for a few simple calculations will dispose of his supposed arguments. As can be seen from Table 12, only one-sixth of the total food intake on the Ark (expressed as dry matter intake) is meat or meat-equivalent. As elaborated below, both fresh and dry meat are relatively dense in nutrients and would have filled only a small fraction of the volumetric capacity of the Ark.

Economizing on Fresh Meat. Insofar as the feeding of fresh meat was necessary at all, Noah did not need to go through the time-consuming procedure of raising mice for the small carnivores and cattle for the larger ones. Giant tortoises could have served as the primary source of fresh meat on the Ark. They have long been used for this purpose on long voyages, as they can go at least several months without being fed (Campbell 1978, p. 53) or given water to drink (Blunt 1976, p. 91). In fact, many tortoises can fast at least the duration of the Ark voyage (1 year: Marcus 1981, p. 65). The use of fresh tortoise meat as food for the carnivorous animals on the Ark is facilitated on the

Table 12. Inventory of Carnivorous Animals on the Ark

(I). NUMERICALLY-SIGNIFICANT CARNIVOROUS ORDERS

CARNIVOROUS ORDER		LOG BODY MASS IN GRAMS:							
		0-1	1-2	2-3	3-4	4-5	5-6	6-7	7-8
Carnivora (whole)	696			86	332	238	40		
Squamata (part)	432			326	96	10			
Therapsida (part)	226			46	82	74	24		
Saurischia (part)	216			4	22	64	66	60	
Falconiformes (whole)	170		6	86	78				
Thecodontia (whole)	144		8	24	26	54	32		
Piciformes (whole)	128	4	94	30					

(Add several small carnivorous orders)

(II). MEAT INTAKE ON THE ARK (DRY-MATTER EQUIVALENTS)

MAMMALS (Log 4-5 Grams)--126 tons
MAMMALS (Log 5-6 Grams)--39 tons
MAMMALS (Log 3-4 Grams)--34.5 tons
SAURISCHIAN DINOSAURS (Log 6-7 Grams)--30.0 tons
SAURISCHIAN DINOSAURS (Log 5-6 Grams)--25.7 tons
BIRDS (Log 3-4 Grams)--16.6 tons
THERAPSIDS (Log 4-5 Grams)--15.7 tons
SAURISCHIAN DINOSAURS (Log 4-5 Grams)--13.5 tons
THERAPSIDS (Log 5-6 Grams)--9.40 tons
BIRDS (Log 2-3 Grams)--7.29 tons

(ADD 13 REMAINING CARNIVOROUS CATEGORIES)

TOTAL: 332 tons, which is 1/6th Total Dry Matter Intake (Table 4) fact that, in nature, many carnivores already eat tortoises on an opportunistic basis. This is true, for instance, of kites (Keeling 1984, p. 12), lions (Pienaar 1969, p. 117), jaguars (Mondolfi and Hoogesteijn 1986, p. 104), and hyenas (Pienaar 1969, p. 134). No manpower need have been expended to cut up the tortoises on the Ark into bite-sized morsels, as carnivores (e.g., jaguars: Mondolfi and Hoogesteijn 1986, p. 104) simply scoop out the flesh from between the carapace and plastron without separating them.

A limited amount of fresh meat could also have been preserved by methods used by the ancients, such as salting, smoking, pickling, etc. (Jensen 1949, p. 181). However, in the event that the carnivores would not accept salted meat, honey could have been used by itself to preserve fresh meat for long periods of time, as had been done by the ancient Romans (Jensen 1949, p. 181).

Fresh-Meat Substitutes. When soaked in water, dried meat closely resembles fresh meat (Mann 1960, p. 140). Most of the fresh-meat ration of the carnivores on the Ark could have been replaced by dried meat. Indeed, captive carnivorous mammals have been successfully maintained largely on biscuits consisting of compressed cakes composed of the following: beef blood, meat, bran, and grain—all hardened by baking for chewing exercise (Blair 1929, p. 30). Furthermore, dried meat or dry-meat based biscuits, supplemented of course with water, could have *completely* replaced fresh meat for many carnivores, as has been done for captive mink (CCAC 1984, vol. 2, p. 97). It is interesting to note that there is a Jewish tradition of the lion on the Ark being fed dry food (Ginzberg 1909, 1988, p. 330), although, according to the tradition, this did not sit well with the lion.

Ark Volume Needed for Carnivores' Food. In my earlier first-order estimate of the volume for feeds on the Ark (Table 5), I allowed, for illustrative purposes, for the entire 1990-ton dry-matter intake to be represented as meat, either fresh or dried. I cited the latter at two different degrees of compression (none and slight), with the smaller volumetric percentage reflecting dried meat compressed to the density of 1.15 as is true of some dried meats (Mann 1960, p. 146; Sharp 1953, p. 57). However, I was conservative in allowing dry meat to be 10% water (by mass) even though some meats are dried to less than 5% moisture (Sharp 1953, p. 3).

Let us now assume, for purposes of discussion, that 90% of the meat intake for the carnivores (amounting to 332 tons dry-matter equivalent: Table 12) was on the Ark in the form of somewhat-compressed dried meat, and the remainder was in the form of live tortoises (each requiring 3 volumetric units of living space per edible volumetric unit of tortoise). The resulting volume of the Ark required for fodder meat (dried and "on-the-hoof") amounts to only about 6%.

Self-Preserved Fresh Fish as Food. Up to now, I have considered animals raised for food as the only source of fresh meat and fish on the Ark. I now discuss some little-appreciated sources. There exist certain fish which can be stored *alive* in a *waterless* state. In nature, they aestivate, remaining dormant until placed in water (Bartlett 1856; Janssens 1964; Smith 1930). There are a number of such fish on the different continents. Whenever the water they live in is drying up, they burrow into the mud and form a cocoon which dries around them. They aestivate and do not awaken again until soaked in water (Smith 1930, p. 99). They can aestivate for up to several years (Janssens 1964, p. 105), and digging them up does not disturb them (Smith 1930, p. 98). Especially relevant to the Ark situation is the fact that transport on ships does not rouse them (Bartlett 1856, p. 312), nor does the careful removal of the mud cocoon which encases them (Janssens 1964, p. 116). Their usage as a food source goes back to ancient times (Johnels and Svensson 1955, p. 133). Moreover, there are a variety of similar aestivators among bivalves and snails (Beadle 1974, p. 274-5) as well as certain frogs (Lee and Mercer 1967, p. 87). All these could have been kept on the Ark in a dormant state and then roused and used as a source of fresh meat whenever desired.

Feeding the Piscivores. Fishing outside the Ark was probably unnecessary to provide a supply of fresh fish for the few strict piscivores on the Ark. As we have seen, the aestivating lungfish could have served this purpose.

Moreover, the need to supply fresh fish to the piscivorous animals on the Ark is nearly eliminated by the fact that so few of them were on the Ark! Indeed, the most strictly piscivorous vertebrates are marine creatures such as predatory fish, marine mammals and reptiles, and true seabirds. Even though they are not commonly thought of this way, true seabirds are essentially marine creatures (Ainley 1980), because they spend 85-90% of their lives at sea. They come on land only to breed, and are just about as intimately connected with the marine ecosystem as are fish. True seabirds can stay out in the open sea, without ever touching land, for many months at a time (Swennen 1977, p. 8). Because of this, they were not taken on the Ark, and could easily have survived the Flood outside it.

Ainley (1980, p. 48) considers the following nine families to be true seabirds: Spheniscidae (penguins), Diomedeidae (albatrosses), Procellaridae (petrels), Hydrobatidae (storm-petrels), Pelecanoididae (diving petrels), Phaethodontidae (tropicbirds), Sulidae (boobies), Fregatidae (frigatebirds), Alcidae (auks), and a few members of Laridae (gulls and terns). These true seabirds should not be confused with other aquatic and semi-aquatic birds whose ecosystem is primarily terrestrial, and which spend a third or more of their time on land (Ainley 1980, p. 49), such as Gaviidae (loons), Podicipedidae (grebes), Pelecanidae (pelicans), Phalacrocoracidae (cormorants), Anatidae (ducks and geese), Scolopacidae (shorebirds), Stercorariidae (skuas), Rynchopidae (skimmers), and most members of the Family Laridae.

Fresh-fish Substitutes. Most fish-eating vertebrates can do without fresh fish, if necessary. For instance, young polar bears in captivity have been maintained on a wafer-based diet without fish (M. Morris 1976, p. 16). It is noteworthy that most of the shorebirds discussed in the previous paragraph, which must have been taken on the Ark, can be fed food other than fish (for details, see Walker 1942, p. 351-2). Gulls are well known for their ability to switch from fish to common foods (Peel 1903, p. 78), such as oats (Darling 1938, p. 67), and even detritus (Perrins 1985, p. 17). Members of Anseriformes (ducks, geese, and swans), have subsisted on pelleted diets, as have Cruiformes (cranes: Wallach and Boever 1983, p. 842-3). As for the more strongly piscivorous members of this group, even at least some of even these can be weaned from fish. For instance, during WWII, when fresh fish was generally unavailable, pelicans at a European zoo were fed meat strips soaked in cod-liver oil (Keeling 1942, p. 45). Furthermore, pelicans, cormorants, and herons have also been switched successfully to a fish-substitute diet (Wallach and Boever 1983, p. 844), and there have been some successes in getting other piscivorous birds to switch, in whole or in part, to a pelleted diet (Swennen 1977, p. 27). These are not isolated instances:

> If fish-eaters have been reared in captivity they can be trained to take trout and poultry pellets, and do so readily. Wild taken birds are not so adaptable (Kear 1975, p. 56).

We thus have yet another reason for Noah having a menagerie before the Flood (Genesis 6:19). He could have experimented with piscivores in captivity to find those individuals that were the most able to forego fresh fish, thus exercising the behavioral filter (Fig. 6).

Flamingoes are piscivorous and molluscivorous in nature. However, they can be maintained on a reconstituted diet of commercial waterfowl pellets, dried shrimp shell, and paprika (Lint and Lint 1981, p. 29), or other kinds of commercial pelleted diets (Wallach and Boever 1983, p. 843). In fact, the bright color of flamingos can be maintained by nothing more elaborate than ground sweet peppers (Poulsen 1960, p. 50-1). While inappropriate diet can lead to loss of plumage coloration (Lint and Lint 1981, p. 29), it does not result in death.

Nectarivores and Frugivores

This section discusses the feeding needs of animals (principally softbilled birds, and bats) which normally subsist on nectar, fruits, and other fresh vegetable matter. Nectarivorous creatures are readily maintained in captivity on nectar substitutes, such as sugar-water (Riggs 1966). Furthermore, even without training or prior captivity, wild lorikeets readily come to drink from honey-water filled bowls supplied by humans (Cherfas 1984, p. 214), and even wild and untrained nectarivorous bats readily come to drink sugar water from hummmingbird feeders (Lee and Clark 1993, p. 3). Not surprisingly, nectarivorous bats have been maintained on honey-based artificial diets (Rasweiller 1977, p. 567), and even on sweetened water for some time (Barbour and Davis 1969, p. 35).

Although some commentators have said that hummingbirds cannot be kept on sugar-water indefinitely (e.g., Lee and Clark 1993, p. 5), Riggs (1966, p. 39) reports no problems in keeping hummingbirds on a sugar-water based nectar substitute for periods of at least one to two years (i.e., comparable to the Ark duration). If necessary, nectarivorous birds can readily be taught to recognize sweet-liquid filled pots as sources of food merely by dipping their beaks into the pot (Nichol 1987, pp. 106-7). Before the Flood, they could have been trained, in like manner, in Noah's menagerie (Fig. 6). On the Ark the sugar could, of course, have been stored in a dry state, to be rehydrated only when ready for feeding. The sugar could also have been pre-mixed with other ingredients and stored dry until needed, as is done with modern commercial nectar substitutes (Brice and Grau 1989, p. 234).

Fresh Fruit on the Ark. Let us now consider the provision of fresh fruit and/or vegetables for the relatively few animals in need of them. There were several sources of fresh fruit and vegetables available on the Ark. In the chapter *The Preservation of Feedstuffs . . ,* I showed that there are fruits and vegetables that could have survived at least a year in the fresh state. Most prominent of these is the wax gourd. It is therefore interesting to note that some captive frugivorous bats have been maintained on a melon/cantaloupe-centered diet (Rasweiler 1977, pp. 558-560).

Most if not all frugivorous bats can live on fruit juice instead of the whole fruit (Rasweiler 1977, p. 561). In fact, Rasweiler and deBonilla (1972, p. 661) have described the maintenance of several captive nectarivorous and frugivorous bats on reconstituted cereal mixed with diluted fruit-juice concentrates. On the Ark, fruit juice could easily have been stored as a dried concentrate (Cruess et al. 1942, p. 30), and then reconstituted as needed. Furthermore, the previously-discussed wax gourd, with its notable yearlong-surviving properties, could easily have been liquefied and served as a juice (Morton 1971, p. 108). Other fruit juices could have been on the Ark up to the full year, preserved with sugars and salt, and stored in bottles stoppered airtight with corks (Anon. 1976, p. 85).

Most if not all frugivores can, if not readily switched to common dry foods, live on non-fruit fresh vegetable matter. Apropos to this, recall that I also discussed, in the *Preservation . . .* chapter, the fact that vegetation could have been easily grown hydroponically from seeds. This, in fact, is commonly done in order to raise tender fresh greens for captive birds (Levi 1957, 487) and reptiles

(Frye 1991, Vol. 1, p. 72). The previously-discussed anhydrobiotic plants, once rehydrated and thereby re-vitalized, must have been another yearlong source of fresh greens on the Ark.

The Preservation of Fruits on the Ark. Let us now consider the preservation of fruits without access to modern technologies (i.e., canning or refrigeration). The ancients (for instance, the Romans: Thorne 1986, p. 14-15) knew how to preserve berries and fruits in sugar syrups and honey. Accordingly, fruits on the Ark could have been preserved in this manner. This is feasible because of the fact that many frugivorous bats have demonstrated at least a tolerance towards fruit mixed with sugar syrup, sugar water, or honey water (Rasweiler 1977, p. 559). The same holds true for many frugivorous softbilled birds, which readily take to fruit that has been canned with sugar syrup (Lint and Lint 1981, p. 178) as a complete diet.

Fruits can conveniently be preserved and stored in the form of jams and jellies. It is thus interesting to note that many nectarivorous and frugivorous bats have been maintained on diets centered on jams, without any supplemental fresh fruit (Rasweiller 1977, p. 565). Furthermore, fruit has been worked into an agar-based jelly to serve as a synthetic diet for a large variety of captive frugivorous birds for up to a year (Denslow et al. 1987). Undoubtedly, dried fruits could also have been made into a similar jelly.

Dried Fruits as Substitutes for Fresh Fruit. Dried fruits, or reconstituted dried fruits, are another dietary option for frugivores. Methods for drying fruits were certainly known in Biblical times (1 Samuel 25:18, 30:12, 2 Samuel 16:1, etc.; Short 1938, p. 28). The ancient Romans, when building aviaries capable of housing thousands of birds, also provided food cakes made of figs and barley for them (Varro 36 B.C., p. 267).

Let us look at the practical dietary implications of dried fruits. Large quantities of dried fruits are used by contemporary zoos to feed their stocks of frugivorous birds (Street 1956, p. 107). The frugivorous parrots (Alderton 1991, p. 374) and frugivorous tropical pigeons (Walker 1942, p. 353) have been maintained on dried fruits. Dried fruits can also be reconstituted if necessary. When fresh fruit is out of season, softbilled-bird keepers commonly switch the birds to reconstituted dried fruits (Alderton 1986, p. 41). For instance, soaked raisins have served as a complete choice to fulfill the fruit requirement of mousebirds and hornbills (Lint and Lint 1981, p. 114, 118). Dates and figs have been equally successful.

Many frugivorous softbills are now completely maintained on commercial mynah pellets, which have dried fruit as their main ingredient (Bates and Busenbark 1970, p. 32). In fact, various softbills (including some of the most frugivorous ones: Bates and Busenbark p. 32, 357, 473) have largely or completely switched to mynah pellets in *preference* to fresh fruit! Moreover, mynah pellets (or, in this case, their antediluvian dried-fruit analogs) save labor because they can be put into hoppers to create a self-feeding situation (Bates and Busenbark 1970, p. 32), as discussed earlier in conjunction with common animal feeds (Table 9).

Fruit Substitutes. In many instances, fruit (in whatever form) can be greatly reduced, or eliminated entirely, from a frugivore's diet. Sponge-cake and brown bread has been used to replace much of the fresh-fruit ration in some frugivorous birds (Hastings 1954, p. 244). Various softbills have successfully been maintained on a diet which replaces most fresh fruits with boiled brown rice and raisins (Bates and Busenbark 1970, p. 38). Many frugivorous bats have seen their fresh-fruit ration replaced with dried fruit (Barnard 1991, p. 21), or with cheeses, animal chows, molasses, etc. (Anon. 1989, p. 13, and see below).

As for the complete elimination of dietary fruit, the normally-frugivorous Megachiropteran bats were, during a shortage of fruit, readily able to switch to common foods such as honey-sweetened oats, milk, and other common foods (Van Dyck 1982, p. 161). In nature, during prolonged dry seasons, bats eat bark and even the wood of trees, even to an extreme extent (Krzanowski 1985, p. 47). I am unaware of any experiments designed to evaluate the suitability of bark or wood as at least a partial fruit-replacement item for bats. During World War II, with fresh fruit unavailable in the London Zoo, a variety of frugivorous birds (among them the toucans and touracos) were successfully switched to non-fruit substitutes (Seth-Smith 1943, p. 129). Even under normative conditions, the complete removal of fresh fruit in the diet has proved feasible in many cases. Lories have been maintained for prolonged periods of time on seeds, but not quite for a whole year (Holshiemer 1981, p. 160). Some frugivorous softbills have been maintained on honey-sweetened sponge cakes (Tollefson 1982, p. 239).

Obligatory Primate Frugivory? Moore (1983, p. 28) displays his ignorance yet again, this time by claiming that primates require fresh fruit. In actuality, most captive primates have been successfully maintained on grain-dominated diets with only small additions of vegetables or fruits (Ratcliffe 1956, pp. 2-7), or on dry foods (e.g., pelleted "monkey chows") *without* supplemental fresh fruits or vegetables (Kerr 1972, p. 422; NAS 1973, p. 38). Even some of the most frugivorous primates in nature have been found to be able to forego fresh fruit, provided that, once again, the correct individual (or pair, in the case of the Ark) is chosen. This is true, for instance, of the callitrichids (Tardif et al. 1988, p. 588). Likewise, the normally-frugivorous mouse lemur has been maintained in captivity on common foods, and without fruits (Petter 1975, p. 189). Likewise, the specialized folivorous *Colobus* monkey does not require fruit in its diet (AAZK 1988).

It should be stressed that, overall, primates readily switch to foods that they do not encounter in nature, including various foods consumed by humans (Roonwal and Mohnot 1977, p. 7). For the mass feeding of captive primates, agar-based foods have proven successful (Newberne and Hayes 1979, p. 112), in addition to the aforementioned "monkey chows." A variety of primates are commonly maintained on cereal-centered pelleted diets (M. Morris, 1976, pp. 16-17), supplemented at least biweekly by a source of vitamin C. The source of vitamin C need not be fruit, but could have been the previously-discussed hydroponic greens. These have been eaten as an inadvertent source of vitamin C since ancient times (Stone 1972, p. 23). Of course, a limited supply of fruits could have been provided for the primates on the Ark, as discussed earlier in conjunction with frugivorous bats and birds. Dried figs would have been especially useful, as many types of tropical primates subsist exclusively on figs, for many months at a time, during the tropical dry season, when there are no other fruits available (Terborgh 1986, pp. 336-9).

Insectivores and Live-Food Eaters

Moore (1983, p. 27) argues that the animals which (presumably) eat only live food (e.g., snakes, and also many insectivorous vertebrates) pose an insuperable difficulty for the veracity of the Ark account. As we shall see in this chapter, such animals are, in actuality, easily fed in captivity, *with or without* the provision of live food.

Snakes and Live Prey. Moore (1983, p. 28) mythologizes snakes as obligatory live-food eaters. His notion is both ludicrously outdated and patently ignorant. The fact that snakes will eat inert prey has been known at least since the late Nineteenth Century (Mitchell and Pocock 1907), although the erroneous belief of snakes eating only live prey had in fact been widespread earlier (Blunt 1976, p. 226). Snakes can be taught to eat inert prey. Moreover, many *untrained* snakes, which would normally eat only live food, will in fact eat inert food if they are hungry enough (Chiszar and Scudder 1980, p. 135). Long ago, Mitchell and Pocock (1907, p. 792) reported that they have *never* met a species of snake that could not be switched from live prey to inert food, or that required any live prey—a fact more recently affirmed by Mattison (1987, p. 68). Moreover, the meat does not even have to be from a recently-killed animal (Mitchell and Pocock 1907, p. 786). Snakes will accept strips of meat (Marcus 1981, p. 64), and even, for that matter, carrion (Burchfield 1982, p. 267). In fact, one Israeli viper (*Pseudocerastes*) is said to sometimes *prefer* carrion (Mendelssohn 1965, p. 206). Almost all other carnivorous reptiles (e. g., carnivorous lizards) will also readily accept dead prey (Barnard 1985, p. 97).

To simplify feeding some more, snakes can even be trained to eat pelleted foods (Campbell 1978, p. 119). In Vietnam, large captive colonies of cobras have been trained to eat dry food pellets *ad lib* (Kien 1984, p. 217), eliminating the cumbersome and time-consuming task of raising large amounts of small animals (e.g., frogs, lizards) to serve as live food for them. Other snakes can be taught to eat various easily-obtainable foods. For instance, the scarlet snake was very difficult to maintain in captivity until it was learned that it could subsist on the yolk of chicken eggs for durations of at least 1.5 years (Brisbin and Bagshaw 1993). In his antediluvian menagerie (Fig. 6), Noah could have trained all the snakes to eat common foods, including dry feed pellets.

The Provision of Live Insects on the Ark. It is interesting to note that there is a Jewish tradition of Noah breeding insect larvae (presumably mealworms) in bran (Ginzberg 1909, 1988, p. 330) for an animal which would not eat common foods. Irrespective of whether or not this particular tradition actually goes back to Noah, it does indicate that the ancients were aware of the fact that certain animals only eat live prey. Let us consider the mass-culturing of live foods on the Ark.

For small bats and birds, fruit flies could have been cultured, as is done by letting bananas become infested with fruit flies (Mobbs 1982, p. 22). On the Ark, the rinds of the wax-gourd (which—as we have seen—could have lasted the entire Flood year) could have been used instead, as fruit flies will readily grow in fruit rinds (Bates and Busenbark 1970, p. 34). However, having a supply of fruits would have been unnecessary for fruit-fly cultures, as reconstituted fruit juices could have served as well. For instance, fruit flies will readily breed in grape juice (Brazier 1987, p. 218). In fact, not even reconstituted fruit juices are necessary. *Drosophila* has been successfully mass-cultured in a variety of cereal-based and molasses-based media (Lint and Lint 1981, p. 192-3).

Mealworms are usually cultured in grain products, such as flour. However, this precious resource need not have been wasted for culturing mealworms on the Ark, as mealworms can also be cultured in some animal manures, such as poultry droppings (Hartman 1970, p. 262). It would have been easy to harvest the mealworms in large numbers by placing two layers of burlap on top of the growth medium (Walker 1942, p. 324). The mealworms would congregate in large numbers between the burlap layers and could be removed conveniently for mass-feeding purposes. To figure mealworm intake, I utilized the data provided by Martin et al. (1976, p. 64-5), as shown in this paragraph. One gram of live mealworms daily can be produced by 101–201 cubic centimeters of bran. However, since mealworms do not become appreciably more prolific with increasing depth of nutrient grains, it is the area of the mealworm-bearing container that is the most relevant for purposes of calculation. Between 25 and 108 square centimeters of grain feed in a dish (assuming about four cm depth) are required to spawn one gram of mealworms daily.

Let us suppose, for purposes of discussion, that only 1% percent of the total area of the three Ark floors had been allocated for the mass culturing of mealworms, and that, owing to the shallowness of mealworm-culturing containers, ten tiers of such containers were stacked on top of each other. This would have resulted in a daily fresh output of between 88 and 375 kg of mealworms. The dry-matter equivalent of this amounts to 35–150 kg. Note that this does not include an earlier-discussed potential source of mealworms—those cultured in the manure pits. Moreover, there are many other live foods that could have been raised. For instance, crickets could have been mass-cultured with a similar small investment of Ark floor space or Ark volume. A 1.2 cubic meter enclosure can raise enough crickets to feed 800 lizards for a week (Langerwerf 1984, p. 168). Obviously, a mere few cubic meters of enclosures could have cultured enough crickets for thousands of animals on the Ark. Earthworms and their egg capsules, the latter of which is relished, for example, by crows (Barrett 1947, p. 72) and by soricids in place of insects (MacDonald 1983, pp. 397-400), could have served as a large live-food source on the Ark. As discussed in the section *Vermicomposting*, the Ark crew could have cultured earthworms to biodegrade animal manure. If this was the case, then vast quantities of excess earthworms would have been available as animal feed as a by-product. The prodigious quantities of earthworms available can readily be appreciated by noting that, during the vermicomposting of animal manure, earthworms can reach concentrations exceeding 65,000 per cubic meter of manure (Barrett 1947, p. 73). If, as discussed earlier, dermestid beetles had been used to destroy manure, these insects could have doubled as a live-food source for various insectivores, notably bats (Stebbings 1988, p. 23).

Live-Food Self-Feeders. In order for the feeding of live foods to have been practical on a large scale on the Ark, it must have been accomplished with a minimal investment of labor. This could have been realized, for instance, by training most of the live-food eaters to respond to a call and come to the person providing the live food, as is commonly done with the feeding of live insects to softbilled birds (Naether 1969, p. 29), bats (Anon. 1989, p. 13), and the hand-feeding of nearly all mammalian insectivores (Wallach and Boever 1983, p. 656). The Roman emperor Tiberius used to feed his pet snakes from his own hand (Bodson 1984, p. 18). In like manner, Noah could have trained the animals to accept hand-proffered food, on command, as he kept them in his menagerie before the Flood (Fig. 6). He could also have trained the insectivorous bats to eat mealworms *en masse* off the floor through a screen through a method that is reviewed by Rasweiler (1977, p. 534).

Let us now consider the mass-feeding of live foods through the use of self-feeders. Some of these live-food self feeders could have mimicked the *de facto* self-feeding situations which occur in nature. For instance, insectivorous bats frequent ranch buildings which contain grain-storing bins, picking off the granivorous insects (Orr 1954, p. 191). They also congregate in large numbers around moth-infested corn-cribs, feeding on the moths that emerge (Lewis 1940, p. 424). Similar insect-infested cribs could have been deliberately kept on the Ark in order to serve as self-feeders of live insects for the insectivorous birds, lizards, and bats.

A more sophisticated arrangement could have been built as follows. A series of pipes, perforated with holes, could have been connected to the insect-infested grain bins, leading to the animal enclosures. A series of bellows could then have been used to blow the insects into the pipes. Once emerging from the holes, the insects would have been eagerly pounced on by the insectivorous animals on the Ark. In fact, the use of exit holes is a technique commonly used in the feeding of animals which eat live insects (Ficken and Dilger 1961, p. 50; Lint and Lint 1981, p. 191; Roots 1970, p. 55). Furthermore, allowing the insectivorous animals to pounce on insects emerging from holes in pipes is not solely a feeding method, but also doubles as a form of exercise for the animals (Lint and 1981, p. 190), as well as behavioral enrichment (Shepherdson et al. 1990, p. 299). Many other types of self-feeding situations can be arranged:

> The problem of leaving birds which will eat only moving insects can be solved in
> several ways. . . . A day's supply of wax moth larvae can be left in a dish of water

where they will float and remain alive for at least eight hours. This method could also be tried with other insects. Cultures of live pupae may also be left in containers from which the larvae or hatched adults can escape one at a time and be captured by the birds (Ficken and Dilger 1961, p. 52).

Replacing Live Insects with Conveniently-Stored Foods. Up to now I have, for the sake of argument, assumed that animals which eat only live foods in nature must necessarily do the same in captivity, which is usually not the case (see below). Yet even when insects are essential in an animal's diet, only small quantities are sufficient to supplement the bulk of the diet, which is common inert foods (Roots 1970, p. 46). For instance, the flycatchers (Muscicapidae: Passeriformes) eat almost nothing but insects in nature, yet in captivity have been fed mainly common, inert foods, with only a few added live insects (Naether 1955, p. 32). Many keepers of softbilled birds have maintained insectivorous birds on *dried* insects and dried ant eggs (Douglas 1981, p. 116; Ficken and Dilger 1961, p. 53). Contrary to some rumors, dried insects are of significant nutritional value (Roots 1970, p. 47). Indians of the American West used to sun-dry vast quantitites of grasshoppers, mix them with berries, seeds, nuts, etc., and then press them into cakes, thus facilitating their long-term storage (Madsen 1989, pp. 22-3). Noah could have done the same, and stocked the Ark with tons of dry insects.

Many live-insect eaters have been switched *entirely* to common foods. Thus, in spite of claims that small birds such as hummingbirds must have live tiny insects (as fruit flies) in their diets, the contrary has been demonstrated. Riggs (1966, p. 38) reports successfully maintaining a variety of hummingbirds on an inert diet, without *any* live insects, for as much as twenty-two months. More recently, Brice and Grau (1989) report a similar experience with captive hummingbirds. This is also true of other birds. For instance, waxbills have been successfully maintained on a bread-based milksop without insectile food (Goodwin 1971). Some insectivorous softbilled birds have been maintained on nothing but moistened wheat bran (Douglas 1981, p. 115), while others have thrived on moistened dog food (Black 1981, p. 44). Lest we hear any Moore-like claim that Noah could not possibly have known this, let it be known that the ancients did maintain their softbilled birds on various common foods (Douglas 1981, p. 112).

Let us now generalize the methods of feeding of captive insectivorous birds. Many softbills are now fed common, inert foods without any live insects (Curio 1976, p. 129). As a whole class, most birds can be fed formulated mixed feeds (Scott 1973, p. 46). In conclusion, most insectivorous softbills do *not* require *any* form of insects (live or dried) in their diet in captivity:

> The day of insectile mixtures is probably past, and live food nowadays may be regarded as an expensive item reserved for birds that are newly acquired and are unused to any other food, or for breeding birds that are feeding young (Douglas 1981, p. 118).

Insectivorous Bats. In maintaining them in captivity, "bat glops" composed of common foods have been used in addition to, or instead of, live insects. Krutzsch and Sulkin (1958, p. 263-4), having found it laborious to keep raising and feeding live mealworms to their bats, successfully maintained them in perfect health, for several months, on a puree made of ground-up insects, cheese, etc. During WWII, with mealworm larvae unavailable, captive insectivorous bats were maintained on milk, cheese, etc. (Ryberg 1947, p. 118). There is a wide variety of recipes for insect-free "bat glops" (Wilson 1988, p. 263).

Although the use of insect-free "bat glops" is generally not recommended for long periods of time because of the attendant nutritional problems (such as intestinal obstruction possibly caused by a lack of dietary chitin: Krutzsch and Sulkin 1985, p. 264), at least some insectivorous bats on the Ark could have tolerated such a diet for one year. Gates (1936, p. 270) kept bats on "glops" for prolonged periods of time without major health problems. Orr (1954, 1958) switched insectivorous bats to a "bat glop" in which crushed mealworms formed only a fraction of the diet. Although some of these bats did show signs of dietary deficiency, this occurred only after a year or two on this diet (Orr 1958, p. 342). Rasweiler (1977, p. 531-2) has reviewed additional successes with prolonged use of "bat glops." Finally, a variety of insectivorous bats have been trained to eat inert meat, with only a small supplement of mealworm larvae added to meet the needs of their digestive physiology (CCAC 1984, vol. 2, p. 61), or even dietary meat for one year with no insect supplement at all (Barbour and Davis 1969, p. 108).

Common Foods for Insectivorous Mammals. Thus far, I have focused on insectivorous bats and softbilled birds. Yet insect-free diets have succeeded for a large number of other typically insectivorous animals. Pangolins have been kept for years in captivity on sweet foods eaten by humans (Prater 1965, p. 303). Most members of the Mammalian Order Insectivora can forgo insects in favor of common foods (Kielan-Jaworowska et al. 1979, p. 254), and the same holds true of the aardwolf (Beddard 1905, p. 106), and various insectivorous marsupials (Dunn 1982, p. 83; Selwood 1982, p. 33). The Echidna will forgo insects in favor of common foods (Wood-Jones 1923, p. 45), as will the platypus (Burrell 1927, p. 203); provided that the right individual is selected. The anteater can readily be switched to common foods (Gersh 1971, p. 62; Roots 1989, p. 55; Wallach and Boever 1983, p. 619). This fact corrects Plimer's (1994, p. 106) hasty assertion that the anteaters on the Ark needed their own supply of ants as food.

Selecting Individual Inert-Food Eaters. Let us now consider how individual animals, which normally are exclusively live-food eaters in nature, could have been carefully chosen for their ability to forego live foods for one year. Since there is a great deal of behavioral variability in a population of animals, it would not have been necessary for God to have changed obligate live-food eaters in order to make them subsist on inert foods. Instead, when God commandeered the animals to come into the Ark, He could have exercised the Divine filter (Fig. 6) by picking those *rare individual animals*, as representatives of the given animal kind, which were *already* capable of eating inert foods as part of their *normal* behavioral repertoire. For instance, out of many softbilled bird kinds, there are commonly some individuals which will spontaneously switch to inert foods (Inskipp 1975, p. 31). The same holds true for some *individual* representatives of various bat kinds that otherwise normally eat only live food (Hopkins 1990, p. 172; Racey 1970, p. 178; Ramage 1947, p. 62).

Yet even this action by God may have been unnecessary. If Noah had a menagerie of animals in anticipation of boarding the Ark (Fig. 6), he and his staff could have trained the recalcitrant live-insect eaters to subsist on inert foods. This could have been achieved, for instance, by several steps of gradual replacement of live foods by inert food (see Ficken and Dilger 1961, p. 51-2 for details). If need be, force-feeding could have been employed, for several days if necessary (Hopkins 1990, p. 172). The Chinese are especially adept in forcing insectivorous insects to switch from live foods to inert meat (Morrison 1947, p. 2). Nor is this a new procedure. For instance, the ancient Romans used to force-feed recalcitrant birds (Levi 1957, p. 475), and the ancient Egyptians did the same with crocodiles (Bodson 1984, p. 16).

In fact, feeding problems with animals can often be solved with force-feeding. For instance, the owlet-nightjars, which are insectivorous birds presently native to Australia, are considered difficult to keep in captivity (Nilsson 1981, p. 93). Upon capture, they steadfastly refuse to eat, and soon die of starvation. However, when force-fed soon after capture, they not only survive by learning to voluntarily accept inert foods, but even come to the trainer for food handouts (Muller and Clayton 1972, p. 139).

Chapter 13

Feeding Challenges II: Animals with Specialized Diets

Before discussing certain animals that have highly specialized diets, they must be put in perspective. Stenophagy (special diet) in nature does not usually imply the same in captivity:

> Despite popular belief (that some zoo people used to share), animals that will eat only one type of food are rather rare. . . . *Most animals that have highly specialized diets in the wild can be switched to more obtainable foods* (Gersch 1971, pp. 60-2). (italics added)

Even these few highly-specialized feeders could have been easily provided for on the Ark, as discussed in this section.

The Vampire Bat and King Cobra

Moore (1983, p. 27) sarcastically asked if Noah got the vampire bat to drink tomato juice. The irony in Moore's arrogant remark is that, were this possible, it would have been more difficult for Noah to supply fresh tomato juice on the Ark than to supply fresh blood!

We now realize that the vampire bat (*Desmodus*) does not, as once believed, suck only the blood of mammals and birds, but also of reptiles and amphibians (Greenhall 1988, p. 112), as well as sea lions (Belwood and Morton 1991, p. 12). A few extra reptiles could have been provided on the Ark for vampires to draw blood from—a minor feat, as there are merely three genera of sanguivorous bats (Fenton 1992, p. 161) to contend with. Moreover, there is a certain flexibility in feeding vampire bats, as they can go at least forty-eight hours without feeding (Ditmars and Greenhall 1935, p. 69). Vampire bats need not bite anyone, as they will readily subsist upon spilled blood (Wimsatt and Guerriere 1961). The constant slaughter of feed animals for the carnivores on the Ark would have provided an endless supply of it. Vampires have also been maintained for a period of several days on reconstituted dried blood (Wimsatt and Guerriere 1961, p. 451). I am not aware if any experiments have been performed to determine if a vampire bat could be maintained for a whole year on such a ration. Yet with or without this, keeping vampire bats on the Ark must have been easy.

Yet perhaps blood meals were unnecessary. The unusual blood-eating habits of a small population of a certain species of finch (Bowman and Billeb 1965) may be instructive in helping us develop a creationist understanding of the origins of vampire-bat sanguivory. There is also a report of *Desmodus* droppings in a cave containing well-digested pulp and seeds (Spanish-language article cited by Greenhall 1988, p. 120), which hints that the vampire bat (or at least a small subpopulation of it) may not be as exclusively a blood-eater as commonly believed.

I now consider the largest of venomous snakes, the king cobra. It is said to eat almost nothing but other snakes. While extra snakes could have easily been provided on the Ark as fodder, they were unnecessary. The king cobra, and other ophiophagus snakes, can be fooled into eating meat if the meat is stuffed into a sloughed snakeskin. This was discovered when a supply of fodder snakes ran out (Street 1956, p. 175), and is frequently practiced today (Mattison 1987, p. 75).

Monophagic Folivores: Colobine Monkey, Three-Toed Sloth, Panda, and Koala

This section demonstrates that the certain specialized leaf eaters, including the monophagic ones (i.e., those that are reputed, correctly or incorrectly, to accept only one kind of plant as food) could have been maintained on the Ark without fresh foliage.

The Colobine Monkey. Most primates are dietary generalists. However, there are a number of highly-specialized leaf-eaters (Hill 1964), of which the best known are the Colobine monkeys, or langurs. They even have a specialized ruminant-like digestive tract and, in terms of ecology, occupy a similar niche to that of the koala and the three-toed sloth. They are often considered difficult to maintain in captivity, but, contrary to common belief, their captive maintenance is not a recent success (Keeling 1984, p. 73). Moreover, their adaptability to captivity is clearly of micro-evolutionary origin, as it varies from species to species of *Colobus* (Oates 1977, p. 451).

In captivity, the *Colobus* monkey's natural diet of foliage is largely replaced by various vegetables, nuts, dried fruits, peanuts, etc. (AAZK 1988). When fresh vegetation is in short supply during the winter in zoos, hydroponic greens (discussed earlier) completely fulfill the dietary requirements for fresh foliage (Neubuser 1968, p. 165). At other times, *Colobus* has been successfully maintained on grain-dominated diets (Ratcliffe 1956, p. 6). Moreover, the Colobine monkeys have been successfully maintained in captivity *without* fresh foliage—in fact, on common foods that humans eat (Hill 1964, p. 229). The key to success is, once again, to select *those few individuals* that can forego their natural foods (Hill 1964, p. 229), which once again underscores the value of the behavioral filter in the antediluvian menagerie (Fig. 6).

This discussion can be extended to other folivorous monkeys. For instance, the howler monkey (*Alouatta*) has been maintained on a cheese-and-pellet food diet, with only small additions of fresh greens, for many years (Collins and Roberts 1978, p. 8). The proboscis monkey (*Nasalis larvatus*) is reputed to be the most difficult of the folivorous primates to keep in captivity (Hill 1964, p. 229), yet there have been instances where *selected individuals* of the proboscis monkey have been maintained, for prolonged periods of time, on many common human foods (Hill 1964, p. 230).

The Three-toed Sloth. There are a variety of live and extinct sloths, but the three-toed sloth (*Bradypus*) is considered to be one of the most difficult animals to maintain in captivity for any length of time. There have been only a handful of instances where this creature has lived more than a few months while in captivity (Goffart 1971, pp. 110-111).

Moore (1983, p. 28) and his parrot, Plimer (1994, p. 122), claim that the three-toed sloth is difficult to keep in captivity by virtue of its reliance on *Cecropia* leaves in its diet. In doing so, they both are repeating an old myth—one that never even enjoyed the support of systematic field study (Montgomery and Sunquist 1975, p. 83). In actuality, three-toed sloths eat a wide variety of plant foods (Montgomery and Sunquist 1975, p. 83; Sunquist 1986, p. 8). Ironically to Moore's argument, some three-toed sloths never visit a *Cecropia* tree (Sunquist 1986, p. 8).

While it is correct that captive sloths not provided *Cecropia* die within a few months, the same is usually true for those captive sloths given unlimited access to fresh *Cecropia* (Crandall 1964, p. 188-9). It is not known why *Bradypus* does so poorly in captivity, but there are a number of hypotheses. These include the sloth's requirement for trace elements provided by either certain ants (Hoke 1976, p. 80; Hoke 1987, p. 98) or tree algae (Aiello 1985, p. 216). Another diet-based theory proposes a highly-specific individual system of leaf preferences combined with gut microorganisms obtained from the mother (Sunquist 1986, p. 9-10). The sloth's poor adaptability to captivity has also been blamed on its supposed docile and timid nature (Collins and Roberts 1978, p. 9), or overall vulnerability to diseases caused by a weak immune system (Hoke 1987, p. 98).

Let us consider these. Apropos to behavior, there is now evidence that these sloths are not as passive and timid as commonly believed (Greene 1989). If sloth immune systems are indeed inherently weak, or else secondarily weakened because sloths are excessively sensitive to the stresses of captivity, then it is probably a matter of individual differences (see paragraph below) in selecting a sloth individual (or pair, in the case of the Ark) that can tolerate a year-long captivity. Indeed, *it has proven possible* to keep a three-toed sloth alive in captivity for well over a year (Herbig-Sandreuter 1964, p. 113), and without any heroic or unusual procedures. It appears to be a matter of finding that very rare individual or pair of three-toed sloths that will differ from its conspecifics by tolerating prolonged captivity. God could have used the Divine filter (Fig. 6) to commandeer that rare pair of three-toed sloths, into the Ark, which He foreknew would tolerate captivity. Of course, Noah could have tried out many three-toed sloths in captivity in his menagerie before he hit upon and selected the pair that did not die in a short period of time.

Of course, the current problems in keeping the three-toed sloth in captivity are probably microevolutionary (and therefore post-Flood) in origin. Indeed, if it is correct that each sloth *individual* has a unique plant/gut-microflora symbiosis (Sunquist 1986, p. 9-10), then this must have arisen by microevolution since the Flood, even if the created kind were no higher than the species. Immune systems also vary by the individual, as demonstrated in countless instances by rare individuals that have survived epidemics.

I now address the dietary needs of the three-toed sloth. It relishes boiled rice while in captivity (Hoke 1987, p. 91). This could have served as the staple of the diet of the three-toed sloths on the Ark provided that the individual sloths could live on it for prolonged periods in captivity. If, however, the sloth's gut microflora was specialized before the Flood, the correct sequence of leaves must have been fed (Sunquist 1986, p. 10). These, however, could have been in the form of reconstituted dried leaves, fed in the proper amounts and sequence (Montgomery and Sunquist 1978, p. 350-1).

The Panda. The panda is widely reputed to eat little else but bamboo shoots, and to require bamboo in captivity (e.g., Roots 1989, p. 55). There even was concern that if giant pandas were maintained without bamboo, they may lose desire for it (Giron 1980, p. 267; Morris and Morris 1981, pp. 139). However, both the red (or lesser) and the giant panda readily eat a variety of foods in captivity (Bleijenberg and Nijboer 1989, p. 45; Dierenfeld 1995; Walker 1942, p. 342), and have a special liking for rice-based gruels (Drummond 1988, pp. 414-5) and sweet foods (Litchfield 1992, p. 76).

The red panda (*Ailurus*) has been successfully maintained for a long time in captivity without bamboo (Bleijenberg and Nijboer 1989, p. 49), even on a permanent basis (Warnell et al. 1989, p. 51). In fact, it has been maintained without *any* kind of bulky feedstuffs (Bartlett 1970, pp. 769-770; Collins and Roberts 1978, p. 10), albeit with possible digestive problems. Of course, red panda individuals with proclivities towards digestive problems, when on a bamboo-free or other low-bulk diet, could have been rejected as prospective passengers on the Ark by Noah and/or God (Fig. 6).

I now discuss the giant panda (*Ailuropoda*). Some individuals have been maintained with only 10–15% of their long-term diets, in terms of dry-matter intake, in the form of bamboo (Bleijenberg and Nijboer 1989, p. 46: Dierenfeld et al. 1995, p. 218). If bamboo had been carried on the Ark, it could have been in the dried state. This is feasible because of the fact that, in nature, giant pandas already subsist on dry, tough bamboo stems for months at a time whenever fresh bamboo becomes seasonally unavailable (Schaller 1993, p. 71). In captivity, pandas will readily eat well-hardened bamboo culms (Dierenfeld et al. 1995, p. 214; McClure 1943, p. 268), and reconstituted dried bamboo leaves. The fiber requirement of pandas can also be fulfilled by such non-bamboo foods as sugar cane (Drummond 1988, p. 414), reeds, corn stalks, etc. (see Dierenfeld et al. 1995). Giant pandas have, in fact, been maintained on bamboo-free diets for prolonged periods of time. Young individuals have been maintained up to a few months solely on rice-based gruels (Schaller 1993, p. 162; Xuqi and Kappeler 1986, p. 35), or, for comparable periods, on reconstituted powdered milk (Harkness 1938). There is an anecdotal report of a half-grown pet giant panda in China that subsisted on grasses and human foods (Anon. 1937, p. 210). Finally, contrary to the notion that captive pandas must have bamboo (e.g., Morton 1995, p. 70), zoos have successfully kept giant pandas on bamboo-free diets for a few months (Giron 1980, pp. 266-7; Harkness 1938, p. 119, 122) all the way up to *two years* (Dierenfeld et al. 1995, pp. 217-218). Clearly, Noah could have done the same, dispensing with bamboo altogether.

The Koala. The koala is widely reputed to be the most specialized vertebrate feeder of all. It subsists on almost nothing but fresh *Eucalyptus* leaves, and then only from a very select number of species. In this section, I demonstrate that, assuming that the koala had indeed been a stenophagic *Eucalyptus*-eater *before* the Flood, Noah could have maintained it on common foods. In the subsequent chapter, I show that, before the Flood, koalas may have subsisted on a broad range of feedstuffs.

Morton (1995, p. 70) recounts the "obligation" of koalas to live on *Eucalyptus* leaves, and imagines the impossibility of its provision on the Ark. Some believers have suggested that *Eucalyptus* might have been cultured on the Ark. While this is unnecessary (see below), it would have been feasible. *Eucalyptus* seedlings could easily have been raised in the shaded recesses of the Ark (Jacobs 1955, pp. 120-1). Maintaining some (small) adult trees would also have been possible, as we know that ancient peoples used to ship whole trees with roots and soil still attached to them (Bostock 1993, p. 8).

All in all, we do not presently understand the basis for the koala's extreme diet selectivity (Hume and Esson 1993, p. 379; Spinney 1994, p. 29). However, some evidence suggests that the amount of simple sugars in a *Eucalpytus* leaf dictate the koala's desire to eat that particular leaf (Osawa 1993, pp. 85-6). If this is correct, the craving of the koala for sweet foods (see below) may be explicable.

There is a growing body of evidence that the koala, while unquestionably dependent upon *Eucalyptus*, is not quite as stenophagic as once believed. There is an anecdotal report that at least some koala individuals can subsist on mistletoe for prolonged periods of time (Pratt 1937, p. 43). It has long been known that koalas occasionally eat the foliage of non-Eucalypts (Lee and Martin 1988, p. 26). There is, in particular, a fascinating recent account of koalas feeding on the Monterey Pine (Lithgow 1982, p. 259). What is particularly interesting is the fact that this tree is not native to Australia. Whereas koalas supposedly had millions of years of coevolution with *Eucalyptus*, this cannot possibly have been the case with this pine, which has only been introduced in the last few centuries. Whether or not koalas can subsist *completely* on pine branches is unknown, but it is considered possible (Lee and Martin 1988, p. 27; Vandenbeld 1988, p. 259). Needless to say, it would have been far easier for Noah to have stored pine needles for the koala than to have cultured fresh *Eucalyptus* leaves! Also, the fact that the koala will eat plants it has never encountered before suggests that there is a much broader range of vegetation that the koala will eat other than the foliage presently native to Australia.

As for captive koalas, efforts are currently underway to develop a synthetic food biscuit for them. Captive koalas have voluntarily foregone half their daily fresh-*Eucalyptus* intake in favor of the biscuit (Pahl and Hume 1990, pp. 125-7), and have been apparently completely maintained on it for unspecified short periods of time (Lee and Carrick 1989, p. 750). Koalas have also been maintained for some time on a glop made of blended common foods mixed with pulverized *Eucalyptus* leaves (Starr 1990, p. 85).

Have there been any instances where a koala was maintained a year or more on something other than fresh *Eucalyptus* leaves? The answer is a resounding "yes!" To begin with, when koalas are young they, like all mammals, subsist on milk. It is possible to keep a young koala on a milk-based diet for at least ten months (Irvine 1992, p. 96). A milk/farinaceous diet can also be used (Savillo Kent 1897, p. 27), as can a bread milk diet (Wood Jones 1924, p. 186). In fact, young koalas that have been hand-reared will accept a wide variety of common foods (Finnie, in discussion with Betts 1978, p. 82; Spinney 1994, p. 29). The first koala to be brought alive to Europe arrived in 1880 at the London Zoo, along with a voluminous supply of *dried Eucalyptus* leaves (Tegetmeier 1880, p. 653). It had arrived from Australia on ship (after all, airplanes were not to be invented for another 23 years!), subsisting on the dried *Eucalyptus* leaves for at least several months (Flower 1880, p. 356; Forbes 1881, p. 180; Grzimek 1967, p. 289).

Pet koalas are sometimes induced to eat common foods, only to usually die of digestive problems in a relatively short period of time. For instance, koalas in captivity commonly acquire a taste for sweet and starchy foods, but die from indigestion caused within a few days (Duncan 1932, p. 13) to a few months (Lewis 1931, p. 346). However, with the *rare* koala individual, and the *right* combination of common foods, it is possible to avoid fatal GI-tract problems, and maintain a koala without either fresh or dried *Eucalyptus* leaves. A Mr. Johnson of San Francisco kept a koala alive for a whole year (the Ark duration) on bread, milk, and *Eucalyptus* oil (Anon. 1933, p. 257). Afterwards, the koala improved in its condition when given fresh *Eucalyptus* leaves. In another instance, (Grzimek 1967, p. 298), a captive koala relished *Eucalyptus* cough lozenges in preference to withered *Eucalpytus* leaves before dying from an unrelated cause. There are other reports of koalas having been successfully maintained on common foods that had been sprinkled or soaked in *Eucalyptus* oil (Serventy and Serventy 1975, pp. 32, 49). Needless to say, the myth of fresh *Eucalyptus* leaves on the Ark is just that, and it would have been easy for Noah to have had *Eucalyptus* oil (liquid or solid) on the Ark.

Assuming that koalas had been stenophagic before the Flood, God could have commandeered those few koala individuals into the Ark who He foreknew would tolerate a year-long diet of dried *Eucalyptus* and/or common foods sprayed with *Eucalyptus* oil (i.e., another use of the Divine filter: Fig. 6). Of course, if Noah did have a menagerie before the Flood, he could have, by trial and error, gone through many koalas before he hit upon a pair that would accept dried *Eucalyptus* leaves and/or the oil-covered common foods in lieu of the usual fresh *Eucalyptus* foliage (i.e., another use of the behavioral filter: Fig. 6).

What about the diet of the koalas immediately after the Flood? By the time the Flood ended and the animals had disembarked from the Ark, many shoots of *Eucalyptus* must already have sprouted, providing an immediate food source for the koalas. Indeed, *Eucalyptus* trees readily regrow by means of vegetative propagation—from fallen trunks and even from individual stems (Jacobs 1955, pp. 145-6). In this respect, the *Eucalyptus* is similar to the olive (Genesis 8:11), which also readily reproduces vegetatively (see chapter: *Olives*). It should also be pointed out that, once established, Eucalypts grow rapidly, reaching twelve meters in height after only two years under favorable conditions (Jacobs 1955, p. 12).

Specialized Diets: A Post-Diluvian Phenomena?

Up to now, I have, for purposes of discussion, tacitly accepted the premise that certain animals before the Flood had dietary specializations identical to their contemporary representatives. However, it is more than possible that dietary specialization arose *only since the Flood* through microevolutionary changes in the animals—the result of variation within the created kind.

One way to determine if dietary specializations arose since the Flood is to examine the taxonomic distribution of specialized eaters. Since we realize that the original created kind is probably somewhere between the species and the family, it is worth examining if dietary specialization is something which primarily occurs above the family level, or if it primarily occurs within the family. If it is the former, it would indicate that dietary specializations *transcend* the kind, and so have been built-in to the creatures since the Creation. On the other hand, if dietary specializations tend to vary within families, genera, and even species, it would provide strong evidence that stenophagy is part of the variation *within* the kind and arose since the Flood.

The evidence clearly shows that dietary specializations vary within the kind. The dietary preferences of various primates (Wolfheim 1983, his Table 193), tropical frugivorous birds (Snow 1981, his Table 2), and insectivorous birds (Muller 1976, the Appendixes I-III) clearly indicate that the specialized frugivores, insectivores, etc., vary *within* families, genera, and even species. In fact, different members of avian families rely on very diverse sources of food (see Morse 1975, his Table 1). For instance, members of Family Sturnidae vary according to species in terms of perceived live-food requirement (Alderton 1986, p. 120).

There is also intriguing evidence that dietary specializations can arise *within* a species. Arnold (1981, 1992) demonstrated that coastal and inland populations of the garter snake, *Thamnophis elegans*, have different diets. The coastal populations are slug-eating, whereas the inland populations are slug-refusing. Proof that these strong dietary preferences are genetically—and not environmentally—determined was provided by Arnold (1992, p. 713). He took naive, newborn snakes from each environment and tested their food preferences. Right from the start, the snakes either preferred or refused slugs, depending upon their respective geographic origins. Had these preferences been environmental, all of the garter snakes would have generally eaten whatever had been provided them, regardless of geographic origin. Obviously these garter snakes represent variation within a kind, even if the kind were no broader than the species. In fact, the two morphs of garter snake freely interbreed, with the offspring having a dietary preference intermediate that of the parental types (Arnold 1981, p. 490).

This example of stenophagy within a species helps illustrate the possibility of the post-Flood origins of stenophagy, especially when coupled with fortuitously selective extinction. Let us thus consider the implications of all inland garter snake populations becoming extinct. The only garter snakes known to us would then have been the coastal ones, and thus garter snakes would carry the reputation of being strict slug-eaters, just as the koala carries the reputation of a strict *Eucalyptus* eater. Prior to the Flood, the koala may have had a relatively catholic diet. After its release from the Ark, some of the koala individuals may have acquired, through microevolution, the strong dietary preference for *Eucalyptus*. Once the other koalas were driven to extinction, only the strict *Eucalyptus* eaters remained. The koala could certainly have acquired its obligatory dietary preference for *Eucalyptus* in only several thousand years since the Flood. Proof that stenophagy can arise rapidly is provided by the example of some Hawaiian moths that have apparently acquired, through microevolution, a strong obligatory dietary preference for the banana (Myers 1985, p. 6; Zimmerman 1960). The banana had been introduced to Hawaii only some 1,000 years ago.

It is likewise possible that the bamboo-centered diet of the panda is of post-Diluvian microevolutionary origin. This can be seen in the strongly bamboo-centered diet seen in a species of the primate *Hapalemur* (Meier et al. 1987). Since other species of this genus are not strict bamboo-eaters (Meier et al. 1987, p. 214), it is obvious that we have a case of variation within the kind, even if the kind were no broader than the species. There is some evidence that the panda's bamboo-centered diet and the koala's *Eucalyptus* diet are degenerative adaptations. This includes the low nutritional quality of the bamboo and *Eucalyptus*, as well as the panda's craving for unnatural foods (e.g., metallic copper and iron: Schaller 1993, p. 61), and the koala's apparent addiction to *Eucalyptus* oil (Spinney 1994).

Chapter 14

Boarding the Ark: The Fallacy
of Climatic Barriers

There is a long history of irrelevant arguments against the veracity of the Ark account based upon the presumed climatic restrictions of different animals, and these canards continue to appear over and over again in anti-creationist literature. For instance, Teeple (1978, p. 70) regurgitates the Nineteenth Century Flood-detractor Jamieson's sarcastic arguments about the misfortunes of the polar and torrid-zone animals when crossing the temperate zone on their way to the Ark. Likewise, Diamond (1985, p. 86) imagines reindeer dropping dead of heatstroke while crossing deserts on their way to Ararat. Similar follies are echoed by Moore (1983, p. 18) and Plimer (1994, p. 134). Whitcomb and Morris (1961, pp. 64-5) pointed out that the antediluvian world probably lacked regions of extreme heat and cold, and this prompted Moore (1983, p. 18) to fantasize that animals now native to geographic areas of high heat or deep cold had no place to live in such a world.

As shown below, these arguments all show an extreme (even pathetic) ignorance of animals' considerable abilities to adapt (both as individuals, and as microevolutionary variants) to widely divergent temperature regimes. Although many of the animals I discuss below were not even on the Ark, I include them in this chapter to show how they could have adapted to the equitable antediluvian climate. There is a broad range of temperatures that even tropical and polar creatures can tolerate, which, as shown below, becomes greatly expanded when animals are allowed to acclimate to temperatures that they don't normally experience in their present-day environment. Finally, microevolutionary changes in animals, sometimes in only a few generations, expands this range even more.

Tropical Faunas in the Cold

Animals that now live in the tropics are often quite sensitive to reduced temperatures (Scholander et al. 1950), but this sensitivity is greatly diminished if they are allowed to acclimate to the lower temperatures encountered seasonally in temperate climes. The nineteenth-century myth that tropical animals require perpetual heat and thus have to be housed in heated enclosures has been soundly dispelled (Street 1956, p. 29). We now realize that tropical animals can be acclimated to outdoor European temperatures, even during severe winters (Street 1956, p. 29, 31, 36). Furthermore, tropical birds and mammals are or were no strangers to cold temperatures:

. . . the error of the common belief as to climate being the principal factor that regulates or controls the distribution of animals. Amongst mammals and birds a vast majority of species and genera regarded as tropical have an actual or recent range into temperate or even frigid climates (Mitchell 1911, p. 543).

More recently, Street (1956, p. 36) and Graham (1992, pp. 82-5) have confirmed Mitchell's statement. As for the aquatic realm, there is a temperature at which polar, temperate, and tropical fish can coexist. It is near or at 15C (Scholander et al. 1953, p. 78). Likewise, arctic and tropical crustaceans can coexist at temperatures in the range of 10–20C (Scholander et al. 1953, p. 79), whereas insects and mollusks from both climes can coexist over an even broader range of temperatures.

Polar Organisms in Temperate Climes

Let us now consider the physiology of cold-adapted creatures. In general, polar creatures show few highly specialized adaptations for life in deep cold (Stonehouse 1989, p. 177), with differences from their non-polar relatives being primarily qualitative in nature (i. e., behavior, plumage and fur, body fat, etc.). To the evolutionist, this low degree of anatomical and physiological differentiation between polar and non-polar life is due to the fact that polar environments have existed for only relatively brief segments of earth history (Stonehouse 1989, p. 105). According to the creationist-diluvialist paradigm, this is due to the fact that the antediluvian world did not have regions of extreme cold, so God evidently did not endow organisms with highly-esoteric adaptations to cold climates. We can get a picture of how the present-day polar animals fared in the warmer antediluvian world by examining their tolerances to warm temperatures. To begin with, polar regions themselves are not areas of perpetual cold, but can get surprisingly warm in summer (20–29C at a stretch in the Russian Arctic: Chernov 1985, p. 13).

Waif Biotas. However, a more obvious indicator of polar animals' heat tolerance occurs when such creatures are forced to live in warmer climates. In nature, these include waif biotas, which are occasional individuals that stray into temperate regions, far equatorward from their natural polar ranges. For instance, fur seals from the Bering Sea have been found breeding off California (Peterson et al. 1968). Walruses have been sighted as far south (44N) as the Bay of Fundy (Wright 1951), with Pleistocene occurrences even further south (Ray 1960). In the southern hemisphere, the very cold-adapted emperor penguin has been found off New Zealand (Henderson 1968). Subantarctic fur seals, in good condition, have been seen off Australia within twenty-seven degrees of the Equator (Gales et al. 1992, p. 136).

Myths About Overheated Polar Animals. The notion that polar animals would have difficulty crossing warmer regions on their way to the Ark not only neglects the difference between antediluvian and extant climates (Whitcomb and Morris 1961, pp. 64-5), but is also based on a hoary myth:

> Polar animals do not, as was once thought, pine for refrigerated conditions—at least not in temperate climates. Surprisingly temperature tolerant, they do need a cool retreat and plenty of clean water in summer—but so do most animals. They take readily to standard feeds; reindeer fortunately do not demand an exclusive diet of reindeer moss, not do polar bears require seals, or penguins' exotic southern species of krill, squid, and fish (Stonehouse 1978, p. 2).

It is clear that the anti-creationist tales about polar bears suffocating in the summer heat (Moore 1983, p. 18) are laughable. Recently, Tarpy (1993, p. 14) took pains to dispel the popular notion that a polar bear in warm climate is akin to a person in a fur coat sitting in a sauna. In fact, polar bears have been kept during the 13th century in the Tower of London (Mullan and Marvin 1987, p. 96), obviously without the possibility of refrigerated enclosures. In Nineteenth Century zoos, polar bears were allowed to range outdoors in the summer amidst temperate wooded areas (Peel 1903, p. 202). Not only could they tolerate the summer temperatures of Europe but, in apparent irony, sometimes disliked being hosed-down despite the summer heat (Peel 1903, p. 170).

Let us consider some other Arctic mammals. The raccoon dog, Arctic fox, and blue fox readily tolerate temperatures of at least 20C with no evidence of discomfort (Korhonen et al. 1985). These are not isolated instances. The classic experiments of Scholander et al. (1950, p. 256) have demonstrated that many Arctic animals have a thermoneutral zone that not only reaches down to very frigid temperatures, but goes as high as 30C. Nor is ice necessary for polar creatures. Pagophilic ("ice-loving") pinnepeds can live and breed on land or rock if ice is not available (Riedman 1990, p. 98).

Polar Animals Acclimated to High Temperatures. When animals are flown from the polar regions into warmer climates, they often experience heat stress. Once acclimated, however, they readily tolerate moderate (and even hot) temperatures. In the probable absence of extreme cold on the antediluvian earth, all presently-polar animals were evidently accustomed to warm temperatures. Let us consider some modern examples of this.

Acclimated walruses do not flee into water until the air temperature rises above 25C (Fay and Ray 1968, p. 10). Fur seal pups also do well in the summer months, with average temperatures of 18–19C (Hubbard 1968, p. 337), and it is no wonder that fur seals have been permanently kept in open enclosures of the northern mid-latitudes (Osburn 1911). The acclimated Antarctic Wedell Seals bask in the sunlight and summer heat as high as 34C (Ray and Smith 1968, p. 43). The sea otter has surprisingly been found to tolerate temperatures as much as 33C (Morrison et al. 1974, p. 228), which is far greater than it ever encounters in Alaska (5C).

I now consider penguins, although we cannot, of course, discuss the (unknown) temperature requirements of the extinct ones (Fordyce and Jones 1990, p. 434). To begin with, most penguins (e.g., King, Humboldt's, Rockhopper, Maccaroni, Galapagos, and Magellan) can live continuously in the temperate outdoors, tolerating temperatures as high as 36C (Nakagawa 1967, p. 40). Based on flipper area and plumage length, Stonehouse (1967, p. 189) rates the Emperor and Adelie penguins as the most strongly adapted to life under Antarctic conditions. It is commonly thought that the Adelie and Emperor penguins can be successfully maintained in temperate climates only within air-filtered and air-conditioned enclosures. The problem is thought to be not only temperature but aspergillosis, a fungal disease. Since Antarctic penguins are not exposed to fungal spores in their native environment, it is reasoned, they have little or no resistance to it (Todd 1978, p. 75). However, this is obviously a matter of individual variation, along with the temperature acclimatization of even the most cold-adapted penguins. Mycosis may be latent, and depend upon the penguin's reaction to the stresses of capture and captivity (Gillespie 1932, p. 56). Moreover, once antarctic penguins have become acclimated to temperate climates, they appear resistant to mycosis (Street 1956, p. 104).

Furthermore, King and Emperor penguins *have* successfully adapted to the warm and fungi-infested environment of the temperate outdoors (Gailey-Phipps 1978, p. 12; 1981, p. 80), even for periods of many years (Mottershead 1967, p. 29). The Emperor penguins are known to tolerate outdoor temperatures of 20–22C for at least several days (Nakagawa 1967, p. 40; Shirai 1967, p. 35), and water temperatures of 21C for long periods of time (Flieg et al. 1971, p. 67). Ironically, the subantarctic King penguins, once acclimated, are said to actually enjoy the heat and sunshine of the temperate summer (Gillespie 1932, p. 55). As for the highly cold-adapted Adelie penguins, they have been successfully maintained in indoor enclosures, for prolonged periods, at the 15–18C range (Nakagawa 1967, p. 40). Even non-acclimated Adelie penguins sometimes do not show heat stress even at ambient temperatures as high as 27C (Murrish 1982, p. 138), tolerating temperatures of 30C with no apparent discomfort (Chappell and Souza 1988, p. 788).

Just as polar animals can become acclimated to high air temperatures, so also can polar fish become acclimated to warm waters. This has been verified by experiment (Baroudy and Elliott 1994).

Polar Plants Climatically Flexible. Having dispelled the myth that polar animals require extreme cold and cannot tolerate moderate temperatures, let us do the same for polar plants. To begin with, many if not most plants can be made to grow in areas of the world far beyond their present natural ranges (MacArthur 1972, p. 132), indicating that the present-day restricted geographic distribution of plants is not only climatic in origin. Various boreal conifers (or their microevolutionary relatives) can grow in gardens of the temperate zone, far equatorward of their natural ranges, so long as they are protected from the competition of the temperate deciduous trees (Woodward 1987, p. 71). In fact, if temperature and precipitation were high and equal, tropical plants and trees would outcompete their temperate counterparts, and temperate plants and trees would outcompete their boreal counterparts. For tropical floras, the limiting factor is not absence of heat but presence of severe cold:

> As a general rule it can be concluded that the poleward spread of a particular physiognomic type of vegetation will be strongly controlled by minimum temperature and the physiological ability to survive low temperatures (Woodward 1987, p. 80).

The poleward spread is also controlled by the heat sum: the number of degree-days in a growing season (Woodward 1987, p. 102). Since this is partly governed by the latitude-determined solar insolation, there was probably a weak poleward floral zonation even in the antediluvian world with its equitable climate. Under present conditions, trees from the boreal, temperate deciduous, and tropical evergreen forest can coexist at a temperature range of about 10–40C (Woodward 1987, p. 25).

Experiments on Antarctic lichens (Kappen and Friedman 1983, p. 231) indicate that the optimum temperature for their photosynthesis, once solar illumination is taken into account, is far above the temperatures they normally encounter. Likewise, experiments on plants from the Arctic (Billings 1987, p. 361), acclimated to temperate climates, indicate optimal temperatures for photosynthesis at close to room temperature. Other tundra plants have an upper temperature limit (for photosynthesis) of 50C (Chernov 1985, p. 78), which is not only higher than any temperature they experience in the Arctic, but higher than most areas on earth presently ever get!

Microevolutionary Changes in Temperature Tolerance. Up to now I have been conservative in my discussion of climatic tolerances of organisms, having assumed, for purpose of discussion, that they were the same before the Flood as they are now. In actuality, temperature tolerances can be readily altered by microevolution. This means that, before the Flood, presently-polar and presently-tropical organisms could have coexisted over a broader range of temperatures that they can today.

To begin with, there is a wide range of temperature tolerances between members of the same family, genus, and even the species. Thus, the frog genus *Rana* and even the species *R. pipiens* display a different range of temperature requirements for developing embryos, depending upon geographic latitude (Moore 1949). The highly cold-adapted Emperor Penguin is congeneric with the minimally cold-adapted King Penguin, and the highly cold-adapted Adelie Penguin is congeneric with the less cold-adapted Chinstrap and Gentoo Penguins (Stonehouse 1967, p. 174). This variation within the kind even shows up even in cases of actual interbreeding between more heat-tolerant and less heat-tolerant animals. For instance, the polar bear can freely interbreed with the brown bear (Kowalska 1969). The less cold-adapted subantarctic and the more cold-adapted antarctic fur seals can also hybridize (Kerley 1983). Likewise, the highly cold-adapted Adelie Penguin can interbreed with the less-strongly cold-adapted Gentoo Penguin (Flieg et al. 1971, p. 71).

Proof of rapid microevolutionary changes in temperature tolerances is provided by the house sparrow. In just 50 years after introduction to North America, it has differentiated into races, with the more northerly populations showing adaptations for cold climate (e.g., increased body size: Johnson and Selander 1964). In the aquatic realm, two populations of pupfish, separated in waters of different temperatures for a period of several centuries to a few millennia, have demonstrated microevolutionary divergences in their respective temperature tolerances (Hirshfield et al. 1980).

When we contemplate the changes in global climate since the Flood, particularly the advent of severely cold temperatures, we realize that the organisms in the pre-Flood world must have been pre-adapted to live in cold climates. But, as a matter of fact, this is true even of many present-day tropical creatures. We are learning that the tropics are not as all-benevolent as once supposed, nor are the conditions there monotonous. For instance, seasonal cycles are not, as once supposed, limited to temperate reptiles. Tropical reptiles also have seasonal cycles, albeit governed by subtle environmental changes (Crews and Garrick 1980, p. 51).

Desert Life in a Desert-Less World

Aridity: Tolerance or Necessity? Arguments about desert animals suffocating upon removal from the desert (Moore 1983, p. 18), or requiring a desert environment in order to exist in the first place (Moore 1983, p. 18) display a grave misunderstanding of the biology of desert creatures. They confuse the creatures' tolerance of desert conditions with an obligation to live under such conditions! To begin with, adaptation to aridity is a matter of degree, and there are large areas of desert so dry that *no* macroscopic form of life can live there (Kirmiz 1962, p. 6).

Secondly, resistance to aridity is altered by microevolutionary changes, which probably arose only since the Flood. For instance, there are desert-adapted cows that can go without water much longer than cows native to lush grasslands (Taylor 1968, p. 198). Most of the species of desert plants and animals are congeneric with, and nearly all are confamilial with, their non-desert counterparts (Kirmiz 1962, p. 7). Finally, desert animals do not have any special organs to enable them to tolerate aridity: their respective adaptations to desert life are simply a matter of degree when contrasted to their nondesert relatives, or simply pre-adaptations for life in nondesert environments. For instance, desert rodents are no different from any other rodents, but simply can live in the desert because their biology allows them to subsist on dry grain without free water (Kirmiz 1962, p. 11), and because many of them burrow and thereby avoid the daytime heat. Likewise, desert reptiles are notable for showing little if any qualitative physiological differences from non-desert reptiles (Bradshaw 1988).

Even the organisms strongly adapted to aridity can survive in wetter environments. Consider, for instance, the camel. The fact that it can go a long period of time without water certainly does not mean that it requires dehydration! Camels can have access to unlimited quantities of water (Crandall 1964, p. 544), and have successfully lived in non-desert regions (Gaultheir-Pilters and Dagg 1981, p. 122-3). Nor do camels require torrid temperatures, as proven by the fact that they once flourished in many cold areas of Eurasia (Gaultheir-Pilters and Dagg 1981, p. 122). Among desert plants, the cactus is notable for not requiring arid conditions to survive. It can tolerate frequent watering so long as the drainage of the soil is good (Nichol 1969, p. 205).

A Modern Picture of Possible Antediluvian Mini-Deserts. Despite having shown the contrary, let us suppose, for the sake of argument, that desert creatures did in fact require arid environments. If it is correct that there were no regional deserts in the antediluvian world, xeric environments, of varying degree, probably still existed. For instance, if the antediluvian mist that watered the land (Genesis 2:6) did not reach all areas with adequate moisture, these areas would have been arid or semi-arid. It is therefore notable that many desert insects are capable of living without free-standing water by drinking very small amounts of water that condense as dew (Crawford 1981, pp. 57-8).

Moore (1983, p. 18) scorned the idea of antediluvian miniature deserts, thereby again displaying his ignorance. Such deserts not only are possible, but exist even today. They are localized, occurring in areas of normal rainfall. The aridity is therefore caused by topographic conditions which cause water to rapidly run off, thus generating a small area of near-perpetual aridity and unabated solar insolation. Such miniature deserts occur in the Ohio Valley and Mississippi Valley of western Illinois (Voigt 1972) and possess a typical desert ecology. In fact, many of the very same plants adapted to aridity (such as cacti) and found in the western deserts of the US also occur in these midwestern mini-deserts (Voigt 1972, p. 30). The same holds true for the insect fauna.

Bats and Reptiles on the Ark

I now focus on the most temperature-sensitive animals on the Ark itself. How could the temperature needs of all the animals on the Ark have been met simultaneously? We need to keep this apparent difficulty in perspective by realizing that most animals on the Ark could have tolerated a wide range of temperature. For instance, the comfort zone of cattle and sheep is 5–21 C (Ensminger 1991, p. 115-6). Most other captive mammals are comfortable at a housing temperature within the range of 15–25 C (CCAC 1984, vol. 1, p. 80). Considering modern bats, there is a large overlap in their respective temperature requirements. For instance, tropical bats can be kept at a temperature of 25–28 C, with temperate bats down to 22 C (Barnard 1991, p. 9). The key to meeting their thermal needs is to provide a temperature gradient (see below).

Let us now consider reptiles. If their temperature and photoperiod requirements are not met, their growth will be limited and their feeding will be reduced (Barnard 1991, p. 20). Sometimes they decline and die. However, this decline is over a relatively long period of time (Frye 1991, Vol. 1, p. 161). I had earlier pointed out that most captive animals show an asymptotic decline in death rate with time after the animals have been in captivity. Likewise, the experiments of Licht et al. (1969, p. 481), involving temperature as a variable, show that captive lizards not only die off with an asymptotically-declining death rate with time, but that the survivors appear to tolerate changes in temperatures quite well. If this can be generalized to other reptiles, then it has a practical application in terms of decreasing the reptilian sensitivity to possibly unfavorable temperatures on the Ark. Had reptiles been in captivity prior to their embarkation on the Ark, those individuals that were more sensitive to temperature changes would have already died off before the time came for

God to commandeer the reptilian pairs into the Ark. (This is another example of the tolerance-to-captivity filter: Fig. 6).

The exact temperature requirements have not been established for many types of reptiles (Mattison 1987, p. 44). The problem of not knowing the specific thermal preferendum of a reptile is solved by providing a temperature gradient in its cage (Gans and van den Sande 1976, p. 30). This creates a thermally-diversified environment, and gives the reptile an opportunity to choose its temperatures. At the same time, we should not overstate the limitations posed by reptilian thermal requirements, as reptiles are not nearly as fragile as Moore (1983, p. 31) makes them out to be. In reality, most reptiles are robust and easily cared for (Mason et al. 1991, p. 84). Numerous snakes have been successfully maintained without specialized temperature conditions, and at near room temperatures (or slightly warmer), for long periods of time (Murphy and Campbell 1987, p. 167). Furthermore, there is some evidence that reptiles can become acclimated to different climatic conditions (Schwaner 1989, p. 398).

A Variable Thermal Environment on the Ark. There are a number of ways that a temperature gradient could have been provided on the Ark for temperature-sensitive animals. For instance, concave mirrors could have been used to concentrate sunlight into certain areas of the Ark. This is feasible because the use of mirrors definitely goes back to early antiquity. For instance, the ancient Chinese knew how to make concave mirrors (CAS 1983, pp. 171-2). These have also been used experimentally to study the effects of sunlight when reflected upon reptiles (White 1973, p. 507). To effect a temperature gradient, for example, elongated reptile-bearing cages could have had one end bathing in heat and the other end in cold.

Post-Flood Origins of Thermal Preferenda. Up to now I have, for the sake of discussion, accepted the present-day thermal preferenda of reptiles and bats as if they had been valid at the time of the Flood. In actuality, these ecological specializations (temperature, photoperiod, etc.) are mostly post-Flood microevolutionary occurrences. One evidence for this is the fact that optimal temperature requirements of iguanid lizards vary according to species (Huey and Kingsolver 1993, p. 526), and the same holds true for many other reptiles (see Table 1 of Heatwole 1976). Furthermore, for reptiles, thermal preferenda vary within species, according to environment, by season of the year, and according to body mass of the individual reptile (Smith and Ballinger 1994, p. 2066).

Chapter 15

Dormancy of Animals on the Ark

I begin by reaffirming the fact that *all* the calculations regarding the logistics and manpower on the Ark, presented in this work, assume *no* suspended animation of the animals of *any* kind. The reason for my deliberate neglect of dormancy is the difficulty of quantifying its effects, due to: 1) scientific ignorance of the manner and degree of dormancy states in many animals, 2) apparent lack of a comprehensive database on animal dormancy (including the precise conditions required for it to occur in given animals), 3) great variability among individuals of even the same species in their ability to enter and remain in a dormant state, and, most important of all, 4) probable microevolutionary changes in the degree and nature of animal dormancy since antediluvian times. This last factor assumes paramount significance, and is discussed in detail in the last part of this section.

In this work, I use the expression dormancy as a general umbrella term to generalize the energy-saving behaviors of animals, irrespective of their physiological origins. After all, we are only interested in the reduction of time necessary for animal care aboard the Ark, and possibly also the reduction of food, water, and waste production. Commensurate with the rest of this work, I do not consider any type of miraculous dormancy.

Critics' Misrepresentations of Animal Dormancy. Let us first consider the deepest and most long-lasting of these dormancy states—hibernation. Whitcomb (1989), in the first (i.e., 1963) edition of his book, correctly answered Ark critics by pointing out that hibernating animals do *not* sleep continuously all winter, and still need to eat periodically. Indeed, Whitcomb, a theologian, has been very perceptive in this matter, as many laymen and even scientists have a distorted view of hibernation:

> The view of hibernation held by most people, and constantly reinforced by children's stories and superficial nature programs, is of a state of deep sleep which starts in autumn and ends in spring. The hibernator is thought to select a site which will permit it to survive throughout the winter. This view has many serious flaws in it, and though they have been pointed out by a number of scientists after conducting field studies in various parts of the world over many decades, it persists (Ransome 1990, p. 81).

Oblivious to this fact, we keep right on hearing from anti-Creationists (e.g., Moore 1983, p. 27) and compromising evangelicals (e.g., Morton 1995, p. 70; Youngblood 1980, p. 132) the old argument that food taken aboard the Ark (Genesis 6:21) vitiates the possibility of hibernation.

Temperature. Moore (1983, p. 25) presents an outdated stereotype of hibernation as a type of winter sleep. In actuality, many animals: 1) don't need winterlike conditions to hibernate, 2) can enter shorter bouts of torpor instead of deep hibernation, 3) can become inactive and/or reduce feeding without entering any apparent state of dormancy. Each of these points is elaborated below.

Let us first examine the temperature/hibernation relationship, and rebut the myth that animal dormancy occurs only at cold temperatures. Episodes of hibernation are not necessarily eliminated, but only shortened, as ambient temperature rises. Such an inverse relationship between temperature and duration of dormancy has been found in various creatures, such as the vespertilionid bats (Twente et al. 1985, pp. 2956-7) and the eastern pygmy possum (*Cercartetus nanus*: Geiser 1993).

Many animals can be in a state of dormancy at or well above 15C. Ground squirrels (*Citellus*) will remain in hibernation even if the ambient temperature stays at 21C for two years (Pengelley and Fisher 1963), and remain torpid for briefer instances at temperatures as high as 23.8C (Wade 1930, p. 168), or even 30C (Kayser 1961, p. 53). Likewise dormice, unless they are kept very warm, will become dormant in wintertime (Bartlett 1899, p. 108), and even experience weeklong bouts of torpor at summer temperatures as high as 15–21C (Johnson 1931, p. 441). Members of Order Insectivora will enter hibernation if their cage temperature drops below 16C (Wallach and Boever 1983, p. 655), and will enter torpor at slightly higher temperatures. The hedgehog will not awaken from hibernation until the temperature reaches 22C (Proctor 1949, p. 108). Some bats (e.g., *Pipistrellus*) have been found hibernating at temperatures over 12C (Tuttle 1991, p. 9) and can experience a large 24-hour temperature change (-5C to 13C) without awakening (Stebbings 1988, p. 7). A similar temperature range (2–16C) was tolerated by hibernating brown bats (Twente and Twente 1987). Some species of the bat genus *Myotis* hibernate at an average temperature of 11.8C (Stones and Wiebers 1965, p. 160), while the big-eared bat (*Corynorhinus*) is in hibernation/torpor at temperatures as high as 14.4C (Layne 1958, p. 232).

A wide variety of reptiles can be kept in hibernation if the ambient temperature is about 10 C (Frye 1991, Vol. 1, p. 30), though some will hibernate at temperatures as high as 15 C (e. g., the ratsnake: Gillingham 1989, p. 88), and remain in hibernation even if the temperature briefly rises to over 20C (Tryon 1987, p. 25). It is interesting to note that at least some reptiles, if given an experimental choice between a warm and cool area, move to cooler areas at various time intervals, apparently in order to become torpid (Regal 1967). If the previously-discussed temperature gradient had been provided on the Ark for the reptiles, they may have chosen coolness and hibernation, instead of warmth, at regular time intervals.

The geographic variation in temperatures experienced by hibernators provides additional evidence that a considerable number of animals can hibernate at relatively high ambient temperatures. Engels (1951) found that chipmunks are nearly as prone to hibernate in the southern US (where winter temperatures are frequently above room temperature (25C) for weeks at a time) as they are in the northeast US (with its brutally cold winters). Tortoises will hibernate even if taken far outside their normal geographic range (Davenport 1992, p. 113).

Seasonality. Moore (1983, p. 26) says that no animal hibernates for an entire year, which is a half-truth. First of all, under the right conditions, certain animals *have* hibernated for an entire year (Kayser 1961, p. 54). But this is besides the point. As discussed in the final section of this work, continuous bouts of dormancy were unnecessary to save greatly on manpower. Moore (1983, p. 26) also claims that, if exposed to cold and dark during the "wrong" time of the year, animals will increase their activity instead of hibernating. Even without taking into account the decoupling of seasonal rhythms from hibernation (discussed in the ensuing paragraph), this claim of Moore is another half-truth. For instance, black and grizzly bears during part of the summer will indeed become more active under adverse conditions. Yet, for part of the spring and summer, they also go through a poorly-understood phase known as walking hibernation (Nelson et al. 1983, p. 285-6), wherein the bears are active yet eat very little or nothing, exhibiting various physiological states similar to hibernation.

Let us now focus on hibernation as a seasonal behavior, taking a closer look at Moore's (1983, p. 26) insistence that hibernation will not occur in the "wrong" time of year. Before the Flood, with greatly reduced seasonal differences in temperatures relative to today, animals were probably much less dependent upon seasonal cues for hibernation than they are today (see below). Yet even without microevolutionary changes, many animals that hibernate have proven to be easily decoupled from the usual seasonality of their hibernation. For instance, in experiments with squirrels, Pengelley and Fisher (1963, p. 1112, 1115), and Lyman et al. (1982, p. 299) have found that the animals entered and left hibernation at a very different time of year than they do in nature. Moreover, Pengelley and Fisher (1963, p. 1112) found that the squirrels gradually became habituated to high temperatures in the sense that the duration of their hibernation became progressively longer and more insensitive to the high temperatures.

Animal Dormancy and Exacting Conditions. Moore (1983, pp. 25-6) imagines that the "exacting conditions" for dormancy could not possibly have been met on the Ark. In reality, the evidence clearly indicates that animals can hibernate under various conditions. Gates (1936, p. 271) noted bats hibernating in his lab even when temperatures fluctuated greatly, reaching to near-room temperature. Twente and Twente (1987) have found that the patterns of hibernation of brown bats are similar under both uncontrolled conditions (with widely varying temperatures) as they are under controlled laboratory conditions at one temperature. Animal dormancy is not an all-or-none proposition even for many of the obligate cold-temperature hibernators. If the temperature conditions for deep and prolonged hibernation are not met, animals can go into a shorter hibernation or torpor instead (Geiser 1994). When, in the lab, the season comes for the bat *Eptesicus* to hibernate, but temperatures are too warm (12.8–21.2C) for this to occur, they go into bouts of torpor instead, each episode of which lasts one or more days (Gates 1936, p. 271). Likewise, when it is too warm and well-illuminated for woodchucks to hibernate, they will nevertheless have periods of dormancy lasting for several days (Clark 1984, p. 191).

It should be pointed out that even this tendency of the duration of torpor bouts to vary inversely with temperature could have been altered by microevolution since the Flood. Indeed, it is possible to find or breed some lineages of hamsters whose tendency to enter torpor, and duration in it, shows little or no differences at varying temperatures (e.g., 5C to 15C: Ruf et al. 1993, p. 111). To the extent that hibernation has constraints based upon seasonality, torpor definitely occurs at any season of the year. Horseshoe bats go into torpor on cool, rainy summer days, often seeking the cooler parts of a house, such as cellars, or under floorboards. (Schober 1984, p. 100). The same holds true for the northern bats in Sweden (Rydell 1990. p. 10). Likewise, the big brown bats (*Eptesicus*) can be torpid during summer cool spells for several days at a time (Hamilton and Barclay 1994, p. 748), and some species of the bat *Myotis* can go into torpor for forty hours during summer cool and/or rainy spells (Kurta 1990, p. 255). The Microchiropteran bats of the Northern Hemisphere readily go into daily torpor (often longer) when the temperature is between 10C and 28C (Kayser 1961, p. 6).

Many animals will go into torpor even at room temperatures, even spontaneously. This is true for many marsupial as well as placental mammals (Geiser 1994, p. 4), and is discussed in more detail in the section below on animals that don't hibernate. Certain marsupials will enter torpor at moderate temperatures (14C–18C), with or without food deprivation, as a function of the individual animal (Collins et al. 1987, p. 54). Finally, some animals will enter dormancy with neither reduced food nor reduced temperatures. Thus, some kinds of hamsters are cued for dormancy solely by a shortening of photoperiod (Ruf et al. 1993), although, for most animals, photoperiod appears to have little effect on the onset and duration of dormancy (Kayser 1961, p. 55).

If, because the conditions have not been met, an animal cannot go into hibernation, but goes into short bouts of torpor instead, the savings in food consumption still are significant. For instance, a mouse not in torpor will need about seventeen grams of food per 100 grams of body weight daily (Tucker 1966, p. 250). Even if in torpor only ten hours daily, the daily food requirement will drop to about 12 grams daily. Similarly, frequently-torpid squirrels consume an average of only about half the food of active ones (Jameson 1965, p. 637).

Dormancy in Captive Animals. Perhaps the strongest evidence for the falsehood of Moore's (1983, pp. 25-7) assertions about animal dormancy only occurring under exacting conditions is the ubiquitous occurrence of dormancy among captive animals even when *no* provision had been made to induce it. This is notably true of bats (Hopkins 1990, p. 172; Ryberg 1947, p. 32), and reptiles. In a set of guidelines for the transport of animals, CITES (1980, p. 69, 75) warns against assuming that lethargic reptiles are ill, because they may only be in torpor. Likewise, Leslie (1970, p. 112) informs uninitiated owners of wild-animal pets that captive chipmunks, while not going into full hibernation, will nevertheless go into bouts of torpor lasting three to four weeks each. Clark and Olfert (1986, p. 732) point out that the "unusual inactivity" reported by owners of captive rodents is a result of the owners' ignorance of the animals' torpor. Investigators have long observed that if laboratory mice are inadequately fed and subject to cold, they may lapse into a state of torpor (Fertig and Edmonds 1969, p. 110).

When it is too warm to hibernate, animals often go through a significant reduction in feeding even without displaying any outward signs of torpor. For instance, the bats described by Gates (1936, p. 271) while not visibly in a state of torpor, were often quiescent. As for snakes, Mitchell and Pocock (1907, p. 786) note that:

> . . . even in a House artificially heated all snakes feed less readily and some of them not at all during the winter months.

More recently, Vance (1990, p. 115) has confirmed this fact. Polar bears exhibit similar behavior:

> Bears kept in temperate climates do not hibernate through the winter, but during severe weather they may become drowsy and take little food or even cease feeding altogether for a week or so at a time (Street 1956, p. 77).

Dormancy and the Non-Problem of Animal Mortality. Another one of Moore's (1983, p. 26) false arguments against hibernation is his claim that, if the Ark animals went into hibernation, most of them would have died from it. The basis of his assertions are some studies which have indicated high rates of mortality among animals after hibernation. First of all, these studies are completely irrelevant to the Ark situation, as they refer to animals hibernating under winter conditions. By far the main cause of death in overwintering hibernation, apart from freeze kill, is premature exhaustion of fat reserves while it is still too cold to find food (Bauwens 1981, pp. 742-3). In addition, the studies cited by Moore (1983, p. 25) have now been shown to be atypical (Costanzo 1989, and references cited therein). More recent studies indicate that only a very small percentage of animals fail to survive a state of hibernation. Overwintering survival rates of animals, which are governed by much more severe conditions than was true for any animal on the Ark, are now known to be in the 95–100% range (Bauwens 1981; Parker and Brown 1974).

Furthermore, it is known that if animals can feed whenever they are awakened from hibernation (as was, of course, the case on the Ark), mortality rates are negligible (Chew et al. 1965, p. 490). For instance, Tryon (1984, p. 25) reports a zero death rate for captive snakes after a prolonged period of hibernation. Elsewhere, in an experiment (Tucker 1966, p. 248), five mice collectively survived 150 periods of torpor without a single death.

Excessive Animal Arousal on the Ark? Moore (1983, p. 25) supposes that animals on the Ark could not have gone into hibernation because of its constant motion. In actuality, creatures in hibernation or torpor show varying degrees of sensitivity to external stimuli, and at least some of the animals could have entered and remained in various states of dormancy even under fairly large amounts of stimulation. For instance, a hibernating hedgehog will not arouse from hibernation if touched (Johnson 1931, p. 448), unless this happens repeatedly. Ground squirrels remain in hibernation in outdoor cages subject to normal weather conditions, as well as disturbances by dogs, children, etc. (Pengelley and Fisher 1963, p. 1105). Minor disturbances will not prevent but only delay the entry of woodchucks into a state of hibernation (Clark 1984, p. 191). Once hibernating, woodchucks can be handled and weighed without awakening (Bartholomew and Cade 1957, p. 67). While some hibernating hamsters are awakened by the opening of their cages, others sleep through this procedure, and are not even awakened if intentionally touched with a pencil eraser (Chaffee 1966, p. 152). A hibernating marmot can sleep through a cardiac puncture with a hypodermic needle (Endres 1930, p. 245).

There are many hibernating animals that can be handled and even carried without awakening. The poor-will, a bird that hibernates, does not awaken even when its back has been stroked (Jaeger 1948, p. 45). At one time, a "dead" tortoise had been painted, labeled, and placed on a museum shelf, only to revive when the room warmed up (Bartlett 1899, p. 188). Hedgehogs in hibernation have been handled and mistaken for dead (Proctor 1949, p. 109). Likewise, a "dead" boa constrictor had been carried out of a ship's hold before reviving near a fireplace (Bartlett 1899, pp. 261-2).

Bats are well-known for their vulnerability to disturbance from hibernation, so Moore (1983, p. 25) deduces that they could not have hibernated on the Ark. In actuality, experiments on individual bats demonstrate that they vary greatly in their sensitivity to arousal from stimuli. Some hibernating bats, when collected, do not begin to awaken until five to ten minutes after being bagged (Layne 1958, p. 232). Bats hibernating in refrigerators may not awaken as a result of motion unless the refrigerator is jarred quite violently (Reeder and Cowles 1951, p. 392). The California Mastiff bat, even when only in torpor, will not readily awaken even if its wings are manually shifted around (Howell 1920, p. 116).

Let us consider bats in the context of their cave environment, and how it differs from their housing on the Ark. We are well aware of the effects of deliberate violent disturbance (vandalism) on bats in caves, but we are not sure how they are, overall, affected by subtle and inadvertent disturbances (McCracken 1988, p. 7). This is also a matter of large individual variation. Some bats hibernating in caves may awaken if approached, while others don't awaken even if flashlights are shone upon them (Folk 1940, p. 313). Surveys of the bat populations in caves (Tuttle 1979, p. 8) suggest that moderately frequent disturbances of caves do not have a severe impact on bat populations as long as the disturbances are not intense.

These anecdotal reports are supported by recent systematic lab studies on hibernating bats (Speakman et al. 1991). The investigation confirms the fact that bats, while sensitive to tactile stimulation, seldom awaken from hibernation as a result of proximate human speech, flashlights, photographic flashes, nor gusts of hot air. A study of bats in their cave environment (Thomas 1995), using infrared motion detectors, indicates that a certain number of bats will apparently rouse from hibernation solely as a result of a casual human visit to the cave. However, the wide individual sensitivity of bats to stimulation is confirmed, with a cascade effect taking place (Thomas 1995, pp. 944–5). In other words, a few very sensitive bats will rouse as a result of casual human activity, and their motion (or inadvertent contact with neighboring bats) will then cause a secondary arousal of many bats which themselves are evidently insensitive to casual stimulation.

The importance of choosing those bat individuals for the Ark prone to hibernate (see below), as well as those which are relatively insensitive to nontactile stimulation, averts such a cascade effect. Moreover, the consequences of premature arousal in a cave and on the Ark were entirely different. In nature, a bat aroused prematurely (and especially if repeatedly), may return to a state of torpor but have insufficient fat reserves left to survive the winter (MacCracken 1988, p. 7). By contrast, on the Ark, even if most bats were regularly disturbed from hibernation, they would not have suffered. They had unlimited food and were not subject to severe cold; a very different situation from a bat overwintering in a cave! This, of course, applies to other creatures besides bats. In an experiment (Mrosovsky and Fisher 1970), a hibernating ground squirrel was deliberately aroused many times during hibernation. It experienced little weight loss because of its access to food. From this we can conclude that, even if the motion of the Ark had been sufficient to rouse animals frequently from dormancy, they would not have been harmed by it. Only some of the savings in food consumption and in manpower expenditures would have been lessened.

Finally, some hibernating or torpid animals can withstand an extraordinary amount of stimulation without awakening. For instance, both Otis (1930, p. 175) and Pengelley and Fisher (1968, pp. 561-2) were able to toss hibernating ground squirrels into the air like balls, and then catch them, without arousing them! Furthermore, Pengelley and Fisher (1968, pp. 561-2) found that ground squirrels become habituated to such extreme stimuli. This suggests that any animals hibernating on the Ark must have become progressively desensitized to its motions.

Let us now consider noise. In an experiment involving hibernating ground squirrels, white noise (such as would be the waves outside the Ark) of over ninety decibels, applied for two to four hours, failed to awaken them (Folk 1960). Hibernating brown bats were not awakened until the sound was above ninety-five decibels (Twente and Twente 1987, p. 1671). As for loud impulsive noise, Strumwasser (1960, p. 305) noted that sharp rapping on the cages of hibernating squirrels aroused them only if it was maintained for a few minutes. Kurta (1990, p. 257) reported an instance where brief but extremely loud hammering of a concrete floor failed to arouse a group of hibernating bats. In general, the threshold of arousal from hibernation is usually much higher than the threshold of arousal from nightly sleep. For instance, the strength of the pulling of a marmot's hair must be several times greater to awaken it from even shallow hibernation than from ordinary sleep (Endres 1930, pp. 246-7).

Moore's (1983) claim that animals would not hibernate on the Ark (because of its motion) is flatly contradicted by the situations where animals *have* hibernated on ships despite the ships' incessant motions. Earlier, I had discussed the account of the boa which had hibernated on a ship for three months and had been assumed to be dead (Bartlett 1899, pp. 261-2). Bats don't require quiet caves to hibernate: they have been found hibernating in occupied man-made structures, including ships (Hamilton and Whitaker 1979, p. 84).

Selecting Animals for Tendency to Hibernate. If hibernation had actually been an important consideration in the care of the animals on the Ark, Noah and/or God could have picked out those individual animals that have the greatest tendency towards hibernation and/or torpor, thus using the filters (Fig. 6). For instance, animals could have been chosen which readily accumulate large amounts of fat throughout their bodies or tails, as such animal individuals are especially prone to enter dormancy (Geiser 1994; Morton 1980). Moreover, for at least some marsupials, very obese individuals begin hibernation with free access to food and water and relatively high ambient temperatures (Geiser 1994, p. 7).

What About Animals that Don't Hibernate? Moore (1983, p. 25) makes much of the fact that most animals do not hibernate. While this is technically correct, at least for modern animals, it is of little significance. What we need is a condition where animals can fast for prolonged periods of time, and are not particularly concerned about its physiological origin.

The earlier-discussed torpor is not limited to animals which normally hibernate but find it too warm to do so. Far from it: animals that never hibernate often go into bouts of torpor. Geiser (1994, p. 4) finds bouts of hibernation among species of marsupials typically lasting between 100 and 600 hours, whereas bouts of torpor of marsupials that never hibernate typically last between 4 and 20 hours.

Many nonhibernating animals will readily slip into bouts of torpor simply by being denied food (French 1992, p. 105). These periods of torpor can range in duration from hours to weeks. For instance, at 10C, the bat *Myotis yumanensis* can go up to three weeks without eating if it is denied food (Ramage 1947, p. 61). Various tropical glossophagine bats, once thought to be free of any tendency towards dormancy, are now known to spend at least a day in torpor if denied food (Rasweiler 1973, p. 400). Moreover, Rasweiler points out that this torpor is independent of seasonal factors and lengthy endogenous rhythms.

Yet even some small animals need not enter into *any* kind of dormancy in order to avoid feeding for long periods of time. Consider the Mexican free-tailed bat *Tadarida mexicana*. It does not hibernate, but does accumulate fat reserves, enabling it to go for considerable periods of time without eating simply by curtailing normal activity (Christensen 1947, p. 60; Tuttle 1994, p. 14). The vampire bat, a tropical bat which does not hibernate, can go without feeding three days (Wimsatt and Guerriere 1961, p. 451), or even four (Ditmars and Greenhall 1935, p. 69). For such a small animal, the duration is notable.

Few birds enter deep hibernation, but many enter bouts of torpor ranging from hours to days at a time, with or without inanition (for tabulation, see Reinertsen 1983). Moreover, certain birds will voluntarily forego eating for periods of time up to a few months (Cherel et al. 1988), and many more birds may have been capable of such prolonged fasts before they lost this capability after the Flood.

Why Do Few Large Animals Enter into Dormant States? Although few large animals hibernate or even go into torpor, it is interesting to note that certain large animals (e.g., some deer, sheep, etc.: Ryg 1983) go into seasonal cycles in feeding, with their metabolic rates being as much as 40% lower in winter than in summer. Presently, this cycle appears to be governed partly by photoperiod, and possibly by degree of animal activity (Ryg 1983, p. 251). Depending upon the nature of any microevolutionary changes in these seasonal cycles since the Flood, these cycles may have played a major role in the reduction of food intake among the larger animals on the Ark.

A probable reason why so few medium and large animals are capable of hibernation is the fact that they don't have to, physiologically speaking. Small animals denied food will starve in a matter of days unless they become torpid (French 1992, p. 113), whereas larger animals can subsist on little or no food for long periods of time without entering any state of dormancy. The physiological basis for this is twofold. First of all, metabolism scales versus body mass at approximately the 0.75 power (Blueweiss et al. 1978, p. 269), so one gram of elephant flesh requires only about 3% of the food energy of one gram of bat flesh. No wonder that the hibernating bear does not need to experience a major drop in body temperature (Nelson 1980, p. 2955), unlike small hibernators.

Furthermore, large animals are much more capable of accumulating fat stores, in terms of percent body mass, than are smaller animals (Calder 1984, p. 16). This is reflected in the ability of medium to large animals to go long periods of time without eating. Horses can go five to six days without food and water, and twenty to twenty-five days without food if water is provided (Hintz 1983, p. 77). Lions can readily fast a week or more without obvious discomfort (Schaller 1972, p. 276). Mammalian and avian predators can go without food for several days (Neubuser 1968, p. 167) so can various other birds (Bartlett 1899, p. 225). Snakes are well known for their prolonged fasts, frequently months at a time (Domalein 1977, p. 186) or even over a year (Wood 1982, p. 112). One undisclosed Nineteenth century zoo kept an elephant alive on less than two kg of wheat cake daily for a prolonged period of time (Peel 1903, p. 173). I am not suggesting that the animals on the Ark were actually subject to such food deprivation, but only want to emphasize the *capability* of large animals going long periods without eating if it had been necessary (e.g., some emergency on the Ark which had prevented the frequent feeding of many of the animals).

One must also consider changes in diurnal sleep, among medium to large animals, as a result of the conditions on the Ark. Ruckebusch (1972, p. 24) reports that pigs sleep about 20% longer than usual when kept in darkness and with reduced sensory stimulation, or under the condition of continuous monotonous sound. This could have been duplicated on the Ark (i. e., the darkness of the inner recesses of the Ark, and the white noise provided by the waves), but any extent that this would have reduced the time needed to care for the animals is not clear from Ruckebusch's study.

Microevolutionary Changes in Dormancy Among Animals. For purposes of discussion I have, up to now, considered present-day tendencies of animal dormancy to have been normative at the time of the Flood. One reason why it is so difficult to quantify the effects of dormancy on captive animals is the fact that the nature of dormancy probably has changed substantially since the time of Noah. Furthermore, many of the conditions of the Flood have not, thus far, been duplicated in experiments on hibernation and torpor. For instance, there is some evidence that hibernation at relatively high ambient temperatures (15C–18C) may be facilitated with the right barometric pressure (Kristofferson and Soivo 1964, p. 19).

The microevolutionary lability of dormancy is proved by several lines of evidence, notably the variation of dormancy (ease of entry, duration, temperatures needed, etc), seen even *within* particular species (Collins et al. 1987; Geiser 1994, pp. 2-3; Lyman et al. 1982, p. 292; Ruf et al. 1993, p. 111; Tannenbaum and Pivorun 1984). Furthermore, the nature of animal dormancy is so malleable that it can be significantly altered by means of selective breeding. Chaffee (1966) subjected two lineages of Syrian hamsters to selective breeding according to their ease of entering hibernation. In just two generations, he had dichotomous lineages: one which largely avoided going into hibernation and another which was very prone to it.

Let us now consider the microevolutionary lability of animals relative to ambient temperature needed to induce dormancy. The required temperature varies greatly from species to species of reptile (see Table 1 of Heatwole 1976). The same holds true for various congeneric species of bats (Davis and Reite 1967), as does bats' ease of arousal from hibernation (McCracken 1988, p. 7). The duration of torpidity in certain mice is also microevolutionarily labile, as demonstrated by its large variability between different species of *Perognathus* (Wolf and Bateman 1978, p. 715). Since, before the Flood, temperatures were less extreme than today, and severe cold was probably nonexistent, animal dormancy (including hibernation) was probably much less governed by season and cold temperatures than it is today. For this reason, animals on the Ark were probably much more prone to enter dormancy at near-room temperatures, and for longer periods, than do animals today.

The taxonomic distribution of animals known to hibernate occurs in many representatives of diverse mammalian orders (Chaffee 1966, p. 153). This suggests that this is a relict physiological state that was much more prevalent, if not universal, in antediluvian times. Further support for this possibility comes from the discovery of an apparent molecular "trigger" for hibernation (Nelson 1980, p. 2957, and citations). This "trigger" molecule is believed to be analogous to insulin: biologically identical (or nearly so) in quite different animals, yet serving the same or similar function. Blood taken from hibernating animals and injected into ones not in hibernation not only triggers hibernation in the same species of animal during summer, but even causes quasi-hibernation states in animals (e.g., rats) that don't hibernate at all (Nelson 1980, p. 2957).

Animal Dormancy on the Ark: an Assessment. Despite the difficulty of quantifying the effects of dormancy on the Ark, the energy-saving implications of possible suspended animation of animals on the Ark can be assessed in general. There is an asymptotic decline in numbers of animals cared for per additional day that they are dormant. Let us consider, as discussed previously, the fact that each person on the Ark cared for 2,000 animals daily. This is under the assumption of no dormancy. If now, on average, animals were dormant every other day, the number of animals to care for was halved—1,000 animals per person per day. If dormant every two days for every one they were awake (a common situation observed with laboratory bats: Gates 1936, p. 271), the number dropped to 667. Note that each additional day of dormancy assumed progressively less importance, as the number of animals to care for daily dropped much more slowly: 500, 400, 333, etc. It is clear that long-term sleep of all or even most animals on the Ark was *not* required in order to have effect a drastic reduction in the number of animals needed to be cared for each day.

Part 3

The Recovery of the Earth's Biosphere After the Flood

Chapter 16

How Organisms Outside the
Ark Survived the Flood

As Aerial Plankton

The propagules of many organisms could have survived the Flood by becoming entrained in air currents, and then coming back down as a biological fallout (or aerial plankton) towards the end of the Flood as the winds subsided. It is seldom appreciated how many airborne biotic particles are present in air, even under tranquil condition. Many types of spores (of fungi, ferns, bryophytes) are readily transported by air currents (Van Zenten 1983). It is also interesting to note that the diaspores of tropical plants, which normally never experience temperatures below c. 15C, are capable of surviving deep-freeze temperatures of the upper atmosphere (as low as -30C: Van Zenten 1983, p. 60).

Moreover, airborne propagules are hardly limited to spore-sized objects. For instance, many kinds of nematode worms are resistant to desiccation, and are candidates for aerial transport (Thornton and New 1988, p. 515). Considering the diversity of nematodes in existence, this is especially noteworthy. Large numbers and diversities of insects have also been found airborne far out at sea (Farrow 1984, and references cited therein), and have been found on or in the water far from land, sometimes in vast quantities (Cheng and Birch 1978). Under the right conditions (such as entrainment in storms, and—on a more long-term basis—in jet streams), much larger particles may be transported, and for much longer periods of time. As demonstrated mathematically by Mollison (1986), a combination of winds and violent vertical atmospheric circulation can allow objects of seed size to be transported trans-continental distances. This means that, depending upon the precise upper-atmospheric conditions during the Flood, large numbers of small to medium-sized seeds (and probably insect eggs, etc.) were able to survive the Flood by remaining airborne throughout its duration.

In the Floodwaters, Which were Tolerable

Of all forms of life, the vast majority were not on the Ark, and could not have become (or remained, for one year) airborne, so must have survived the Flood on or in the water itself. Detractors of the Ark account have shown themselves as prone to raise fallacious arguments against the survival of the organisms outside the Ark as they are for organisms in it. Let us consider some of these arguments.

Did the Oceans Boil During the Flood? Soroka and Nelson (1983) have presented some impressive-looking calculations "proving" the fact that certain alleged events during the Flood must have made the earth intolerably hot. However, the heat-producing events which they attribute to the Flood are absurd in the extreme. All that these critics have done is build a ludicrous straw-man of the Flood. In terms of specifics, their scenario includes the following: 1) all rain during the Flood coming from water vapor *simultaneously* stored in the atmosphere (as if they had never heard of the hydrological cycle); 2) all floodwater originating from hydrothermal springs (who said this had to be so?); 3) all "excess" water for the Flood coming from comets (a self-originated fantasy); 4) all mountain-covering waves coming from a constant stream of bolide impacts (same as #3).

However, Soroka and Nelson (1983) have been outdone in pseudo-reasoning by Moore (1983, p. 10–11), who has blindly extrapolated information from some volcano (Bullard 1976; MacDonald 1972) and has arrived at a mind-boggling 3.65 octillion calories supposedly generated by volcanic action during the Flood. I have checked the plausibility of his gargantuan figure through the use of actual data on heat production from a cooling and congealing basaltic magma (Baker et al. 1989, p. 9247-8). Allowing a temperature drop from 1100C to 20C, while assuming a worst-case scenario of *complete* magma cooling during the Flood year, *perfectly efficient* heat transfer from magma to water, and *no* cooling of waters during the Flood year itself, comes out to a fantastic 3,190 million cubic kilometers of lava supposedly extruded during the Flood. To put this number in perspective, the *entire* volume of Phanerozoic rock is only 640 million cubic kilometers (Ronov 1982, p. 1369).

Clearly, Moore's computations have no semblance to reality. Furthermore, who said that the largest ancient lava flows, which dwarf in volume those of recent volcanoes (Simpkin and Siebert 1994, p. 25), need have formed *and completely cooled* during the Flood year itself? Moreover, the largest lava flows on land (e.g., flood basalts such as the Deccan Traps, as well as volcanic islands such as Iceland) are generally not interbedded between fossiliferous sediments, so they could have formed and gradually cooled long after the Flood. Most Flood-related igneous activity manifested itself not in volcanism but in plutonism. Plutons, of course, gradually gave up their heat for long periods after the Flood, so could not possibly have contributed to any mythical intolerable heat buildup on earth. Of course, the igneous rocks encountered in shield regions and among Precambrian basement rocks probably all date back to Creation Week, as do most large batholiths, which are rootless. We do not know, even approximately, the total volume of submarine volcanics (Simkin and Siebert 1994, p. 10), much less what fraction of them formed and cooled during the Flood year itself.

For volcanic heat to have been a potential problem during the Flood, not only its amount but also the rate of its dissipation need have been excessive. Earlier, I had assumed, for purposes of illustration, the complete cooling of Flood-extruded lavas within one year. This was far from the case. Lavas extruded underwater tend to develop a "skin" of solidified rock which greatly inhibits the rate of their cooling (Emiliani et al. 1981, p. 327), particularly if lava flows are thick. Much heat from volcanoes originates from volcanic gases, yet the pressure from overlying water tends to inhibit and even prohibit the explosive release of volcanic gases (Simkin and Siebert 1994, p. 10).

Apart from all this, Moore's (1983, p. 10–11) arguments about excessive volcanic heat revolve about the fallacious premise that heat from volcanoes readily spreads throughout the water. Apart from severe geographic inhomogeneities in the distribution of volcanics (Simkin and Siebert 1994), the heat emanating from underwater volcanic action does not even heat water subequally on a regional scale. The force from the earth's rotation acts as a powerful invisible cordon to confine superheated water to localized small circular areas of the ocean—even for decades at a time (Emiliani et al. 1981, p. 327; Emanuel et al. 1995, pp. 13, 763–4), except at the Equator. During the

Flood, this must have guaranteed the persistence of floodwaters cool enough for the survival of life, even if there had been enough volcanogenic heat, if distributed evenly, to have made the entire shoreless ocean too hot for any living thing.

Of course, all the foregoing discussion is not meant to imply that there were not vast areas of floodwater-covered continents subject to extreme heat, and in which probably no macroscopic life survived. In fact, certain widespread deposits (e.g., cherts, and possibly dolomites), difficult to explain by actualistic analogies with modern sedimentary environments, probably owe their origin to this large regional heating of floodwaters. Less intensely heated waters could have been tolerable to some aquatic life. For instance, many fish have a lethal temperature that is many degrees higher than what they normally experience (Alabaster and Lloyd 1982, pp. 56–60).

Muddy Water or Muddy Thinking? Moore (1983, p. 10) has taken the total volume of oceanwater (representing the total water of the Flood) and divided it by the total volume of sedimentary rock, arriving at a ratio of 2.06 to 1. From this ultra-naive computation, he makes the illogical argument that the floodwater would have been too muddy for anything to have lived in it. First of all, even if, for the sake of argument, his figure had been valid, it would tell us absolutely nothing about the actual distribution of sediment in the floodwater. For instance, one volumetric unit of floodwater may have entrained clastics at a water/sediment ratio of 1.03 to 1, leaving another unit relatively unaffected by sediment even though the overall ratio remained at 2.06:1. Organisms could, of course, have survived the Flood in the relatively sediment-free unit.

Turbidity currents provide a classic example of the unevenness of the distribution of sedimentary particles in the water column. The clastics occur at such a high concentration that the turbidite flows as a slurry. Above the turbidity current, however, water may be nearly pristine. This clearly makes any attempt to quote an average figure for sediment entrained in water, as Moore does, quite meaningless.

Most of all, Moore's argument becomes debunked once it is remembered that there is no requirement for *all* the sediment to be in suspension in the floodwater *simultaneously*! As the floodwaters moved, they carried sediment, deposited it, and then picked up more sediment. Using Moore's logic, one could argue that a large pile of coal could never be removed by a shovel because the pile could not fit in the shovel. Finally, even if only a minuscule fraction of the total volume of floodwater had remained tolerable to marine organisms, they would still have survived the Flood. This follows from the ubiquitous distribution of propagules in water. For instance, astronomical numbers of eggs and larvae are produced by individual fish (Hempel 1979, pp. 24-5) and marine invertebrates (Jokiel 1990b, p. 66), and they achieve a wide geographic distribution. Typically, only very small numbers of these spawn actually survive (Dahlberg 1979), but the prodigous numbers guarantee that at least a few of them will fortuitously end up in waters compatible with their survival (Jokiel 1990b, p. 66). Furthermore, the eggs of the same spawn vary greatly in size (Hempel 1979, p. 26), which may contribute to a further diversity of conditions compatible with the survival of a given fish kind.

Finally, let us suppose, for the sake of argument, that *all* the sea bottoms were intolerably muddy during the Flood. Benthic organisms such as reef animals (including corals and fish) could have survived the Flood as passengers on floating bits of pumice (see Jokiel 1989, and discussion below). The same holds for fish. They can survive within spaces between floating pumice blocks (Jokiel 1989, p. 491; Simkin and Fiske 1983, p. 152 and 438), and also amongst drift logs (Jokiel 1990b, pp. 70-1). This is true not only of reef fish but also of large numbers and diversities of fish in general (Jokiel 1990b, p. 71). Furthermore, many fish lay their eggs in vegetation (Dahlberg 1979,

p. 9; Hempel 1979, pp. 33-5), and many other fish eggs must have gotten commingled with floating vegetation during the Flood. This flotsam would have given the eggs some protection from excessive heat or cold, salinity, and—especially—wide fluctuations of environmental conditions, thus facilitating their survival. Finally, owing to the fact that fish eggs are often preserved for some time by cold waters (Hempel 1979, pp. 42-3), some eggs of marine organisms could have survived the Flood in this manner if there had been incipient glaciation during the Flood itself. Obviously, all these avenues of survival must have obviated any potential problems with excessively muddy water.

Bypassing the Water Column Entirely. Apart from the aerial plankton discussed earlier, there is another manner by which at least some aquatic organisms could have survived the Flood irrespective of the environmental conditions of the floodwater itself. They could have been buried in sediment at the start of the Flood, survived there for several months, and been fortuitously re-exhumed towards the latter stages of the Flood. This would have been possible if the organisms avoided being crushed by the overburden, and could tolerate anoxia and darkness.

We now know that certain foraminifers and their algal symbionts can survive at least several months of darkness (Smith and Hallock 1992). Experiments with certain fish (Mathur 1967, pp. 318-319) have demonstrated their ability to survive for months in anoxic conditions. This invites speculation that, if some fish were buried alive in sediment during the Flood, and were protected by associated debris from being crushed by the overburden, they may have been still alive when re-exhumed towards the latter stages of the Flood. However, I have been unable to locate further sources of information on this phenomenon in order to follow it up with more research.

Deep-Sea Fish. Moore (1983, p. 11, 18) imagines grave difficulties for any Flood model because of the existence of fish adapted for life at great depths. His thinking is fuzzy: does he fantasize that all deep-sea fish were somehow forced to shallow waters during the Flood? He also exaggerates the aquatic organisms' sensitivity to changes of pressure resulting from changes in depth. In actuality, with the exception of fish brought from great depths, severe barotrauma is usually only a problem when fish are brought *rapidly* towards the surface (Parrish and Moffitt 1993, p. 29). Most fish can tolerate considerable changes in *relative* pressure without severe problems (as in relatively gradual change in depth from 65–90 meters to 30 meters: Parrish and Moffitt 1993, p. 31). Since the majority of fish are native to relatively shallow depths (see below), this fact assumes particular importance.

In terms of both diversity and number of individuals, the ocean depths are virtually barren of fish. In fact, of all fish species presently in existence, only about 5% occur beyond continental shelves and slopes and at depths in excess of 200 meters (Cohen 1970, p. 344). Fishes of the great ocean depths (e.g., hadal domain) amount to only a tiny fraction of 1% of all fish species (Parin 1984, p. 33). Essentially the same few kinds of specialized fish occur all over the deeper parts of the world's oceans (Parin 1984, pp. 30-1). This may be due to the fact that few deep-sea fish were created in the first place (precisely what Moore (1983) scoffed at), and/or survived the Flood. Hence a very low diversity of fish has come to occupy a geographically broad ecological niche.

Survival of Aquatic Organisms in Perspective. This chain of reasoning can be extended to all aquatic organisms. It is probable that most kinds of marine organisms did not survive the Flood, precisely because most of the floodwaters were intolerable for them. Consider the fact that there are only about 200,000 species of aquatic invertebrates and plants (Briggs 1994) in contrast to millions of species of terrestrial invertebrates. By contrast, at the level of the phylum, marine life is more diverse than terrestrial life (Briggs 1994, p. 133). These observations suggest that present-day marine life is but an impoverished remnant of that which had originally been created and had existed before the Flood.

Chapter 17

Biological Effects of
Semi-Saline Floodwaters

Most organisms are adapted to a restricted range of salinities, or to virtually no ambient salinity. Critics from time immemorial have wondered how all the organisms could have survived within the same floodwater. In this section, I first consider the actual salinity tolerances of various organisms (principally fish and amphibians), and then discuss the actual salinity levels of floodwater. From a biological standpoint, the relative proportions of solutes are usually less biologically important than total osmo-concentration (Kinne 1964, p. 290).

By way of introduction, extant seawater (hereafter abbreviated SW) has a concentration of 35 ppt (parts per thousand) of dissolved salts, whereas fresh water (hereafter abbreviated FW) is defined as having fewer than one-half of one ppt dissolved salts (Kinne 1964, p. 283). Full saturation of water with salts occurs only at 260–280 ppt dissolved salts. For a review of the salinity levels of the earth's major bodies of water, see Gibbs (1970).

Some creationists have noted the fact that fish can gradually become accustomed to a wide range of ambient salinities. Moore (1983, p. 9) has derided this, but, for his information, a wide variety of studies have established this fact (Kinne 1964, p. 323; Norton and Davis 1977, p. 426; Parry 1966, p. 398). In fact, this has long been known (Beadle 1943, p. 176; Krogh 1939, pp. 137-8; Sumner 1905, p. 65, 68). For instance, goldfish will die within two to three hours if placed suddenly in half-strength SW, but will survive indefinitely in that medium if gradually acclimated to it (Lahlou et al. 1969, p. 1427). There are also some SW mollusks which, if allowed to acclimate to waters of decreasing salinity, will tolerate pure FW (Beadle 1943, p. 176), and some FW mollusks which, if transferred gradually, will tolerate full-strength SW (Beadle 1943, p. 179). Amphibians also have greater salinity tolerances if allowed to acclimate gradually to waters of different salinities (Licht et al. 1975, p. 127).

What, Exactly, is a Euryhaline Organism? Moore (1983, p. 10) claims that few fish are euryhaline, which is a half-truth, largely dependent upon the definition of euryhalinity. For instance, Gunter (1956a, pp. 345-6) defines a euryhaline fish as one that not only can tolerate SW and FW, but one that also has actually been *observed* living in both SW and FW. (In Fig. 7, I depict a euryhaline organism as the line which spans the entire range of salinities from FW to SW). There are many estuarine organisms that are not recognized by Gunter as euryhaline (Martin 1990, p. 232) even though they can tolerate *almost* the entire range of salinities from SW down to FW. Secondly, the fact that a particular organism is found exclusively in either FW or SW is no proof of

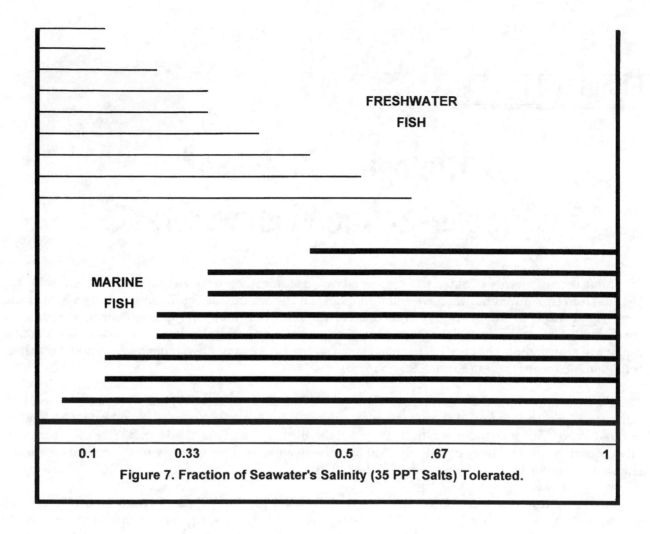

Figure 7. Fraction of Seawater's Salinity (35 PPT Salts) Tolerated.

its physiological intolerance of the other medium. For instance,the Roofed Turtle *Kachuga* was, until recently, never known outside of FW (Rashid 1991, p. 39), and the same was claimed for some of the FW chelyid turtles (Neill 1958, p. 69). The diamondback terrapin *Malaclemys* is never encountered in FW even though it can live in it (Dunson 1984, p. 118). The American crocodile usually occurs only in SW even though it can live perfectly well in FW (Neill 1958, p. 37). The same holds for the walrus (Atz 1958, p. 66). The cichlid fish *Tilapia grahami* occurs only in waters of high salinity, but can maintain itself in FW (Beadle 1974, p. 264). Likewise, the FW crab *Telphusa* is never found in SW, but can live in it (Beadle 1943, p. 178). A variety of Australian mussels, found only in FW, can tolerate considerable salinity (Williams and Campbell 1987, pp. 161-2).

In general, there are probably many more euryhaline organisms than currently recognized, as most organisms encountered in only SW or only FW have not been well studied with respect to their salinity ranges (Norton and Davis 1977, p. 425). Finally, while most aquatic animals cannot tolerate the *entire* range of salinities from the near-zero salinity of the most pristine FW all the way to the

35ppt (parts per thousand) salinity of SW, most can tolerate a large fraction of this 0–35 ppt range. This is even true of most so-called stenohaline fish. For instance, Maceina et al. 1980 (p. 616) use the label "stenohaline FW fish" for some fish that have been shown to tolerate nearly half the salinity of SW.

Floodwater Salinity and Freshwater Organisms. In terms of a global generalization, most stenohaline FW organisms cannot tolerate more than 5–10 ppt salinity (Beadle 1974, pp. 143-4; Khlebovich 1969, p. 338), which corresponds to a range of 1/7th—1/3rd of the salinity of SW (Fig. 7). This upper level, 1/3rd, is nearly isosmotic with the fishes' body fluids, and is at or near the upper salinity tolerances of the gudgeon and roach (Black 1951, p. 56), grass carp and tench (Furspan et al. 1984, p. 773), the shiner (Matthews and Hill 1977, p. 90), as well as many other FW fish (Eddy 1982, p. 130; Karpevich 1977, p. 31; Privolnev 1977, pp. 371-2). In fact, this is also typical of many FW invertebrates. Consider the Aral Sea (before its recent increase in salinity). Although its average salinity was nearly 1/3rd that of SW, it supported a mostly FW fauna (Micklin 1994, p. 114).

Certain types of fish encountered in FW can tolerate close to half the salinity of SW (this is depicted by the longer lines pertaining to FW fish in Fig. 7). These include various FW fish of Europe (Sumner 1905, p. 65), the US (Renfro 1960, p. 90), Russia (Privolnev 1977, p. 372), Australia (Merrick 1990, p. 11), and Africa (Beadle 1974, p. 264). Consider, for instance, the goldfish. Although usually considered to be a stenohaline FW fish, it tolerates half-strength SW (Lahlou et al. 1969, p. 1427). It should be added that tolerance of brackish water by FW fish can be for prolonged periods of time, as hypotonic solutions of dilute SW do not appear to be any more detrimental to FW fish than is FW itself (Garrey 1916, pp. 319-319). Moreover, many of the studies cited above show a sharp asymptotic dropoff of fish deaths, after a few days, in a given level of salinity, provided, of course, that the level is nonlethal. This indicates that, if fish can tolerate a certain salinity level for at least several days, most of them can also tolerate it for considerably longer periods of time.

Floodwater Salinity and Marine Organisms. In general, ostensibly-stenohaline SW fish are much more tolerant of reduced salinity than stenohaline FW fish are of salinity increases (Keup and Bayless 1964, p. 122; Khlebovich 1969, p. 338). A wide variety of stenohaline marine fish can survive at least a halving (Fryer and Iles 1972, p. 391; Hempel 1979, p. 50; Kilby 1955, p. 242) or a quartering (Parry 1966, p. 397) of the salinity of SW for considerable periods of time. Still other marine fish can tolerate a severalfold dilution of seawater, at least for limited (but nontrivial) periods of time (Hulet et al. 1967, p. 686). In some estuaries, stenohaline marine fish are encountered in water whose salinity is only 3% that of SW (Geoghegan et al. 1992, p. 252). Such tolerance is not limited to marine fish, but is also found, to varying degrees, in a wide variety of marine organisms (Beadle 1943, p. 173; Gunter 1956b). For instance, the so-termed stenohaline American lobsters can tolerate reductions in salinity ranging downward from 1/3rd to 1/6th that of SW (Jury et al. 1994, p. 24).

Osmotic stress on teleost marine fish is at a minimum in water whose salinity amounts to about 1/3rd that of seawater (Job 1959, p. 281). The eggs of some marine fish are notably resistant to changes in ambient salinity (Hempel 1979, p. 60). For instance, larvae of herring and plaice can tolerate reductions in salinity down to 1/7th that of SW (Almatar 1984), and those of the lumpsucker down to 1/10th of the same (Kjorsvik et al. 1984, p. 318). In brackish waters, marine organisms predominate over FW ones at salinity levels down to one-tenth of the salinity of SW (Keup and Bayless 1964, p. 122).

In Fig. 7, the large range of salinities tolerated by ostensibly stenohaline marine fish is depicted by the longer horizontal lines in contrast to the FW fish. It should be noted that the ability of SW fish to tolerate drastic reductions in salinity is not limited to the coastal marine fish. For instance, the capelin (*Mallotus villosus*) seldom experiences water less saline that full SW (Davenport and Stene 1986, p. 157), but can tolerate water down to 1/6th that of SW (Davenport and Stene 1986, p. 154). Of course, since the vast majority of ocean fish live near the coasts (Cohen 1970, p. 344), they must occasionally encounter dilutions of SW caused by FW runoff from land, and so must be adapted to tolerate varying degrees of reduction in ambient salinity.

Experiences with saltwater aquariums have confirmed the ability of SW fish to tolerate considerable reductions in ambient salinity. One recent guide to SW aquariums (Mowka 1981, p. 14) recommends that SW fish be kept in water whose salinity is as low as 77% of SW. Sumner (1905, p. 68) reports successful maintenance, for many years, of 173 species (comprising 72 different families) of SW fish in aquaria whose salinity rarely much exceeding 50% that of SW, and seasonally went down as low as 5% of SW. Similarly, Hoese (1960, p. 334) cites his unpublished studies which have demonstrated that several stenohaline marine fish can tolerate salinity reductions down to 10% that of SW.

There are even conditions under which stenohaline marine organisms can survive in virtually-zero salinity, that is FW. One of these involves the presence of suitable water temperatures. There is considerable evidence that marine organisms can tolerate more extreme reductions of ambient salinity in warmer than in colder water (Hoese 1960, p. 332). In fact, some marine organisms that tolerate only brackish water in temperate regions can tolerate FW if the waters are warm (i.e., tropical temperatures: Kinne 1964, pp. 327-8). It is obvious that, if large areas of floodwater-covered terrain were warmed (i.e., by volcanic action), some marine fish could have survived in waters of near-zero salinity. Interestingly, many fish have a lethal temperature that is many degrees higher than what they normally experience (Alabaster and Lloyd 1982, pp. 56-60).

Another circumstance in which SW fish can survive in FW (or near-FW) occurs when there are significant quantities of calcium salts dissolved in the water. This occurs when many marine fish frequent Florida's FW streams and lakes (Breder 1934; Carrier and Evans 1976; Evans 1975, p. 493; Hulet et al. 1967). It is possible that most or even all marine fish can be made to live in FW with the right combinations of dissolved calcium salts, along with other factors (Breder 1934, p. 82; Evans 1975, p. 495). The implication of this fact is enormous: large numbers of SW fish could have survived in calcium-rich floodwater, even in regions where its salinity approached or reached the near-zero concentrations typical of FW. The dissolved calcium salts must have been readily available as a result of the leaching of terrigenous regolith.

Post-Flood Changes in Organisms' Salinity Tolerances. Up to now, I have, for purposes of discussion, assumed that the restricted salinity tolerances of aquatic organisms as seen today (Fig. 7) were also true during the Flood. However, when variations within the kind are taken into account, it becomes obvious that the antediluvian organisms were tolerant of much greater ranges of ambient salinity than are extant ones. Therefore, the salinity (or lack thereof) of the floodwaters was a much less limiting factor than would be the case were the Flood to re-occur today.

To substantiate this, let us begin by noting that there is a great deal of individual variation in salinity tolerance among species of the same genus. This can be seen among different species of flounder, a SW fish (Black 1951, p. 61), as well as African fish such are *Tilapia* and *Ambassis* (Martin 1990, p. 232). Different species within the same genus of barnacle also show this pattern (Dineen and Hines 1994). Among American FW fish, the catfish and bullheads (*Ictalurus* sp.) vary in their respective salinity tolerances from less than one-third to half the salinity of SW (Chipman 1959, p. 300; Kendall and Schwartz 1968, p. 104). Overall, many FW species, intolerant of more than one-tenth the salinity of SW, are congeneric with species that can tolerate one-third or more of the salinity of SW [see Table 2 of Keup and Bayless (1964, p. 121)]. In the genus *Fundulus*, we see the entire range of commonly-occurring salinities (0–35ppt) spanned by its constituent species (Griffith 1974), and much the same is true of the African/Indian clupeoid genus *Sardinella* (Lowe-McConnell 1987, p. 227).

Consider now the variations, in terms of salinity tolerance, of different individuals within the same *species*. Commonly a few individual organisms are found to tolerate significantly greater ranges of salinity than most of their conspecifics. For instance, among FW fish, the median salt toxicity for *Lepomis cyanellus* was reported as just over one-tenth the salinity of SW, yet some individuals of *L. cyanellus* were found to be able to tolerate at least one-fourth of the salinity of SW (Chipman 1959, p. 301). The salinity tolerance of largemouth bass (*Micropterus salmoides*) also varies by individual: ranging from one-fourth to almost one-half the salinity of SW (Renfro 1959, pp. 176-7). Different populations of *Cyprinodon variegatus* also vary in the extent and magnitude of their tolerance to elevated salinities (Martin 1968). In a broader context, this fairly large individual variation of salinity tolerance is reflected by the distribution of FW and SW fish in brackish water. There is a gradual numerical decline of both FW and SW fish in waters whose salinity is variably intermediate between that of SW and FW [see Table 1 of Echelle et al. (1972, p. 113) and Table 1 of Renfro (1960, p. 86)]. As for brackish-water invertebrates, there are varieties of isopods, amphipods, and mollusks that, even within the same species, are either tolerant or intolerant of FW (Beadle 1943, p. 175-6).

The implications of this individualized variation for the survival of organisms in floodwater is considerable. Since members of a genus or even members of a species have individuals with diverse salinity tolerances, it thus becomes all the more likely that at least a few individuals of each aquatic kind encountered salinities compatible with its survival through the Flood. Moreover, microevolutionary changes in salinity tolerance could have occurred in only the few thousand years since the Flood. Plimer (1994, p. 103) is completely wrong in his assertion that FW fish could not have arisen from microevolutionary changes in SW ones, certainly not in thousands of years. In fact, many FW organisms in Scandinavian lakes must have arisen, since the glaciation thousands of years ago, not once but several times, from ancestors that require at least some dissolved salts in their water (Croghan and Lockwood 1968, p. 154, 157), and this post-glacial microevolution in salinity tolerance is not an isolated instance (Griffith 1974, pp. 328-9). In addition, there is evidence that a species of *Fundulus* has lost the ability to tolerate FW in only a few decades (Griffith 1974, p. 326). As if that were not enough, we have evidence of measurable changes in the salinity tolerances of organisms in only *one generation*, in the case of the euryhaline sea bass. It had been subject to simulated natural selection in FW, giving rise to "races" with different degrees of tolerance to FW (Allegrucci 1994).

Nevertheless, it is unnecessary to suppose that all present-day FW fish arose from SW ones since the Flood, or vice-versa. Only relatively small changes in the presently-seen salinity tolerances of aquatic organisms would have been decisive in their survival of the Flood. For instance, in Fig. 7, one can imagine all the horizontal lines (depicting the ranges of salinity tolerance) being significantly, though not completely, extended in length. For example, the very stenohaline FW organisms that presently can tolerate no more than 1/10th the salinity of SW (i.e., the very short line on the left side of Fig. 7) could have once tolerated up to 1/3rd of it, as do many other FW organisms. This would have made the effective range of floodwater salinities, compatible with *all* aquatic organisms, in the range of 3–12 ppt (see below).

Aquatic Organisms' Survival During the Flood. I now combine the information discussed in this section into an explanation of how organisms with varying salinity tolerance survived the Flood. However, we must review some basic factors in the geographic and bathymetric distribution of fish. As noted earlier, most of the ocean volume is virtually barren of fishes. Around 90% of all marine fish species occur within 200 meter depths of water, and that over the continental shelves (Cohen 1970, p. 341). Overall, FW fish are far more diverse than SW ones, so we have 41.2% of *all* fish species (the FW ones) living in less than one one-hundredth of 1% of all global water (Horn 1972, p. 1296). However, much of this diversity must have arisen since the Flood, as species of fish hybridize readily (especially the FW ones: Hubbs 1955, p. 17).

Conditions before and during the Flood must have actually facilitated the existence of high diversity among FW fish compared with SW ones, as well as the greater sensitivity of FW fish to salinity changes than SW ones. First of all, the antediluvian seas were probably considerably less saline than contemporary seas (Austin 1990, p. 27), so there was much less dissolved salt to dilute than would have been the case had a global flood occurred today. Consider also the relative volumes of the antediluvian FW and SW. Suppose, for illustrative purposes, that the antediluvian marine water was only 20ppt saline (instead of the 35 ppt today), and that FW before the Flood accounted for 50% of all earth's surface water (instead of the tiny percentage today). During the Flood, if completely homogenized, the resulting mixture would, of course, have been 10ppt saline (or just under 1/3rd of the salinity of contemporary SW). Let us now allow for minor nonhomogeneities in the salinity of the shoreless ocean, conservatively assuming that the difference in salinity in different layers of floodwater and/or different geographic regions of floodwater was only on the order of plus or minus 5 ppt (parts per thousand). This means that the floodwaters would have had a salinity range of 5–15 ppt dissolved salts. As we have seen, the vast majority of stenohaline SW and FW fish could have survived the Flood in waters of such a salinity range, even without taking into account any considerable microevolutionary changes since the Flood, nor any strong stratification of floodwater layers with respect to salinity, which is discussed next.

Floodwaters Layered by Salinity. Going along with this idea, creationists (e.g., Smith and Hagberg 1984, and earlier-cited works) have suggested that distinct SW and FW layers could have developed in the floodwater, and this salinity stratification could have persisted throughout the Flood, allowing stenohaline organisms with widely divergent salinity tolerances to survive. Moore (1983, p. 10) has belittled these experiments by pointing to the ease with which a fish in a fishbowl can homogenize such layers. Only someone ignorant of hydrodynamics would try to equate the lack of permanence of such layers at the scale of a fishbowl to the scale of an ocean depth! Only sophisticated modeling can evaluate how stable such layers would be, and to what extent floodwater turbulence would stay de-coupled, one layer from another. In addition, there are other factors to consider besides the density differences of the stratified waters which account for the stability of such layers. For instance, consider bottom topography. The relatively dense high-saline water stagnates for months or years in fjords (Edwards and Grantham 1986, pp. 196-7). Similar sheltered cracks could have formed on the ocean bottom during the Flood, allowing high-saline waters with their fauna to be protected from mixing with the less-saline waters above them.

It must be added that aquatic and semi-aquatic organisms did not survive the Flood just by fortuitously occurring in regions of osmo-concentration compatible with their biology. Many organisms are capable of escaping from intolerable salinities by horizontal and vertical migration (Foreword 1989; Keup and Bayless 1964, p. 119; Kinne 1964, p. 293). This would have been feasible even if there had been relatively small vertical and lateral differences in salinity in the floodwaters. It is also interesting to note that the threshold salinity necessary to induce a behavioral response to unfavorable salinity varies with species of crustacean larvae (Foreword 1989, p. 229), demonstrating that even this behavior is microevolutionarily malleable.

Finally, the dynamics of extinction after the Flood must have sharpened the presently-seen large dichotomy between SW and FW fish. Consider the earlier-discussed range of salinities tolerated by different species of *Fundulus*. Had the fate of extinction fortuitously fallen on all the brackish-water species of that genus, only the FW-dwelling species would be extant, and *Fundulus* would now be labeled a FW genus. It is possible that there were many more *Fundulus*-like genera before and during the Flood than there are today.

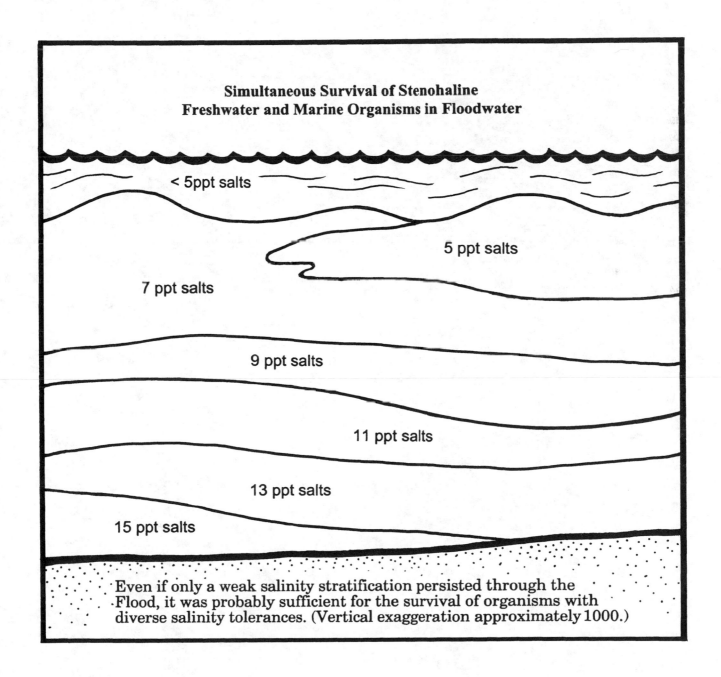

Simultaneous Survival of Stenohaline Freshwater and Marine Organisms in Floodwater

< 5ppt salts

5 ppt salts

7 ppt salts

9 ppt salts

11 ppt salts

13 ppt salts

15 ppt salts

Even if only a weak salinity stratification persisted through the Flood, it was probably sufficient for the survival of organisms with diverse salinity tolerances. (Vertical exaggeration approximately 1000.)

Chapter 18

How Amphibians Survived the Flood

Amphibians are often regarded as fragile creatures. For instance, they are supposed to be very vulnerable to the effects of acid rain. However, actual experiments with various amphibians (reviewed by Pierce 1985) demonstrate that, as a group, amphibians are no more sensitive to acid than are most other FW aquatic organisms. Moreover, those species of amphibians that are highly acid-intolerant are congeneric with relatively acid-tolerant ones (Pierce 1985, p. 239). Hence, sensitivity to acids probably arose by microevolutionary processes only since the Flood. However, acidity of waters was probably not a relevant factor for most of the floodwaters. As for other pollutants, FW organisms of many diverse types (including amphibians) are more sensitive to dissolved potassium salts than they are to dissolved sodium salts (Padhye and Ghate 1992, p. 21). As shown in this section, the survival of amphibians in floodwater closely parallels that of the other FW organisms because all amphibians are, during at least part of their life cycle, dependent upon water.

Claims about most amphibians being killed by even small amounts of saltwater (Morton 1995, p. 69) are fallacious. In actuality, there are many reports of amphibians being found in brackish water or even seawater (see Neill 1958, Taylor 1943, and more recent citations below). The overall pattern of their tolerance to dissolved salts in water is very much like that of stenohaline FW fish (Fig. 7). Thus, although most amphibians cannot even briefly tolerate half the salinity of SW (Licht et al. 1975, p. 131), many can tolerate up to 1/3rd the salinity of SW for prolonged periods of time (Abe and Bicudo 1991, p. 313; Christman 1974, p. 775; Licht et al. 1975, p. 123; Ruibal 1959, p. 320). As is the case with FW fish, the most salt-intolerant species are often or usually congeneric with forms that can tolerate at least 1/3rd the salinity of SW. Thus, different species of the salamander genus *Batrachoseps* (Licht et al. 1975, p. 123) have different survival times in dilute SW: some members of this genus can tolerate more than half the salinity of SW (Jones and Hillman 1978, p. 1). This is also notably true of different species within the genera *Bufo* (which is by far the most common genus of toad). The spawn of most species of *Bufo* cannot tolerate more than 1/6–1/5th of the salinity of SW (Beebee 1985, p. 15; Ely 1944, p. 256). These figures are comparable with prolonged survival of *B. bufo* in 1/7th salinity of SW (Hagstrom 1981, p. 187), though tadpoles of at least some *Bufo* species can tolerate nearly 1/3rd the salinity of SW for at least a week (Beebee 1985, p. 14). *B. boreas* can tolerate 2/5ths of the salinity of SW on a permanent basis whereas, by contrast, *B. viridis* can indefinitely tolerate half the salinity of SW (Gislen and Kauri 1959, p. 294; Gordon 1965, p. 223). [Over briefer periods, *B. viridis* can tolerate as much as 3/4th of the salinity of SW (Gordon 1962, p. 261; Katz 1973, p. 795; Tercafs and Schoffeniels 1962, p. 19)]. The fact that these different salinity tolerances between species are merely variations within the kind is also evident by the fact that very many species of the frog genus *Bufo* can produce fertile hybrids (for a tabulation, see Wilson et al. 1974). For instance, the relatively salt-sensitive *B. bufo* and the much more salt-tolerant *B. viridis* can interbreed (Gislen and Kauri 1959, p. 294).

As for the widespread frog genus *Rana*, we see a similar pattern of interspecific variation in salinity tolerance. For instance, *R. pipiens* has been encountered in brackish water at salinities up to one quarter that of SW (Ruibal 1959, p. 317), and similar limits of salinity tolerances have been determined for *R. esculenta* and *R. temporaria* (Ackrill et al. 1969, p. 1320). By contrast, *R. cancrivora* can tolerate as much as 4/5th the salinity of SW (Dunson 1977, p. 378).

In parallel with FW fish, salinity tolerances of amphibians vary even *within* species; as within populations of *Rana sphenocephala* (Christman 1974), *Salamandra salamandra* (Degani 1981), and species of *Batrachoseps* (Licht et al. 1975, p. 123). In each of these three examples, the more salt-tolerant populations live near salt water, and so had been previously subject to natural selection for salinity tolerance. As a result, the relatively salt-tolerant populations of *Salamandra* can live in waters having as much as 44% of the salinity of SW, whereas their conspecifics, living inland and away from salt waters, can tolerate only 27% of the salinity of SW (Degani 1981, p. 133). Among green toads (*Bufo viridis*), salinity tolerances of certain populations native to specific geographic regions have been as high as 3/4th that of SW (Gordon 1962, p. 261). Moreover, indicators of osmotic and ionic regulation vary considerably among different populations of *B. viridis*, demonstrating the fact that even the basic physiological mechanisms of salinity tolerance are under microevolutionary control (Khlebovich and Velikanov 1982).

As has been shown to be the case with fish, there is a wide range of *individual* differences in terms of salinity tolerance. For instance, most individuals of the African pipid frog *Xenopus laevis* (a normally FW dweller: McBean and Goldstein 1970, p. 1115) cannot tolerate more than 1/4th the salinity of SW, yet some individuals of this species could tolerate 2/5th the salinity of SW for at least several days (Munsey 1972), or even greater salinity for briefer periods of time (Romspert 1976).

As was the case with the previously-discussed FW organisms, many amphibians must have survived the Flood by mimicking aquatic organisms and living freely in the water. Others rode out the Flood as passengers on floating objects. Indeed, various salamanders have been found attached to wooden objects out at sea (Ferguson 1956, p. 120; Hardy 1952, pp. 181-2). Amphibians are pre-adapted for such transport as many of them normally lay and attach their eggs to sticks, foliage, or logs already present in the water (Duellman and Trueb 1986, p. 112). In fact, salamanders are commonly encountered under logs and driftwood (Licht et al. 1975, pp. 123-4). Frogs could also have been shielded within floating mats or clumps of vegetal debris (Boyd 1962, p. 269, and see below). Mitchell (1990, p. 102) points out that frogs found in certain Pacific islands could have been transported as eggs (which he considers to be more resistant to salinity), attached to leaf bases of trees, and washed out to sea.

Chapter 19

Alleged Problems
Facing Post-Diluvian Plants

Salty Soils After the Flood?

After the Flood retreated, the land surface was supposedly impregnated with salt. Detractors of the Bible, beginning with the Seventeenth and Eighteenth Century rationalists (Allen 1963, p. 88), have long raised this false issue. Moore (1983, p. 13) also trots out this old chestnut. In reality, the salt left by the retreating sea (assuming, for argument's sake, that the floodwater was as saline as contemporary ocean water) is readily removed by leaching caused by rainfall or even water used for irrigation (Wittwer et al. 1987, pp. 83-9). One good rainfall can drastically reduce the salt content of the soil, provided that the drainage is good (Wittwer et al. 1987, p. 89). In the immediate post-Flood world, the cleansing effects of rainwater must have been particularly acute because of the excellent drainage engendered by the ubiquitous presence of recently-eroded gullies. Large areas of land must have been leached of salt in a matter of days or weeks of last floodwater inundation, allowing even salt-sensitive plants to germinate and grow.

In addition, there are significant differences within individual plants, of common species, in terms of tolerance for salt (NRC 1990, pp. 4-5; Wainwright 1980, pp. 224-5). This would have allowed these individual plants to begin growth in areas that had not yet been well leached of the salt ostensibly left by the Flood.

Arguments About Seeds that Will Not Float

The title of this section intentionally has a dangling modifier. The phrase "will not float" refers to both the seeds and the unrealistic arguments regarding their survival through the Flood. In addition to Howe's (1968) study of seeds in a simulated Flood context, many other investigators (e.g., Guppy 1917, and his earlier-cited works; Smith 1991, and works cited theirein) have proved that many kinds of seeds can stay afloat not only months but even for several years, and these seeds are not limited to those of littoral plants (Smith 1990, p. 19; 1991, p. 368).

Moore (1983, p. 12) has cited Gunn and Dennis (1976, p. 4), who suppose that only about 1% of tropical plants' seeds float for even a month, and then imagined the same for all the seeds in the floodwater. His argument is disingenuous, for several reasons. To begin with, there are many ways besides flotation of seeds by which plants could have survived the Flood (see below). The Gunn and

Dennis (1976) compilation itself is hardly comprehensive (Smith 1990, p. 13), and their cited "guesstimate" of seed floatability is an assertion devoid of any experimental support. It becomes even more unbelievable when we consider the huge range of durations which different individual seeds of the same kind of plant exhibit in terms of flotation and resistance to seawater (e.g., coconut: Ward and Brookfield 1992, p. 471). The list of seeds which turn out to be able to float, for prolonged periods of time, keeps growing (e.g., Hacker 1990, p. 23). Needless to say, the Gunn and Dennis (1976) compilation can only show a strong bias towards littoral plants whose proximity to the ocean allows their seeds to fall into the ocean on a frequent basis (e.g., see Carlquist 1981). As discussed in the ensuing chapter, they are next to useless in predicted seed flotation in a catastrophic situation. Even seed flotation itself is largely a microevolutionary phenomena as demonstrated by the fact that non-floating seeds are often congeneric with seeds that do float (Carlquist 1974, p. 464), so many non-floating seeds could have lost the ability to float only since the Flood.

Most significant of all, there is a fundamental difference between the flotation of mature seeds discharged regularly by plant life, and the flotation of seeds that have been massively liberated by the Flood. Under normative (i.e., non-catastrophic) conditions, seeds are discharged by the parent plant only when ripe. By contrast, under catastrophic conditions, large numbers of trees, along with their seeds, are uprooted (as seen, for instance, after the Krakatoa eruption: Simkin and Fiske (1983, p. 437). Pine cones can remain on trees 30 years or more (Turrill 1957, p. 37) containing viable seeds. Some of these cones could have remained sealed in floodwater, thus protecting the seeds. The ability or inability of the seeds themselves to float becomes unimportant, because the seeds are still usually attached to a fragment of the parent plant or tree, which often does float (Carlquist 1974, p. 465). This fact is also applicable to situations where seeds become commingled in other flotsam which does float. Thus, in contrast to Moore's (1983) dogmatic statements about non-floating seeds, Carlquist (1974, p. 74), Fridriksson (1975, p. 63), and Stephens (1966, p. 207) recognize and emphasize the fact that the inability of seeds to float for any significant period of time is no argument against their ability to cross oceans, because the nonfloating seeds can be attached to debris (pumice, tangled masses of vegetation, floating logs, etc.) which does float. Driftwood and pumice have been observed with seeds attached (Ridley 1930, pp. 252-3). In fact, had Moore (1983) read Howe (1968) a little bit more carefully, he would have noticed that Howe (1968, p. 109) also documented the fact that seeds can survive as passengers on floating debris. Furthermore, very many kinds of seeds can retain viability and dormancy even while soaked in floodwater (see *Overcoming Seed Dormancy*).

Let us now consider the fate of the seeds that *did* sink in the floodwater. This need not have doomed them: they still could have germinated once the floodwaters drained off the land and left them behind as lag deposits. Note that this is entirely different from the ocean-floating situation (i.e., Gunn and Dennis 1976) wherein, once a seed sinks to the bottom of the ocean, it has virtually no chance of being brought to the surface again, and placed on land, for an opportunity to germinate.

Finally, seeds are not the only way that plants reproduce, and this is even more evident during catastrophes. Uprooted plants and trees themselves can survive a long time in salt water (Carlquist 1974, p. 74). Torn-off vegetation with roots, apparently viable, has been observed in the ocean far from land (Ridley 1930, p. 253). It is interesting to note that, for many plants, the ease of vegetative propagation appears to be inversely related to the ease of meeting the needs for seed germination (USDA 1948, p. 40), suggesting that plants with difficult-germinating seeds have largely circumvented seed-based propagation, as a primary reproductive strategy, in favor of vegetative propagation (USDA 1948, p. 40). This matter is discussed in more detail under *Vegetative Propagation*. . . .

Floating Rafts or Floating Objects? I now elaborate on the flotational properties of the flotsam in the floodwater. This included mats of vegetation (Whitcomb and Morris 1961, p. 70). Today, these are often encountered at sea (Powers 1911), or freshly beached on islands (Thornton and Kew 1988, p. 498). Moore (1983, p. 13) presents a red herring by arguing that floating mats tend to break up in rough seas. His claim is contradicted by Power (1911, p. 305), who observed a large floating mat, over 1500 km from shore, that had survived a severe storm. There is also evidence that, if the volume of floating vegetation is very great (as during the Flood), rough waters will tend to *concentrate* rather than disperse the flotsam (Junk 1973, p. 84). Moreover, when there is a large amount of debris at sea, it tends to concentrate into windrows (Jokiel 1989, p. 491; 1990a, p. 666) which are often massive in character (Jokiel 1990a, p. 666). Even small amounts of vegetation debris tend to be rolled into tight clumps or balls, and these have a firm consistency themselves (M'atee 1925, p. 299). Finally, if, for the sake of argument, *all* vegetation rafts had broken up during the course of the Flood, organic propagules could survive as passengers on *small* floating drift (Matthew 1915, p. 207). The roots and rhizomes of the dispersed pieces could still remain tightly entangled in large clumps (Junk 1973, p. 12), facilitating the protection of insects, eggs, seeds, etc., inside a particular clump. As long-term accumulations of vegetation in water often develop into a consistency of peat (Junk 1973, p. 91), some forms of life must have been protected within such windrows owing to their consistency, even if the rafts themselves had broken into small pieces.

Empirical evidence supports the foregoing statements. Logs floating out in the ocean are frequently found to have roots with soil or gravel still attached to them (Jokiel 1990b), the latter of which is often teeming with live insects and/or insect eggs (Ball and Glucksman 1975, p. 438). Individual bits of flotsam have been found to carry an astonishing diversity of terrestrial life (Heatwole and Levins 1972). Of course, crevices in flotsam also serve as a haven for a great diversity of marine life as well (Carlton 1985). Experiments and observations on ant colonies (Wheeler 1916) have demonstrated that ant colonies not only can stay attached to floating logs out at sea, but are themselves very resistant to submersion in seawater if the nest-entrances are closed. (Perhaps the high diversity and biomass of ants on earth has something to do with this capability: i.e., their ability to have survived the Flood, especially in relatively large numbers). Even vegetation from land is unnecessary, as clumps of floating kelp can yield an astonishing diversity of fauna on it in the middle of the ocean (for tabulation of these faunas, see Table 3 of Edgar 1987), and such clumps of kelp have been shown by Helmuth et al. (1994, p. 425) to entrain organisms for at least several months at sea.

Apart from all this, the Flood produced another major source of flotsam—pumice—and it is much more durable than vegetation (Guppy 1917, p. 248; Williams and McBirney 1969). Pumice can float on the ocean for years (Jokiel 1989, p. 488; Simkin and Fiske 1983, p. 15). Large blocks of pumice at sea are durable enough to provide cover and support for larger reef organisms such as corals, crustaceans, mollusks, and even reef fishes (Jokiel 1989, p. 491; Simkin and Fiske 1983, pp. 152, 438). Pumice must have been very widespread owing to the volcanoes erupting during the Flood, and is believed to be underrepresented in the sedimentary record (Fiske 1969). It should be added that there was no threat to the Ark from the pumice, as ships can cut right through a pumice field without damage. This is even the case when the pumice is durable enough for a person to walk on it (Simkin and Fiske 1983, p. 153).

Seeds Buried and Then Re-Exhumed. Up to now, I have considered seed survival within the floodwater itself as a *sine qua non* of its subsequent viability. In actuality, very many seeds must have missed most of the Flood (and its prolonged soaking) when buried in the early-Flood deposits, only to be fortuitously re-exhumed later on. Clearly, Moore's (1983, p. 12) assumption that the seeds would need to grow through many kilometers of sedimentary rock completely neglects the fact that the Flood was an erosive agent as much as it was a depositional agent. This allowed for the uncovering of seeds at the latter stages of the Flood, including those that had been deeply buried during its early stages.

After being buried, many seeds must have been protected from being crushed by the penecontemporaneous cementation of sediments. Nevertheless, it is interesting to note that many seeds can tolerate pressures as high as several tons (Porter 1949, p. 256). There is no doubt that seeds can survive a long time in sediments, as demonstrated by the recovery of viable seeds from adobe bricks after 211 years (Spira and Wagner 1983). The dryness of the adobe bricks is irrelevant: seeds could equally have survived in sediment even if it had retained a significant amount of moisture. This fact is proved by the many instances of seeds surviving in wet soil for years, decades, and even centuries (see papers in Leck et al. 1989, and discussion below).

The absence of light and the anoxic conditions of burial must have facilitated the dormancy of seeds (Priestley 1986, pp. 100-101) until unearthed by late-Flood and post-Flood erosive events. Furthermore, the absence of oxygen tends to greatly prolong the viability of seeds which are viable only for short periods of time under normal subaerial conditions (Crocker 1938, p. 241). Had carbon dioxide percolated through some of the Flood-deposited sediments, it must have also imposed a narcotic effect on many seeds (Kidd 1914), including at least some that would not otherwise have survived prolonged burial in a viable condition. For instance, the rubber plant (*Hevea braziliensis*) is notorious for the short period of viability of its seeds under normative conditions. Yet when narcotized by carbon dioxide, the seeds can survive in a viable state for at least several weeks (Kidd 1914, pp. 620-1) and, if present in sufficient numbers, a few individual seeds out of a great number initially buried may have survived the Flood year.

Overcoming Seed Dormancy

Did Seeds in Floodwater Germinate Prematurely? Moore (1983, p. 12) has alleged that the seeds, subject to warmth and moisture, necessarily germinated in the floodwater and died from lack of oxygen. His argument is patently fallacious for many, if not most, plant types, as moisture and warmth themselves are often insufficient to break seed dormancy (see below). Nor is Moore's assertion invariably true even for prompt germinators—those seeds which germinate soon after being warmed and moistened. At least some variants within the seed populations must have had coats thick enough to withstand prolonged soaking. This is even more true if some of these seeds were entangled and well-wrapped in the (previously-discussed) clumps of vegetation. This would have shielded them from complete soaking, forestalling their premature germination until the Flood had ended. Yet even if the clumps of vegetation had been unable to prevent the seeds from being imbibed, the slowing down of the rate of imbibing must have increased their chance of surviving the Flood in an imbibed condition. The inverse relationship between the rate of imbibing, and eventual viability, has been demonstrated experimentally (Perry and Harrison 1970, p. 504, 511).

It is most interesting to note that the plants whose seeds tend to germination upon wetting include nearly all crop plants (Fenner 1985, p. 67). These, of course, are the very ones which were on the Ark with Noah as sources of food (Whitcomb and Morris 1961, p. 70). Even more interesting is the fact that their wild relatives (e.g., certain grasses) show a microevolutionary variation in terms of tolerance to soaking without premature germination. That is, within the same genus, the seedling of a grass species whose environment includes waterlogged soils is resistant to anoxia, whereas one native to dryer areas is sensitive to it (Barclay and Crawford 1982, p. 548). It is thus possible that most, if not all, of the species which now germinate soon after soaking, and asphyxiate if they remain in water, are post-Diluvian microevolutionary derivatives of the species whose seedling *can* survive prolonged soaking without premature germination.

Yet even without this factor, the seedlings that did germinate in the floodwater were not necessarily doomed. Had floating clumps of vegetation been sufficiently durable, they could have supported the germination and growth of seedlings through the Flood (notably wild rice: M'atee 1925, p. 296). The temperature of the floodwaters is also of great relevance. Barclay and Crawford (1981) have showed that the buildup of ethanol, which asphyxiates the pea seedling in water, is greatly reduced when the temperature of the water is under 5C. If there were regions of cold floodwater, as during incipient glaciation, it is possible that some seedlings could have survived even a year in floodwater under those conditions.

I now consider the recalcitrant crop seeds, a group of mostly-tropical and subtropical plants whose seeds lack dormancy mechanisms. They soon either germinate or die, and cannot normally spend a year in the ground, in water, nor in conventional storage. However, experiments (e.g., Van der Vossen 1979; King and Roberts 1980) have demonstrated that many of these *can* survive a year if buried, provided that certain conditions of oxygenation, temperature, and moisture are met. If buried and then re-exhumed under fortuitously appropriate conditions, many such plants could have survived the Flood. Finally, plants possessing recalcitrant seeds are notably prone to vegetative reproduction (see below).

The Soak-Resistant Seeds. Up to now, I have considered only the seeds which germinate readily soon after being soaked. Many plants whose embryos lack dormancy once imbibed (notably the leguminous plants: Ewart 1908, p. 192) tend to have thick seeds which resist the entry of water for long periods of time (Crocker 1938, p. 260). Therefore, such seeds can soak in water over a year without even becoming imbibed (Priestley 1986, p. 122). In fact, many kinds of seeds have retained viability although soaked in water for many years (Salter 1857, White 1886, Crocker 1938, p. 263, and references therein). In particular, Shull's (1914) experiments demonstrated the ability of many types of seeds to survive prolonged submergence in a viable state, even for years.

Furthermore, a seed's permeability or nonpermeability to seawater varies within the genus (Carlquist 1974, p. 430) and even the species (Ward and Brookfield 1992, p. 471), so easy seed permeability to water is probably a post-Flood microevolutionary adaptation. If the antediluvian world had been wetter than the contemporary one, many more seeds must have been adapted to soaking and/or imbibing without premature germination, thus facilitating their later survival through the Flood.

In addition, many other seeds survive even if the coat is breached and the embryo *does* become imbibed (Crawford 1977, p. 511; Ewart 1908, p. 192). The ability of seeds to be soaked and yet not germinate is proved by the existence of seed banks in soil which can persist for many years (Leck et al. 1989, and contained papers). Various experiments (Kivilaan and Bandurski 1973, pp. 143-5; Wesson and Wareing 1967; Vazquez-Yanes and Smith 1982, and many others) have clearly demonstrated that moisture is a necessary but not sufficient cause for seed germination.

It is now recognized that light is *the* major factor required for seeds to germinate (Baskin and Baskin 1989, p. 58). In regions where the floodwaters had been murky, the light requirement would not have been met and the seeds would have survived even if imbibed (Priestley 1986, p. 100, 103). Such dormancy in a dark and imbibed state has been shown to last at least a year (Vazquez-Yanes and Smith 1982, p. 481). Secondly, since many seeds require fluctuating temperatures to germinate

(Baskin and Baskin 1989, p. 61), seeds in floodwater would not germinate until the floodwaters drained off and the seeds became exposed to a regimen of fluctuating environmental temperatures.

Seed Germination: Exacting Conditions? Moore (1983, pp. 12-13) portrays seed germination as something that occurs only when a set of narrow conditions is met precisely. Again, were he correct, it would be amazing that plant life (and hence all life) did not become extinct long ago. As is shown in this and succeeding paragraphs, what is necessary for seed germination is not the exact fulfillment of several narrow requirements, but a fulfillment of *one of several alternate requirements*, at least one of which may be broad in character. Consider, for example, extreme temperatures as a condition for dormancy. Most seeds can germinate if they experience *either* low winter temperatures *or* high summer temperatures, because that is what is necessary to make the seed coat permeable (Baskin and Baskin 1989, pp. 62-3). Yet seeds that require sharply fluctuating temperatures in order to break seed dormancy will still germinate even if the fluctuating-temperature requirement is not met, provided that an alternative requirement is met instead. This alternative requirement is often simply a relatively high constant temperature (e.g., 25 to 30 C: Thompson et al. 1977, p. 147; Thompson and Grime 1983, p. 151). In fact, it appears that the amplitude of temperature variation becomes progressively less important for successful seed germination in general as higher absolute temperatures become the norm (Murdoch et al. 1989). This latter condition could easily have been satisfied in the post-Flood world, if not through meteorological conditions, then by microclimatic factors, such as proximity to hot water from geothermal springs. However, even the absence of forest canopy after the Flood must have facilitated seed germination, in and of itself, by allowing seeds to experience large diurnal fluctuations in temperature (Thompson and Grime 1983, p. 154) and light, along with unmoderated high daytime absolute temperatures.

There is an even more fundamental reason why seeds of the same plant could have germinated under very different conditions after the Flood. This is the fact that plants and trees "hedge their bets" for survival by producing seeds that vary greatly in their respective individual requirements for germination (Kivilaan and Bandurski 1973, pp. 144-5; Thompson and Grime 1983, pp. 148-9; USDA 1848, p. 39). For instance, seeds typically requiring large temperature fluctuations to germinate usually include some individual seeds that will germinate with little or no such fluctuation of temperatures (Thompson et al. 1977, p. 148). This physiological heterogeneity of seeds of the same plant is true even in the case of apparently genetically-uniform seedlot (Murdoch et al. 1989, p. 98). Even many tropical seeds can experience delayed germination (for months or years) *with or without* seasonally-adverse periods (Garwood 1989, pp. 152-3). Finally, the nature and extent of seed dormancy is probably a post-Flood microevolutionary development, as it varies according to species in a genus (USDA 1948, p. 40).

Moore (1983, p. 13) also greatly exaggerates the difficulty seeds have in germinating, and becoming established, if they land in foreign environments. Such is far from the case. In fact, the reason why plants and trees produce such an astronomical number of seeds is precisely to guarantee that a few of them will fortuitously land in a suitable environment to germinate and reach adulthood. Furthermore, the seeds available after the Flood were not solely those attached to the plants uprooted by the Flood, but also the vast numbers washed out of the antediluvian seedbanks. Extant seedbanks average, to the nearest power of ten, about 1,000 seeds per square meter (Fenner 1985, p. 57). When we add the seeds still on the plants and trees, and suggest an immediate post-Flood seedling emergence rate of 1 seedling per 100 square meters of land, we see that only on the order of *one out of a million* seeds that had been in existence at the start of the Flood need have survived it. This, of course, does not include the additional plants and trees that survived as seeds on the Ark, nor as vegetative propagules (see below).

The timing of germination is also crucial in the plant being able to defeat adverse environmental circumstances, provided that the adverse circumstances are not permanent. Experiments have demonstrated that a few individual seeds germinate long after the rest have done so (Kivilaan and Bandurski 1981, p. 1292). This must have created a large span of time during which seeds from the pre-Flood world were germinating after the Flood, thus tending to guarantee that some of them would fortuitously germinate at the same time that conditions were right for the plants to become established.

Of course, plants possess a great deal of phenotypic plasticity in adapting to various environments. This is proved, for example, by the successes of plants and trees in geographic regions and climes where they are not native. Furthermore, experiments have shown that plants can become acclimated to various temperatures, even to the extent that the optimum temperature for maximally-efficient photosynthesis can change by 5C or more *in the same plant* as a result of this acclimatization (Mooney and West 1964, p. 827).

Finally, it should be added that the ability of seeds to grow in foreign environments is not limited to weed species. For instance, experience with the Mt. St. Helens eruption has demonstrated that tolerant late seral and climax herbaceous species often behave like pioneer plants (Del Moral and Bliss 1993, p. 52)

Must Seeds be Scarified in Order to Germinate? In criticizing creationist Howe's (1968) experiment on seed germination, Moore (1983, p. 12) has argued that some seeds would be scarified by Flood action and germinate prematurely, whereas others could not germinate at all after the Flood, as there was no one around to scarify them. Moore's argument is preposterous. Why should seeds be limited to either premature scarification or no scarification at all? Secondly, if seeds actually required scarification by someone as a *sine qua non* of germination, the plant kingdom (and all life, for that matter) would have become extinct a long time ago. In reality, nearly all seeds germinate without so much as being touched by humans, and it is now recognized that the overall importance of scarification in seed germination has been exaggerated (Baskin and Baskin 1989, pp. 59-60).

In nature, seed coats are removed or sufficiently weakened by the action of sedimentary particles (USDA 1948, p. 33) as well as biological agents (e.g., bacteria and fungi: Crocker 1938, p. 261). Mechanical scarification (e.g., as done by Howe 1968) is *not* a precondition for germination; it only increases the *rate* of germination (Howe 1986, p. 142). Furthermore, even seeds with thick pericarps often have a few individual seeds that will germinate without having undergone significant amounts of scarification (Priestley 1986, p. 122). Some seeds have their hard coats largely dissolved or abraded by passing through the digestive tract of animals, but the significance of this has also been exaggerated in the past (Baskin and Baskin 1989, pp. 59-60). Furthermore, there is no plant which *requires* passage of its seeds through an animal tract as an absolute prerequisite for germination (Temple 1977, p. 885). The one possible exception (*Calvaria*) is a taxonomic synonym of a plant genus (*Sideroxylon*) which has thin pericarps requiring no such scarification (Temple 1977, p. 886).

Plant-Pollinator Symbioses

Entomophilous plants are plants which reproduce because of pollination by insects. Moore (1983, p. 13) doubts that such plants could have grown after the Flood, for some ill-defined reason. To the extent that his argument has any coherence, it revolves around two fallacious premises: 1) that there actually were no insects right after the Flood, and 2) entomophilous plants *must* be pollinated by insects as an unalterable condition for the setting of seed.

Consider the availability of insects. As discussed in a section below, insect populations must have multiplied explosively towards the later stages of the Flood. Therefore, they would have been around in large numbers before *most* plants would have flowered for the first time after the Flood! Introduced plants themselves typically find an equivalent pollinator in the location of their introduction (Vogel and Westerkamp 1991, p. 161). It is also recognized, even within the evolutionary paradigm that, just because there is a close morphological "match" between floral anatomy and that of the pollinating organism (e.g., hummingbird, butterfly) does not in itself prove that the two co-evolved together (Schemske 1983, p. 89).

Let us now consider the second premise underlying Moore's fallacious argument, whereby he supposes that insects are indispensable for seed set. In reality, many, if not most, entomophilous plants will set seed by self-pollination or wind pollination if insects are unavailable. This has been verified by experiments where netting was tied around flowers to prevent pollination by insects (Chernov 1985, pp. 150-4; Gross and Werner 1983, p. 102; Karoly 1992, p. 51; Steiner 1983, p. 12, 15). In most cases, pollination occurred anyway, albeit at a much lower rate than would been the case had insects been allowed to pollinate the flowers. This reduction (not elimination) of seed-set is a recognized consequence of pollinator absence (Linhart and Feinsinger 1980, p. 757). Owing to the large barren areas after the Flood, even a low rate of reproduction must have been sufficient for the flora to become established. The supposed lack of insect pollinators later became rectified by nature.

Some flowers with bagged infloresences will not set any seed. However, in nearly every case, such plants are congeneric with plants that will set at least a few seeds with neither an insect pollinator nor with manual selfing (Chernov 1985, pp. 151-4; Gross and Werner 1983, p. 102, 111). Thus the obligatory requirement of an insect pollinator, seen in only a certain minority of plants, is microevolutionary in origin.

Specialized Pollinator-Plant Symbioses? The vast majority of entomophilous plants can be pollinated by an entire guild of insects: a fact equally true of polar, temperate, and tropical floras (Chernov 1985, pp. 147, 150-1; Howe 1984, p. 767; Vogel and Westerkamp 1991, p. 161). Only a very few plants are dependent on one pollinator (Faegri and can der Pijl 1979, p. 45; Howe 1984, p. 767), and many, if not most, of these associations are merely ecological associations (Howe 1984, p. 772), not genetically-determined obligatory mutualisms. Furthermore, plants having a symbiotic relationship with one pollinator can often set some seeds without it (Linhart and Feinsinger 1980, p. 745), although probably not to the extent of plants, denied insect pollinators, that are normally visited by many of them.

To the extent that these mutualisms originate in the genetics of the organisms, such highly-specialized insect/plant relationships tend to occur on a species-specific basis (Chernov 1985, pp. 148, 153-4; Estes et al. 1983, p. 542; Howe 1984, p. 772; Ramirez 1970), indicating that they are of microevolutionary origin. Furthermore, recent evidence (Singer et al. 1993) indicates that highly specific plant-animal symbioses can arise by microevolution in only a few decades. In fact, there exists a close (although not exclusive) weed-plant/bee pollinator symbiosis that is believed to have developed recently through microevolution (Faegri and van der Pijl 1979, p. 44).

Up to now, I have tacitly assumed that pollination of flowers is the only way that entomophilous plants could have reproduced after the Flood. In actuality, it is particularly noteworthy that most of the plants which have specialized pollinators "hedge their bets," in terms of successful reproduction, by being also able to reproduce vegetatively (Bond 1994, p. 86). For instance, the figs and wasps have a very specialized pollinator symbiosis whereby one species of wasp pollinates only one species of fig. There are no seeds at all if the appropriate wasp is unavailable, but this most certainly does not doom the fig to extinction. Figs simply reproduce vegetatively for years until the geographic range of the specific wasp species catches up to the range of the specific fig species (Ramirez 1970, p. 684).

Vegetative Propagation and the Olive Branch

As noted earlier, all of the "problems" discussed earlier (seed flotation, seed dormancy, entomophily, scarification, etc.) have an additional solution to them, because the plant's survival of the Flood is not contingent upon any of its seeds remaining viable after the Flood. This is vegetative reproduction, which is exceedingly common in the Plant Kingdom. Vegetative propagation occurs in many deciduous and ornamental plants, shrubs, and trees (Hartmann et al. 1981, p. 94; Mukherjee and Majumder 1973). For instance, fallen oaks can regenerate from fallen branches only 2 meters long (Anon. 1994, p. 6). Vegetative propagation is especially notable in a considerable variety of fruit trees (Mukherjee and Majumder 1973; Zohary and Spiegel-Roy 1975). Many trees and plants that have short-lasting seeds readily propagate vegetatively. This is true, for instance, of willows and poplars (Hartmann et al. 1981, p. 94), as well as very many of the subtropical and tropical recalcitrant seed plants (e.g., citrus fruits, rubber, mango, durain: Chin 1980, p. 117, 125).

Vegetative propagation could have begun even before the Flood had retreated. Large numbers of uprooted trees, often still in upright position, have been seen after the Krakatoa Eruption (Simkin and Fiske 1983, p. 131). Furthermore, such uprooted trees found floating in the ocean can be seen to have fresh and healthy sprouts arising from the trunk (Ball and Glucksman 1975, p. 438). Some plants could also have been buried early in the Flood and survived the burial until their re-exposure by late-Flood erosive events. There is a surprising variety of plants and trees that can survive for considerable periods of time in a vegetative state although buried. For instance, plants and trees buried under volcanic ash have resumed growth, once re-exhumated, as much as 8 years after burial (Zobel and Antos 1992, p. 700). Moreover, it must be stressed that these comprise a wide variety of common foliage, surviving in waterlogged soils (Griggs 1919, p. 196-7), *not* just a narrow suite of plants ostensibly adapted for life in regions of volcanic activity.

The Olive Branch. Plimer (1994, p. 91) has asserted, without a shred of evidence, that *all* olive trees must have been deeply buried by sediment in the Flood. His unfounded claim does not square with the fact that wood fragments tend to float. Whitcomb and Morris (1961, pp. 104-6) have demonstrated that the olive branch (Genesis 8:11) could have arisen by means of vegetative propagation towards the close of the Flood. Moore (1983, p. 13) has ridiculed the suggestion that olive trees are hardy, and challenged creationists to learn some botany. As shown in this section, Moore (1983) is the one in need of a botany lesson. Whitcomb and Morris (1961) have, if anything, understated the ability of the olive tree to reproduce by vegetative propagation. I hereby supplement their excellent discussion with some more details about the regeneration of olive trees after the Flood.

There is no doubt that olives are hardy. They can survive diseases and drought (Belousova and Denisova 1992, p. 154), and tolerate higher salinities and lower temperatures than can most other evergreen orchard species (Chandler 1950, pp. 364-5). They are also tolerant of boron in the soil, as well as wide ranges in soil ph (Hartmann et al. 1981, p. 617). Olive trees can not only grow where there is little soil and water (Bitting 1920, p. 14), and in stony ground (Chandler 1950, p. 365), but also under precipices (Belousova and Denisova 1992, p. 153). This fact must have facilitated their establishment on the initially-barren post-Diluvian mountains. Olive trees are also hardy in a genetic sense. Wild and domesticated varieties cross easily (Zohary and Spiegel-Roy 1975, p. 321). The repeated siring of olive trees by vegetative propagation does not diminish their viability in the slightest (Brichet 1943, pp. 92-3).

The olive can regenerate not only from branch tips and from ovuli (Whitcomb and Morris 1961), but also from virtually any tree fragment. This means that just about any piece of olive-tree debris, left stranded after the Flood, could have given rise to an olive seedling, given the right local conditions. Thus, olive trees can regenerate from side shoots only 5–10 cm long (Sheat 1965, pp. 283-4, branch fragments only 23 cm long and 1.9 cm in diameter (Holder 1903, p. 209), thick firewood-like truncheons (Bitting 1920, p. 11; Chandler 1950, p. 367), bases of trunks with the roots and trunk length severed off (Bitting 1920, p. 12). Olive trees can even regenerate from bark fragments (Casella 1931, p. 113), as well as large roots (Porter 1905, p. 61). Furthermore, the orientation of the olive-tree debris, left in the ground, is of little importance. Olive trees can be regenerated from branches driven as stakes in the ground as well as branches laid horizontally, or at any diagonal in between (Muguerza 1944, p. 8).

Whitcomb and Morris (1961, pp. 104-6) have noted that enough time elapsed from the emergence of the mountain peaks as a result of floodwater retreat, and the bird bringing the olive leaf (*not* olive branch), for the olive's vegetative propagules to have rooted and sent out shoots. Indeed, seven to eight weeks are sufficient for rooting (Mencuccini et al. 1988, p. 264), with durations of time as short as thirty days being sufficient under other conditions (Sheat 1965, p. 284). Some of the conditions peculiar to the Flood must have facilitated the vegetative propagation of olive trees. For instance, olive cultivars root better under low light, and putrescine promotes earlier rooting of olive propagules (Rugini et al. 1988, p. 439). The semi-darkness could have occurred when some of the olive-tree fragments had been covered by decaying flotsam. The putrescine, an amine breakdown-product of decomposition, must have come from the decaying material.

Chapter 20

End-Flood Events:
Why the Ark in the Mountains?

This section considers the events on the Ark during the latter stages of the Flood. Special emphasis is put on the "problems" of its landing in the mountains of Ararat.

Noah's Release of the Birds. The release of the birds (Genesis 8:7-12) from the Ark in order to determine the abatement of the floodwaters was a very practical procedure. The early Norse sailors also released live birds to determine the nearness of land (Long 1981, p. 10). Plimer (1994, p. 91) has made the strange assertion that the failure of the dove to return to the Ark means that doves should be extinct. In actuality, nothing in Scripture tells us how far these scout birds went from the Ark, much less why they could not have returned to the Ark's general vicinity and subsequently been re-united with their mates once all the passengers had been released from the Ark.

The Removal of the Ark Covering. Noah removed the covering of the Ark to see the scenery after the Flood (Genesis 8:13; H. Morris 1976, p. 210). This probably implies that the Ark roof was gabled, for, had it been flat, there would have been little or no advantage in vantage-point for Noah to have done this, instead of just having looked out the under-eave window. Pictorial depictions of the Ark by the Jewish scholar Ben Uri (1975; see also Friedler 1967), and the Dutch boatbuilder van der Werff (1980) show it having a gabled roof.

Moore (1983, p. 33) and his disciple Plimer (1994, p. 132) have made a complete farce of the events described in Genesis 8:13. They fantasize Noah tearing off the entire roof of the Ark and thereby exposing the animals to the elements for several months. Needless to say, Scripture makes no such claim. In actuality, Noah probably made the hole in the roof covering just large enough for him to peer out. He must have largely sealed it back up if necessary. This is feasible, as even a small opening at the apex of a gabled roof can serve for ventilation and illumination (Bruce 1978, p. 165). Incoming rain poses no problem if the slot width itself is no more than a few centimeters in width. It is therefore probable that Noah did not close up the entire opening that he had made in the roof (originally to observe the immediate post-Flood scenery) in order to have another opening for ventilation. Since the winds of the Flood had probably died down by then, the opening in the roof must have played a major role in the continued ventilation of the Ark. Indeed, this arrangement (i. e. under-eave inlets and slotted-roof opening at the apex of a gabled roof) is a very efficient one for the ventilation of animal houses (Bruce 1978).

The PostFlood Change in Human-Animal Relations. I now discuss a probable reason why God put the fear of man into the animals after they had been released from the Ark (Genesis 9:2-3). It has been a recurring problem with many freed wild animals that they remain attached to humans. For instance, large cats raised by humans and subsequently released into the wild have no natural fear of humans, and commonly resort to cattle-eating and even man-eating (Panwar and Rodgers 1986, p. 941). By instilling the fear of man into the animals (Genesis 9:2-3), God protected Noah's family and descendants, as well as the domesticated animals.

Why Did the Ark Not Land in a Plains Region? I once heard an anti-creationist say that a mountainous region is just about the worst place for the Ark to have landed. Moore (1983, p. 34) has repeated this, embellishing it with various baseless fantasies of the animals released from the Ark being forced to contend with burning volcanoes and the like. Who ever said that Ararat must have been erupting at the time of the Ark landing? Obviously, Moore has never heard of, or has chosen to disregard, the episodic nature of volcanic eruptions and lava flows.

Moreover, despite the common notion that the Ark landed on a mountain top (or even on Mount Ararat itself), it is agreed by creationists (Schmich 1978), compromising evangelicals (Young 1995, p. 22, 33), and modernists (Bailey 1989, p. 58) that Scripture does not teach this. It only states that the Ark landed in the *mountains* of Ararat (Genesis 8:4), saying nothing about the topography, elevation, etc., of the immediate site of the Ark landing. All the arguments of Moore (1983, p. 34) about the unsuitability of the mountain peak for the Ark are therefore vacuous.

In a clumsy attempt to discredit Scripture, McKown (1993, p. 47, 63) has asserted that the Biblical claim of the Ark landing in Ararat stems from the Biblical writers' ignorance of world geography (i.e., their mistaken belief that the mountains of Ararat were the tallest mountains on earth). McKown's claim is absurd: nowhere in the Bible does it claim that the mountains of Ararat are the tallest mountains on earth! It is bad enough when skeptics imagine the existence of errors and contradictions in Scripture, but it is even worse when they resort to outright falsehoods about the Word of God.

It is, of course, possible that God let the Ark land in a mountainous region in order to preserve it and eventually reveal it's existence. While we may not fully understand God's purposes in allowing the Ark to land on Ararat, at least this side of eternity, we can deduce some of the advantages of the Ark landing where it did. The most obvious of these is that the highland regions of the earth were the ones first freed from the floodwaters. This created a few months of time between the abatement of the floodwaters and the disembarkation of the Ark. This span of time must have been valuable for several reasons. First of all, it allowed the mountainous regions to dry out from the floodwater. It also gave a few months for the plants to sprout, grow somewhat, and become available as food by the time the passengers of the Ark disembarked.

There is also a possible climatic reason for the Ark landing in the mountains of Ararat. In my work on post-Flood biogeography (the first paper in Woodmorappe 1993), I discussed the probable fact that extensive regions of the earth were probably too cold to support life immediately after the Flood due to the reduction of surface-reaching sunlight by volcanic dust. Since there had been an atmospheric temperature inversion, mountainous regions were warmer than plains regions, and therefore more conducive to post-Flood life in the immediate post-Flood period.

Ecological Consequences of a Montane Landing. Apart from these considerations, probably the most obvious advantages of the Ark landing are ecological in nature. For instance, there is a greater diversity of microclimates in a mountainous region. In fact, some mountains today have very ecologically-complex associations of organisms (Carson and Templeton 1984, p. 101). The montane landing guaranteed that the Ark animals had a variety of temperatures from which to choose. A montane region also facilitated shading from the sun as needed. For instance, elephants in montane regions tend to be healthier than those in lowland regions, because the former are better able to retreat to shaded thickets during the heat of the day (Sikes 1968, p. 255).

There must have been a greater source of carrion, as an alternative to live prey, in the mountainous regions than in the lowlands immediately after post-Flood. Mountainous regions, because of their rugged topography, have many more outcrops than do plains regions. Owing to deep erosions in the earlier-deposited Flood strata, this must have facilitated the re-exhumation of dead animals, with the carrion serving as an important post-Flood food source (see below).

A montane region also must have facilitated the fragmentation of the populations of the Ark-released animals, conferring several advantages to the fledgling populations of animals involved. A patchy, heterogenous environment can support a greater diversity of life than a unitary, homogenous one (Lomnicki 1980, p. 192). Extinction is probably less likely to occur if there are several subdivided populations of a kind than just one population (Griffith et al. 1989, p. 478; Loeschcke and Tomiuk 1991, p. 280). For instance, a disease epidemic is less likely to wipe out a population if the population is subdivided (Young 1994). The landing of the Ark in a mountainous area also must have facilitated the development of stable predator/prey relationships among the animals. Spacial patchiness is necessary in order for prey-only and predator-prey regions to exist (May 1991, p. 156). Moreover, the fledgling populations of ungulates must have been relatively protected from predators when they were solitary, well-dispersed, and difficult to locate in the rugged topography (Bailey 1993, p. 223).

A Montane Landing: Effects on Genetics and Speciation. There is some evidence that a subdivided population is more successful in conserving genetic remaining diversity than an equal-sized panmictic population (Egan and Grant 1993, p. 80; Templeton 1991b, p. 187), and is also more likely to retain new alleles caused by mutations. Thus, if a species is split into separate subpopulations with no gene flow between them, alternate alleles may be fixed in different subpopulations, permanently retaining them in the total population (Hedrick and Miller 1992, p. 40). Finally, genetic polymorphisms are more likely to be maintained when the population is in a heterogenous environment (Hall 1993, p. 141).

Landing in a mountainous region must have also facilitated the rapid diversification of the created kinds released from the Ark. Moore (1983, p. 8) foolishly asserts that there was "no impetus for speciation in post-Diluvian Armenia." For his information, not only is rapid speciation possible (see below) and possibly facilitated by population bottlenecks (see below) but also many theories of speciation *predict* a greater chance of speciation when the initial population structure is subdivided (Templeton 1980, p. 1029). This is borne out by actual evidence. For instance, the topographic relief of the Andes mountains has been implicated in the rapid speciation of the native bird fauna. The habitats readily enlarged, shrank, and become isolated (Arctander and Fjeldsa 1994, p. 222). This forced the creatures to experience sharp but variable microevolutionary pressures, followed by isolation of the gene pool, often culminating in rapid speciation.

Even mutation rates, responsible for increased variation in a population (with or without concomitant speciation) may be subject to increases in montane regions. Vorontsov and Lyapunova (1989, pp. 132-3) have found that plants occurring in tectonically-active regions have many more karyomorphs than conspecifics elsewhere. Seismicity is correlated with a concentration of various mutagenic factors (X-rays, radon water, salts of heavy metals, etc.) in tectonically-active regions.

Chapter 21

Food Sources in the "Barren" Post-Flood World

Not content to invent and attribute many false problems to the Ark itself, detractors of Scripture have also generated a huge web of rather vacuous arguments about the impossibility of the animals having anything to eat once they had been released from the Ark. McGowan (1984, p. 58) and Morton (1995, p. 71) are among those who have repeated this tomfoolery. In addition, Teeple (1978, p. 71) and Morton (1995, p. 71) suppose that the Ark-released carnivores turned on the other Ark animals for want of anything else to eat; a fantasy also entertained by the Eighteenth Century zoologist Eberhardt Zimmerman (Browne 1983, p. 26).

All these canards presuppose that nothing edible existed after the Flood besides what had been on the Ark. In actuality, the post-Flood world was not totally barren, much less sterile. There was, first of all, flotsam left behind from the Flood, some of which must have served as an immediate food source. The bark on logs is edible, and has served as an emergency food source for various animals such as rabbits (Myers et al. 1994, p. 119), porcupines (Eisenberg and Lockhart 1972, p. 100), and elephants (Dasmann 1964, p. 38; Moss 1992, p. 144). Earlier, we noted the time lag of a few months between the emergence of land, and the disembarkation of animals from the Ark, giving plenty of time for plants to sprout. These need not have been tall. Folivorous animals (e.g., elephants) need not wait around for trees to grow, but could have subsisted on the fast-growing small plants, such as grasses (Eisenberg and Lockhart 1972, p. 100). Finally, as discussed in the ensuing section, seaweed must have been available, as a food source, over vast areas of recently-flooded land.

Seaweed. The continents had been flooded and terrestrial vegetation destroyed. Yet the same need not have been true of aquatic vegetation. Furthermore, aquatic vegetation could have recovered sooner than land vegetation after the Flood. Moreover, as vast areas covered by residual floodwaters continued to be drained off, much seaweed must have been left behind in residual pools of water, readily available as a major, or even sole, food component.

Even today, many terrestrial mammals will eat seaweed if it is available. Moose are well known for eating seaweed, and so are buffalo (Ridpath 1991, p. 178). Elephants have been known to eat aquatic grasses (Melland 1938, p. 111). The sheep of Iceland are grazed exclusively on seaweed for up to eighteen weeks a year when the grassland is snowbound (Halsson 1964, p. 399). This aquatic diet is even more true of the Orkney sheep, which subsist almost entirely on seaweed (Jewell 1978). Rabbits have also been known to graze on seaweed for prolonged periods of time (Sheail 1971, p. 51).

Seaweed has also served as a major food source for cattle, horses, foxes, and bears (Russell 1975, p. 121; South and Whittick 1987, p. 273). Of course, Noah and his descendants can also have used this food source. Even today, many cultures (notably Asiatic ones: Zaneveld 1959) include algae as a major component of their diet.

Edible Fungi. Humans, with their propensity to include mushrooms, truffles, and yeast in their diets, are just one of very many kinds of mammals (to say nothing of other creatures) known to include fungi as a significant component of their diet (see Claridge and May 1994, and citations). After vegetation (including the remains of trees) had been left stranded *en masse* by the Flood, many types of fungi must have sprung up and proceeded to break down this debris, thus serving as a widely-available food source for the post-Diluvian organisms. Owing to the fact that thick branches and tree trunks often take a long time to break down by the fungi which encrusts them, the fungi must have been available as a major food source for a duration of many years after the Flood.

Re-exhumed Carrion. Untold numbers of animals had been killed by the Flood. Of those carcasses which floated on water, most must have decomposed within two months of death (Schafer 1972, pp. 3-34). However, there are a number of ways that the decomposition of carcasses must have been hindered long enough for many of them to have lasted long after the Flood had ended.

Let us first consider the preservation of carcasses in the floodwater itself. Those carcasses which had sunk deeply into water (200 atmospheres pressure) experienced a major reduction in the rate of bacterial decomposition (Allison et al. 1991, p. 82), enabling them to survive as carrion when the Flood drained away and stranded them. However, even carcasses which remained in shallow water had a chance to be preserved, provided that a saponification reaction of body fat and water took place. This reaction gives rise to adipocere ("grave wax"), enabling corpses in water to be preserved for at least five years (Cotton et al. 1987, p. 126) if the requisite conditions are met.

Burial is a major protector of corpses not only against scavengers, but also bacteria. Even today, the Innuit peoples collectively bury thousands of fish in large pits. The fish rot, attaining the consistency of jelly. This mass is then eaten by dogs as well as people (Eidlitz 1969, p. 109). Probably the main source of carrion after the Flood was the deeply-buried corpses that had become fortuitously re-exhumed towards the latter stages of the Flood or in the early post-Flood period. Experiments with buried unembalmed human cadavers (Mann et al. 1990, p. 106; Rodriguez and Bass 1985, p. 842; Spinney 1995, p. 14) demonstrate that years can pass, under many circumstances, before such corpses are skeletonized. The animal carcasses which had been re-exhumed must have served as a source of edible carrion not only just after the Flood, but even for some years afterward. In addition, had there been areas where Flood-deposited sediments could dry out, the entombed carcasses would have been preserved by natural mummification (Weigelt 1989, p. 12).

Creatures that will eat carrion are most certainly not limited to a few scavengers (e.g., vultures). Among the medium to large mammalian predators, it is well known that hyenas and jackals will eat carrion, but it is seldom realized that so will civet cats (Bailey 1993, p. 321), lions and tigers (Prater 1965, p. 56, 66; Schaller 1972, p. 276), ratels (Prater 1965, p. 163), cheetahs (Pienaar 1969, p. 131), leopards (Bailey 1993, p. 216; Norton et al. 1986, p. 47; Pienaar 1969, p. 124), foxes and wolves (Yom-Tov et al. 1995, p. 21), etc. Otters will take carrion when normal foods are unavailable (Mason and MacDonald 1986, p. 20), as will the goosander (Hewson 1995). Carrion is a seasonally important food source for grizzly bears (Cole 1972). Even normally herbivorous animals have been known to opportunistically include carrion in their diet. This is true of wild pigs (Prakash 1991, p. 244) and even elephants (Melland 1938, p. 118).

When hungry, various snakes readily eat carrion (Chiszar and Scudder 1980, p. 136; Frye 1991, Vol. 1, p. 42) even when it is in an advanced stage of decomposition (Burchfield 1982, p. 267). An Israeli viper (*Pseudocerastes*) is notable for its *preference* for carrion (Mendelssohn 1965, p. 206). Crocodiles will also take even putrid carrion (Street 1956, p. 144). Likewise, various carnivorous lizards, notably many kinds of varanids, will eat carrion (Bennett 1992), regardless of its degree of decomposition (Ward and Carter 1988, p. 22).

Moore (1983, p. 34) doubts if the Ark-released carnivores would eat carrion since live prey (i.e., the Ark-released herbivores) was available. For his information, lions are more allured by carrion than by the finest herd of zebras or antelope (Beddard 1905, p. 94). In fact, Pienaar (1969, p. 117) states that lions will even eat the most putrid meat with about the same relish as they will a freshly-killed animal. Likewise, Bailey (1993, p. 220) points out that leopards will feed on carrion, even if live prey is abundant, provided that the carrion is easy to obtain. Owing to the fact that the carrion after the Flood must have been much more plentiful than the live herbivores released from the Ark, it is very likely that the predators subsisted on carrion instead of the live prey for a long time after the Flood.

Residual Aquatic Life. Although the earth's fish populations must have been decimated by the Flood, at least some of these populations must have rebounded soon afterwards. This owes to the fact that many types of fish enjoy rapid, if not explosive, population growth if the water is full of nutrients, as is the case after floods (Ross and Baker 1983, p. 10). As the floodwaters drained off the continents, residual pools of inland water must have persisted for some time after its final retreat. As these gradually dried up or drained away, various kinds of aquatic life, dead or still alive, were stranded. These animals were available as an important source of meat, for the carnivores, in the immediate post-Flood period. Of course, they need not have all been alive or even fresh. For instance, otters and foxes will eat old and rotten fish as well as fresh ones (Hewson 1995, p. 63).

A large variety of normally non-piscivorous animals will eat fish on an opportunistic basis. In fact, so efficient are terrestrial predators in taking advantage of the plight of fish stuck in shrinking pools of water that such fish are difficult to study (Tramer 1977, p. 472). Many kinds of animals (e.g., lions: Guggisberg 1963, p. 128; Pienaar 1969, p. 117), hyenas (Pienaar 1969, p. 134), jaguars (Mondolifi and Hoogesteijn 1986, pp. 107-8), and even baboons (Hamilton and Tilson 1985) have been observed going into shallow pools that were drying out in order to catch and eat the struggling fish. Hawks have been seen doing the same (Smith 1915, p. 43), as well as taking fish from overflowing river banks (Finley 1905, pp. 6-7). Pigs have been known to habitually graze the seacoast during low tide in search of molluscs, fish, etc. (Riedman 1990, p. 50), as have rats (Hendrickson 1983, p. 85).

Whether under unusual or normative conditions, animals hardly reputed as piscivorous often include fish as a significant component of their diet. Thus, when rodents and hares are unavailable, foxes near coastal regions will subsist on aquatic food (Burton 1979, p. 47; Hewson 1995). In winter, the normally-insectivorous platypus includes molluscs and fish eggs as a major, or even dominant, part of its diet (Grant 1982; pp. 235-6). When seals are unavailable, polar bears will sometimes eat a significant amount of fish (Russell 1975, p. 127). Tigers eat fish opportunistically (Markowitz 1982, p. 101; Prater 1965, p. 66), as do wolves (Moore and Smith 1990, p. 267), and leopards (Norton et al. 1986, p. 47).

Let us now consider birds of prey in some detail. Many (e.g., the osprey, many kinds of eagles) already eat fish as part of their normal diet, but so can most if not all other carnivorous birds. Bent (1937, 1938) has recorded numerous observations of normally non-piscivorous birds of prey including fish in their diets, such as the caracara (*Polyborus*), vultures (*Cathartes*), hawks (*Buteo, Urubitinga*), and various owls (*Strix, Bubo, Otus, Nyctea, Speotyto*, etc). More recently, the experiments of Bunn et al. (1982, p. 91) have verified that the normally rodentivorous barn owl will eat fish if it is available. Various crows have also been observed eating molluscs and fish (Barber 1993, p. 11; Clegg 1972, p. 249; Hewson 1995).

Among reptiles, a wide variety of snakes are known to consume fish, including dead fish (Mitchell and Pocock 1907, p. 790-1; for details, see Table 1 in Barnard 1985). Among the elapids (whose usual diet is snakes, lizards, and frogs), the Banded Krait (*Bangurus fasciatus*) is known to eat fish at times (Liat 1990, p. 414). As for carnivorous lizards, the Komodo Monitor already includes fish in its diet (Auffenberg 1981, p. 226), as does the tuatara (Neill 1958, p. 68).

Even normally-herbivorous animals will eat aquatic flesh. For instance, the normally granivorous sparrows will eat molluscs and crustaceans from the sea shore (Summers-Smith 1988, p. 161). Rats, of course, will eat virtually anything, including seafood (Hendrickson 1983, p. 39). Badgers living near seashores have been known to include molluscs as a major component of their diet (Pigozzi 1991, p. 304), and primates living on islands have been observed eating fish (Watanabe 1989, p. 125, 130). Some captive camels have come to relish fish (Blunt 1976, p. 55), and there are anecdotal reports of elephants including fish and molluscs in their diet (Melland 1938, p. 118).

In some instances, fish and other aquatic life has served as the *sole* food source, for prolonged periods of time, for normally non-piscivorous animals. Such is the case with the Northern Barred Owl (*Strix varia*: Bent 1938, pp. 189-190), and, in captivity, with certain horses, sheep, and cattle (Anon. 1827b, p. 357). A leopard stranded on an island in Kariba Lake, Africa, and completely bereft of its normal prey, became adapted to an all-fish diet (Mitchell et al. 1965, p. 304). Certain lions frequenting the coasts of South Africa subsist on marine sources of food (Jones 1987, p. 297). Between November and January, salmonid carcasses serve as an important food source for various birds and mammals along the Scottish coast (Hewson 1995, p. 63). Amphibians were an additional alternative, or supplemental, food for various forms of post-Flood animal life. Various carnivores have been found to include amphibians (especially frogs) in their diets, such as tigers (Markowitz 1982, p. 101), badgers (Pigozzi 1991, p. 304), and several kinds of snakes (Frye 1991, Vol. 1, p. 42).

Chapter 22

The First Post-Diluvian Food Chains

With the decimation of the fauna and flora by the Flood, the survivors were few and far between. However, since they now faced no competitors in a near-vacant biosphere, they must have undergone explosive population growth. This is notably true of insects and earthworms and—among the Ark released animals—the rodents. It is these animals which must have been at the base of the first post-Diluvian food chains. By contrast, the populations of the larger animals could only grow much more slowly and become ecologically significant much later.

Insects. Many individual small arthropods must have survived the Flood. For instance, ants can survive flooding by entering hibernation if the temperature is usually below 8C (Davenport 1992, p. 113). Even the debris left after the Flood must have served as a huge spawning ground for many types of insects. For instance, the "filth flies" will flourish not only in carrion, but also in decomposing vegetation and seaweed (Anderson 1966, p. 22). In fact, phytophagous insects are the first to become established on a devastated area, feeding as they do on plant debris (Carlquist 1974, p. 13). Insects are legendary for the rate of their population increase. At a very favorable intrinsic rate of natural increase, a population of 1 milligram insects could enjoy a 120-billion fold population increase in just six months (Bluewciss 1978, p. 267). Three hundred ants could multiply into several billion within a year (Wilson 1984, p. 34). This all means that, allowing only a fraction of this rate of increase in order to be realistic, insect populations must have been already fairly plentiful towards the latter stages of the Flood; months before the grounding of the Ark. The Ark-released animals must have found many insects to eat, at least in many locations.

In fact, most vertebrates are at least facultatively insectivorous. For instance, many normally non-insectivorous birds of prey will eat insects on an opportunistic basis (e. g., the little owl, buzzard, and kestrel: Bunn et al. 1982, p. 92), especially if their usual prey (principally rodents) is in short supply (Lack 1966, p. 139). On some islands, foxes are almost entirely insectivorous (Regal 1985, p. 70). Moreover, insects can serve as a supplemental source of food for such large animals as wild pigs (Prakash 1991, p. 244), tigers (Markowitz 1982, p. 101), leopards (Hamilton 1986, p. 455), lions (Guggisberg 1963, p. 128; Pienaar 1969, p. 117), grizzly bears (McLellan and Hovey 1995, p. 706), and wolves (Moore and Smith 1990, p. 267).

Earthworms. The lowly earthworm could have survived the Flood itself in appreciably numbers. Morton (1995, p. 68) has cited the common observation of worms on sidewalks after the rain, and from this has made the abysmally ignorant assertion that earthworms could not have survived the floodwater. In actuality, experiments (Roots 1956, pp. 33-34) have demonstrated that earthworms can survive a year in waterlogged mud, and for many continuous weeks suspended in water itself. Of course, this is not the only way for earthworms to have survived the Flood. Earthworm capsules are often transported in the roots of plants, for thousands of kilometers, at sea (Barrett 1947, p. 100). If the water temperatures were below 10C, the earthworm capsules themselves would have survived the Flood in a state of dormancy (Barrett 1947, p. 98). Towards the recessional stages of the Flood, the earthworms must have multiplied very rapidly. Shields (1974, pp. 10-11) has showed that, allowing only one quarter of the normal increase under ideal conditions, 1,000 breeding earthworms could multiply 73-fold in six months and 883-fold in one year. Because of their plenitude by the time the Ark landed, they must have been a significant post-Flood source of food for many creatures.

Everyone knows that most birds eat worms, but it is seldom realized how many other animals will do likewise, especially if there is a shortage of other live foods. Many snakes eat earthworms (MacDonald 1983, p. 394). When the normal prey (e.g., rodents) of carnivorous birds is in short supply, the birds of prey will include earthworms in their diet (Lack 1966, p. 139; MacDonald 1983, pp. 394-5). Likewise, many carnivorous mammals (e.g., foxes, badgers, weasels, viverrids, raccoons, and opossums: Lee 1985, p. 148; MacDonald 1983, pp. 402-3) include earthworms as a significant, and sometimes major, component of their diet. Likewise, members of the mammalian Order Insectivora often subsist on earthworms (MacDonald 1983, pp. 397-400).

Rodents. These little mammals are legendary for their population growth rates, especially when unhindered by competitors. Not long after leaving the Ark, the rodents must have grown explosively in numbers: theoretically, a single pair of rats having 15,000 descendants in a year (Hendrickson 1983, p. 76), and a pair of field mice actually siring 2,557 animals in ten months (Hendrickson 1983, p. 180). Furthermore, the rodent population growth must have been facilitated by the (previously-discussed) abundance of insects and earthworms at the end of the Flood. This owes to the fact that very many types of rodents include insects in their diet (for a tabulation of rodent insectivory, see Landry 1970, and Funmilayo and Akande 1979). In fact, some rodent individuals even subsist on insect-*dominated* diets (Landry 1970).

Possibly as early as several weeks after the Flood, rodents were fairly common, and available as a food source for many carnivorous animals, and certainly not only the small ones. Most, if not all, large-mammal predators are at least facultatively rodentivorous, consistent with the fact that large predators commonly eat a much larger range of prey than do small predators (Cohen et al 1993). Especially when large prey is not available, lions can and will subsist at least a few months on medium to large rodents (Guggisberg 1963, pp. 127-8; Owens and Owens 1984, p. 237, 286-7; Pienaar 1969, p. 117; Seidensticker et al. 1973, p. 23) and hares. The same is true for leopards (Hamilton 1986, p. 455; Johnson et al. 1993, p. 648), jackals (Owens and Owens 1984, p. 52), cheetahs (Pienaar 1969, p. 130-1), and wolves (Prater 1965, p. 115). Grizzly bears include rodents in their diet at an approximately inverse proportion to the availability of ungulates (McLellan and Hovey 1995, p. 706). Even herbivores will eat rodents, especially if they occur locally in large numbers. This is true, for instance, of lemmings eaten by reindeer (Chernov 1985, p. 176), and various rodents eaten by wild pigs (Prakash 1991, p. 244).

Slow-Growing Populations Protected by Buffers. Animals which take a relatively long time to multiply to large numbers were unlikely to have been immediately eaten by the predators released from the Ark, owing to the much greater abundance of the other food sources. Leopold (1933, p. 231) has defined buffers as alternative food sources for predators. This is an apt term, since the buffers take the pressure off the main prey while the population of the prey is low. After the Flood, first the carrion and aquatic life, followed by insects and rodents, must have served as buffers, allowing the populations of large ungulates (i.e., the normal prey of large mammalian predators) to multiply to large numbers.

Part III

The Adequacy of Single Pairs in the Repopulation of the World

Chapter 23

Demographic Ramifications of Single-Pair Founders

Animals Which "Breed Only in Flocks"

Moore (1983, pp. 14-15) asserts that single pairs of colonial breeders, released from the Ark, would have been incapable of siring any offspring. There are several levels of fallacies in his argument, not least of which is his premise that, since some animals *presently* breed, or are *believed* to breed, only when in groups, then they must be *obligate* group-breeders, and/or must have *always been* obligate group-breeders.

To begin with, the breeding of birds in flocks is especially prevalent among just those birds which were least likely to have been on the Ark—various oceanic birds (Darling 1938, pp. 100-1). Secondly, many animals which usually breed colonially, such as sea lions and squirrel monkeys, *will* in fact breed in solitary pairs, although sometimes at reduced rates of fecundity (Young and Isbell 1994, p. 129). However, owing to the open ecological niches right after the Flood, reduced fertility was more than made up by the survivorship of the fledglings. Likewise, in the case of many, if not most, colonial-breeding birds, solitary pairs appear to have no problem in the siring of offspring (Immelman 1973, p. 134). Only the season of breeding is slightly altered. It is now recognized that, even in the case of difficult breeders like flamingos, the fulfillment of some mythical exacting conditions is not necessary for successful breeding to take place (Ogilvie and Ogilvie 1986, p. 107). Moreover, the widely-held notion of their obligatory group-breeding has been questioned:

> The fact that very small flocks of flamingos will breed suggests that large mass displays may not be essential to stimulate breeding in captive flamingos. . . . Factors other than flock size may play an important role in determining whether flamingos will breed (Pickering et al. 1992, p. 233).

Another fallacy in Moore's (1983, pp. 14-15) argument is his implicit claim that only members of the same species can stimulate a colonial breeder to sire offspring. In reality, many, if not most, colonial breeders released from the Ark could have been stimulated to breed by the sight of the numerous *other* birds released from the Ark and/or the oceanic birds which had survived the Flood outside the Ark. Note that pelicans (Order Pelecaniformes) are stimulated to breed not only by the sight of other pelicans, but also by the sight of cormorants and even birds belonging to other orders, such as Ciconiiformes (Brouwer et al. 1994, and citations therein).

I now consider probable changes in group-breeding behavior *since* the Flood. The reproductive biology of many animals (notably birds) is quite variable even within a species, to say nothing of microevolutionary differences between species. For instance, some bird individuals that frequent islands have different nesting strategies from conspecifics elsewhere, even though the islands have been in existence for only thousands of years (Williamson 1981, p. 141). The same plasticity in reproductive behavior applies to group breeding. In the case of the Australian Zebra Finch, for instance, colonial breeding appears to be more pronounced in the arid interior of the continent than in the coastal regions (Immelman 1973, p. 138). For all their very divergent breeding-flock sizes, the flamingos are not only members of the same kind, but can actively hybridize with each other (Duplaix-Hall and Kear 1975, pp. 132-3). Whereas some flamingos breed by the thousands, others have bred in colonies of under ten pairs in nature (Ogilvie and Ogilvie 1986, p. 107) and in captivity, in a flock of only four (Pickering et al. 1992). Pelicans, another colonial-breeding bird, have sired offspring in groups as small as six (Brouwer et al. 1994).

Evidence that breeding biology is governed by easily-altered microevolutionary factors is further demonstrated by the Bewicks's Swan, a high Arctic breeder. Breeding cannot take place until the male performs a wing-display show, and he does not do it until the day is exceedingly long (as in the late spring of the Arctic). Yet there have occurred instances where this swan has bred under the photoperiodic conditions of the temperate zone (Luoma 1987, p. 147-8), probably as a result of a rare genetic haplotype. This inherited variability in breeding biology is, of course, hardly limited to birds. Consider Belyaev's (1979) experimental domestication of the fox. While breeding foxes for tameness, he inadvertently altered their estrous cycle. In conclusion, it appears that colonial breeding did not develop until after the Flood, and so was not a relevant factor at the time of the disembarkation of the Ark.

Viable Populations Founded by Single Pairs

Moore (1983, p. 15) has argued that the founding of populations by the single pairs (and even seven pairs) released from the Ark would have given them a nil chance of survival in the post-Flood world. His assertion is fallacious, and soundly contradicted by numerous examples of populations fledged by single-pair founders:

> The extreme, naturally occurring case, wherein a population is founded by a single such propagule, is not only biologically feasible, but provides a degree of operational simplicity for theoretical purposes (Carson and Templeton 1984, p. 100).

The genetic diversity of single-pair founders is discussed in a later section.

Single-Pair Introductions: the Ramifications. To begin with, it must be remembered that there was a tradeoff between post-Flood survivorship and the capacity of the Ark. Let us also put the "problem" of self-sustaining post-Diluvian populations in perspective. We are told that Noah took the animals to allow flesh to survive (Genesis 6:20), but nothing in Scripture indicates that it was God's will for *all* the kinds alive in the antediluvian world to succeed in the post-Diluvian one. We know from the fossil record that there are many more extinct genera of vertebrates (notably mammals) than extant ones, so it follows that the majority of animals released from the Ark did *not* succeed in the post-Flood world. Thus, Plimer's (1994, p. 124) assertion that the Ark would have been a failure if even one kind died out is completely wrong.

While it is not hard to guess that a multitude of introduced founders is more likely to give rise to a lasting population than is a single introduced pair, the picture is not so simple. For instance, not only are there many modern examples of viable populations started by a single pair of founders (see below), but also not a few instances of even hundreds of founders failing to give rise to a lasting introduced population (see, for instance, Appendix 1 in Newsome and Noble 1986). Experimental introductions of animals demonstrate that a large founder population has only a limited advantage, in terms of eventual success, over a single-pair founder. For instance, Griffith et al. (1989, p. 479) determined that the advantage of introducing progressively more founder individuals quickly levels off asymptotically, so that a population started by 400 birds is only 2.5–5.7 times, certainly not 200 times, more probable to persist than is a population started by only two birds. Moreover, a single pair of founders released into a habitat that is rated "excellent" has as much chance of survival as does an introduced population of 400 founders placed in a habitat that is rated only as "good" (Griffith et al. 1989, p. 479). In a study of the probability of extinction in an introduced bird population as a function of the number of founding members, Pimm et al. (1988, p. 771) found that populations started by single founders do not necessarily go extinct more frequently than do pairs started by several founders. Finally, not only are many factors involved in the eventual success of a founder population, but the studies of successfully-transplanted faunas are limited by the fact that they tend to be after-the-fact studies of the successful colonists (Brown 1989, p. 102).

Successful Single-Pair Founders: Case Histories. The ability of single pairs to give rise to growing and relatively permanent populations is not merely a theoretical possibility, but is a demonstrable fact. Thus, many birds transplanted within Australia have been started by single pairs of innoculi (see Appendix 1 in Newsome and Noble 1986). The introduced Laysan Finch on one of the Hawaiian Islands may have descended from a single pair of birds (Conant 1988, p. 256; Pimm 1988, pp. 290-1). Likewise, a population of American Gray Squirrel, started by one pair of founders, flourishes in Victoria, Australia (de Vos et al. 1956, p. 179). Populations of larger animals have also been successfully started by single pairs. This is true, for instance, with the rock wallaby introduced to Hawaii (Tomich 1986, p. 17), rabbits introduced to the Balearic Islands by the ancient Romans (Flux and Fullagar 1992, p. 151), rabbits introduced to some Australian islands in the 19th century (Flux and Fullagar 1992, p. 182), raccoons introduced to the Bahamas (Sherman 1954, p. 126), koalas introduced to French I Island (George 1990, p. 191; Wilmer 1993, p. 177), the elk introduced to California (McCullough 1978, p. 174), sheep introduced to Ile Haute Island (Chapuis et al. 1994, p. 100; Lesel and Derenne 1975, p. 487), and possibly the macaques introduced to Mauritius Island (Lawler et al. 1995, p. 138).

Many other viable populations have been started by not many more than two individuals, of which I will only cite only a few examples. These include the: reindeer introduced to Ile Haute Island (three founders: Lesel and Derenne 1975, p. 485), American muskrat introduced to Europe (five founders: Mohr 1933), Virginia opossum brought to Oregon (possibly four founders: Jewett and Dobyns 1929), European horses once living ferally in vast herds in South America (five founders: Clutton-Brock 1992, p. 83), various European birds introduced to South Africa (few to several founders each: Bigalke 1937, p. 51), Chinese pheasants introduced to Europe (three founders: Delacour 1951, p. 197) and nearly all Syrian hamsters currently existing in captivity (three founders: Van Hoosier and Ladiges 1984, p. 125).

Explosive Population Growth Rates Aid Single-Pair Founders. The absence of competitors (certainly true of the post-Flood world) is of crucial importance in the successful establishment of an introduced population (Brown 1989, p. 98, 104; Chapuis et al. 1994, p. 97; Griffith et al. 1989, p. 478). Also, when a population starts from only a few founders, it is of paramount importance for it to grow quickly to a large size, for several reasons. First of all, larger populations are less likely it to grow quickly to a large size, for several reasons. First of all, larger populations are less likely to be driven to extinction by stochastic events. Second, rapid population growth greatly reduces the loss of genetic variability in the founded population (see below). There is no necessarily simple relationship between founder size and ensuing population growth rate. Experimental introductions of mice (Pennycuik and Reisner 1990, p. 483) have shown that the differences between populations started by five founders versus those started by twenty founders tend to disappear in a relatively short period of time. Owing to the explosive population growth of animals after the Flood (see below), the consequences of using only two founders (as opposed to many more) must have been minimized.

It is interesting to note that many animals appear to have a build-in mechanism to take advantage of empty niches. They have the capability to have many more offspring than usual when food sources are abundant and competitors few. This is true, for instance, of deer and rodents (Lack 1954, p. 70), as well as wolves (Jordan et al. 1967, p. 249) and cheetahs (Mills 1991, p. 87). No doubt this must have facilitated rapid post-Flood population growth.

We know from contemporary experience that introduced populations can grow at astonishing rates. For instance, the Collared Dove, introduced to Britain as four individuals (Hudson 1965, p. 129), grew to at least 19,000 birds within nine years (Hudson 1972, p. 143), amounting to a 100% annual increase (Hudson 1972, p. 144). In a US example, two pairs of birds released multiplied to at least 2,000 in only five years (Phillips 1928, p. 16): a staggering 347% annual increase. Many other such instances could be cited (Phillips 1928, p. 6). Rapid population growth can also occur in larger animals (subject, of course, to the limitations of their generally lower reproduction rates). For instance, the population of macaques on Mauritius Island numbers 25,000–35,000, and all are descendants of a very few founders introduced by sailors some 400 years ago (Lawler et al. 1995). A feral cattle population on Amsterdam Island (South Indian Ocean) grew from five innoculants to 1,500 in sixty years despite nonideal conditions (Micol and Jouventin 1995, p. 202). Irruptive population increases are well known in deer (Scheffer 1951) and sheep (Melville 1994, p. 6). To a lesser extent, this is even true of the largest animals (e.g., elephants):

> . . . it should be remembered that the maximum rate of increase is associated with optimal conditions, usually in a small population that has been introduced into a new habitat, or a population that has been reduced to levels well below its carrying capacity. Under these conditions, fecundity approaches the physiological maximum, and mortality is extremely low (Calef 1988, p. 324).

However, all the foregoing discussion should not be taken to imply that those animals whose population remained small for some time after the Flood were necessarily doomed to extinction. For instance, a viable population of cranes in Japan has existed, for over a century, numbering only thirty to forty individuals (Masatomi 1991). Canada Geese introduced to England remained at only about 100 birds for a period of eighty years before undergoing a period of near-exponential growth (Parking and Cole 1985, p. 22). The Palm-Nut Vulture in South Africa has had, for a long time, self-sustaining populations of only several breeding pairs, and even these are not all in the same location (Steyn 1982, p. 7). As for large animals, the Javan Rhinoceros, thought to have been driven to extinction in Vietnam several decades ago, turns out to have a remnant, apparently self-sustaining population of ten to fifteen individuals (Schaller et al. 1990). There is a population, consisting of several tens (each) of rhinos, giraffes, and elephants, maintaining itself in a desert region of South West Africa (Walker 1982). As discussed earlier, predator populations probably remained relatively low for some time after the Flood, until there were sufficient numbers of prey animals available. This often occurs today. For instance, the Gir lion population of Gujarat State,

India, fell to less than twenty individuals and remained below 250 individuals for some eighty years (O'Brien et al. 1987, p. 100).

The fate of post-Flood populations need not have been left solely to the mercy of nature. It is possible that Noah and his family had been involved, after the Flood, in allowing at least some of the large animals to multiply in numbers, within enclosures under their partial care, before releasing them into the wild. This would have meant a *de facto* release of several founders instead of just two. Such a procedure has been followed in the successful introduction of the European Wild Boar to Tennessee, USA (Stegeman 1938).

Let us now briefly consider human population growth rates soon after the Flood. These must have been very high because of the long human lifespans then prevalent. However, even without this factor, human populations can grow very rapidly. Consider the Hutterites. In just seventy years, the population of this sect has increased from 443 to 8,532 persons (Eaton and Mayer 1953), largely without the assistance of modern medicine or other life-prolonging technology.

The Extent of Post-Flood Ecological Differentiation

The Created Kind: a Practical Concept. Early in this work, I had refuted the charge that the created kind is arbitrary and ill-defined. In this section, I consider some of the ecological implications of variation within the kinds released from the Ark. Some anti-Creationists have raised a bogus issue by asserting that there is no way of telling which morphology is the result of variation within the kind, and which goes back to Creation. Even if it were true, it would be a nonproblem, as there is nothing which requires God to provide markers in living things in order to inform us where His direct creative ability leaves off and where natural phenotypic variation begins.

As a matter of fact, it *is* possible to tell the two apart by comparative taxonomy. Those biological attributes which vary *within* families, genera, or species are clearly variations within a kind. An example of this is viviparity and oviparity among reptiles. A live-bearing reptile is commonly confamilial, congeneric, and even conspecific with another reptile which lays eggs (Blackburn 1982, p. 193; Frye 1991). By contrast, among mammals, oviparity and viviparity have an all-or-none distribution not only at the family level and below, but also at the ordinal level. All members of Order Monotremata lay eggs, and all members of other mammalian orders bear live young. Among mammals, therefore, the contrast between viviparity and oviparity is clearly not variation within the kind subsequent to Creation, but differences *between* different kinds from the time of Creation. In general, the large morphological differences *between* created kinds are qualitatively different from the primarily-ecological variations *within* the kind:

> Differences between major taxa, such as agnathans, elasmobranchs, teleosts, amphibians, reptiles, birds, and mammals are generally more than niche-specific features such as range of hearing which might be regarded as *ecological adaptations within the same grade of complexity*, that is, lateral radiations. Instead, we may notice at least four vertical grades (Bullock 1991, pp. 15-16). (italics added)

The Created Kind: Ecological Differentiation. Moore (1983, pp. 6-8) imagines that the descendants of single pairs could not possibly have the built-in potential to suffice for the post-Flood world, let alone producing descendants as ecologically variable as seen within modern families, or even genera. His arguments display ignorance of even the basics of population biology, not to mention significant ecological changes that are routinely observed to occur in organisms in a matter of *generations*.

The ability for substantial differentiation within the kind to occur in only 5,000 years is also proved by microevolutionary changes within populations in very short periods of time, with or without the concomitant origin of new species and genera. The earlier-discussed examples of island birds are an obvious example of variation of closely-related organisms into different ecological spaces:

> Given the plasticity and adaptability of natural populations, and the great amount
> of genetic variation in them, it is to be expected that cases of niche shift, whether
> based on genetic change or just phenotypic adaptability, will be found quite com-
> monly (Williamson 1981, p. 148).

Let us consider some specific examples of this. In less than twenty years, the population of introduced Laysan Finches, started by one pair of founders, has undergone profound differentiation in beak morphology (Pimm 1988, p. 290). In fact, introduced birds have repeatedly adapted to new environments, in terms of microevolutionary changes in plumage, beak morphology, etc., in a matter of generations (for review and citations, see Diamond et al. 1989, p. 704).

Turning to the aquatic realm, let us, first of all, consider the mosquitofish (Stearns 1983). In only seventy years, introduced members of this fish acquired, through variation within the kind, significant changes in the time to reach maturity as compared with the parental stock. The selection pressure had been the fluctuations in water levels within the reservoir to which the fish had been introduced. Weiner (1995) summarized experiments with guppies which demonstrate significant microevolutionary changes in body color and sexual selection in a matter of generations. Elsewhere, populations of aquatic worms have adapted, through microevolution, to a metal-polluted environment in only a handful of generations (Klerks and Levinton 1989). There are also examples of rapid variation within the kind among plants, such as the case of the plant *Poa annua* (Till-Bottraud et al. 1990). In only twenty-five years, annual and perennial versions of the same plant have arisen as a result of contrasting modes of precipitation between their respective geographic areas.

In conclusion, Moore's (1983, p. 18) cavalier dismissal of variation within the kind as meaningless only speaks of his ignorance. Moreover, as we shall see, the rapid genetic differentiation of an introduced population into an alien environment can even give rise to new species in a short period of time.

Rapid Post-Flood Speciation

Factors Facilitating Rapid Post-Flood Speciation. If the kinds on the Ark were at the level of the genus (Table 1, 2, etc.), it follows that the species found today must have arisen since the Flood. Let us consider some of the dynamics of rapid speciation. To begin with, the founder effect often causes a disruption of coadapted genetic complexes, alters pleiotropic balance, and thus allows for significant changes in the founded population in short periods of time. Among plants, Singer et al. (1993, p. 682) noted that a highly-specific plant/butterfly symbiosis arose as a result of a population bottleneck of butterflies. Vermeij (1987, p. 41) has cited and discussed several instances where introduced populations, often started by only a few founders, have resulted in the founder populations having a much greater range of individual variation than the respective parent populations.

The fluctuating physical environment characteristic of the immediate post-Flood period must have facilitated the rapidity of speciation. For instance, in the case of the cichlid fishes speciating within 200 years (Owen et al. 1990), discussed below, changes in bottom topography have been implicated as a major factor in the rapidity of the speciation. The ability of environmental stresses, such as would have been common after the Flood as the earth re-adjusted itself, to trigger speciation, is also supported by indirect evidence. Certain rodents show a positive correlation of chromosomal diversity with environmental stress (Nevo et al. 1994), and speciose rodent genera show a high rate of chromosomal repatternings (Reig 1989, p. 277). However, studies which link enhancement of chromosomal mutations with extrinsic factors are still in their infancy (Reig 1989, p. 280; for further discussion, see *Rapid Recovery . . .*).

There are various models (e.g., founder-flush) which predict founder-induced speciation (see Carson and Templeton 1984, pp. 115-119). Single pairs of founders, introduced into novel or stressful environments, are excellent candidates for rapid speciation, even within a few generations. Conservation projects which involve the outcrossing of individuals coming from several formerly-isolated inbreeding-demes may technically result in a new species (Templeton 1986, p. 115). These conclusions are supported by empirical evidence. For instance, Conant (1988, p. 256) points out that an introduced population of rock wallabies, started by a single pair of founders (Tomich 1986, p. 17), has become so differentiated from its parental stock, in only several decades, that they should be considered a new species.

Modern Examples of Rapid Speciation. Both creationists (Jones 1982; Lester and Bohlin 1989, pp. 123-5; Brand and Gibson 1993, p. 72) and evolutionists (Briggs 1974, pp. 442-3) have compiled numerous examples of various invertebrates and vertebrates giving rise to new species and genera in thousands of years (or even less). Some of these examples have subsequently been subject to detailed studies. For instance, Berry (1992b) has updated the long-available evidence for speciation in mice in only a few decades, whereas Kornfield (1978) has investigated the origin of reproductively-isolated species of African cichlid fishes in only 5000 years. As if this were not enough, Owen et al. (1990) have recently shown that some cichlid fish species have arisen in merely 200 years.

One consequence of the glaciation several thousand years ago is that the tropics must have undergone profound climatic changes, because belts of rainfall must have shifted considerably during glacial and interglacial intervals (see Haffer (1974) for details). As a consequence, many species in the tropics must have arisen within only the last several thousand years. Nagel (1986) has provided evidence that species of central African beetles have arisen within only 5000 years, and Moreau (1966) has allowed for extensive speciation among tropical birds within a comparable period of time. The conditions immediately after the Flood (single-pair founders of new populations, vacant niches, novel environments, and other factors) must have facilitated the rapid diversification within the kinds released from the Ark, culminating in the rapid origin of present-day species.

The Timing of Post-Flood Speciation. Morton (1995, p. 50) has argued against the possibility of extensive post-Flood speciation on the basis of the fact that many familiar animals (e.g., cattle, jackals) supposedly look identical to their modern counterparts in ancient statues and pictures. There are several fallacies in his argument. To begin with, the interpretation of ancient animal depictions is fraught with pitfalls. Ancient pictographs are subject to multiple interpretations (Brewer et al. 1994, p. 121). More significantly, any detail that *is* present may be misleading, because it reflects cultural or artistic styles instead of anatomy (Brewer et al. 1994, p. 116; White 1994). Finally, interpretations are hardly free of standard uniformitarian bias. The archeologist would, of course, be laboring under the evolutionistic preconception that the animals a few thousand years ago were the same as those today (compare Rosen 1994 with White 1994).

Let us however, for the sake of argument, assume that the animals depicted in ancient cultures *are* in fact identical to modern animals. The ultimate fallacy of Morton's argument is his supposition that many thousands of years would have been necessary to generate new species. As we have seen in this section, new species can be generated in a matter of *years* or *decades*. There could thus have been a rapid burst of speciation events immediately after the Flood, followed by a relative (or absolute) quiescence in the origin of new species. By the time the ancient civilizations developed, about the only animals encountered would have been substantially no different from those of today.

Chapter 24

Avoiding the Hazards of Inbreeding

Inbreeding Depression and Single-Pair Founders

Inbreeding occurs whenever close relatives sire offspring, and often causes various problems (e.g. infant mortality, genetic defects, etc.) collectively known as *inbreeding depression*. It has historically been blamed on the expression of "genetic load" (O'Brien 1994, p. 478), which includes the sudden expression of many previously-accumulated deleterious recessive alleles. In addition, other interactive genetic processes are now also believed to contribute to inbreeding depression (Brewer et al. 1990, p. 265; Templeton and Read 1994, p. 94). However, there are no universal predictive models for the effects of inbreeding with regard to any particular species or its populations (Rabb 1994, p. 161).

A certain degree of inbreeding was inevitable after the animals had been released from the Ark, as the ensuing populations had been started by single pairs (or seven pairs), and all of their progeny had to be closely related. Morton (1995, p. 71) has raised the issue of inbreeding problems among the Ark-animal descendants caused by the small number of Ark founders. His argument is fallacious, for several reasons discussed in this section. First of all, owing to the rapid growth of most post-Flood populations, matings between close relatives must have been largely limited to the first post-Flood generation or so. In fact, there is a rapid asymptotic dropoff in the extent and severity of inbreeding in a rapidly expanding population started by a few founders [for a graphical display of this phenomenon, see Shields (1993, p. 159)], which greatly blunts the impact of potential inbreeding depression. Note that this is very different from the inbreeding depression which is likely to occur in a *sustained* small population (Frankel and Soule 1981, p. 144).

Ralls et al. (1988) have shown that the consequences of inbreeding vary greatly between different animals, and the common consequence of inbreeding is an increase of about 30% in the juvenile mortality rate. However, owing to the vacant niches in the post-Flood world and initial rarity of predators, any increased juvenile mortality was probably more than offset by other conditions favoring juvenile survivorship (e.g., large numbers of juveniles sired).

However, all the foregoing discussion is rather academic, as it is unlikely that inbreeding depression occurred at all among the descendants of the Ark animals. First of all, many contemporary animals have undergone severe population reductions without undergoing any obvious inbreeding depression, such as certain populations of waterfowl (Swengel 1987, pp. 514-515), field mice (Brewer et al. 1990), European bison (Slatis 1960), and certain regional populations of koalas (Wilmer 1993, p. 186). In some cases, this was evidently due to the animals fortuitously not bearing deleterious recessive alleles (Brewer et al. 1990, p. 265). Such chance successes in inbreeding can be seen most obviously in a few highly-inbred lineages of experimental animals which, in contrast to most other lineages, persist for many generations under repeated, close (i.e. brother-sister) interbreeding (Brewer et al. 1990, p. 258; Frankel and Soule 1981, pp. 66-9, 144; Levi 1957, p. 348). There is even experimental evidence that the differential sensitivity to inbreeding depression, commonly seen within a given population, is a heritable trait (Pray and Goodnight 1995).

The elimination of inbreeding depression can also occur if deleterious alleles are gradually removed during episodes of decreasing population size, which allows them to be periodically expressed phenotypically as a result of their occurrence in the homozygous state, and thus removed from the population (Hedrick and Miller 1992, p. 38; O'Brien 1994, p. 478). Such a mechanism has been credited with the apparent lack of impact of inbreeding depression in many of the instances mentioned in the earlier paragraph (Wilmer 1993, p. 186). In addition, the elimination of inbreeding depression by gradual reduction of a population prior to the bottleneck has been demonstrated experimentally in the case of the Speke's gazelle (Templeton 1987, p. 266; Templeton and Read 1983, 1984). Populations of animals can naturally have mildly-inbreeding demes (Grobbelaar 1989), with deleterious alleles undergoing continuous purging, yet this type of mild inbreeding does not itself lead to a loss of overall genetic variation (see Pray and Goodnight 1995, p. 186; and Templeton and Read 1994, p. 97).

To the extent that God selected the animals which went on the Ark (i.e., the Divine filter: Fig. 6), He could have chosen those pairs from Noah's menagerie and/or the wilderness which He foreknew would not have problems with inbreeding as a result of the alleles they were bearing and/or which lacked a heritable tendency to inbreeding depression (Pray and Goodnight 1995, p. 187). Since, as we have seen, inbred lines which experience no inbreeding depression are by no means rare, it follows that, even if the "genetic load" in organisms had been as high then as it is today, His choice of animals to enter the Ark need not have been particularly selective. Of course, had Noah bred animals in his menagerie for several generations before the Flood, he could have purged the deleterious recessive alleles through mild inbreeding, thus effecting a genetics filter (Fig. 6). It should be noted that pedigree breeding goes back many thousands of years in various ancient cultures (Levi 1957, p. 346) and there is no reason why the antediluvians should have been any less familiar with it.

Thus far, I have only discussed those factors reducing inbreeding depression which took place before the Flood. There are also post-Flood-world factors that must have diminished the impact of inbreeding even further. Many animals are known to have mechanisms to reduce the level of inbreeding (see Schwartz et al. 1986, p. 185, and citations therein). Once the post-Flood populations reached appreciable size, these mechanisms would have greatly reduced the instances of inbreeding, and would have acted to reduce inbreeding apart from the aforementioned size of the population itself (e.g. Shields 1993). Of course, it is possible that Noah's family was involved in the breeding of some animals after the Flood, especially in the crucial first few generations. If disassortive mating (Egan and Grant 1993, p. 80; Templeton and Read 1994, p. 94) had been practiced, inbreeding would be further minimized, as only those descendants of the Ark animals which were as unrelated to each other as possible would have been involved in mating.

Inbreeding Among Noah's Descendants

How could the human race, rebuilt after the Flood from the eight members of Noah's family, have escaped the effects of inbreeding? Some believers have suggested that the genetic load (i.e., deleterious recessive mutations which become expressed during inbreeding) was nonexistent at the time of Adam and Eve, and was very low at the time of Noah, so the descendants of these founding pairs of humans need did not experience any problems with inbreeding. While this is certainly possible, I now show that, depending upon the antediluvian population structure, Noah's descendants need not have suffered any consequences from the inevitable inbreeding even if there had in fact existed a significant genetic load.

The earlier-discussed implications of mild, prolonged inbreeding apply also to humans. For instance, some tribal populations in India often engage in consanguineous marriages, yet there is no perceptible evidence of inbreeding depression. This is because there have been consanguineous marriages going on among them for over 2,000 years, and any deleterious mutations must have been previously expressed and removed (by death) from the population (Ghosh and Majumder 1979, p. 206; Rao and Inbaraj 1980, p. 32). Likewise, had Noah's ancestors practiced mild inbreeding, his pedigree would have been virtually free of deleterious alleles. Therefore Noah's immediate descendants would have had no problem with inbreeding depression caused by any consanguineous marriages.

Chapter 25

The Ark Animals: Carriers of Adequate Genetic Diversity

Introduction. A constellation of arguments asserts that the single pairs (or even the seven pairs) released from the Ark would have been inadequate to found the post-Flood populations of animals that we see today. These assertions typically center upon the premises (Lammerts 1975; Moore 1983, pp. 6-7) that a few founders would carry insufficient genetic variation for the populations to function in new environments and, even if they could, would not account for the genetic diversity currently observed among the land animals. Such arguments continue to crumble in the face of steadily accumulating evidence to the contrary (see Fray and Goodnight 1995, and citations therein). Genetic diversity is commonly expressed in terms of percent polymorphic loci (P), number of alleles (N), and heterozygosity (H). Templeton (1994) provides an excellent tutorial on the meaning and derivation of these indices. Cavalli-Sforza et al. (1994, pp. 6-15) provide a very basic introduction to genetic polymorphism. In recent years, we have found that the genetic diversity of organisms at the DNA level far surpasses that uncovered by, for example, electrophoretically-detectable protein variants. However, the vast majority of this diversity at the DNA level appears to have little biological meaning (Bittles and Neel 1994, p. 121).

In all our discussion, we must keep in mind the fact that the importance of genetic variation remains essentially unquantified for almost all organisms (Brakefield and Saccheri 1994, p. 165). In addition, there is much that we do not even know about genes themselves. For instance, the number of genes in the human genome may be anywhere from 14,000 to 300,000 (Fields et al. 1994, p. 346; Mitton 1993, p. 24). Even the very notion of the gene may have to be overthrown, as there now is evidence genes cannot be considered as "beads on a string." We now realize that transcription units of DNA may encode multiple, unrelated proteins, may overlap, or may not even be contiguous (Fields et al. 1994, p. 345). Finally, we do not fully understand how genes interact to manifest themselves phenotypically.

The Myth of the 50/500 Rule.

Moore (1983, p. 50) and Morton (1995, p. 71) have argued against the viability of the Ark-released single pair founders by citing population-conservationists' estimates that a minimum of 50 (and preferably at least 150) founding animals are necessary to adequately conserve the genetic diversity of a population. Their use of these figures is extremely inaccurate and misleading.

Furthermore, the 50/500 rule, upon which their argument is based, has now fallen into disrepute (Soule and Mills 1992, p. 57).

The 50/500 rule had a very tenuous foundation to begin with (for historical survey, see Templeton 1994, pp. 61-63), and never had been more than a crude guess (May 1994, p. 13), despite being imbued with a precision never intended by its author (May 1991, p. 150). The number 500 of the "50/500 rule" came about as a result of a single experiment on the bristles of the fruit fly (*Drosophila*) (Dawson et al. 1987, p. 215). Even then, the interactive properties of genes had been neglected:

> It is disturbing that a single experiment on bristle number in one strain of one species of fruit fly is being used as a general guide for conservation management policy. . . . In the context of the time, the 50/500 rule was a reasonable working hypothesis, although the results summarized here indicate that this hypothesis can now be rejected both theoretically and empirically. . . . Unfortunately, it is common-place to treat the 50/500 proposition as a "rule" rather than as a hypothesis (Templeton 1994, p. 63).

Earlier, I discussed the many instances where lasting populations have been founded by as few as two founders, and it is recognized that such occurrences are clear evidence against the inviolability of the 50/500 rule (Hedrick and Miller 1992, p. 38; Hengeveld 1989, p. 137). Furthermore, a single pair of founders most definitely *can* have the same genetic diversity as fifty founders, and without any miraculous or unusual procedures:

> Hence, a founder population of two lizards collected from different local popula-tions would display more genetic variation for all diversity measures with the possible exception of N than a sample of 50 lizards from a single local population (Templeton 1994, p. 62).

Also, in the case of the Speke's gazelle (discussed below), four founders (of which two were responsible for most of the lasting genetic diversity; Templeton 1991b, p. 186) satisfied the "50 rule" (Templeton 1994, p. 61). Finally, Templeton (1994, p. 62) concludes that, when a panmictic population is sampled, an inbreeding effective size of 50 will almost always occur regardless of the census founding size.

The number 500 in the 50/500 rule is a rule-of-thumb for conservation biologists dealing with essentially static populations, and is of no relevance to the post-Flood situation. It tells us nothing about the original number of founders, nor the dynamics of a continuously-expanding population. Consider the recent conservationists' attempt to preserve 80% of the heterozygosity of the black-footed ferret, for a targeted duration of 200 years, using the recommended carrying capacity of 500 animals (Ballou and Cooper 1992, pp. 198-9). This could be achieved, under the condition of rapid population growth, with eight founders and the 500 animals. With only five founders, a population of 800 becomes necessary. After the Flood, of course, the situation was entirely different from that of a modern conservation-biology project. The post-Flood population was under no constraint to preserve some arbitrary fraction (e.g., 80%) of original heterozygosity (but see below on the conservation of heterozygosity), and, of course, populations rapidly grew to much larger sizes than 500 or 800.

Not all the Ark-released post-Flood populations had only two founders. Aside from the seven-pair clean-animal founders, some of the female animals on the Ark could have boarded it in a pregnant state, carrying offspring sired by males other than the ones which entered the Ark with them. This would have meant at least two male founders in the lineage, increasing the genetic diversity of the post-Flood population. In addition, many female reptiles can store sperm for up to four years (Stewart 1989, p. 99), affording the possibility that, in some cases, the post-Flood reptilian hatchlings had been sired by different fathers from the pre-Flood world.

Fallacies of "Beanbag" Genetics

Commensurate with his mistaken notion that single pairs carry insufficient genetic diversity (discussed earlier), Moore (1983, p. 6) imagines that the pairs released from the Ark would have been forced to carry the *full ensemble* of traits later manifested in all members of the given family represented by the pair, including those living in very diverse environments. His argument is absurd in the extreme, as it grossly misrepresents genes and their effects, portraying them as essentially independent containers filled with biological information. It would be as if all the genes in a population were beans in a huge beanbag, and a single pair of founders were a mere handful of beans taken out of it (Berry 1986, p. 223). Each founder would then need to contain some "beans" to enable some of its descendants to live in torrid climates, and also be endowed with some other "beans" so that its other descendants could adapt to frigid climates (paraphrase of Moore 1983, p. 7).

In contrast to the erroneous "beanbag" concept, genes do not behave as cans of biological information waiting to be "opened" and expressed as traits, but instead are highly *interactive*, that is pleiotropic. For this reason, just a few genes interacting one way may produce a phenotype very well adapted to torrid climates, and just a few genes (possibly even the same ones) interact another way to produce an organism well tolerant of tropical heat. That is how, as discussed earlier under *Extent of PostFlood Ecological Differentiation*, descendants of single-pair founders were able to diverge phenotypically in order to fit diverse environments. It is, of course, possible that at least some of the important pre-Flood genetic variance has been lost, and not all biologically-important alleles have been carried over from the antediluvian world. If this is so, then modern-day founders, burdened by a reduction in originally-created genetic diversity not once but twice over, are nevertheless still able to not only function but flourish.

The fallacies of the beanbag approach to genetics can perhaps be best noted by appreciating the viability of repeatedly-inbred animals (e.g., mice) in spite of them lacking most of their natural genetic variation. If genes were not highly interactive and also quite redundant in phenotypic effects, such creatures could not even live. Instead, the lack of so many alleles would cause them to be as dysfunctional as a machine missing many critical parts. Altukhov (1990, p. 43) called attention to the "enormous reserves of hidden hereditary variability in almost all species" which go far beyond genetic polymorphism. The significance of genetic architecture has been generally ignored, and we know far too little about its importance and resilience (Berry 1992b, p. 115). In fact, Berry (1983, p. 151) suggests that the next major advance in evolutionary biology will be an understanding of genetic architecture and its significance for conservation genetics.

Gene Pleiotropy and Supergenes. Gene pleiotropy means that many traits are influenced simultaneously by just a few genes, and vice-versa. For instance, loci controlling the color of mouse fur also have gross effects on the morphology of the mouse (Wright 1980). In his classic experimental domestication of the fox, Belyaev (1979) showed that by simply selecting animals for docility, he also influenced various other traits, such as the the timing within the reproductive cycle, the anatomy of the extremities, and pigmentation of the skin. Plants (notably crops: Williamson 1992,

p. 144) selected for increased yield also experience gene frequency changes at many different loci. Another implication of gene pleiotropy is the converse: one trait is affected by many loci. Out of the 1300 gene loci identified in mice, over 200 of them affect behavior, and they are distributed over nineteen of the twenty mouse chromosomes (Berry 1992a). Now consider human intelligence. Estimates of the number of genes governing this trait ranges from as low as ten to as high as 50,000 or more (Seligman 1992, p. 72, 211). These examples can hardly be considered exhaustive: we do not understand the full extent of genetic pleiotropy among organisms (Barton and Turelli 1989, p. 339). On the flip side, we also do not know to what extent genes are redundant in terms of phenotypic expression (see Thomas 1993). This is especially true of phenotypic effects:

> However, it is not the number of base pair configurations that is of primary concern but the number of distinct allelic effects. An allelic effect includes not only redundances in the code but all other configurations that have the same qualitative effect. The number of allelic effects is not known, of course, but may not be large (Cockerham 1994, p. 99).

Creationists have called attention to supergenes, and genetic diversity as manifested by quantitative characters. A supergene is a cluster of closely-linked genes which functionally behaves as a single gene. Supergenes are often acted on together by natural selection, and can modulate the intensity and direction of the selection depending upon their composition (Altukhov 1990, p. 136). Moore (1983, p. 7) imagines that the governing of many traits by supergenes somehow negates their significance, while Plimer (1994, p. 114) even states that they don't exist.

Merrell (1981) provides good background material on supergenes, to which I refer the interested reader. The vertebrate HLA complex (discussed below) is an excellent example of a supergene complex (Hedrick 1994, p.946), as are some of the human immunoglobulin genes (Cavalli-Sforza et al. 1994, p.131). Among insects, the mimetic traits of certain butterflies are a classic example of a supergene in action (Charlesworth and Charlesworth 1976), as are the esterase loci in the common fruit fly (Altukhov 1990, p. 136). In contrast to Moore's (1983, p. 7) misrepresentation of supergenes vis-a-vis 2 founders, Berry (1992a, p. 115) points out that supergenes are protected by genetic architecture, and that this genetic architecture *can* in fact survive a population bottleneck:

> The power of genetical architecture to protect variation cannot be measured at the present moment, but it is undeniably strong. There is abundant evidence that inherited variants persist to a theoretically surprising extent under either intense selection or close inbreeding, and natural populations which have been through a bottleneck in numbers do not seem to be adversely affected in any way (Berry 1983, p. 151; 1986, p. 223).

Furthermore, when alleles occur at intermediate frequences in a population because of balanced polymorphism (regardless of whether this is a result of supergenes, gene blocks, etc.), they are all the more likely to pass through a population bottleneck (Carson 1990, p. 228). Genetic polymorphism can arise and multiply as a result of supergenes: multiple loci hitch-hike with each other (Kaufman et al. 1995, p. 67). Supergenes can even be responsible for the origin of new species that are sharply different from their progenitors owing to the simultaneous effect of selection on many different phenotypic traits (Hindar 1994, p. 329).

Moore (1983, pp. 7-8) asserts, without any supporting evidence, that supergenes would have resulted in various misfit creatures owing to the simultaneous appearance of many deleterious pleiotropic effects. Long ago, Clarke and Sheppard (1962, p. 224) showed that misfit combinations resulting from the expression of supergenes are no problem because organisms can easily go from one adaptive peak to another as a result of ecological changes. Furthermore, strong natural selection can quickly remove any potential misfits resulting from deleterious pleiotropic effects (Barton and Turelli 1989, p. 359). In conclusion, Moore's argument about deleterious pleiotropic effects is a common but outdated one (for further detail, see Barton and Turelli 1989, pp. 358-9), resting upon the mistaken notion that natural selection is invariably weak. In actuality, selective forces in natural populations are extremely intense (Carson and Templeton 1984, p. 113), even approaching the intensity seen in man-made selective breeding of animals and plants (Barton and Turelli 1989, p. 360).

Was a Miracle Necessary to Restore Genetic Diversity? Lammerts (1975) presupposes a very strict beanbag model of genetics in insisting that, unless God had intervened to restore genetic diversity in the post-Flood populations, Noah would have had to be heterozygous for all of the many thousands of genes which humans are believed to possess. To begin with, a lack of alleles would only be a serious problem for an organism if all the alleles found in the parent population were of vital importance, non-redundant in phenotypic effects, and non-interactive. In humans and animals, most gene loci are monomorphic to begin with (see below). Furthermore, most individuals are not even heterozygous at the so-called polymorphic loci (see, for instance, Table 9.1 in Berry 1983, p. 147), yet they survive well. As far as heterozygosity itself is concerned, it is not a *sine qua non* for viability (see below).

Since genes are highly interactive and phenotypically redundant, it is not surprising that organisms can function well even if they lack most of the genetic variance of the parent population. We do not know the number of loci responsible for most quantitative genetic variation: it can be as small as five or twenty, or as large as 100 or more (Barton and Turelli 1989, p. 340). The alleles responsible for quantitative traits (i.e., including those responsible for traits that govern individual fitness) must readily pass through population bottlenecks (Carson 1990, p. 228), or we would not observe the progeny of bottlenecked animals even surviving. Much of a species' overall genetic diversity is present in the form of individual heterozygosity (Templeton 1991b, pp. 183-4), for it is the common alleles which account for most heterozygosity (H) and polymorphism (P).

While the selection (for the Ark) of individuals possessing more (H) and (P) than most members of the parent population was desirable (see below), the choice of astronomically-rare individuals, endowed with extremely high (H) and (P)—as suggested by Lammerts (1975)—was unnecessary. As elaborated in the next section, even a single pair possesses most of the genetic diversity of the parent population. The infrequently-occurring alleles (i.e., the vast majority of all the alleles in a population) are biologically unimportant, and are easily replaced. We can therefore conclude that Noah did *not* have to be heterozygous at most loci, and God did not need to perform miracles after the Flood in order to create new genetic diversity in post-Flood populations.

Let us now consider the even-greater genetic diversity conserved in the seven pairs of clean animals as opposed to the earlier-discussed individual pairs. The number fourteen is recognized as nearly ideal in this regard:

> The Ark was stocked with seven pairs of each species (Genesis, Ch. 14). This wisdom in collecting a significant gene pool representing, more than 97% of the average genetic variance or heterozygosity of the species, reflects the practical animal husbandry skills of these peoples (Seal and Flesness 1981, p. 301).

In fact, fourteen founders is near the inflection point of the asymptotic curve which depicts the progressive unimportance of additional founders in terms of conserving heterozygosity (Tangley 1984, p. 608; for a tabulation of this effect, see Barrett and Richardson 1986, p. 22).

The Bottleneck at the Time of the Flood

We do not fully understand the genetic consequences of population bottlenecks (Bancroft et al. 1995, p. 263), nor how often they occur in nature (Maruyama and Fuerst 1985, p. 686). It was once commonly believed that, whenever a population goes through a bottleneck (a severe reduction in numbers followed by recovery), it possesses only a small fraction of the original genetic diversity of the parent population (for old citations, see Nei et al. 1975, p. 1). Moore (1983, p. 7) has also cited this old assumption as fact. We now realize that even severe bottlenecks in and of themselves do *not* cause a drastic decrease in genetic diversity. Some of these studies have been cited and discussed by Brand and Gibson (1993, p. 72). A more recent experimental demonstration of this fact is discussed as follows:

> A population bottleneck is generally believed to limit the evolutionary potential of a population by decreasing its additive genetic variance. For example, in conservation, the loss of genetic variability that results from a period of reduced population size and the consequent loss of evolutionary potential to respond to new selective pressures may be as important as the immediate manifestation of inbreeding depression. . . .The results of our first experiment provide evidence that a population's evolutionary potential is *not* limited after a bottleneck (Pray and Goodnight 1995, pp. 186-7; emphasis added).

Nei et al. (1975, p. 4) has shown that a population started by a single pair will not suffer a large loss in genetic variation (H), provided that the population grows rapidly (see also Barrett and Richardson 1986, p. 22). This conclusion has subsequently been supported by many other investigators (Ballou and Cooper 1992, pp. 198-9; Barrett and Richardson 1986, p. 21; Berry 1986, p. 224; Frankel and Soule 1981, pp. 36-7; Howard 1993, p. 126), and is in agreement with field studies (Janson 1987; Lawler et al. 1995; Leberg 1992). Let us consider one historical bottleneck. A very small number (probably a single pair) of macaques had been introduced to Mauritius island by Dutch sailors some 400 years ago. The presently-large population, exhibits low MtDNA diversity when compared with the macaques on the Philippines. Yet (H), the average heterozygosity, as measured by allozymes, is *greater* than that found among macaques on the Philippines (Lawler et al. 1995, p. 139).

It is also recognized that, counterintuitively, quantitative variation can *increase* after a bottleneck (Abplanalp 1988; Bancroft et al. 1995, and citations; Carson 1990; Galiana et al. 1989, p. 71; Pray and Goodnight 1995, and citations). One reason why genetic diversity can actually increase after a severe population bottleneck is the sudden bringing together, in a homozygous state, of large numbers of genes, formerly unexpressed because of their rarity in the outbred population (Grobbelaar 1989, pp. 366-7). Since formerly-rare alleles may now be common (Barton and Turelli 1989, p. 343), this may increase the heterozygosity of a locus or series of loci (Leberg 1992, p. 491).

Genetics and the Selection of Ark Animals

Up to now, I have considered the effects of bottlenecks on genetic diversity having assumed that the founders were a random sample of the original population. Yet even in nature, it is more likely that the more heterozygous members of a population will survive a population bottleneck, thus facilitating the conservation of heterozygosity (Carson 1990, p. 229). As noted earlier, the animals on the Ark were probably chosen by Noah and/or God so as to avoid problems with inbreeding depression. The same kind of genetics filter and/or Divine filter (Fig. 6) could have been used to increase the genetic diversity [(H) and (P)] available from two founders. With regards to average individual heterozygosity (H), suppose that (H) of pre-Flood animals was (x). If most of the animals commandeered by God into the Ark were individuals with an (H) of (1.5x), the animals, inevitably losing about 35% of (H) as a result of a single-pair bottleneck (Carson 1990, pp. 228-9), would have left descendants with an average (H) once again close to (x).

The choosing of animals for the Ark was similar to a certain modern conservation biology project, where only a few gazelles were available to start a population:

> The Speke's gazelle program was designed with the idea that the adaptation to pedigree inbreeding is due to both selection *for* alleles or gene combinations as well as to selection *against* recessive, deleterious alleles (Templeton and Read 1994, p. 94). (emphasis in original)

Although the entire captive herd of Speke's gazelle are descendent from four founders, only two founders account for most of the surviving genetic diversity in the captive herd (MacCluer et al. 1986, p. 153; Templeton 1991b, p. 186). So successful has the conservation of genetic diversity been that the level of protein polymorphism (P) in the descendants, 14%, is, ironically, somewhat *greater* than that found in most mammals! Variation as measured by heterozygosity (H) is comparable to that of non-bottlenecked mammals (Templeton 1994, p. 61). Mitochondrial DNA diversity is low, but is still higher than that found in humans (Templeton, Davis, and Read 1987, p. 310).

Noah may have purposely gathered animals from different pedigrees for his menagerie (Fig. 6) in order to increase their heterozygosity. Overall, it is a common strategy to maximize genetic variability from a few founders by doing this:

> Dissassortative mating can greatly increase the opportunity for new genetic combinations to arise, and thereby increase the overall level of genetic variation upon which selection can operate (Templeton and Read 1983, p. 253).

In the next two sections, I discuss how the alleged problems (of viability and outbreeding depression), resulting from dissassortative mating, could have been avoided.

Is Heterozygosity Inversely Correlated with Viability? Moore (1983, p. 7) has argued against the choosing of animals, for the Ark, with high heterozygosity because of their supposed low viability. As discussed below, outbreeding depression usually does not occur as a consequence of highly-outcrossed matings.

Let us first consider the implications of high (H) itself. A recent review of the effects of overall heterozygosity (H) on fitness (Turelli and Ginzburg 1983) has found no consistent trend between the two. If anything, high heterozygosity is *more* likely to be associated with higher overall fitness. Hedrick and Miller (1992, p. 42) warn against trying to infer population fitness from the level of heterozygosity. Carson (1990, p. 229) suggests that individuals which are more heterozygous than most members of the population are *more* likely to be successful founders after a population bottleneck. The few studies suggestive of reduced fitness, as a function of increasing numbers of heterozygous loci, usually indicate only a minor loss of fitness (Altukhov 1990, pp. 176-9).

Barrett and Richardson (1986) have evaluated the genetic attributes of successful biological invaders, and report finding a wide range of heterozygosity among successful founders, including some with little variation. They concluded (p. 23) that there is no necessary relationship between levels of inherited variation, and success as colonizers. Clearly, high levels of genetic diversity are not necessary for success as invading species (Barrett and Richardson 1986, p. 24). Moore's (1983, p. 7) claim of the certainty of the failure of the post-Diluvian organisms, due to their lack of genetic variation (assuming the truth of that premise), is patently wrong. For instance, we cannot conclude that a population with 8% heterozygosity has twice the probability of surviving 1,000 years as one with 4% heterozygosity (Soule and Mills 1992, p. 59).

Outbreeding Depression. The term refers to a decreased fertility or viability (Templeton 1986) potentially manifest in the offspring of parents of very different pedigrees. Thus, whereas *inbreeding* depression results from the crosses of parents that are too *closely* related, *outbreeding* depression (to the extent that it exists at all) results from the crosses of parents that are too *distantly* related. The dangers of outbreeding depression may be overblown, as evidence for outbreeding depression among outcrossed mammals is scant (Ballou 1989, p. 59). For instance, the outcrossing of isolates among cercopithecoid primates reveals no obvious evidence of outbreeding depression (Smith et al. 1987).

Let us first consider any animals that had been chosen by God from the wild (Fig. 6), for the Ark, in such pair combinations that maximize the (H) of the Ark-released progeny. It is known that, if outcrossed populations can disperse widely in relation to distances separating breeding groups of individuals, outbreeding depression is unlikely to occur (Templeton et al. 1986). If such was a characteristic of pre-Flood animal populations, outbreeding depression would have been virtually nonexistent, even without God having chosen specific animals to circumvent this problem.

Let us now consider the fate of animals in Noah's menagerie (Fig. 6). Earlier, we had noted that Noah could have subjected his animals to mild inbreeding so as to purge them of the deleterious recessive alleles that could cause inbreeding depression. To maximize the heterozygosity of the post-Flood animals, he may then have chosen each member of the Ark pair from different inbreeding demes. If Noah had indeed done this, the high levels of individual heterozygosity between previously homozygous blocks of genes could potentially have caused outbreeding depression (Templeton 1991a, pp. 24-5). However, even if members of formerly-inbreeding demes are crossed, this will not necessarily result in an outbreeding depression. Such was the experience of Templeton (1986, 1996) in his program of breeding individuals gathered from different long-isolated highly-inbred populations of collared lizards from the Ozarks (central USA). At this writing, the founded populations of lizards are flourishing, and possess a high genetic variability (Templeton 1996).

Finally, even if it *does* occur, most of the effects of outbreeding depression show up by the F_2 generation (Templeton et al. 1986, p. 117; Templeton 1991a, p. 25). To circumvent this problem, mixing in captivity should be done so that healthy F_2 or later-generation individuals are available (Templeton 1991b, p. 192). If several generations of animals had been in Noah's menagerie, God could have, in the event of outbreeding depression in their respective lineages, selectively commandeered only the healthy F_2 or later generations of animals into the Ark.

Two Founders: Maximizing the Number of Alleles Per Locus. Let us now consider the sampling of the allelic diversity of the antediluvian populations by the single-pair founders taken on the Ark. If alleles had been distributed with very unequal frequencies in the antediluvian world, then single pairs could only carry one to two alleles per locus, regardless of the number of total alleles in the population (Frankel and Soule 1981, p. 35). By contrast, if the antediluvian animals had at least twenty or twenty-five alleles per locus, with the alleles equally distributed (or close to it), then single pairs should carry four alleles solely by chance (Allendorf 1986, p. 183). It is interesting to note that most loci of present-day animals contain between one and five alleles (Mani 1984, p. 282), although the MHC complex, discussed separately below, contains many more. Since the pre-Flood animal pairs could have carried four alleles per locus, this means that, in most cases, no mutations need have taken place since the Flood to generate the one to five alleles per locus seen today. Of course, most loci have fewer than four alleles per locus because the Ark animals did not always carry the maximum possible four per pair, and/ or some alleles have been lost since the Flood by genetic drift.

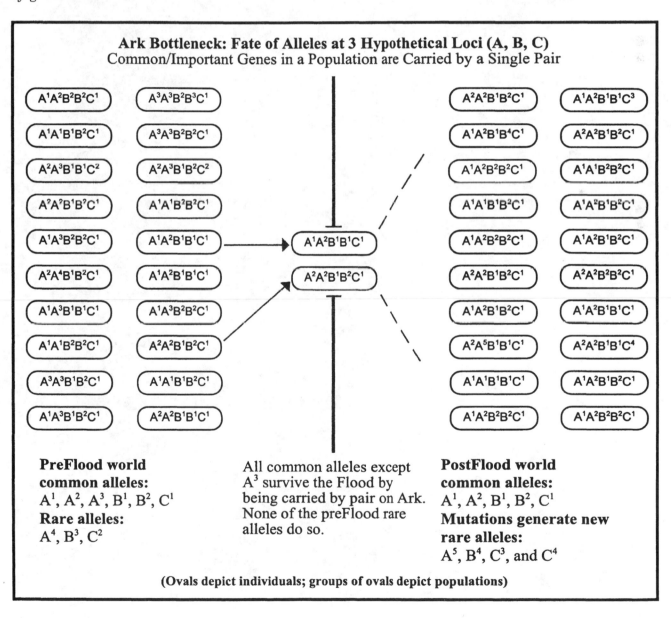

Ark Bottleneck: Fate of Alleles at 3 Hypothetical Loci (A, B, C)
Common/Important Genes in a Population are Carried by a Single Pair

**PreFlood world
common alleles:**
A^1, A^2, A^3, B^1, B^2, C^1
Rare alleles:
A^4, B^3, C^2

All common alleles except A^3 survive the Flood by being carried by pair on Ark. None of the preFlood rare alleles do so.

**PostFlood world
common alleles:**
A^1, A^2, B^1, B^2, C^1
Mutations generate new rare alleles:
A^5, B^4, C^3, and C^4

(Ovals depict individuals; groups of ovals depict populations)

Chapter 26

The Post-Flood Generation of Rare Alleles

Let us now consider, for the sake of argument, that many organisms indeed had lost a great deal of genetic variation as a result of the Ark bottleneck. Lande [(1980, p. 474; 1988, p. 1457; see also May (1991), and Samson et al. (1985, p. 427)] have shown that, because of the pleiotropic effects of genes, even when most genetic variability is lost due to a population bottleneck, mutations can restore heritable variance, in quantitative traits, in only 100-1,000 generations. Obviously this is sufficient time, for the vast majority of organisms, to regain this type of diversity in the 5,000 years since the Flood. It should be noted that this is not organic evolution in any way. It is merely the shuffling around of biological information, not the origin of biological novelty.

Genetic Monomorphism Need Not be Harmful

I now focus on genetic diversity as reflected in the genome itself. Post-Flood organisms were not doomed to extinction if they happened to lose much of their pre-Flood genetic diversity. I have already shown that there is no relationship between the genetic diversity and success of a colonizing animal. In addition, there are many animals alive today, and evidently successful, with low genetic diversity. These include, but are not limited to, the cheetah (O'Brien 1994, and earlier-cited works), elephant seal (Hoelzel et al. 1993, and earlier-cited works), and certain rhinos (Merenlender et al. 1989). Some of this low genetic diversity is known to be (i.e., elephant seals) or suspected to be (i.e., the cheetah) the consequence of a severe population bottleneck. Likewise, the koalas tend to have a low diversity, albeit in terms of mitochondrial DNA (Wilmer 1993, p. 185).

Overall, we do not know if genetic monomorphism is necessarily harmful (Merenlender et al. 1989, p. 381), and this is even more true on a young-earth time scale. No simple generalization can be given for even modern-day bottlenecks and any ensuing loss of genetic diversity:

> Each population bottleneck is different and qualitatively unpredictable. . . . These examples suggest that the consequences of a population bottleneck are determined by both the quantity of variation lost as well as the stochastically determined quality of allelic representation that remains (O'Brien 1994, pp. 475).

As far as modern populations are concerned, average levels of (H) and (P) are known to vary dramatically between species (for refs, see Merola 1994, p. 963). Apart from a relatively few cases of genetic monomorphism, we cannot say for sure what levels should be considered "low" heterozygosity (H), as the levels are relative. The (H) of a particular creature or set of creatures can only be compared to the (H) of some ostensibly normal reference population (Merola 1994, p. 964).

As a result of the Flood, nearly all animals may have lost some heterozygosity (H) and at least some of them may not regained all their pre-Flood (H) yet. Consequently, the "normal" range of (H) we see today may be significantly depressed relative to the (H) characteristic of the antediluvian animals. It is interesting to note that the Ark animals (Aves, Mammalia, and Reptilia) appear to have lower average (H) than do Amphibia, Insecta, and non-insect invertebrates (Merola 1994, p. 963). This may be because the first group, repopulating the earth from the single-pair Ark founders, had lost more of its pre-Flood (H) than did the animals which were not taken on the Ark and whose populations were usually rebuilt from many individual survivors of the Flood. There is also some controversial evidence that large mammals tend to have lower (H) than smaller ones (Merola 1994, p. 363; Wooten and Smith 1985). This may be caused by their long generation times, with insufficient number of generations having elapsed since the Flood for them to regain (H).

Much the same can be said about (P), the proportion of polymorphic loci. Animals vary greatly in the extent of loci found to be at a polymorphic state. Among some marine creatures, 100% of known loci are polymorphic, whereas among mammals, a fraction of them are (Mitton and Raphael 1990). It may be that, before the Flood, up to 100% of the loci of all creatures had been polymorphic. If this is correct, then not enough time has elapsed since the Flood for all loci to re-establish their formerly polymorphic status through the generation of new alleles by mutation, and the subsequent increase of allele frequency to appreciable levels.

Loss of Alleles. It is inevitable that rare alleles will be lost whenever there is a small number of founders, even if the population rebounds in size quickly (Dixon et al. 1991, pp. 208-9; Miller and Hedrick 1991, p. 557). However, as with heterozygosity, the loss of the more-frequently occurring alleles will be retarded if the population expands rapidly (Maruyama and Fuerst 1985, p. 687), notably in the F_1 generation (Ballou 1984, p. 317). In fact, the reason why a bottleneck erodes allelic diversity to a greater extent than it does heterozygosity is the fact that the easily-lost rare alleles contribute little to average heterozygosity. By contrast, the more common alleles which contribute the most to average heterozygosity are relatively difficult to lose from a population, even after a single-pair founder bottleneck (Fuerst and Maruyama 1986, p. 174).

Moore (1983, p. 7) and Morton (1995, p. 48) exult in the fact that a founder group could not possibly reflect the allelic frequencies of the parent population. Their claims are true but unimportant, as rare alleles (which are the majority of all alleles, and the very ones usually missed by founders) are evidently of doubtful significance in terms of individual and population fitness (Tangley 1984, p. 609). The existence of many viable populations bereft of rare alleles suggests their relative unimportance, at least in a young-earth timescale. Further evidence for this is the rarity of balanced polymorphism among most higher eukaryotes (Hedrick 1994, p. 945). Nevertheless, I later demonstrate how allelic diversity could have been recovered in several thousand years.

Alleles and Heterozygosity: Rates of Increase

Regaining Allelic Diversity. With the notable exception of the MHC complex (discussed separately below), the overwhelming majority of polymorphic loci have no more than four alleles per locus (e.g., see Table 1.3.1, pp. 8-9, in Cavalli-Sforza et al. 1994), very rare variants excepted. Furthermore, when we look at the relative abundances of these alleles in a population, we see a very lopsided (in fact bimodal: see Altukhov 1990, pp. 206-9) distribution of frequencies. There is usually a single allele occurring at high frequency (at least 85%), with one to three other alleles (rarely more) found at frequencies of 1–15% (Hughes 1991, p. 249). In fact, of all alleles, most exist at low frequency (Fuerst and Maruyama 1986, p. 174). This is further borne out by the very definition of a polymorphic locus: one where the most common allele occurs at no more than 95% frequency in the population (Templeton 1994, p. 60). To a less extreme extent, this uneven distribution of alleles also shows up at the microsatellite DNA level (Valdes et al. 1993).

This lopsided pattern of allelic frequences is readily explicable in terms of founder effects (Altukhov 1990, p. 206), in this case Flood-related ones. The 1–3 frequently-occurring alleles at polymorphic loci are probably the ones which were carried by the two founders on the Ark, and the rarely-occurring alleles have arisen, by mutation or other means, only since the Flood. Of course, other loci (e.g., globins: Klein 1986, p. 613) have variant alleles so rare in the population that the most frequently-occurring allele exceeds the maximum 95% or 99% allowed for the definition of a polymorphic locus. In fact, Templeton (1994, p. 62) suggests that most infrequently-occurring alleles are one-step mutational derivatives of more-common alleles. Not enough time has elapsed since the Flood for most of them to have assumed a greater frequency in populations. The same holds for deleterious recessive mutations, which also take a long time to purge from the population (Kaufman et al. 1995, p. 66).

Whenever alleles do survive a population bottleneck, they can undergo major shifts in frequency, relative to the parent population, in only a relatively few generations. This can be seen in animals as disparate as birds (Baker and Moeed 1987) and fish (Vuorinen et al. 1991). This means that, whatever genetic diversity does survive the population bottleneck itself, it becomes widely available to members of the founding population in a relatively short period of time.

Regaining Heterozygosity. Measurements of average heterozygosity (H) must be interpreted with some caution in view of the fact that electrophoretic surveys may only survey 30–50 genes out of a total of many tens of thousands (Mitton 1993, p. 24).The conventional view is that it takes on the order of a million generations to recover lost heterozygosity (Nei et al. 1975, p. 4; Lande 1988, p. 1457). This, however, assumes a mutation rate on the order of 10^{-6} to 10^{-8} per locus per generation, as well as the selective neutrality of alleles. A value of 10^{-8} to 10^{-7} is based on *Drosophila* (Chakraborty and Nei 1977, p. 350), although it is recognized that the mutation rate may be much higher at some loci. Moreover, mutation rates can increase by orders of magnitude under stressful conditions, as must have been the case after the Flood (see next chapter). Finally, there is no reason why the mutation rates in a fruit fly should necessarily be comparable to that of vertebrates.

As a practical matter, Gooch and Glazier (1986, p. 61) as well as Lande (1988, p. 1457) were willing to entertain an average mutation rate of 10^{-5} per locus per generation. This would allow the recovery of heterozygosity in about 10^5 generations. However, if the mutation rate per locus could be accelerated to 10^3 per generation, heterozygosity could be restored in under 500 generations (i.e., the first few centuries after the Flood, for most vertebrates), even if alleles were neutral and the population expanded rapidly (based on the formula in Chakroborty and Nei 1977, p. 354).

Since the time to restore lost genetic variation (in terms of heterozygosity) is an approximate reciprocal of the mutation rate, it is obvious that the time needed to restore genetic diversity could be compressed to only a few thousand years (or less) if the mutation rate could be accelerated by two to four orders or magnitude. Such an acceleration is elaborated shortly.

Neutrality vs. Selection of Alleles. Up to now, I have tacitly assumed that most mutations are selectively neutral, at least with regards to the recovery of allelic diversity and heterozygosity. However, it is, in fact, virtually impossible to prove that a given enzyme locus is in fact neutral (Tatarenkov and Johanesson 1994, p. 106), and absence of evidence for selection is not proof of neutrality. At the same time, there is a growing body of evidence that even those alleles long held to be selectively neutral in fact are not (Cook 1984, pp. 8-9).

This would reduce the earlier-cited estimates, for the recovery of allelic diversity and even heterozygosity, even more. For instance, in a population of 100,000, a neutral mutation would require an average of 400,000 generations to become fixed, but this would drop to only a few hundred generations if the mutation were favorable and had a selection coefficient within the range 5–10% (Ayala et al. 1994, pp. 6789-6790). A selection coefficient of 5–10% enables a novel allele, initially occurring at a frequency of one per 100,000 individuals, to become common enough (1 per 100), to be considered part of a polymorphic system (i.e., rendering the most common allele at less than or equal to 99% abundance: Cavalli-Sforza et al. 1994, p. 7). At the quoted 5-10% selection coefficient, this takes place in only one or two hundred generations (Cavalli-Sforza et al. 1994, pp. 12-13; see also Table 4 in Takahata (1993b, p. 14), which, even in slowly-reproducing organisms such as humans, comes out to only a few thousand years.

It must be emphasized that the selection coefficients applicable to human alleles are largely unknown (Cavalli-Sforza et al. 1994, p. 12). Of course, alleles change in their selective advantage given a change in environment, so that alleles which now appear to confer no selective advantage to their bearers may have done so in the immediate post-Flood period. Human cultural factors can also raise the selection coefficient of an allele from a very small value (or perhaps none at all) to around 10% (Cavalli-Sforza et al. 1994, p. 13). Furthermore, there is evidence that population crashes can cause an unexpected and unpredicted enrichment of relatively rare alleles in the surviving population (Bancroft et al. 1995). We must also keep in mind that most evolutionistic models of mutations and selection assume that the two are in balance with each other. if, however, there had been a sudden increase of mutations (see below), this would have contributed to a rapid increase in genetic variation.

It is recognized that some alleles probably originated only a few thousand years ago, as in the case of some of the thalassemias (Cavalli-Sforza et al. 1994, p. 152). The sickle-cell trait is another example (Wiesenfeld 1967), as is the recently-described HLA antigen (Hill et al. 1994, p. 381). However, most of the alleles at various loci are assumed to be ancient (Cavalli-Sforza et al. 1994, p. 154) because of their geographic distribution combined with evolutionistic premises about the antiquity of the human race. Once these evolutionistic notions are dispelled, no temporal dichotomy needs to be recognized between so-called ancient, and recent, ones. Therefore, most infrequently-occurring (and also some frequently-occurring) alleles can be recognized as being of recent origin—the 5,000 years since the Flood.

Greatly-Accelerated Post-Flood Mutation Rates. As far as quantitative characters are concerned (discussed earlier), the total mutation rate affecting them is 3–4 orders of magnitude faster than the inferred per-locus mutation rate (Lynch 1988). Barton and Turelli (1989, p. 342) have called it a paradox that the measured per-character mutation rate of 10^{-2} contrasts with the accepted per-locus mutation rates of 10^{-6} to 10^{-5}. They suggested that this may be because hundreds of loci contribute to character states, or the mutation rates of loci that contribute to quantitative variation may be much higher than those upon which the 10^{-6} to 10^{-5} rate is based.

Mutation rates per locus could be estimated from nucleotide-substitution rates. These are derived from "molecular clocks" which are calibrated according to time since phylogenetic split of two particular organisms. Such clocks, of course, presuppose the validity of organic evolution and the geological time-scale, and have no temporal meaning in the creationist-diluvialist paradigm. Instead, we can try to rely on empirical measurements of mutation rates. These are difficult to come by, as methods of detecting mutations may not be sensitive enough to detect all mutations, and the sample size of laboratory animals to make meaningful judgements of mutation rates may be impossibly large (Klein 1986, p. 73). Studies on mutation rates in humans do not give unambiguous results. For instance, a study of electrophoretically-detectable mutations in over 1.2 million humans (Neel et al. 1986) can be interpreted as indicative of a mutation rate of several times 10^{-5} per locus per generation. However, various errors, uncertainties, and assumptions can also make the data compatible with a rate over ten times lower. Even so, it is much higher than previously-supposed mutation rates (Neel et al. 1986, pp. 392-3). Of course, even if valid, these rates are based on contemporary normative conditions, and much higher rates can occur under stressed conditions (see below).

Some loci are known to be mutational "hot spots," experiencing mutation rates many orders of magnitude higher than the rates accepted by evolutionists. This is possibly true, for instance, of a gene responsible for color blindness in humans (Cavalli-Sforza 1986, pp. 305-6), as well as a K(*b*) gene in mice (Klein 1986, p. 73). The immunoglobin V segment is known to be affected by hypermutations (Yelamos et al. 1995). Other "hot spots" are not genomic but geographic. Animals native to specific regions sometimes show a greatly elevated mutation rate inexplicable by known mutagens (Wallace and Berry 1978). A mutator gene may be responsible for such instances, or it may be caused by physiological stressors.

It has long been known that mutation rates can be modified by environmental influences (Gillis 1991, p. 205). Radiation is a well-known mutagen, and areas of high radioactivity may have been common after the Flood. The high population growth rates of post-Flood animals must have more than made up for attritional losses caused by the harmful effects of the radiation. In fact, this can be seen today among the many kinds of animals whose populations have multiplied in the no-man's land near the Chernobyl reactor despite the 3,000-fold elevation of radiation above background levels (Williams 1995, p. 304), all the while experiencing greatly elevated mutation rates.

Brand and Gibson (1993, p. 72) have cited and discussed evidence that stressful environments themselves increase the rate of mutations. A variety of physiological stressors in an animal can alter its neurohormonal balance, accelerating the rate of crossing over and of spontaneous mutations (Belyaev and Borodin 1982). A single episode of elevated temperature proved sufficient to induce a massive increase in mutations in fruit flies, affecting multiple and simultaneous genetic changes (Ratner and Vasilyeva 1989, pp. 172-3).

Transposable elements of the genome (also called transposons, jumping genes, or retroviruses) occur in all creatures and, when activated, may play a major role in the rapid restoration of heritable variation:

> Transposons therefore appear to provide a mechanism whereby mutational events increase dramatically during periods of environmental challenge, and the consequent periods of organismic stress. Does it follow that precisely at those challenging moments in evolutionary history when there is a premium on major adaptive shifts, the probability that the appropriate variants will be produced is increased? Much more needs to be known about the nature and role of environmentally-induced responses, and detailed studies of laboratory stresses simulating field stresses are needed (Parsons 1987, p. 145).

The significance of transposable elements in the rapid recovery of genetic variation, after population bottlenecks, also remains to be assessed (Fontdevila 1989, p. 92; Howard 1993, p. 135;

McDonald 1989, p. 196). Preliminary evidence indicates that transposon activity can elevate rates of mutation, for many quantitative traits simultaneously, by a factor of 100 (Lynch 1988, p. 146), over the usually-seen polygenic-mutation maximum of 5×10^{-2}. Transpositional bursts appear to be related to inbreeding and other forms of genomic or environmental stress (Biemont et al. 1987; McDonald 1989, p. 200; 1995, p. 125), which was certainly the norm after the Flood. We do not know to what extent the acceleration of mutations governing character traits does proportionally the same to the magnitudes-slower per-locus mutation rates. (I have discussed this matter with leading geneticists, and have been informed that it is very difficult to measure per-locus mutation rates directly.)

Rapid PostFlood Origin of Pseudogenes. Transposable elements may also solve the creationist "problem" of pseudogenes. Evolutionists have seized upon the existence of these apparently nonfunctioning genes as evidence against Creation. Employing a molecular-biology version of the old vestigial-organ argument, they argued that an Intelligent Designer would not create nonfunctioning genes. Creationists have responded by noting that at least some so-called pseudogenes may have an unknown function, while other pseudogenes may be the result of degenerative changes in living organisms only since the Fall, not relics of past evolutionary events. Apropos to this, it is most fascinating that Carlton et al. (1995) report observing a retrovirus inactivate a gene and turn it into a pseudogene. Carlton et al. (1995) also note that this points to the significance of retroviruses in this process. Indeed, the widespread action of retroviruses soon after the Flood not only enabled the drastic increase in mutation rates to take place, but may have given rise to the pseudogenes found in the genomes of living organisms.

Do Built-in Mechanisms for the Rapid Recovery of Genetic Diversity Exist? Earlier, I had discussed the acceleration of mutation rates, whether by endogenous or exogenous factors. In addition, we have evidence that natural selection itself can indirectly favor a very high mutation rate (Yund and Feldgarden 1992, p. 450). This may have been the norm after the Flood.

Ranker (1994) reports that a small and isolated population of Hawaiian fern, colonizing a volcanic substrate only 350–500 years old, showed unexpectedly high genetic diversity. One of his proposed explanations for this unexpected phenomenon is the possibility that this plant has a means of greatly increasing mutation rates in order to rapidly regain genetic diversity following a population bottleneck (Ranker 1994, p. 22). If this is correct, one wonders if *all* plants and animals originally had this property when first created. If so, they would have used it to regain any lost genetic diversity right after the Flood. Afterwards, most of them may have lost this capability. A much more thorough understanding is obviously needed of this intriguing phenomenon before it can be pursued further.

The MHC Complex and the Trans-Species Hypothesis

Introduction. The Major Histocompatibility Complex (hereafter abbreviated MHC) complex of alleles is vital in the function of the immune system (for a primer on the MHC, see Klein 1986, and Hedrick 1994). It is by far the most polymorphic set of loci known in many creatures, including humans. Several loci in humans have a few tens of known alleles each (Hedrick 1994, p. 948), while the DRB1 locus has 106 known alleles (O'hUigin 1995, p. 124). Apart from the extreme profusion of alleles per locus, the MHC complex differs from all the other loci in that the alleles do not follow the classic bimodal or J-shaped distribution discussed earlier. Instead, many of the alleles occur in the population at intermediate frequencies (Bergstrom and Gyllensten 1995, p. 13). Moore (1983, p. 7) and Morton (1995, p. 48) have pointed out the impossibility of a single pair carrying more than

4 different alleles per locus. In this section, I suggest how this polymorphism could have arisen in the 5,000 years since the Flood, and explore possible alternatives to the evolutionistic notion that many MHC alleles diverged before humans and chimps did.

To begin with, the huge number of alleles, while true of the human race as a whole, obscures the fact that only a few alleles need have arisen (since the Flood) in any one particular geographical location:

> Natural selection can clearly act to select new alleles, but in no indigenous population is there evidence for the large numbers of alleles found in modern urban populations. It seems likely that the large numbers of alleles found in city populations are the results of admixture. For example, if the two Brazilian tribes we studied were to form a single population, then the number of alleles would almost double and it would require relatively few such amalgamations to bring the number of alleles up to those found in a provincial town of Europe or Asia (Parham et al. 1995, p. 177).

Shared Human/Chimp Allelic Lineages? The trans-species hypothesis (Ayala et al. 1994; Klein 1987; Klein, Takahata, and Ayala 1993; Mayer et al. 1988) is based on the premise that allelic lineages can be traced in different organisms, as certain alleles are more similar between species than they are to adjoining alleles within a species. The human-chimp similarities in the MHC are believed to be so great that the alleles must have originated *before* the supposed chimp/human evolutionary divergence. It also asserts that no population bottlenecks lower than several hundred individuals could ever have occurred in either humans or chimps, or else this shared similarity would have been lost (although McAdam et al., 1995, are willing to entertain the possibility of a later bottleneck among chimps to explain away the *dissimilarities* in MHC between humans and chimps).

An obvious assumption of the trans-species hypothesis is the premise that the human/chimp similarity could not have arisen independently. In contrast to this, I provide counterexamples to suggest how extreme human/chimp similarities could have arisen through convergence, being thus compatible with a four-pair bottleneck (humans) and one-pair bottleneck (chimps) disembarking from the Ark 5,000 years ago.

Flaws in the Trans-Species Hypothesis. To begin with, the trans-species hypothesis assumes not only organic evolution but also the close evolutionary relatedness of primates:

> In general, it is difficult to understand the evolutionary history of HLA class II polymorphism without attempting a phylogenetic analysis of sequences derived from different primate species (Erlich and Gyllensten 1991, p. 414).

One reason why the independent origin of MHC alleles is not generally favored is the consequence of evolutionary preconceptions. It would mean that more polymorphisms have arisen in MHC loci in 600,000 years than other loci did in seventy-five million years (Klein 1987, p. 157). The scientific creationist is, of course, not constrained by such mental boxes limiting his thinking.

A second line of evidence against independent acquisition of MHC loci is the fact that certain human MHC allelic organizational patterns are more similar to their chimp counterparts than they are to other human MHC alleles (Mayer et al. 1988, p. 2765). This premise is correct if and only if organic evolution is true. The original human/chimp similarities in allelic organizational patterns (as opposed to numerous alleles now found in these regions), must have originated through God's use of common design during Creation. Furthermore, the recent astonishing evidence that certain alleles are more similar between *phyla* than within them (Quiring et al. 1994) indicates that God chose to use similar allelic organizational patterns in otherwise very dissimilar creatures. The observed similarity of allelic organizational patterns itself could have survived even a single-pair population bottleneck (after all, each locus can carry no less than 1 allele). By contrast, most of the forty-odd alleles which are supposed to have predated chimp/human speciation (Ayala et al. 1994, p. 6791) must instead have arisen independently since the Flood (see below).

A third line of evidence against convergence at MHC loci is the claim that, had they originated independently in chimps and humans, the codons coding for them should not be identical (Kasahara et al. 1990, p. 69). In actuality, we now know that convergence can operate even at the nucleotide level (see below). More significant, it is recognized that the identical-codon argument is invalidated by the fact that the nucleotide bases not only are not random, but are distributed very unevenly in the genome: Cytosine and Guanine account for the vast majority of the bases in these alleles (Hughes et al. 1994, p. 363). This greatly limits the possibilities for substitution, making the independent origins of similar if not identical codons virtually inevitable.

A fourth line of evidence against independent origins of MHC alleles involves claims of different degrees of substitution arising in the coding vis-a-vis non-coding regions of DNA. One problem with this is, as stated by Neel et al. (1986, p. 393): "The amount of silent DNA is steadily shrinking." The lack of strong selection pressure in untranslated regions of nucleotides is acknowledged to be an assumption (Kasahara et al. 1990, p. 69-70). Silent bases may not be exempt from natural selection, but may in fact be subject to variable selection (Cook 1984, p. 9). In fact, Koop and Hood (1994) called attention to 100 kilobases of T-receptor DNA which is strikingly similar between humans and mice, and transcends both coding and non-coding regions of DNA. From this, they cautioned against denoting all chromosomal noncoding regions as junk.

A fifth line of evidence involves the non-continuous distribution of HLA alleles. Proponents of the trans-species hypothesis propose that, had the HLA polymorphism arisen independently in humans, there should be a continuous spectrum of alleles bridging the unrelated HLA alleles (Kasahara et al. 1990, p. 65). This is, of course, valid only if one accepts the evolutionistic notion that the human race is very old, and that mutations have continuously occurred in the past at slow rates. By contrast, had there been a burst of mutations among Noah's immediate post-Flood descendants, followed by a drastic decrease of mutation rate along with a rapidly-expanding population, this would account for the handful of unbridged allelic patterns ubiquitous to the entire human race.

Sixth, we have the argument of biochemical similarities related to MHC loci. In fact, the similarity is a matter of degree, and even distantly-related mammals show unexpected similarities. For instance, certain MHC motifs are shared by primates, ungulates, and rodents, and evolutionists wonder whether to accept these as resulting from distant common ancestry, or convergence (see O'hUigin 1995).

Evolutionistic claims about human/simian (and particularly human/chimp) similarities at MHC loci are internally inconsistent. For instance, the human genome includes two allelic lineages, one of which has been lost, respectively, in chimpanzees and gorillas (Parham et al. 1995, p. 173). The TAP allele is said to be similar in humans and chimps, but very dissimilar between humans and gorillas (Kronenberg et al. 1994, p. 6). By contrast, the MHC-DQB1*15 lineage is found in chimpanzees and several Old World monkey species, but not in humans (Bontrop et al. 1995, p. 35). In a similar vein, the MHC-DRBW9 lineage occurs in chimps and gorillas, but not humans (Bontrop et al. 1995, p. 37). Whereas the human HLA-DRB1*0701 and the chimp *Patr*-DRB1*0702 alleles differ by only two nucleotides out of 246 sequenced, most other MHC class II haplotypes differ greatly between nonhuman primates (including chimps) and humans (Bontrop et al. 1995, pp. 42-3). Close examination reveals the fact that only one of the six Class I A-locus alleles in chimps can be said to be closely related to the human one (McAdam et al. 1995). The HLA-B locus is, on the whole, very dissimilar between humans and chimps, and this is said to be an exception to the trans-species hypothesis (Hughes et al. 1993, p. 669, 678; McAdam et al. 1994, p. 5894).

In the end, the human/chimp similarity in the HLA complex turns out to be rather general:

> Despite the structural similarities between A, B, and C alleles in humans, chim-
> panzees and gorillas, no alleles seem to be shared by these species. Even the most
> similar alleles differ at one of more peptide binding residue(s) of the antigen-recog-
> nizing site . . . , indicating that no class I antigen-presenting specificity present in
> the common ancestor has been retained to the present time. This behavior is very
> different from that of other proteins, many of which have identical amino acid
> sequences in humans, chimps, and gorillas (Parham et al. 1995, pp. 173-4).

For the trans-species hypothesis to be tenable, strong selective pressures of unknown origins must have existed to prevent the close MHC similarities between certain mammals from being scrambled over many millions of years (Golding 1992). It may instead be more reasonable to accept the recent origin of this similarity.

Finally, there is no unambiguous criterion to demarcate just how many alleles are supposed to have been shared by humans and chimps before their supposed evolutionary divergence. In contrast to the forty-odd alleles which are claimed to have predated chimp/human speciation (Ayala et al. 1994, p. 6791), I have talked to specialists who were willing to accept the ancestral status of only ten such alleles. Some studies (Erlich and Gyllensten 1991) allow for many alleles overall to have arisen only recently. In fact, Titus-Trachtenberg et al. (1994, p. 165) disagree with the claim that much of the DR8 diversity predates human/chimp divergence, and even allow for some of it to have arisen only thousands of years ago.

Why the Trans-Species Similarity? As noted earlier, the human-chimp similarities in the organizational patterns at MHC loci must date back to Creation. As for most of the alleles at these loci, they and their similarities to those of other animals must have arisen by convergence, as the founders on the Ark could not have carried most of them.

The question boils down to how much similarity can arise by convergence and how much similarity is so precise that it could only have come from shared evolutionary ancestry. I have discussed this matter with several specialists in the MHC complex and the trans-species hypothesis, and was unable to get a definitive answer. Instead, I was told that "it seemed probable" that the human/chimp similarities at MHC loci were the result of shared ancestry and not convergence. Generally, evolutionists are predisposed to downplay the significance of convergence. They usually assume convergence only when shared similarities cannot be accounted for by phylogeny (O'hUigin 1995, p. 128). Since very detailed similarities among evolutionarily-unrelated life forms are believed to be uncommon, evolutionists conclude that detailed biochemical convergence is rare. This, of course, begs the question of evolutionary vs. nonevolutionary origins.

It is known that, in mammalian genomes, there is a preference for specific patterns of adjacent nucleotides (Hughes et al. 1993, p. 673, and earlier-cited works). A limited number of amino acid replacements are favored at particular sites at MHC loci (O'hUigin 1995, p. 131), and may even be favored by natural selection in response to the same pathogen (Takahata 1995, p. 235). The degeneracy of codons ironically facilitates convergence at the amino acid level (Takahata 1995, p. 233). The lysozomes of the cow, langur, and hoatzin (Kornegay et al. 1994; Stewart et al. 1987) show convergence at five amino acid residues, demonstrating that there is only a limited number of ways to make stomach lysosomes. It is also known that complex nucleotide motifs, whose origin by accumulated independent single substitutions is astronomically improbable, can arise instead by concerted mutagenesis (Ripley 1991).

Working, of course, within an evolutionary framework, Hughes et al. (1994) have attempted to gauge the extent of convergence at MHC loci. They noted (pp. 363-4) that shared polymorphism at the individual amino acid residue position and even of two amino-acid motifs occur frequently even between different mammalian orders. By contrast, three amino-acid motifs were found only in closely-related organisms (i.e., humans and chimps). From this, Hughes et al. (1994, p. 364) conclude that three amino-acid motifs could only come about through shared ancestry, whereas two amino-acid and individual-residue similarities could either occur by shared ancestry or by convergence. Obviously, this is a suggestion and not a proof.

If convergence can produce the same two amino-acid motifs independently, then perhaps it can also produce the same three amino-acid motifs independently, especially when we remember that more closely-related organisms (i.e., humans and chimps) share more of the same pathogens than do more dissimilar organisms (i.e., humans and cattle). Most interesting of all is the fact that there are MHC motifs shared by very-different mammals. Motifs consist of a short chain (but sometimes more than a dozen) of shared nucleotides or amino acid sequences. These motifs are believed to have arisen by convergent evolution, possibly because mammalian orders share some of the same parasites (Klein and O'hUigin 1995, p. 108). It is claimed that MHC allelic lineages persist for millions of years because of their successful immune response to bacterial antigens (Bontrop et al. 1995, p. 41). Could it be instead that the specificity of bacterial antigens helped to strongly constrain the convergence between human and chimp MHC alleles to very similar lineages?

Convergence of MHC loci is demonstrated by the fact that certain substitutions must have occurred more than once. This is true of a glycine/valine exchange at position 86 in some DRB1 alleles (Apple and Erlich 1992). Expanding this reasoning, close convergences at MHC loci in humans and chimps owe to the (previously-discussed) common allelic organizational pattern which goes back to Creation. This could have helped predispose certain independently-derived alleles in humans and chimps to resemble each other more closely than adjoining alleles within the same creature, thus generating the illusion of trans-species allelic lineages.

Independent Post-Flood Origins of MCH Alleles. A possible line of evidence for the independent origins of MHC polymorphism in humans and chimps is the fact that presumably orthologous loci differ greatly in the number of their respective alleles (see Table 1 in Klein, O'hUigin et al. 1993, p. 55). For instance, the MHC-DRB3 and MHC-DRB5 loci are very polymorphic in chimps but oligomorphic in humans (Bontrop et al. 1995, p. 38). It is interesting to note that at least some of the respective human and chimp MHC alleles behave similarly to the same antigen (Bontrop et al. 1995, pp. 44-5). Perhaps this is because they had to deal with the same pathogens, so arose independently.

Since each pair on the Ark could only carry, at most, four alleles per locus, it follows that the remainder of the alleles must have arisen since the Flood. Although there are tens of alleles per locus and the HLA alleles tend to be relatively evenly distributed in the population, there are about four of them that occur almost all over the world at nontrivial frequencies (Cavalli-Sforza 1994, p. 130). These are the alleles which Noah's family probably bore. The remainder must have arisen through mutation or recombination. It should be added that, to the extent that the post-Flood creatures were bereft of MHC polymorphism, it need not have harmed them in any way, as there are successful present-day animals with limited MHC polymorphism (Bergstrom and Gyllensten 1995, p. 13), including that resulting from population bottlenecks (Klein 1987, p. 160).

To carry up to the maximum four different alleles per pair, each member of the Ark may have been chosen to be highly heterozygous at the HLA loci (and other loci, as discussed earlier). Moore (1983, p. 7) has objected to this suggestion by questioning the viability of a person highly heterozygous at the HLA loci. His claim is devoid of merit, if only because many humans today have HLA heterozygosities as high as 80% (Hughes et al. 1993, p. 669). Yet even if the highly heterotic individuals taken on the Ark had decreased genetic viability, the effect was probably small and short-lived. Takahata (1994, pp. 242-3) has shown that the relative fitness, expressed as number of heterozygous loci at the MHC complex caused by the hybridization of antigenically diverged individuals, decreases by only a few percent when going from an optimum of three all the way to twelve heterozygous loci.

Facilitating the Rapid Origins of HLA Polymorphism. For so many HLA alleles to have reached appreciable frequencies in the human population in only 5,000 years, they must have been subject to strong natural selection. We do not yet fully understand the selective advantages which the various MHC polymorphisms convey to their hosts (Golding 1992, p. 270). However, there is now convincing empirical evidence that HLA associations are important in the combatting of pathogens (Hill et al. 1994). In fact, one allele is now known to facilitate its bearer's survival of malaria to such an extent that its frequency could have increased manyfold in only a few thousand years (Hill et al. 1994, p. 381). It is also interesting to note that MHC alleles can be subject to strong selection aside from immunity considerations, and these factors can contribute to a rapid increase in frequency of rare alleles. For instance, spontaneous-abortion rates in humans appear to be inversely related to differences at MHC loci of the parents, and there is some evidence that at least some animals tend to mate with partners having a different MHC type (Hedrick and Miller 1994, pp. 191-2). The same appears to hold for humans (Wedekind et al. 1995).

Is there evidence that HLA genes can mutate rapidly? The conventional view, based on molecular "clocks," is that HLA loci mutate no more rapidly than do other loci (Ayala et al. 1994, p. 6790). However, Pease (1985, p. 228) discusses genetic changes which have given rise to histocompatibility variants in only a single generation, as evidenced by the results of thousands of animals tested by reciprocal skin-grafting. One locus in the mouse MHC, the K(b) gene, is known to undergo an unusually high mutation rate (one mutation per 5,000 gene duplications), involving complex changes in several nucleotides at different positions (Klein 1986, p. 748).

A recent study of HLA variants in human sperm (Zangenberg et al. 1995, p. 413) indicates that MHC "alleles" can arise rapidly through segmental exchange (gene conversion), or recombination. Of course, the MHC "alleles" are really haplotypes of over fifty genes (Gilpin and Wills 1991, p. 555). As noted earlier, since the MHC complex is a supergene, the closely-linked genes hitch-hike with each other, thereby facilitating the origin and multiplication of genetic polymorphism (Kaufman et al. 1995, p. 67). The possibility of rapid increase in allelic diversity by even simple mutations is facilitated by the simplicity of the changes necessary to generate large numbers of alleles. For instance, it appears that the most polymorphic locus of the MHC complex also has the most easily-generated diversity of HLA alleles. Of the forty-four known alleles of the DRB1 locus (Apple and Erlich 1992, p. 69), ten pairs of these alleles differ from each other by only one residue at position

86 (Titus-Trachtenberg et al. 1994, p. 165). Other alleles differ from each other only at position 57 (Apple and Erlich 1992).

We have actual evidence of an extremely rapid recovery of HLA alleles after a population bottleneck. A fascinating study (Yund and Feldgarden 1992) discovered that a colonial ascidian recovered allelic diversity (at historecognition alleles) at a rate which is *several orders of magnitudes faster* than predicted by conventional evolutionistic nucleotide-substitution rates. As noted earlier, this may be caused by natural selection indirectly favoring loci with very high mutation rates (Yund and Feldgarden 1992, p. 450). If this is so, it would be most interesting to discover what post-Flood events gave rise to the natural selection of genes which mutate the MHC loci at very high rates.

In contrast to the previously-discussed alleles which are supposed to predate human/chimp divergence, other ones are believed to have arisen only thousands of years ago through recombination from a limited number of founding MHC haplotypes. This applies to certain South American Indian tribes (Belich et al. 1992; Titus-Trachtenberg et al. 1994; Watkins et al. 1992). The recent origin is based on the fact that these tribes do not share the alleles with their neighbors, and the fact that Palaeo-Indians did not colonize the New World until 11,000–40,000 years ago. Since the Creationist is not beholden to organic evolution nor to the evolutionary-uniformitarian time-scale, this temporal dichotomy between "ancient" and "recent" alleles has no meaning in his paradigm. Instead, the recent post-Flood origin of nearly all the MHC alleles can be contemplated.

Morton (1995, p. 49), after uncritically accepting old studies which indicate that mutations (including those affecting mouse and human MHC) occur at very slow rates, has made a most amusing assertion. He claims that if MHC mutations occurred at a very rapid rate, ancient animals (such as the cows featured in statues of ancient Crete) would look different from their modern counterparts. The rank absurdity of his argument can best be appreciated by briefly indulging in his fantasy. Just think for a moment how the science of genetics would be revolutionized were it indeed possible to determine mutation rates in cows, or MHC diversity in cows, just by looking at a herd of them (or—better yet—at statues of cows).

The Post-Flood Generation of HLA Alleles. Let us recall that no local population has more than a few of the MHC alleles typical of the human race as a whole (Parham et al. 1995, p. 177). When human populations are subdivided and relatively monomorphic at MHC loci, nearly any new allele arising by mutation may be advantageous to its bearer by allowing the presentation of a more complex immune system to the pathogen (Belich et al. 1992, p. 328). Once a few mutants arise, even a small number of them will rapidly become subequal in frequency within the population. This follows from evidence that a small number of MHC alleles in a population tends to even out as a result of balancing selection (Markow et al. 1993). Under various realistic conditions, subdivided populations can acquire an aggregate of a large number of alleles in a short time:

> My main conclusion is that, if selection is effective within demes ($Ns > 1$) and the number of demes is large ($L > 10$), the interplay between balancing selection and population structure can produce an enormous amount of alleles. This is because each deme can be polymorphic by selection and different demes tend to maintain different alleles owing to restricted gene flow (Takahata 1993a, p. 19).

The (N) refers to the population size, and the (s) refers to the selection coefficient.

Placed into a creationist context, we can see how the subdivided human populations in the post-Flood world (notably after the Tower of Babel) could have rapidly acquired novel MHC alleles, no doubt facilitated by the ever-changing pathogen-rich post-Flood world. When the subdivided postDiluvian populations subsequently merged, each of these small numbers of distinctive alleles, occurring at relatively high frequency, eventually amalgamated to form the large number of intermediately-occurring MHC alleles now characteristic of the human race as a whole. That is how the extensive MHC polymorphism we know today came to be in only the 5,000 years since the Flood.

For further discussion of how the explosive population growth of humans, combined with natural selection favoring the emergence of allelic diversity at MHC loci, facilitates the rapid incorporation of new alleles into the population, see Takahata (1993a, pp. 14-15). Of course, Takahata (1993b, p. 18) believes that most HLA alleles are of ancient origin because, following the dictates of evolutionary branching patterns and the conventional uniformitarian time-scale, they do not coalesce into the recent past. However, if both organic evolution and the geologic time-scale are discarded, there is no need to buy into the trans-species hypothesis. Instead, the recent origin of most of the HLA alleles becomes tenable, as *the rapid origin of considerable numbers of alleles is certainly possible:*

> One possible explanation is that the modern human population began to explode with the agricultural revolution. This period of time (10,000 years) amounts to only about 500 generations, yet it is possible that many new alleles were restored in such a rapidly growing population. This is particularly true for overdominant alleles, and the number of such new alleles can be very large if $M=N_e u \geq 1$ (Takahata 1993b, p. 17).

Note that this occurs when the product of the population N_e and the mutation rate u equals or exceeds one. Takahata's time estimate needs only to be halved in order to bring it within the Biblical time-frame of the Flood.

Chapter 27

The Restoration of Variation in Mitochrondrial DNA

Up to now, I have considered genetic variation solely in terms of phenotypic effects as manifested by the genes in the nuclear DNA. However, DNA is also present in the mitochondria. Largely because its inheritance is matrilineal, and not subject to the complications of sexual reproduction (as is nuclear DNA), evolutionists have used it as a "molecular clock" to date the time of divergence of certain groups of organisms. For instance, the divergence of different groups of humans has been placed within a time span of several tens of thousands of years to about 200,000 years (Cavalli-Sforza 1994, pp. 154-5; Harpending et al. 1993; Rogers and Jorde 1995). The large diversity of mtDNA among populations of most organisms has been used to argue against the occurrence of recent population bottlenecks. This argument has been picked up and parroted by Morton (1995, pp. 49-50). In this section, I provide evidence that is contrary to these widespread premises, and show how the presently-observed mtDNA is compatable with single-pair founders of land-vertebrate populations only 5,000 years ago.

To begin with, the interpretation of mtDNA divergences as a "clock" is fraught with difficulties. When the extent of such divergences is calibrated by evolutionists according to their time scale, the rates of divergence vary widely between different vertebrates (see Prager et al. 1993, p. 116 and citations therein). There are notable instances of severe contradictions between the results of mtDNA and other evidence accepted by evolutionists (e.g., Orti et al. 1994).

Anomalous Built-In MtDNA Polymorphism. There is a growing body of evidence that polymorphisms in mtDNA can arise much faster than commonly supposed, and may not be rare (Olivo et al. 1983, p. 402). The conventional view is that a lineage descended from one female should have very monomorphic mtDNA, and it should take a long time for mutations to generate polymorphisms in that lineage. Hauswirth and Laipis (1982) report the appearance of DNA polymorphism within a lineage of maternally-related cattle. The implied rate of origin for this polymorphism comes out to three orders of magnitude greater than conventionally-accepted mutation rates (Hauswirth and Laipis 1982, p. 4689). In fact, mutation alone is recognized to be insufficient to account for this rapid polymorphism (Hauswirth et al. 1984, p. 1001). To explain this intriguing phenomenon, Olivo et al. (1983, p. 402) suggest that there may be a novel mutational mechanism in that part of the mtDNA, or that nuclear genes may predispose some species, breeds, or lineages to mtDNA variation. If so, it would be analogous to mutator genes vis-a-vis elevated mutation rates in nuclear DNA (discussed previously). If such mutator genes had been common soon after the Flood, the organisms would have enjoyed a very rapid increase in the polymorphism of their mtDNA. The significance of elevated mutation rates is discussed shortly.

It is also possible that the females on the Ark had polymorphism already built-in to their mtDNA. In fact, Hauswirth et al. (1984, p. 1006), in order to explain the unusual polymorphism among cows descended from one female, have suggested that the common maternal ancestor contained heterogenous mtDNA within her mitochondrial genotype, passing this build-in diversity to her daughters.

MtDNA Mutation Rates. As is the case with the previously-discussed mutation rates of nuclear DNA, the mutation rates of mtDNA are assumed to be extremely low (i.e., on the order of 10^{-8}/nucleotide), and these estimates are used in actual studies of population bottlenecks *vis-a-vis* mtDNA (e.g., Hedrick 1995). The requirement of hundreds of thousands, if not millions of years, for the restoration of mtDNA diversity after a population bottleneck thus becomes a foregone conclusion. As previously shown for nuclear DNA, the mutation rates in mtDNA can be accelerated by orders of magnitude. This has actually been observed among the many kinds of animals whose populations have multiplied in the no-man's land near the Chernobyl reactor despite the 3,000-fold elevation of radiation above background levels (Williams 1995, p. 304).

MtDNA has a number of properties which play a major role in the way mutations become either fixed or eliminated. Owing to the fact that the mitochondrion is the cell's "powerhouse," combined with the fact of its matrilineal inheritance, deleterious mutations are readily expressed and are likely to afflict the carriers with severe or fatal metabolic diseases (Wallace 1987, p. 158); hence the probable rapid removal of such mutations from the population. Conversely, beneficial mutations are likely to rapidly sweep through the population because the mtDNA behaves as a single locus owing its lack of genetic recombination (Brookfield 1994, p. 652).

The use of mtDNA as a "molecular clock," along with the large spans of time apparently indicated by this "clock" is predicated not only on the validity of low mutation rates, but also on their selective neutrality. Evidence continues to accumulate that, contrary to evolutionistic preconceptions, mtDNA is in fact subject to natural selection (see Malhotra and Thorpe 1994, and citations therein). As noted earlier in conjunction with mutations affecting nuclear DNA, positively-selected mutations will become common in populations many orders of magnitudes faster than will neutral ones.

The Greatly-Accelerated PostFlood MtDNA "Clock." Let us put all the foregoing discussion in perspective. Consider the "African Eve" hypothesis. It need not mean that there was once only one human female on earth, but that only one matrilineal lineage has survived to the present, with all other matrilineal lineages having left no descendants (Cavalli-Sforza 1994, p. 155). This means that only one of the four human matrilineal lineages represented on the Ark persists to the present. Although the African origins of the "African Eve" can no longer be maintained (Rogers and Jorde 1995, p. 2), it is still recognized that, according to the standard assumptions behind the mtDNA "clock," all human mtDNAs coalesce approximately 200,000 years ago, and provide no information about human population structure before that time (Harpending et al. 1993, p. 494).

The implications of increased mutation rates (whether exogenous or endogenous) and the existence of natural selection are that conventionally-used mtDNA "clocks" can be accelerated by some orders of magnitude, and the 200,000 years can be compressed to within the Biblical time frame. Likewise, the drastic expansion and later subdivision of the human population, now dated between the interval of 30,000 to 150,000 years ago (Harpending et al. 1993; Rogers and Jorde 1995), collapses to within the 5,000 years since the Flood.

My discussion of greatly-accelerated "mtDNA clocks" does not apply to all organisms, as some of them have evidently not been successful in regaining their mtDNA diversity in the short time since the Flood. This is one possible explanation for the observed low diversity of mtDNA in the cheetah (along with other evidences of a population bottleneck several thousands of years ago: Menotti-Raymond and O'Brien 1993), as well as the extraordinarily low diversity among humans of both mtDNA (Ruvulo et al. 1994) and the patrilineally-inherited Y-chromosome (Dorit et al. 1995).

In a Matrilineal Lineage:
Built-In Mitochondrial-DNA Diversity

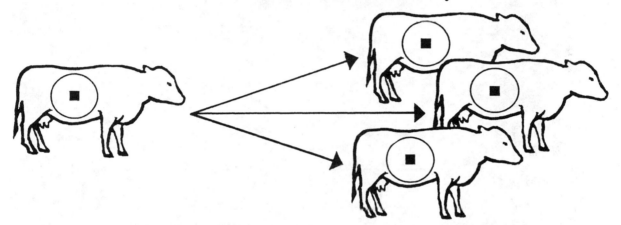

Conventional Evolutionistic Belief: A female can only pass monomorphic mtDNA to her progeny. It takes a long time for mutations to restore mtDNA diversity in her lineage.

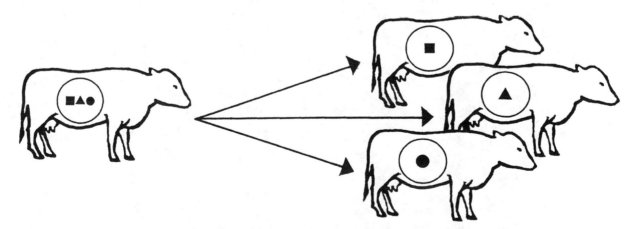

Contrary Evidence: A female can pass on diverse mtDNA to her daughters, generating instantly-diverse postFlood mtDNA lineages.

Chapter 28

Was Noah Afflicted with Diseases?

A number of anti-creationists (e.g., Moore 1983, Plimer 1994) have argued that all the inhabitants of the Ark must have been repositories of all the pathogens and parasites which can possibly live in them, or else these diseases would have become extinct at the time of the Flood. These arguments would only be valid if pathogens and parasites were all extremely host-specific, never changed, and could only be transmitted host-to-host.

To begin with, the claim that Noah's family had to be simultaneously afflicted with all human diseases (Moore 1983, p. 19) ignores the fact that the animals on the Ark were also reservoirs of human diseases. Nelson (1982, p. 182) estimates that over 80% of human diseases can be transmitted from animals. Probably most parasites are not host-specific (Murdoch and Oaten 1975, p. 35), and pathogens can change over time (as discussed below).

Humans and common domestic animals share a large number of parasites (Southwood 1987). In addition, one of the dangers in modern times is people taking in wild animals as pets, exposing humans to the dangers of transmitted diseases, especially those carried by reptiles, psittacine birds, and primates (Keyser 1972, p. 379). There is an entire catalogue of diseases known to be readily transmitted from primates to humans (e.g., see Table 44-2 of Martin 1986, p. 670). In fact, it is recommended (CCAC 1984, Vol. 2, p. 170) that it be *assumed*, as a precaution, that every captive monkey is carrying a disease which is transmissible to humans! There were no less than 412 primates on the Ark (Table 2) as potential carriers of ancient as well as present-day human diseases, and it is doubtful if Noah's family was afflicted with any disease. Of course, the disease carriers on the Ark could easily have been asymptomatic (Nelson 1982, p. 182; Smith 1982, pp. 207-8; Wieland 1994a). Finally, our understanding of the potential of infectious diseases to be harbored by wildlife is rather limited (Smith 1982, p. 208). By the clearing of many wildlands, the human race is presently being exposed to a whole set of hitherto-rare animal-borne viral diseases (Culliton 1990).

What about those diseases that are host-specific? To begin with, many so-called host-specific pathogens turn out to be able to infect other hosts. For instance, it was believed that canine distemper could never infect felines, until the contrary was demonstrated (Morell 1994). Diseases can also change their mode of transmission in a short period of time, with or without microevolutionary changes. Fleas can change hosts, as demonstrated by mammals introduced to islands (Pugh 1994). It is common for viruses to show markedly enhanced virulence when transferred from their natural host to another animal (Smith 1982, p. 209). The ability of canine distemper to infect lions may be the result of a recent mutation (Morell 1994). Most human diseases are believed to have arisen in only the last several thousand years (Johnson 1986). Human lentiviruses, such as HIV, are believed to have arisen in the last thousand years from nonhuman primates, who in turn got them earlier from ungulates (Moriyama and Gojobori 1991, pp. 298-9). The rate of parasite/host evolution in fleas is assumed to be slow based on evolutionary phylogenies, but rests on virtually no direct evidence (Traub 1985, p. 419). Parasitic nematodes can change hosts completely (i.e., become unable to parasitize their original hosts) as a result of only three years of microevolutionary changes (Jaenike 1993).

The Ark critics' arguments about humans being the only carriers of their diseases has taken on vile and offensive proportions. Noah, a herald of righteousness (2 Peter 2:5) has been charged with cannibalism (Plimer 1994, p. 125) and with being afflicted with sexually-transmitted diseases (Moore 1983, p. 19; Plimer 1994, p. 125). These offensively unjustified arguments again fail to consider changes in diseases with time. For instance, kuru need not be transmitted only by cannibalism of human brains, but also by touching contaminated flesh (Wieland 1994b). Diseases which currently spread through sexual contact need not have done so at the time of the Flood. For instance, syphilis may have originated from yaws, a non-venereal disease spread by skin-to-skin contact (Cavalli-Sforza et al. 1994, p. 129).

Let us now consider the fate of the pathogens and parasites not spread directly from one creature to another. Fleas can be transmitted by dung, hay, and other fodder (Pugh 1994, p. 214). Some of the materials which Noah brought into the Ark could have been contaminated by pre-Flood animals which were not themselves taken on the Ark. Wieland (1994a) has showed that pathogens and parasites could have survived outside the Ark in corpses, or in a frozen state if there had been incipient glaciation. Indeed, if, as suggested earlier, re-exhumed carrion had been a major food source after the Flood, it must have also been a major bridge, between the antediluvian and post-Flood worlds, in the transmission of pathogens and parasites.

Part 5

Conclusion

Chapter 29

Conclusion

It is obvious from this work that the oft-repeated pseudo-intellectual arguments against the Ark are without foundation. Nor is a constant stream of *ad hoc* Divine miracles necessary, as critics charge, to "prop up" the Ark account. I personally cannot help but visualize Noah in heaven getting a hearty laugh out of the foolish arguments of the Ark critics.

Of course, it is not surprising that the Ark account is the butt of ridicule today (note, for instance, the insulting cartoon of the hole-filled Ark, reproduced in Moore (1983) from a newspaper editorial). Fallen humans do not want to be reminded of God's judgement in the past any more than they want to be informed about God's judgment in the future. No doubt humanists will continue repeating the same old false claims about the Ark and the Flood, or perhaps even dream up some new ones. The compromising evangelicals will continue promoting the local-flood copout because of their uncritical acceptance of such anti-Biblical claims ("after all, so many scientists can't be wrong"), and go on twisting the Bible–no matter how grotesque the contortions. But no matter: the evidence clearly shows that the Ark account and global Flood could have happened exactly as the Bible teaches. Far from actually being the modernistic travesty of "believing what you know isn't true," faith in God and His Word are eminently reasonable.

References

AAAZK (American Association of Zoo Keepers). 1988. *AAZK Diet Notebook*. Volume 1, Mammals. Privately Published, Topeka, Kansas.

Abe, A. S., and J. E. P. W. Bicudo. 1991. Adaptations to salinity and osmoregulation in the frog *Thoropa miliaris* (Amphibia, Leptodactylidae). *Zoologischer Anzeiger* 227:313-318.

Acker, D. 1983. *Animal Science and Industry.*, 3rd ed. Prentice-Hall, New Jersey.

Ackrill, P., Hornby, R., and S. Thomas. 1969. Responses of *Rana temporaria* and *Rana esculenta* to proloned exposure to a saline environment. *Comparative Biochemistry and Physiology* 28:1317-1329.

Adams, C. 1975. *Nutritive Value of American Foods in Common Units*. United States Department of Agriculture Handbook No. 456, Washington, D. C.

Adams, J. 1981. *Wild Elephants in Captivity*. Privately published.

Adams, R. L. 1971. The dry deep-pit system: one way to handle manure. *Poultry Tribune* 77(4): 26-8.

Adolph, E. F. 1949. Quantitative relations in the physiological constitutions of mammals. *Science* 109(2841): 579-585.

Aiello, A. 1985. Soth hair: unanswered questions (pp. 213-218) *in* Montgomery, G. G., ed., *The Evolution and Ecology of Armadillos, Sloths, and Verminguas*. Smithsonian Institution Press, Washington, D. C.

Ainley, D. G. 1980. Birds as marine organisms: a review. *California Cooperative Oceanic Fisheries Investigations Report* 21:48-53.

Akridge, G. R. 1981. The Hebrew Flood even more devastating than the English translation depicts. *Creation Research Society Quarterly* 17(4): 209-213.

Alabaster, J. S., and R. Lloyd. 1982. *Water Quality Criteria for Freshwater Fish*, Second Edition. Butterworths Scientific Publishers, London, Boston.

Alderton, D. 1986. *The Complete Cage and Aviary Handbook*. T. F. H. Publications, New Jersey.

Alderton, D. 1991. *The Atlas of Parrots*. T. F. H. Publications, New Jersey.

Alexander, J. 1969. The indirect evidence for domestication (pp. 123-9) *in* Ucko, P. J., and G. W. Dimbleby., eds., *The Domestication and Exploitation of Plants and Animals*. Aldine Publishing Co., Chicago.

Alison, R. M. 1978. The earliest records of aviculture. *Aviculture Magazine* 84(4): 213-223.

Allegrucci, G., Fortunato, C., Cataudella, S., and V. Sbordoni. 1994. Acclimation to fresh water of the sea bass: evidence of selective mortality of allozyme genotypes (pp. 486-502) *in* Beaumont, A. R., ed., *Genetics and Evolution of Aquatic Organisms*. Chapman and Hall, London)

Allen, D. C. 1963. *The Legend of Noah*. University of Illinois Press, Urbana.

Allen, R. P. 1956. *The Flamingos*. National Audubon Society, New York.

Allendorf, F. W. 1986. Genetic drift and loss of alleles versus heterozygosity. *Zoo Biology* 5:181-190.

Allison, P. A., Smith, C. R., Kukert, H., Deming, J. W., and B. A. Bennett. 1991. Deep-water taphonomy of vertebrate carcasses: a whale skeleton in the bathyal Santa Catalina Basin. *Paleobiology* 17(1): 78-89.

Almatar, S. M. 1984. Effects of acute changes in temperature and salinity on the oxygen uptake of larvae of herring (*Clupea harengus*) and plaice (*Pleuronectes platessa*). *Marine Biology* 80: 117-124.

Altukhov, Y. P. 1990. *Population Genetics: Diversity and Stability*. Harwood Academic Publishers, London, Paris.

Amundsen, V. S. and F. W. Lorenz. 1955. Pheasant-turkey hybrids. *Science* 121:307-8.

Anderson, J. R. 1966. Biological interrelationships between feces and flies (pp. 20-23) *in* ASAE. 1966, *op. cit.*

Anderson, D. P., Cherms, F. L., and R. P. Hanson. 1964. Studies on measuring the environment of turkeys raised in confinement. *Poultry Science* 43: 305-318.

Anderson, G. A., Smith, R. J., Bundy, D. S., and E. G. Hammond. 1987. Model to predict gaseous contaminants in swine confinement buildings. *Journal of Agricultural Engineering Research* 37:235-253.

Anderson, H. M., and J. M. Anderson. 1970. A preliminary review of the biostratigraphy of the Uppermost Permian, Triassic, and lowermost Jurassic of Gondwanaland. *Palaeontologia Africana*, Supplement to Volume 13, Chart 1.

Andrews, R. M. and F. H. Pough. 1985. Metabolism of squamate reptiles: allometric and ecological relationships. *Physiological Ecology* 58:214-231.

Anon. 1827a. Food for horses. *Journal of the Franklin Institute* 4: 207-8.

Anon. 1827b. Cows, horses, and sheep fed on fish, in Persia. *Journal of the Franklin Institute* 3:357.

Anon. 1846. IV. Method of preserving eggs in China. *Journal of the Franklin Institute*, 3rd Series, 12:284.

Anon. 1855. *The Elephant as He Exists*. Harper and Brothers, New York.

Anon. 1918. German substitutes for cattle feed. *Scientific American* 118(14): 313.

Anon. 1921. Mechanical hired men. *Scientific American* 124(18): 351, 359.

Anon. 1933. More about koalas. *Nature Magazine* 21(5): 256-7

Anon. 1937. Captive giant panda's death attributed to wrong diet. *China Journal* 27:209-210.

Anon. 1954. Beats the silage tub. *Farm Journal* 78(May 1954): 62.

Anon. 1961. He cut silage-feeding time to half an hour. *Successful Farming* 59(3): 100.

Anon. 1967. Squab Raising. *United States Department of Agriculture Farmers' Bulletin* No. 684.

Anon. 1968a. Gas from manure pits can kill. *Farm Journal* 92(9): 36L.

Anon. 1968b. All concentrate. *Farm Journal* 92(1): B-12.

Anon. 1976. *Workshop on Food Preservation and Storage*. United Nations Economic Commission for Africa, New York.

Anon. 1983. *Solar Livestock Housing Handbook*. Iowa State university, Iowa.

Anon. 1989. For the love of bats. *Bats* 7(3): 12-13.

Anon. 1994. Chopped up cork tree springs back to life. *New Scientist* 141(1913): 6.

Abplanalp, H. 1988. Selection response in inbred lines of white leghorn chickens (pp. 360-373) *in* Wier, B. S. ed., *Proceedings of the Second International Conference on Quantitative Genetics*. Sinauer Associates, Inc., Sunderland, Massachusetts.

Apple, R. J., and H. A. Erlich. 1992. Two new HLA DRB1 alleles found in African Americans: Implications for balancing selection at positions 57 and 86. *Tissue Antigens* 40:69-74.

Archer, M. 1981. Systematics: an enormous science rooted in instinct (pp. 125-150) *in* Archer, M. and G. Clayton, ed. 1981. *Vertebrate Zoogeography and Evolution in Australasia*. Hesperian Press, Australia.

Archibald, G. W., and R. F. Pasquier. 1987. *Proceedings of the 1983 International Crane Workshop*. International Crane Foundation, Baraboo, Wisconsin.

Arctander, P., and J. Fjeldsa. 1994. Andean tapaculos of the genus *Scytalopus* (pp. 205-225) *in* Loeschke, *op. cit.*

Arends, J. J. 1988. Insect and fly control in poultry waste (pp. 34-5) *in* Anon. *Proceedings of the National Poultry Waste Management Symposium*. Ohio State University.

Armario, A., Ortiz. R., and J. Balasch. 1984. Effect of crowding on some physiological and behavioral variables in adult male rats. *Physiology and Behavior* 32:35-7.

Armstrong, K. 1993. *A History of God*. Alfred A. Knopf, New York.

Arnold, S. J. 1981. Behavioral variation in natural populations. I. Phenotypic, genetic and environmental correlations between chemoreceptive responses to prey in the garter snake, *Thamnophis elegans*. *Evolution* 35(3): 489-509.

Arnold, S. J. Behavioural variation in natural populations. VI. Prey responses by two species of garter snakes in three regions of sympatry. *Animal Behavior* 44:705-719.

Arsdall, R. N. van. 1980. Some economics of animal production (pp. 16-40) *in* Hoefer, J. A., and P. J. Tsuchitani, eds. *Animal Agriculture in China*. National Academy Press, Washington, D. C.

ASAE (American Society of Agricultural Engineers). 1966. *Management of Farm Animal Wastes*. Michigan State University, East Lansing.

Ashbrook, F. G. 1955. *Butchering, Processing, and Preservation of Meat*. Van Nostrand Reinhold, New York.

Atkeson, F. W., and H. Beresford. 1935. Portable elevator as a labor-saving device on the dairy farm. *Agricultural Engineering* 16(4): 149-150.

Atz, J. W. 1958. Olaf: 1,000 pounds of Walrus charm. *Animal Kingdom* 61(3): 66-72.

Auffenberg, W. 1981. *The Behavioral Ecology of the Komodo Monitor*. University of Florida Press, Gainesville.

Austin, S. A. 1990. The sea's missing salt: a dilemma for evolutionists (pp. 17-30) *in* Walsh, R. E., and C. L. Brooks, eds., *Proceedings of the Second International Conference on Creationism*, Pittsburg.

Awbrey, F. T. 1981. Defining "kinds"—do creationists apply a double standard? *Creation/Evolution* 5:1-6.

Ayala, F. J., Escalante, A., O'hUigin, C., and J. Klein. 1994. Molecular genetics of speciation and human origins. *Proceedings of the National Academy of Sciences (USA)* 91:6787-6794.

Babinski, E. T. 1995. If it wasn't for agnosticism, I wouldn't know what to believe (pp. 207-231) *in* Babinski, E. T., ed., *Leaving the Fold: Testimonies of Former Fundamentalists*. Prometheus Books, New York.

Bailey, L. R. 1989. *Noah*. University of South Carolina Press, Columbia, South Carolina.

Bailey, R. M. 1942. An intergeneric hybrid rattlesnake. *American Naturalist* 76: 376,385.

Bailey, T. N. 1993. *The African Leopard*. Columbia University press, New York.

Baker, A. J., and A. Moeed. 1987. Rapid genetic differentiation and founder effect in colonizing populations of common mynas (*Acridotheres tristis*). *Evolution* 41(3): 525-538.

Baker, E. T. et al. 1989. Episodic venting of hydothermal fluids from the Juan de Fuca Ridge. *Journal of Geophysical Research* 94(B7): 9237-9250.

Bakker, R. T. 1986. *The Dinosaur Heresies*. William Morrow, New York.

Ball, E., and J. Glucksman. 1975. Biological colonization of Motmot, a recently-created tropical island. *Proceedings of the Royal Society of London* B190:421-442.

Ballou, J. D. 1984. Strategies for maintaining genetic diversity in captive populations through reproductive technology. *Zoo Biology* 3:311-323.

Ballou, J. D. 1989. Inbreeding and outbreeding depression in the captive propagation of black-footed ferrets. (pp. 44-68) *in* Seal, U. S., ed., *Conservation Biology and the Black-Footed Ferret*. Yale University Press, New Haven and London.

Ballou, J. D., and K. A. Cooper. 1992. Genetic management strategies for endangered captive populations: the role of genetic and reproductive technology. *Symposium of the Zoological Society of London* 64:183-206.

Bancroft, D. B. et al. 1995. Molecular genetic variation and individual survival during population crashes of an unmanaged ungulate population. *Philosophical Transactions of the Royal Society of London* B347:263-273.

Bantin, G. C., F. I. A. T., and P. D. Sanders. 1989. Animal caging: Is big necessarily better? *Animal Technology* 40(1): 45-54.

Barber, E. M. 1974. *A Study of the Production and Control of Hydrogen Sulfide from Anaerobic Swine Manure*. Master's Degree Thesis, University of Alberta, Edmonton.

Barber, T. X. 1993. *The Human Nature of Birds*. St. Martin's Press, New York.

Barbour, E. 1870. *The Timber Trees of India and of Eastern and Southern Asia*, 3rd Edition. Higginbotham and Co., Madras, India.

Barbour, R. W., and W. H. Davis. 1969. *Bats of America*. University of Kentucky Press, Lexington.

Barclay, A. M., and R. M. M. Crawford. 1981. Temperature aned anoxic injury in pea seedlings. *Journal of Experimental Botany* 32(130): 943-9.

Barclay, A. M., and R. M. M. Crawford. 1982. Plant growth and survival under strict anaerobiosis. *Journal of Experimental Botany* 33(134): 541-9.

Barlow, P. 1832. Experiments on the strength of different kinds of wood. *Journal of the Franklin Institute (New Series)* 10:49-52

Barnard, S. M. 1985. Reptile Care, Part 9. *Animal Keeper's Forum* 12:97-102.

Barnard, S. M. 1991. *The Maintenance of Bats in Captivity*. Privately printed.

Barnes, B. J., and E. R. Orskov. 1982. Grain for ruminants. *World Animal Review* No. 42, pp. 38-44.

Baroudy, E., and J. M. Elliott. 1994. The critical limits for juvenile Arctic charr *Salvelinus alpinus*. *Journal of Fish Biology* 45:1041-1053.

Barrett, T. J. 1947. *Harnessing the Earthworm*. Bruce Humphries, Boston.

Barrett, S. C. H., and B. J. Richardson. 1986. Genetic attributes of invading species (pp. 21-33) *in* Groves and Burdon, *op. cit.*

Barrick, R. E., and W. J. Showers. 1994. Thermophysiology of *Tyrannosaurus rex*: Evidence from oxygen isotopes. *Science* 265:222-4.

Bartholomew, G. A., and T. J. Cade. 1957. Temperature regulation, hibernation, and aestivation in the little pocket mouse *Perognathus longimembris*. *Journal of Mammalogy* 38(1)60-72.

Bartlett, A. D. 1856. Observations on a living African *Lepidosiren* in the Crystal Palace. *Proceedings of the Zoological Society of London* 1856:312-347.

Bartlett, A. D. 1870. Remarks on the habits of the panda (*Ailurus fulgens*) in captivity. *Proceedings of the Zoological Society of London* 1870:769-772.

Bartlett, A. D. 1899. *Wild Animals in Captivity*. Chapman and Hall, London.

Barton, N. H., and M. Turelli. 1989. Evolutionary quantitative genetics: how little do we know? *Annual Review of Genetics* 23:337-370.

Baskin, J. M., and C. C. Baskin. 1989. Physiology of dormancy and germination in relation to seed bank ecology (pp. 53-66) *in* Leck et al., *op. cit.*

Bates, H., and R. Busenbark. 1970. *Finches and Soft-Billed Birds*. TFH Publications, New Jersey.

Batten, P. 1976. *Living Trophies*. Thomas Y. Crowell, New York.

Baur, M. E., and R. R. Friedl. 1980. Application of size-metabolism allometry to therapsids and dinosaurs (pp. 253-286) *in* Thomas, R. D. K., and E. C. Olson., eds., A Cold Look at the Warm-Blooded Dinosaurs. *AAAS Selected Symposium* 28.

Bauwens, D. 1981. Survivorship during hibernation in the European common lizard, *Lacerta vivipara*. *Copeia* 1981(3): 741-4.

Baxter, S. H. 1984a. *Intensive Pig Production*. Granada, London.

Baxter, S. H. 1984b. *The environmental complex in pig production* (pp. 1-49) *in* L. C. Hsia (ed). Environment and Housing for Livestock. Pig Research Institute, Taiwan.

Beadle, L. C. 1943. Osmotic regulation and the faunas of inland waters. *Biological Reviews* 18(4): 172-183.

Beadle, L. C. 1974. *The Inland Waters of Tropical Africa*. Longman Group Limited, London.

Beddard, F. E. 1905. *Natural History in Zoological Gardens*. Archibold Constable and Co., Ltd., London.

Beebe, F. L., and H. M. Webster. 1964. *North American Falconry and Hunting Hawks*. World Press, Utah.

Beebee, T. J. C. 1985. Salt tolerances of Natterjack Toad (*Bufo calamita*) eggs and larvae from coastal and inland populations in Britain. *Herpetological Journal* 1:14-16.

Belich, M. P., and 7 others. 1992. Unusual *HLA-B* alleles in two tribes of Brazilian Indians. *Nature* 357:326-9.

Belousova, L. S., and L. V. Denisova. 1992. *Rare Plants of the World*. A. A. Balkema, Rotterdam.

Belwood, J. J., and P. A. Morton. 1991. Vampires: the real story. *Bats* 9(1): 11-16.

Belyaev, D. K. 1979. Destabilizing selection as a factor in domestication. *Journal of Heredity* 70:301-8.

Belyaev, D. K., and P. M. Borodin. 1982. The influence of stress on variation and its role in evolution. *Biologisches Zentralblatt* 101:705-714.

Bendiner, R. 1981. *The Fall of the Wild, the Rise of the Zoo*. E. P. Dutton, New York.

Bennett, D. 1992. Note on *Varanus panoptes rubidus* (Storr 1980) in Wanjarri, Western Australia. *British Herpetological Society Bulletin* No. 39.

Bent, A. C. 1937. Life histories of North American Birds of Prey I. Smithsonian Institution Bulletein 167.

Bent, A. C. 1938. Life histories of North American Birds of Prey II. Smithsonian Institution Bulletein 170.

Benton, M. J. 1990. Reptiles (pp. 279-301) *in* McNamara, K. J., ed., *Evolutionary Trends*. Belhaven Press, London.

Bergstrom, T., and U. Gyllensten. 1995. Evolution of Mhc class II polymorphism; the rise and fall of class II gene functions in primates. *Immunological Reviews* 143:13-31

Berry, R. J. 1983. Genetics and conservation (pp. 141-156) *in* Warren, A., and F. B. Goldsmith, eds, *Conservation in Perspective*. John Wiley and Sons, New York.

Berry, R. J. 1986. Genetics of insular populations of mammals. *Biological Journal of the Linnean Society* 28:205-230.

Berry, R. J. 1992a. The role of ecological genetics in biological conservation (pp. 107-123) *in* Sandlund et al., *op. cit.*

Berry, R. J. 1992b. The significance of island biotas. *Biological Journal of the Linnean Society* 46:3-12.

Berthold, P., Helbig, A. J., Mohr, G., and U. Querner. 1992. Rapid microevolution of migratory behaviour in a wild bird species. *Nature* 360:668-9.

Berthold, P., and F. Pulido. 1994. Heritability of migratory activity in a natural bird population. *Proceedings of the Royal Society of London* B257:311-315.

Bertram B. 1984. Breeding ostriches (pp. 28-31) *in* Partridge, J. (ed.), *The Management of Cranes, Storks, and Ratites in Captivity.* ABWAK (Association of British Wild Animal Keepers), Bristol, England.

Besch, E. L. 1985. Definition of laboratory animal environmental conditions (pp. 297-315) *in* G. P. Moberg, ed. *Animal Stress.* American Physiological Society, Maryland.

Besch, E. L. 1991. Temperature and humidity control (pp. 154-166) *in* T. Ruys, ed. *Handbook of Facilities Planning*, Vol. 2. Van Nostrand Reinhold, New York.

Betts, T. J. 1978. Koala acceptance of *Eucalyptus globulus labill.* as food in relation to the proportion of sesquiterpenoids in the leaves (pp. 75-85) in Bergin, T. J., ed., The Koala: *Proceedings of the Taronga Symposium.* Sydney, Australia.

Biemont, C., Aouar, A., and C. Arnault. 1987. Genome reshuffling of the *copei* element in an inbred line of *Drosophila melanogaster. Nature* 329:742-4.

Bigalke, M. A. 1937. The naturalization of animals: with special reference to South Africa. *South African Journal of Science* 33:46-63.

Billings, W. D. 1987. Constraints to plant growth, reproduction, and establishment in Arctic environments. *Arctic and Alpine Research* 19(4): 357-365.

Bird, S. H., and R. A. Leng. 1978. The effects of defaunation of the rumen on the growth of cattle on low-protein high-energy diets. *British Journal of Nutrition* 40:163-167.

Bitting, K. G. 1920. *The Olive.* Glass Container Association of America, Chicago.

Bittles, A. H., and J. V. Neel. 1994. The costs of human inbreeding and their implications for variations at the DNA level. *Nature Genetics* 8(2): 117-121.

Black, R. G. 1981. *Nutrition of Finches and Other Caged Birds.* Copple House Printing, Georgia.

Black, V. S. 1951. Osmotic regulations in teleost fishes (pp. 53-89) *in* Hoar, W. S., Black, V., S., and E. C. Black, eds., Some Aspects of the Physiology of Fish. *University of Toronto Biological Series* No. 59.

Blackburn, D. G. 1982. Evolutionary origins of viviparity in the Reptilia. I. Sauria. *Amphibia-Reptilia* 3:185-205.

Blair, W. R. 1929. *In the Zoo*. Charles Scribner's Sons, New York, London.

Bleijenberg, M. C. K., and J. Nijboer. 1989. Feeding herbivorous carnivores (pp. 41-50) *in* Glatston, *op. cit.*

Blueweiss, L., Fox, H., Kudzma, V., Nakashima, D., Peters, R., and S. Sams. 1978. Relationships between body size and some life history parameters. *Oecologia* 37:257-272.

Blunt, W. 1976. *The Ark in the Park*. Hamish Hamiltod Ltd., London.

Bodson, L. 1984. Living reptiles in captivity: a historical survey of origins to the end of the XVIIIth century. *Acta Zoologica et Pathologica Antverpiensia* 78:15-32.

Bond, W. J. 1994. Do mutualisms matter? Assessing the impact of pollinator and dispersal disruption on plant extinction. *Philosophical Transactions of the Royal Society of London* B334:83-90.

Bonner, W. N. 1982. *Seals and Man*. University of Washington Press, Seattle, London.

Bontrop, R. E., Otting, N., Slierendregt, B. L., and J. S. Lanchbury. 1995. Evolution of major histocompatibility complex polymorphisms and t-cell receptor diversity in primates. *Immunological Reviews* 143:33-62.

Bostock, S. C. 1993. *Zoos and Animal Rights*. Routledge, London, New York.

Bowman, R. I., and S. L. Billeb. 1965. Blood-eating in a Galapagos Finch. *The Living Bird* 4:29-44.

Boyd, C. E. 1962. Waif dispersal in toads. *Herpetologica* 18(4): 269.

Bradbury, P. 1974. *Horse Nutrition Handbook*. Cordovan Corporation, Houston, Texas.

Bradshaw, S. D. 1988. Desert reptiles: a case of adaptation or pre-adaptation. *Journal of Arid Environments* 14:155-174.

Brainard, G. 1989. Illumination of laboratory animal quarters (pp. 69-74) *in* Anon. 1989. *Science and Animals*. Bethesda, Maryland.

Brakefield, P. M., and I. J. Saccheri. 1994. Guidelines in conservation genetics and the use of population cage experiments with butterflies to investigate the effects of genetic drift and inbreeding (pp. 165-179) *in* Loeschcke et al., *op. cit.*

Brand, L. R., and L. J. Gibson. 1993. An interventionist theory of natural selection and biological change within limits. *Origins* 20(2): 60-82.

Brazier, T. L. 1987. Breeding and maintenance of *Drosophila melanogaster*. *Animal Technology* 38(3): 211-8.

Breder, C. M. 1934. Ecology of an oceanic fresh-water lake, Andros Island, Bahamas, with special reference to its fishes. *Ecology* 18(3): 57-88.

Bressler, G. O. 1950. Labor saving on Pennsylvania poultry farms. *Pennsylvania Agricultural Experiment Station Bulletin* No. 532.

Brewer, B. A., Lacy, R. C., Foster, M. L., and G. Alaks. 1990. Inbreeding depression in insular and central populations of *Peromyscus* mice. *Journal of Heredity* 81:257-266.

Brewer, D. J., Redford, D. B., and S. Redford. 1994. *Domestic Plants and Animals: The Egyptian Origins*. Aris and Phillips, Ltd., Warmister, England.

Brice, A. T., and C. R. Grau. 1989. Hummingbird Nutrition: Development of a purified diet for long-term maintenance. *Zoo Biology* 8:233-7.

Brichet, J. 1943. Should selected olives by propagated from cuttings or grafted on seedling stock? *Horticultural Abstracts* 13:92.

Briggs, J. C. 1974. *Marine Zoogeography*. McGraw Hill Book Company, San Francisco.

Briggs, J. C. 1994. Species diversity: land and sea compared. *Systematic Biology* 43(1): 130-5.

Brink, A. S. 1982. Illustrated bibliographic catalogue of the Synapsida. *Geological Survey of South Africa Handbook* 10, Part 1.

Brisbin, I. , and C. Bagshaw. 1993. Survival, weight changes, and shedding frequencies of captive scarlet snakes, *Cemophora coccinea*, maintained on an artificial liquid diet. *Herpetological Review* 24(1)27-9.

Brody, S. 1945. *Bioenergetics and Growth*. Reinhold Publishing Co., New York.

Brookfield, J. F. Y. 1994. A new molecular view of human origins. *Current Biology* 4(7): 651-2.

Broom, R. 1932. *The Mammal-like Reptiles of South Africa*. F.& G. Witherby, London.

Brown, H. J. 1989. Patterns, modes, and extents of invasions by vertebrates (pp. 85-109) *in* Drake, J. A., and 6 others, eds., *Biological Invasions: a Global Perspective*. John Wiley and Sons, Chichester, New York.

Brown, J. H., and V. Powell-Smith. 1984. *Horse and Stable Management*. BSP Professional Books, Oxford, London.

Brown, L. H., Cargill, B. F., and B. R. Bookhout. 1950. Pen-type dairy barns. *Michigan Agricultural Experiment Station Special Bulletin* No. 363.

Browne, J. 1983. *The Secular Ark*. Yale University Press.

Brouwer, K., Hiddinga, B., and C. E. King. 1994. Management and breeding of pelicans *Pelecanus* sp. in captivity. *International Zoo Yearbook* 33:24-39.

Bruce, J. M. 1978. Natural convection through openings and its application to cattle building ventilation. *Journal of Agricultural Engineering Research* 23:151-167.

Bruhn, H. D., Zimmerman, A., and R. P. Niedermeier. 1959. Developments in pelleting forage crops. *Agricultural Engineering* 40(4): 204-7.

Bryan, J. J., Kroner, W. M., and R. P. Leslie. 1981. *Daylighting: a Resource Book*. Rensselaer Polytechnic, New York.

Budiansky, S. 1992. *The Covenant of the Wild*. Wm. Morrow and Co., New York.

Bullard, F. M. 1976. *Volcanoes of the Earth*. University of Texas Press, Austin.

Bullock, T. H. 1991. Comparisons of major and minor taxa reveal two kinds of differences: "lateral" adaptations and "vertical" changes in grade (pp. 15-19) *in* Webster D. B., Fay R. R., and A. N. Popper. 1991. *The Evolutionary Biology of Hearing*. Springer Verlag, New York, Berlin.

Bullock, T. H. 1993. How are more complex brains different. *Brain, Behavior, and Evolution* 41(2): 88-96.

Bunn, D. S., Warburton, A. B., and R. D. S. Wilson. 1982. *The Barn Owl*. Buteo Books, Vermillion, South Dakota.

Burchfield, P. M. 1982. Husbandry of Reptiles (pp. 265-285) *in* Sausman, K., ed., *Zoological Park and Aquarium Fundamentals*. American Association of Zoological Parks and Aquariums, Wheeling, West Virginia.

Burrell, H. 1927. *The Platypus*. Angus and Robertson, Sydney, Australia.

Burton, R. 1979. *Carnivores of Europe*. B. T. Batsford, London.

Butler, J. L., and H. F. McColly. 1959. Factors affecting the pelleting of hay. *Agricultural Engineering* 40(8)442-6.

Byers, G. B. 1952. Effect of work methods and building designs on building costs and labor efficiency for dairy chores. *Kentucky Agricultural Experiment Station Bulletin* No. 589.

Cain, A, J. 1956. The genus in evolutionary taxonomy. *Systematic Zoology* 5:97-109.

Calder, W. A. 1984. *Size, Function, and Life History*. Harvard University Press, Massachusetts.

Caldwell, J. S. 1918. Farm and home drying of fruits and vegetables. *USDA (United States Department of Agriculture) Farmers Bulletin* No. 984.

Calef, G. W. 1988. Maximum rate of increase in the African Elephant. *African Journal of Ecology* 26(4): 323-7.

Campbell, S. 1978. *Lifeboats to Ararat*. Times Books, New York.

Carlquist, S. 1974. *Island Biology*. Columbia University Press, New York, London.

Carlquist, S. 1981. Chance Dispersal. *American Scientist* 69:509-516.

Carlton, J. T. 1985. Transoceanic and interoceanic dispersal of coastal marine organisms: the biology of ballast water. *Oceanography and Marine Biology Annual Review* 23:313-371.

Carlton, M. B. L., Colledge, W. H., and M. J. Evans. 1995. Generation of a pseudogene during retroviral infection. *Mammalian Genome* 6:90-5.

Carrier, J. C., and D. H. Evans. 1976. The role of environmental calcium in freshwater survival of the marine teleost, *Lagodon rhomboides*. *Journal of Experimental Biology* 65:529-538.

Carroll, R. L. 1988. *Vertebrate Paleontology and Evolution*. W. H. Freeman and Company, New York.

Carson, H. L. 1990. Increased genetic variance after a population bottleneck. *TREE (Trends in Ecology and Evolution)* 5(7)228-230.

Carson, H. L., and A. R. Templeton. 1984. Genetic revolutions in relation to speciation phenomena: the founding of new populations. *Annual Review of Ecology and Systematics* 15:97-131.

Carter, D. G., and W. E. Carroll. 1943. Labor-saving equipment for hog production. *University of Illinois Agricultural Experiment Station Circular* 554.

Carter, R. M. 1943. Labor saving through farm job analysis. *Vermont Agricultural Experiment Station Bulletin* 503.

CAS (Chinese Academy of Sciences). 1983. *Ancient China's Technology and Science*. Foreign Languages Press, Beijing.

Casady, R. B. 1971. Commercial Rabbit Raising. *United States Department of Agriculture: Agriculture Handbook* No. 309.

Case, T. J. 1978. Speculations on the growth rate and reproduction of some dinosaurs. *Paleobiology* 4(3): 320-8.

Casella, P. 1931. A new method of olive propagation. *Horticultural Abstracts* 1:113.

Casson, L. 1971. *Ships and Seamanship in the Ancient World*. Princeton University Press, Princeton, New Jersey.

Catton, C. 1990. *Pandas*. Facts on File, New York, Oxford.

Cavalli-Sforza, L. L. 1986. African Pygmies, an evaluation of the state of research (pp. 361-426) *in* Cavalli-Sforza, L. L., ed., *African Pygmies*. Academic Press, Orlando, San Diego.

Cavalli-Sforza, L. L., Menozzi, P., and A. Piazza. 1994. *The History and Geography of Human Genes*. Princeton University Press, New Jersey.

CCAC (Canadian Council on Animal Care). 1984. *Guide to the Care and Use of Experimental Animals*, 2 Volumes. Ottawa.

CCIGC (Central Commission for Investigation of German Crimes in Poland). 1982. *German Crimes in Poland*. Howard Fertig, New York.

Censky E. J. and C. J. McCoy. 1988. Female reproductive cycles of five species of snakes (Reptilia: Colubridae) from the Yucatan Peninsula, Mexico. *Biotropica* 20(4): 326-333.

Chadwick, D. H. 1992. *The Fate of the Elephant*. Sierra Club Books, San Francisco.

Chaffee, R. R. J. 1966. On experimental selection for super-hybernating and non-hibernating lines of Syrian hamsters. *Journal of Theoretical Biology* 12:151-154.

Chakraborty R., and M. Nei. 1977. Bottleneck effects on average heterozygosity and genetic distance with the step-wise mutation model. *Evolution* 31:347-356.

Chandler, W. H. 1950. *Evergreen Orchards*. Lea and Febiger, Philadelphia.

Chang, K. 1986. *The Archaeology of Ancient China*, 4th Edition.

Chappell, M. A., and S. L. Souza. 1988. Thermoregulation, gas exchange, and ventilation in Adelie penguins (*Pygoscelis adeliae*). *Journal of Comparative Physiology* B:783-790.

Chapuis, J. L., Bousses, P., and G. Barnaud. 1994. Alien mammals, impact and management in the French Subantarctic Islands. *Biological Conservation* 67:97-104.

Charlesworth, D., and B. Charlesworth. 1976. Theoretical genetics of Batesian mimicry II. Evolution of supergenes. *Journal of Theoretical Biology* 55:305-324.

Cheeke, P. R., Patton, N. M., Lukefahr, S. D., and J. I. McNitt. 1987. *Rabbit Production* (6th edition). Interstate Printers, Danville, Illinois.

Cheng, L., and M. C. Birch. 1978. Insect flotsam: an unstudied marine resource. *Ecological Entomology* 3:87-97.

Cherel, Y., Robin, J.-P., and Y. LeMaho. 1988. Physiology and biochemistry of long-term fasting in birds. *Canadian Journal of Zoology* 66:159-166.

Cherfas, J. 1984. *Zoo 2000*. British Broadcasting Corporation, London.

Chernov, Yu. I. 1985. *The Living Tundra*. Cambridge University Press, London, New York.

Chew, R. M., Lindberg, R. G., and P. Hayden. 1965. Circadian rhythm of metabolic rate in pocket mice. *Journal of Mammalogy* 46(3): 477-494.

Chimits, P. 1957. *Tilapia* in Ancient Egypt. *FAO Fisheries Bulletin* 10:211-5.

Chin, H. F. 1980. Seed production and processing (pp. 111-133) *in* Chin, H. F., and E. H. Roberts, eds., *Recalcitrant Crop Seeds*. Tropical Press, Kuala Lumpur, Malaysia.

Chinsamy, A. 1993. Image analysis and the physiological implications of the vascularisation of femora in archosaurs. *Modern Geology* 19: 101-8.

Chinsamy, A., and P. Dodson. 1995. Inside a dinosaur bone. *American Scientist* 83:174-180.

Chipman, R. K. 1959. Studies of tolerance of certain freshwater fishes to brine water from oil wells. *Ecology* 40(2): 299-302.

Chiszar, D., and K. M. Scudder. 1980. Chemosensory searching by rattlesnakes during predatory episodes (pp. 125-141) *in* Muller-Schwarze, D., and R. M. Silverstein, eds., *Chemical Signals*. Plenum Press, New York, Oxford.

Christensen, E. 1947. Migration or hibernation of *Tadarida mexicana*. *Journal of Mammalogy* 28(1): 59-60.

Christman, S. P. 1974. Geographic variation for salt water tolerance in the frog *Rana sphenocephala*. *Copeia* 1974:773-8.

Church, D. C. 1991. *Livestock Feeds and Feeding*, 3rd edition. Prentice Hall, New Jersey.

CITES (Convention on International Trade in Endangered Species of Wild Fauna and Flora). 1980. *Guidelines for Transport and Preparation for Shipment of Live Wild Animals and Plants*. UNIPUB, New York.

Clark, J. D. 1984. Biology and diseases of other rodents (pp. 183-206) *in* Fox, J. G., Cohen, B. J., and F. M. Loew, eds., *Laboratory Animal Medicine*. Academic Press, Orlando, San Diego.

Clark, J. D., and E. D. Olfert. 1986. Rodents (Rodentia) *in* Fowler, *op. cit.*

Clarke, C. A., and P. M. Sheppard. 1962. Disruptive selection and its effect on a metrical character in the butterfly *Papilio dardanus*. *Evolution* 16:214-226.

Claridge, A. W., and T. W. May. 1994. Mycophagy among Australian mammals. *Australian Journal of Ecology* 19:251-257.

Cleaver, T. 1952. Time-travel studies on dairy farms. *Agricultural Engineering* 33(3): 137-9, 142.

Clegg, S. 1852. Action of the sea-worm on timber, and the best means of protection. *Journal of the Franklin Institute*, 3rd Series, Vol. 23: 38-40.

Clegg, M. 1972. Carrion crows feeding on marine molluscs and taking fish. *Bird Study* 19(4): 249-250.

Clifton, M. 1991. Killing. *The Animal's Agenda* 11(3): 41

Close, R. L. and P. S. Lowry. 1990. Hybrids in Marsupial Research. *Australian Journal of Zoology* 37:259-267.

Cloudsley-Thompson, J. L. 1971. *The Temperature and Water Relations of Reptiles*. Merrow, Watford, England.

Clutton-Brock, J. 1992. The process of domestication. *Mammal Review* 22(2): 79-85.

Cockerham, C. C. 1994. Further observations on the evolution of additive genetic variation with mutation. *Theoretical Population Biology* 45:92-100.

Cogger, H. G. 1992. *Reptiles and Amphibians of Australia*. Cornell University Press, New York.

Cohen, D. M. 1970. How many recent fishes are there? *Proceedings of the California Academy of Sciences*, 4th Series, 38(17): 341-6.

Cohen, J. E., Pimm, S. L., Yodzis, P., and J. Saldana. 1993. Body sizes of animal predators and animal prey in food webs. *Journal of Animal Ecology* 62(1): 67-78.

Colbert, E. H. 1962. The weights of dinosaurs. *American Museum Novitates* No. 2076.

Cole, G. F. 1972. Grizzly bear-elk relationships in Yellowstone National Park. *Journal of Wildlife Management* 36:556-561.

Collins, D. H. 1977. Was Noah's Ark stable? *Creation Research Society Quarterly* 14(2): 83-7.

Collins, B. G., Wooler, R. D., and K. C. Richardson. 1987. Torpor by the Honey Possum, *Tarsipes Rostratus* (Marsupialia: Tarsipedidae) in Response to food shortage and low environmental temperature. *Australian Mammalogy* 9(1-2): 51-7.

Collins, L., and M. Roberts. 1978. Arboreal folivores in captivity (pp. 5-12) *in* Montgomery, G. G., ed., *The Ecology of Arboreal Folivores*. Smithsonian Institution Press, Washington, D. C.

Conant, S. 1988. Saving endangered species by translocation. *BioScience* 38(4): 254-257.

Conrad, J. H., and V. B. Mayrose. 1971. Animal waste handling in confinement production of swine. *Journal of Animal Science* 32(4): 811-5.

Cook, L. M. 1984. The problem (pp. 1-12) *in* Mani, G. S., ed., *Evolutionary Dynamics of Genetic Diversity*. Springer-Verlag, Berlin, Heidelberg, New York.

Cooper, M. R. 1917. Cost of keeping farm horses and cost of horse labor. *United States Department of Agriculture Bulletin* No. 560.

Cornish, V. 1934. *Ocean Waves*. Cambridge University Press, Cambridge.

Cosper, L. C., and H. B. Logan. 1951. *How to Grow Vegetables*. Duell, Sloan, and Pearce, New York.

Costanzo, J. P. 1989. Effects of humidity, temperature, and submergence behavior on survivorship and energy use in hibernating garter snakes, *Thamnophis sirtalis*. *Canadian Journal of Zoology* 67:2486-2492.

Cotton, G. E., Aufherheide, A. C., and V. G. Goldschmidt. 1987. Preservation of human tissue immersed for five years in fresh water of known temperature. *Journal of Forensic Sciences* 32(4)1125-1130.

Cowan, D. F. 1980. Adaptation, maladaptation, and disease (pp. 191-6) *in* Murphy and Collins, *op. cit.*

Crandall, L. S. 1964. *The Management of Wild Mammals in Captivity*. University of Chicago Press, Chicago and London.

Crawford, C. S. 1981. *Biology of Desert Invertebrates*. Springer-Verlag, Berlin, Heidelberg.

Crawford, R. M. M. 1977. Tolerance of anoxia and ethanol metabolism in germinating seeds. *New Phytologist* 79:511-7.

Crews, D., and L. D. Garrick. 1980. Methods of inducing reproduction in captive reptiles (pp. 49-70) *in* Murphy and Collins, *op. cit.*

Crocker, W. 1938. Life-span of seeds. *Botanical Review* 4:235-274.

Croghan, P. C., and A. P. M. Lockwood. 1968. Ionic regulation of the Baltic and fresh-water races of the isopod *Mesidotea (Saduria) Entomon* (L.). *Journal of Experimental Biology* 48:141-158

Cruess, W. V., Joslyn, M. A., and G. MacKinney. 1942. *Adapting Fruit and Vegetable Products to War Needs*. University of California Press, Berkeley.

Culliton, B. J. 1990. Emerging viruses, emerging threat. *Science* 247:279-280.

Cummins, K. W., and J. C. Wuycheck. 1971. *Caloric Equivalents for Investigations of Ecological Energetics*. Internationale Vereinigung fur Theoretische und Angewandte Limnologie Mitteilung No. 18.

Cunha, T. J. 1991. *Horse Feeding and Nutrition*, 2nd Edition. Academic Press, New York, London.

Curio, E. 1976. *The Ethology of Predation*. Springer-Verlag, Berline, Heidelberg, New York.

Curtis, S. E. 1983. *Environmental Management in Animal Agriculture*. Iowa State University Press, Ames, Iowa.

Dahlberg, M. D. 1979. A review of survival rates of fish eggs and larvae in relation to impact environments. *Marine Fisheries Review* 41(3): 1-12.

Damuth, J. 1987. Interspecific allometry of population density in mammals and other animals: their independence of body mass and population energy-use. *Biological Journal of the Linnean Society* 31:193-246.

Daniel, R., Kadlec, J. E., Morris, W. H. M., Jones, H. W., Conrad, J. H., Hinkle, C. N., and A. C. Dale. 1967. Productivity and cost of swine farrowing and nursery systems. *Purdue University Agricultural Experiment Station Research Progress Report* No. 315.

Darling, F. F. 1938. *Bird Flocks and the Breeding Cycle*. Cambridge University Press, England.

Dasman, R. F. 1964. *African Game Ranching*. Pergamon Press, London, New York.

Davenport, J. 1992. *Animal Life at Low Temperature*. Chapman and Hall, London, New York.

Davenport, J., and A. Stene. 1986. Freezing resistance, temperature and salinity tolerance in eggs, larvae and adults of capelin, *Mallotus villosus*, from Balsfjord. *Journal of the Marine Biological Association of the United Kingdom* 66:145-157.

Davis, J. 1968. River otters, sea-otters, and part-time otters, Part III. *Animal Kingdom* 71:8-12 (December).

Davis, S. J. M. 1987. *The Archaeology of Animals*. B. T. Batsford Ltd., London.

Davis, W. H., and O. B. Reite. 1967. Responses of bats from temperate regions to changes in ambient temperatures. *Biological Bulletin* 132(3): 320-8.

Dawson, W. R., Ligon, J. D., Murphy, J. R., Myers, J. P., Simberloff, D., and J. Verner. Report on the scientific advisory panel on the Spotted Owl. *Condor* 89(1): 205-229.

Decker, W. M., and J. H. Steele. 1966. Health aspects and vector control associated with animal wastes (pp. 18-20) *in* ASAE 1966, *op. cit.*

Degani, G. 1981. Salinity tolerance and osmoregulation in *Salamandra salamandra* (L.) from different populations. *Journal of Comparative Physiology* 145:133-7.

Del Moral, R., and L. C. Bliss. 1993. Mechanisms of primary successionL insights resulting from the eruption of Mount St. Helens. *Advances in Ecological Research* 24:1-66.

Delacour, J. 1951. *The Pheasants of the World*. Country Life Limited, London.

Denslow. J. S., Levey, D. J., Moermond, T. C., and B. C. Wentworth. 1987. A synthetic diet for fruit-eating birds. *Wilson Bulletin* 99(1): 131-5.

Desy, D. H., Risbeck, J. S., and L. A. Neumeier. 1973. Research finds methane can ignite by frictional sparks between aluminum alloys and rusty steel. *Coal Age* 78(12): 65-8.

Diamond, J. 1985. Voyage of the overloaded ark. *Discover* 2(2): 82-92.

Diamond, J., Pimm, S. L., Gilpin, M. E., and M. LeCroy. 1989. Rapid evolution of character displacement in myzomelid honeyeaters. *American Naturalist* 134(5): 675-708.

Dierenfeld, E. S., Qui, X., Mainka, S., and W. Liu. 1995. Giant panda diets fed in five Chinese facilities: an assessment. *Zoo Biology* 14:211-222.

Dilger, W. C., and J. Bell. 1982. Caging and environment (pp. 11-17) *in* Petrak, M. L., ed., *Diseases of Cage and Aviary Birds*. Lea and Febiger, Philadelphia.

Dineen, J. F., and A. H. Hines. 1994. Effects of salinity and adult extract on settlement of the oligohaline barnacle *Balanus subalbidus*. *Marine Biology* 119:423-430.

DiSilvestro, R. L. 1991. *The African Elephant*. John Wiley and Sons, New York, Chichester.

Ditmars, R. L., and A. M. Greenhall. 1935. The vampire bat. *Zoologica* (New York) 19(2): 53-76.

Dixon, A. M., Mace, G. M., Newby, J. E., and P. J. S. Olney. 1991. Planning for the re-introduction of scimatar-horned oryx (*Oryx dama*) and addax (*Addax calatus*) into Niger. *Symposium of the Zoological Society of London* 62:201-216.

Dobie, J. B., Curley, R. G., and P. S. Parsons. 1964. Economics of hay wafering. *Agricultural Engineering* 45(2): 74-7.

Dodson, P. 1990. Counting dinosaurs: how many kinds were there? *Proceedings of the National Academy of Sciences (USA)* 87:7608-7612.

Domalain, J. Y. 1977. *The Animal Connection*. William Morrow and Co., Inc., New York.

Donham, K. J. 1987. Human health and safety standards for workers in livestock housing (pp. 86-95) *in* Anon. 1987. *Latest Developments in Livestock Housing*. American Society of Agricultural Engineers. Illinois.

Donnelly, I. A. 1930. *Chinese Junks and Other Native Craft.*, 2nd Ed. Kelly and Walsh, Ltd., Shanghai, China.

Dorit, R. L., Akashi, H., and W. Gilbert. 1995. Absence of polymorphism at the ZFY locus on the human Y chromosome. *Science* 268:1183-5.

Douglas, A. 1981. Feeding softbills—an historical synopsis (pp. 112-120) *in* Risser et al., *op cit.*

Downey, N. E., and J. F. Moore. 1980. The possible role of animal manures in the dissemination of livestock parasites (pp. 553-71) *in* Gasser, J. K. (ed). *Effluents from Livestock*. Applied Science Publishers, London.

Dresner, S. H. and S. Siegel. 1959, 1966. *The Jewish Dietary Laws*. Burning Bush Press, New York.

Drummond, L. A. 1988. Panda magic at the Calgary Zoo. *Animal Keeper's Forum* 15:412-6.

Duellman, W. E. 1979. The numbers of amphibians and reptiles. *Herpetological Review* 10(2): 83-84.

Duellmann, W. E., and L. Trueb. 1986. *Biology of Amphibians*. McGraw Hill Book Co., New York, St. Louis.

Duley, F. L. 1919. Handling farm manure. *University of Missouri Agricultural Experiment Station Bulletin* 166.

Dumelow, J. 1993. Unbedded self cleaning sloped floors as alternatives to fully slatted floors for beef cattle housing (pp. 209-216) *in* Collins, E., and C. Boon, eds., *Livestock Environment IV*. American Society of Agricultural Engineers, Michigan.

Duncan, W. 1932. Australian "bears." *Nature Magazine* 20(1): 13-16.

Dunham, A. E., Miles, D. B., and D. N. Resnick. 1988. Life history patterns in squamate reptiles (pp. 441-523) *in* Gans, C. ed., *Biology of the Reptilia*, Vol. 16, Alan R. Liss, Inc., New York.

Dunn, R. W. 1982. Gliders of the genus *Petaurus*: their management in zoos (pp. 82-5) *in* Evans. 1982. *op. cit.*

Dunning, J. B. 1993. Body masses of birds of the world (pp. 3-310) *in* J. B. Dunning, ed., *CRC Handbook of Avian Body Masses*. CRC Press, Boca Raton, Florida.

Dunson, W. A. 1977. Tolerance to high temperatures and salinity by tadpoles of the Phillipine frog *Rana cancrivora*. *Copeia* 1977(2): 375-8.

Dunson, W. A. 1984. The contrasting roles of the salt glands, the integument, and behavior (pp. 107-129) *in* Requeux, A,, Gilles, R., and L. Bolis, eds., *Osmoregulation in Estuarine and Marine Animals*. Springer-Verlag, Berlin, Heidelberg, New York.

Duplaix-Hall, N., and J. Kear. 1975. Breeding requirements in captivity (pp. 131-141) *in* Kear, J., and N. Duplaix-Hall., ed., *Flamingos*. T and Ad Poyser, Berkhamsted, England.

Dyck, Van S. 1982. Management of captive Megachiroptera (pp. 161-4) *in* Evans. 1982. *op. cit.*

Earle, I. P. 1950. Compression of complete diets for horses. *Journal of Animal Science* 9:255-260.

Eaton, J. W., and A. J. Mayer. 1953. The social biology of very high fertility among the Hutterites. *Human Biology* 25(3)206-264.

Echelle, A. A., Echelle, A. F., and L. G. Hill. 1972. Interspecific interactions and limiting factors of abundance and distribution in the Red River Pupfish, *Cyprinodon rubrofluviatilis*. *American Midland Naturalist* 88(1)109-130.

Eddy, F. B. 1982. Osmotic and ionic regulation in captive fish with particular reference to salmonids. *Comparative Biochemistry and Physiology* 73B(1): 125-141.

Edgar, G. J. 1987. Dispersal of faunal and floral propagules associated with drifting *Macrocystis pyrifera* plants. *Marine Biology* 95:599-610.

Edwards, A., and B. E. Grantham. 1986. Inorganic nutrient regeneration in Loch Etive bottom water (pp. 195-204) *in* Skreslet, S., ed., *The Role of Freshwater Outflow in Coastal Marine Ecosystems*. Springer-Verlag, Berlin, Heidelberg, New York.

Edwards, N. A. 1975. Scaling of renal functions in mammals. *Comparative Biochemistry and Physiology* 52A:63-6.

Edwardes, S. M. 1923. A note on the durability of Indian Teak. *Indian Forester* 49(3): 165-8.

Eftink, B., and L. Searle 1973. Models for handling solid manure. *Successful Farming* 71:28 (October).

Egan, V. T., and W. S. Grant. 1993. Breeding the striped puff adder *Bitis arictans*. Inbreeding avoidance. *South African Journal of Wildlife Research* 23(3): 78-81.

Eidlitz, K. 1969. Food and emergency food in the circumpolar area. *Studia Ethnografica Upsaliensia* 32:1-175.

Eisenberg, J. F. 1981. *The Mammalian Radiations*. University of Chicago Press, Chicago and London.

Eisenberg, J. F., and M. Lockhart. 1972. An ecological reconaissance of Vilpatta National Park, Ceylon. *Smithsonian Contributions to Zoology* No. 101.

Eitam, D. 1987. Research of the oil industry during the Iron Age at Tel Miqne (pp. 37-56) *in* Heltzer and Eitam, eds., *op. cit.*

Ellis, D. V. 1985. *Animal Behavior and its Implications*. Lewis Publishing Co., Chelsea, Michigan.

Ellis, R. H., and E. H. Roberts. 1980. Improved equations for the prediction of seed longevity. *Annals of Botany* 45:13-30.

Elton, R. H. 1979. Baboon behavior under crowded conditions (pp. 125-138) *in* Erwin, J., Maple, T. L., and G. Mitchell, eds., *Captivity and Behavior*. Van Nostrand Reinhold, New York.

Ely, C. A. 1944. Development of *Bufo marinus* larvae in dilute sea water. *Copeia* 1944(4): 256.

Emanuel, K. A., et al. 1995. Hypercanes: A possible link in global extinction scenarios. *Journal of Geophysical Research* 100(D7): 13, 755-13, 765.

Emiliani, C., E. B. Kraus, and E. M. Shoemaker. 1981. Sudden death at the end of the Mesozoic. *Earth and Planetary Science Letters* 55:317-334.

Endres, G. 1930. Observation on certain physiological processes of the marmot. *Proceedings of the Royal Society of London* B107:241-7.

Engels, W. L. 1951. Winter inactivity of some captive chipmunks (*Tamias striatus*) at Chapel Hill, North Carolina. *Ecology* 32(3): 549-555.

England, M. D. 1974. A further review of the problem of "escapes." *British Birds* 67(5): 177-197.

Ensminger, M. E. 1980. *Poultry Science*. Interstate Publishers, Illinois.

Ensminger, M. E. 1991. *Animal Science Digest*. Interstate Publishers, Illinois.

Epstein, H. 1971. *The Origin of the Domesticated Animals of Africa*. Africana Publishing Co., New York, London.

Erlich, H. A., and U. B. Gyllensten. 1991. Shared epitopes among HLA class II alleles: gene conversion, common ancestry, and balancing selection. *Immunology Today* 12(11): 411-414.

Ernst, A., and J. Weiss. 1984. The influence of various housing conditions on the ocular fundus in Wistar rats. *Laboratory Animals* 18:221-3.

Ernst C. H. and R. W. Barbour. 1989. *Turtles of the World*. Smithsonian Institution Press, Washington, D. C.

Esmay, M. L. 1977. Layout and design of animal feedlot structures and equipment (pp. 49-77) *in* Taiganides. 1977. *op. cit.*

Esmay, M. L., and D. B. Booker. 1953. Horizontal self-feeding silos. *Agricultural Engineering* 34(9): 620-3, 630.

Estes, J. R., Amos, B. B., and J. R. Sullivan. 1983. Pollination from two perspectives: the agricultural and biological sciences (pp. 536-554) *in* Jones, C., E., and R. J. Little, eds., *Handbook of Experimental Pollination Biology.* S and AE Editors, New York, Cincinnati).

Evans, D. D. 1982. *The Management of Australian Mammals in Captivity.* Zoological Board of Victoria, Melbourne, Australia.

Evans, D. H. 1975. Ionic exchange mechanisms in fish gills. *Comparative Biochemistry and Physiology* 51A:491-5.

Ewart, A. J. 1908. On the longevity of seeds. *Proceedings of the Royal Society of Victoria* 21(New Series), Part 1, 1-210, plates.

Faegri, K., and L. van der Pijl. 1979. *The Principles of Pollination Ecology*, 3rd Edition. Pergamon Press, Oxford, New York.

Fairbanks, F. L., and A. M. Goodman. 1926. Dairy-stable ventilation. *Cornell University Extension Bulletin* 151.

Faivre, M. I. 1973. *How to Raise Rabbits for Fun and Profit.* Nelson-Hall Co., Chicago.

FAO (Food and Agriculture Organization of the UN). 1990. *Manual on simple methods of meat preservation.* United Nations, Rome.

Farlow, J. O. 1976. A consideration of the trophic dynamics of a Late Cretaceous large dinosaur community (Oldman Formation). *Ecology* 57: 841-857.

Farrow, R. A. 1984. Detection of transoceanic migration of insects to a remote island in the Coral Sea, Willis Island. *Australian Journal of Ecology* 9:253-272.

Fay, F. H., and C. Ray. 1968. Influence of climate on the distribution of walruses *Odobenus rosmarus* (Linnaeus). I. Evidence from thermoregulatory behavior. *Zoologica* (NY) 53(1): 1-18.

Fenner, M. 1985. *Seed Ecology.* Chapman and Hall, London, New York.

Fenton, M. B. 1992. Wounds and the origin of blood-feeding in bats. *Biological Journal of the Linnean Society* 47:161-171.

Ferguson, D. E. 1956. Notes on the occurrence of some Oregon salamanders close to the ocean. *Copeia* 1956, No. 2, p. 120.

Fertig, D. S., and V. W. Edmonds. 1969. The physiology of the house mouse. *Scientific American* 221(4): 103-110.

Ficken, R. W., and W. G. Dilger. 1961. Insects and food mixtures for insectivorous birds. *Aviculture Magazine* 67:46-55.

Fields, C., Adams, M. D., White, O., and J. C. Venter. 1994. How many genes in the human genome? *Nature Genetics* 7:345-6.

Finley, W. L. 1905. Photographing the Aerie of a western Red-Tail. *Condor* 7(1): 3-7.

Fisher, J. 1967. *Zoos of the World*. Natural History Press, New York.

Fiske, R. S. 1969. Recognition and significance of pumice in marine pyroclastic rocks. *Geological Society of America Bulletin* 80:1-8.

Flieg, G. M., Foerster, H., and H. Sanders. 1971. Penguin exhibit at St. Louis Zoo. *International Zoo Yearbook* 11:67-73.

Flower, W. H. 1880. The secretary on additions to the menagerie. *Proceedings of the Zoological Society of London* 1880 (No. 24): 24-5.

Flux, J. E. C., and P. J. Fullagar. 1992. World distribution of the rabbit *Oryctolagus cuniculus* on islands. *Mammal Review* 22(3/4): 151-205.

Folk, G. E. 1940. Shifts of population among hibernating bats. *Journal of Mammalogy* 21(3): 306-315.

Folk, G. E. 1960. Day-night rhythms and hibernation. *Bulletin of the Museum of Comparative Zoology (Harvard University)* 124:209-231.

Fontdevila, A. 1989. Founder effects in colonizing populations: the case of *Drosophila buzzatii*. (pp. 74-96) *in* Fontdevila, *op. cit.*

Fontdevila, A. 1989. *Evolutionary Biology of Transient Unstable Populations*. Springer-Verlag, Berlin, Heidelberg.

Foose, T. J. 1982. Trophic Strategies of Ruminant Versus Nonruminant Ungulates. *University of Chicago PhD Dissertation*.

Forbes, W. A. 1881. On some points in the anatomy of the koala (*Phascolarctos cinereus*). *Proceedings of the Zoological Society of London* 1881:181-1.

Forbes-Watson, A. D. 1987. Frugivorous pelicans: fish or fig? *Scopus* 11(1)23.

Fordyce, R. E., and C. M. Jones. 1990. Penguin history and new fossil material from New Zealand (pp. 419-446) *in* Davis, L. S., and J. T. Darby, eds., *Penguin Biology*. Academic Press, San Diego, New York.

Forst, B. 1993. *The Laws of Kashrus*. Mesorah Publications, New York.

Fortelius, M. 1993. The largest land mammal ever imagined. *Zoological Journal of the Linnean Society* 107:85-101.

Forward, R. B. 1989. Behavioral responses of crustacean larvae to rates of salinity change. *Biological Bulletin* 176:229-238.

Fosgate, O. T., and M. R. Babb. 1972. Biodegradation of animal waste by *Lumbricus terrestris*. *Journal of Dairy Science* 55(6): 870-2.

Fowler, M. E. 1986. Common and scientific names of animals classed as domestic (p. 1067) *in* Fowler, *op. cit.*

Fowler, M. E. 1986. *Zoo and Wild Animal Medicine*. 2nd Edition. W. B. Saunders and Company, Philadelphia.

Frair, W. 1991. Original kinds and turtle phylogeny. *Creation Research Society Quarterly* 28(1): 21-24.

Frankel, O. H., and M. E. Soule. 1981. *Conservation and Evolution*. Cambridge University Press, Cambridge.

Frankel, R. 1987. Oil presses in western Galilee and the Judaea—a comparison (pp. 63-80) *in* Heltzer and Eitam, eds, *op. cit.*

Fraser, D. 1989. Role of ethology in determining farm animal well-being (pp. 95-102) *in* Anon., *Science and Animals*. Bethesda, Maryland.

French, A. R. 1992. Mammalian dormancy (pp. 105-121) *in* Tomasi, E., and T. H. Horton., eds., *Mammalian Energetics*. Cornell University Press, Ithaca and London.

French C. E., McEwen L. C., Magruder N. D., Ingram R. H., and R. W. Swift. 1956. Nutrient requirements for growth and antler development in the white-tailed deer. *Journal of Wildlife Management* 20(3): 221-232.

Fridriksson, S. 1975. *Surtsey*. John Wiley and Sons, New York, Toronto.

Friedler, Y. 1967. What the Ark was really like. *Jerusalem Post* 37(12083): 5. (October 10, 1967).

Frye, F. L. 1991. *Biomedical and Surgical Aspects of Captive Reptile Husbandry*. (2 Volumes), Krieger Publishing Company, Malabar, Florida.

Fryer, G., and T. D. Iles. 1972. *The Cichlid Fishes of the Great Lakes of Africa*. T.F.H. Publications, New Jersey.

Fuerst, P. A., and T. Maruyama. 1986. Considerations on the conservation of alleles and of genic heterozygosity in small managed populations. *Zoo Biology* 5:171-179.

Funmilayo, O., and M. Akande. 1979. Body weight, diet, and reproduction of rats and mice in the forest zones of south-western Nigeria (pp. 136-141) *in* Ajayi, S. S., and L. B. Halstead, eds., *Wildlife Management in Savannah Woodland*. Taylor and Francis, Ltd., London.

Furspan, P., Prange, H. D., and L. Greenwald. 1984. Energetics and osmoregulation in the catfish, *Ictalurus nebulosus* and *I. punctatus*. *Comparative Biochemistry and Physiology* 77A(4): 773-8.

Futuyma, D. J. 1983. *Science on Trial*. Pantheon Books, New York.

Gailey-Phipps, J. J. 1978. A world survey of penguins in captivity. *International Zoo Yearbook* 18:7-12.

Gailey-Phipps, J. J. 1981. Management of penguins in captivity (pp. 80-92) *in* Risser et al., *op. cit.*

Galiana, A., Ayala, F. J., and A. Moya. 1989. Flush-crash experiments in *Drosophila* (pp. 58-74) *in* Fontdevila, *op. cit.*

Gales, N. J., Coughran, D. K., and L. F. Queale. 1992. Records of subantarctic fur seals *Arctocephalus tropicalis* in Australia. *Australian Mammalogy* 15:135-8.

Gans, C., and A. P. van den Sande. 1976. The exhibition of reptiles: concepts and possibilities. *Acta Zoological et Pathologica Antverpiensia* 66:3-51.

Garrey, W. E. 1916. The resistance of fresh water fish to changes of osmotic and chemical conditions. *American Journal of Physiology* 39:313-329.

Garwood, N. C. 1989. Tropical soil seed banks: a review (pp. 149-209) *in* Leck et al., *op. cit.*

Gates, W. H. 1936. Keeping bats in captivity. *Journal of Mammalogy* 17:268-273.

Gaughwin, M. D. 1982. Southern hairy-nosed wombat *Lasiorhinus latifrons*: its maintenance, bahaviour, and reproduction in captivity (pp. 144-157) *in* Evans. 1982. *op. cit.*

Gaulthier-Pilters H., and A. I. Dagg. 1981. *The Camel*. University of Chicago Press, Chicago and London.

Gay, C. W. 1924. *Productive Horse Husbandry*, 3rd Edition. J. B. Lippincott Co., Philadelphia and London.

Geiser, F. 1993. Hibernation in the Eastern Pygmy Possum *Cercartetus nanus* (Marsupialia: Burramyidae). *Australian Journal of Zoology* 41:67-75.

Geiser, F. 1994. Hibernation and daily torpor in marsupials: a recies. *Australian Journal of Zoology* 42(1): 1-16.

Geist, V. 1971. *Mountain Sheep*. University of Chicago Press, Chicago and London.

Gelder, R. G., Van. 1977. Mammalian hybrids and generic limits. *American Museum Novitates* 2635: 1-25.

Geoghegan, P., Mattson, M. T., Reichle, J. J., and R. G. Keppel. 1992. Influence of salt front position on the occurrence of uncommon marine fishes in the Hudson River Estuary. *Estuaries* 15(2): 251-4.

George, G. G. 1982. Cuscuses *Phalanger* spp.; their management in captivity (pp. 67-73) *in* Evans. 1982. *op. cit.*

George, G. G. 1990. Monotreme and marsupial breeding programs in Australian zoos. *Australian Journal of Zoology* 37:181-205.

Gersh, H. 1971. *The Animals Next Door*. Fleet Academic Editions, New York, London.

Ghosh, A. K., and P. P. Majumder. 1979. Genetic load in an isolated tribal population of South India. *Human Genetics* 51:203-8.

Gibbs, R. J. 1970. Mechanisms controlling world water chemistry. *Science* 170(3962): 1088-1090.

Gillespie, T. H. 1932. *A Book of King Penguins*. Herbert Jenkins Limited, London.

Gillingham, W. B. 1989. The first North American captive breeding of the Mandarin Ratsnake (*Elaphe mandarina*) (pp. 87-9) *in* Gowen, *op. cit.*

Gillis, A. M. 1991. Can organisms direct their evolution? *BioScience* 41(4): 202-5.

Gilpin, M., and C. Wills. 1991. MHC and captive breeding: a rebuttal. *Conservation Biology* 5(4): 554-5.

Gimpel, J. 1976. *The Medieval Machine*. Holt, Rinehart, and Winston, New York.

Ginzberg, L. 1909, reprinted 1988. Noah and the Flood in Jewish Legend (pp. 319-355) *in* A. Dundes, ed. *The Flood Myth*. University of California Press, Berkeley.

Giron, J. A. T. 1980. Giant pandas *Ailuropoda melanoleuca* in Chapultepec Park Zoo, Mexico City. *International Zoo Yearbook* 20:264-9.

Gish, D. T. 1993. *Creation Scientists Answer Their Critics,* Institute for Creation Research, El Cajon, California.

Gislen, T., and H. Kauri. 1959. Zoogeography of the Swedish amphibians and reptiles. *Acta Vertebratica* 1(3): 191-397.

Glatston, A. R. 1989. *Red Panda Biology*. SPB Academic Publishers. The Hague, Netherlands.

Gleeson, G. 1933. *London Zoo*. National Travel Club, New York.

Glynn, I. M. 1993. The evolution of consciousness: William James's unresolved problem. *Biological Reviews* 68: 599-616.

Goffart, M. 1971. *Function and Form in the Sloth*. Pergamon Press, Oxford, New York.

Gohl, B. 1981. *Tropical Feeds*. United Nations (FAO), Rome.

Gold, M. 1983. *Assault and Battery*. Pluto Press, London.

Gold, T. 1987. *Power From the Earth*. J. M. Dent and Sons, London, Melbourne.

Gold, T. 1992. The deep, hot biosphere. *Proceedings of the National Academy of Sciences (USA)* 89:6045-6049.

Golding, B. 1992. The prospects for polymorphisms shared between species. *Heredity* 68:263-276.

Gooch, J. I., and D. S. Glazier. 1986. Levels of heterozygosity in the amphipod *Gammarus minus* in an area affected by Pleistocene glaciation. *American Midland Naturalist* 116(1): 57-63.

Goodman, A. M. 1940. Dairy stable ventilation. *Agricultural Engineering* 21(8): 301-2, 309.

Goodwin, D. 1971. Soft foods for waxbills. *Aviculture Magazine* 77(2): 66-9.

Goodwin, D. 1984. Some aspects and problems of sexual dimorphism in birds. *Aviculture Magazine* 90(1): 48-59.

Gordon, I. J. 1991. Ungulate re-introductions: the case of the scimitar-horned oryx. *Symposium of the Zoological Society of London* 62:217-240.

Gordon, M. S. 1962. Osmotic regulation in the green toad (*Bufo viridis*). *Journal of Experimental Biology* 39:261-270.

Gordon, M. S. 1965. Intracellular osmoregulation in skeletal muscle during salinity adaptation in two species. *Biological Bulletin* 128(2): 218-229.

Goss-Custard, J. D., Wilkins, P., and J. Kear. 1971. Rearing wading birds in captivity. *Avicultural Magazine* 77(1): 16-19.

Gowen, R. L. 1989. *Proceedings of the Northern California's Herpetological Society's 1989 Conference on Captive Propagation and Husbandry of Reptiles and Amphibians.*

Graham, R. W. 1992. Late Pleistocene faunal changes (pp. 76-91) *in* Peters, R., and L. E. Lovejoy., eds., *Global Warming and Biological Diversity*. Yale University Press, New Haven, London.

Grant, T. R. 1982. Food of the Platypus, *Ornithorhynchus anatinus*. *Australian Mammalogy* 5(3-4): 235-6.

Green, C. 1977. *Stable Management Explained*. Arco Publishing Co., New York.

Greene, H. W. 1989. Agonistic behavior by three-toed sloths, *Bradypus variegatus*. *Biotropica* 21(4): 369-372.

Greenhall, A. M. 1988. Feeding behavior (pp. 111-131) *in* Greenhall, A. M., and U. Schmidt, eds., *Natural History of Vampire Bats*. CRC Press, Boca Raton, Florida.

Greenhill, B. 1976. *Archaeology of the Boat*. Adam and Charles Black, London.

Greenough, P. R., MacCallum, F. J., and A. D. Weaver. 1981. *Lameness in Cattle*. J. B. Lippincott, Philadelphia, Toronto.

Greer, G. E. 1916. An underground mine stable. *Coal Age* 9(24): 998-9.

Griffith, R. W. 1974. Environment and salinity tolerance in the genus *Fundulus*. *Copeia* 1974(2): 319-331.

Griffith, B., Scott, J. M., Carpenter, J. W., and C. Reed. 1989. Translocation as a species conservation tool: status and strategy. *Science* 245:477-480.

Griggs, R. F. 1919. The character of the eruption as indicated by its effects on nearby vegetation. *Ohio Journal of Science* 19(3): 173-209.

Grobbelaar, C. S. 1989. Crisis inbreeding: rapid evolution in large, ecologically intact populations. *Evolutionary Theory* 8:365-395.

Gross, R. S., and P. A. Werner. 1983. Relationships among flowering phenology, insect visitors, and seed-set of individuals: experimental studies on four co-occurring species of Goldenrod (*Solidago*: Compositae). *Ecological Monographs* 53(1): 95-117.

Groves, R. H., and J. J. Burdon. 1986. *Ecology of Biological Invasions*. Cambridge Univesity Press, Cambridge, London.

Grundey, K. 1980. *Tackling Farm Waste*. Farming Press Limited, Suffolk, England.

Grunfeld, D. I. 1972. *The Jewish Dietary Laws*. Soncino Press, London, Jerusalem.

Grzimek, B. 1967. *Four-Legged Australians*. Hill and Wang, New York.

Guggisberg, C. A. W. 1963. *Simba*. Chilton Books, Philadelphia, New York.

Gulland, F. M. D., Albon, S. D., Pemberton, J. M., Moorcroft, P. R., and T. H. Clutton-Brock. 1993. Parasite-associated polymorphism in a cyclic ungulate population. *Proceedings of the Royal Society of London* B254:7-13.

Gunn, C. R., and J. V. Dennis. 1976. *World Guide to Tropical Seeds and Fruits*. Demeter Press, New York.

Gunter, G. 1956a. A revised list of euryhalin fishes of North and Middle America. *American Midland Naturalist* 56(2): 345-354

Gunter, G. 1956b. Some relations of faunal distributions to salinity in estuarine waters. *Ecology* 37(3): 616-9.

Guppy, H. B. 1917. *Plants, Seeds, and Currents in the West Indies and Azores*. Williams and Norgate, London.

Guyer C. and M. A. Donnelly. 1990. Length-mass relationships among assemblages of tropical snakes in Costa Rica. *Journal of Tropical Ecology* 6: 65-76.

Hacker, J. B. 1990. Drift seeds and fruit on Raine Island, northern Great Barrier Reef, Australia. *Journal of Biogeography* 17:19-24.

Haffer, J. 1974. Avian Speciation in Tropical South America. *Publications of the Nuttall Ornithological Club* No. 14.

Hagenbeck, D. 1966. Report on the hand-rearing of an Indian Rhinoceros (*Rhinoceros unicornis*) at Hamburg Zoo. *International Zoo Yearbook* 6:82-87.

Hagstrom, T. 1981. Tadpoles of the common toad (*Bufo bufo* L.) found in brackish water. *Amphibia-Reptilia* 2:187-8.

Hall, G. 1970. Data to calculate heat and moisture balance (pp. 28-45) *in* Anon., *Ventilation Workshop for Confinement Swine and Beef*. University of Illinois (Urbana).

Hall, G. P. 1993. Management options for preserving genetic diversity in western Australian mammals. *Israel Journal of Zoology* 39:139-146.

Hallsson, S. V. 1964. The uses of seaweeds in Iceland (pp. 398-405) *in* A. D. DeVirville, and J. Feldmann, eds., *Proceedings of the Fourth International Seaweed Symposium*, MacMillan, New

Hamilton, P. H. 1986. Status of the leopard in Kenya (pp. 447-459) *in* Miller and Everett, *op. cit.*

Hamilton, I. M., and R. M. R. Barclay. 1994. Patterns of daily torpor and day-roost selection by male and female big brown bats (*Eptesicus fuscus*). *Canadian Journal of Zoology* 72: 744-9.

Hamilton, W. J., and R. L. Tilson. 1985. Fishing baboons at desert waterholes. *American Journal of Primatology* 8:255-7.

Hamilton, W. J., and J. O. Whitaker. 1979. *Mammals of Eastern United States*, (Second edition). Cornell University Press, New York.

Hand, S. J. 1990., *Care and Handling of Australian Native Mammals*. Surrey Beatty and Sons, Norton, New South Wales, Australia.

Haneda, Y. 1955. Luminous organisms of Japan and the Far East (pp. 335-385) *in* Johnson, F. H., ed., *The Luminescence of Biological Systems*. American Association for the Advancement of Science, Washington, D. C.

Hanski, I., and Y. Cambefort. 1991. Appendix A.12: Estimated dung production of nonvolant terrestrial mammals (pp. 375-6) *in* I. Hanski and Y. Cambefort (eds.) *Dung Beetle Ecology*. Princeton University Press, New Jersey.

Hardy, J. D. 1952. A concentration of juvenile spotted salamanders, *Amblystoma maculatum* (Shaw). *Copeia* 1952, No. 3, pp. 181-2.

Harkness, R. 1938. *The Baby Giant Panda*. Carrick and Evans, New York.

Harpending, H. C., Sherry, S. T., Rogers, A. R., and M. Stoneking. 1993. The genetic structure of human populations. *Current Anthropology* 34(4): 483-496.

Harris, J., ed., *Proceedings of the 1987 International Crane Workshop*. International Crane Foundation, Baraboo, Wisconsin.

Harrison, C. J. O. 1972. The space requirements of small birds. *Aviculture Magazine* 78(2): 49-50.

Harrison, R. G. 1990. Hybrid zones: windows on evolutionary process. *Oxford Surveys in Evolutionary Biology* 7:69-128.

Hart, E. B., McCollum, E. V., Steenbock, H., and G. C. Humphrey. 1919. Balanced rations from restricted sources. *Scientific American Supplement* No. 2256, p. 202.

Hartman R. C. 1970. Biological fly control works. *Poultry Digest* 29(340): 262-5.

Hartmann, H. T., Flocker, W. J., and A. M. Kofranek. 1981. *Plant Science*. Prentice-Hall Co., Englewood Cliffs, New Jersey.

Hartung, J., and V. R. Phillips. 1994. Control of gaseous emissions from livestock buildings and manure stores. *Journal of Agricultural Engineering Research* 57: 173-189.

Hasel, G. F. 1978. Some issues regarding the nature and universality of the Genesis Flood narrative. *Origins* 5(2)83-98.

Hastings, P. H. 1954. The use of nectar in feeding birds. *Aviculture Magazine* 60(6): 244.

Haswell. C. H. 1860. Strength of Materials. *Journal of the Franklin Institute (3rd Series)* 40:337-342.

Hauswirth, W. W., and P. J. Laipis. 1982. Mitochondrial DNA polymorphism in a maternal lineage of Holstein cows. *Proceedings of the National Academy of Sciences (USA)* 79:4686-4690.

Hauswirth, W. W., Van de Walle, M. J., Laipis, P. J., and P. D. Olivo. 1984. Heterogenous mitochondrial DNA D-loop sequences in bovine tissue. *Cell* 37:1001-7.

Hayes, M. H. 1969. *Stable Management and Exercise* (6th edition). Arco Publishing Co., New York.

Heatwole, H. 1976. *Reptile Ecology*. University of Queensland Press, St. Lucia.

Heatwole, H., and R. Levins. 1972. Biogeography of the Puerto Rican Bank: flotsam transport of terrestrial animals. *Ecology* 53(1): 112-117.

Hediger, H. 1968. From cage to territory (pp. 9-20) *in* Kirchshofer, *op. cit.*

Hedrick, P. W. 1994. Evolutionary genetics of the major histocompatibility complex. *American Naturalist* 143:945-964.

Hedrick, P. W. 1995. Elephant seals and the estimation of a population bottleneck. *Journal of Heredity* 86(3): 232-5.

Hedrick, P. W., and P. Miller. 1992. Conservation genetics: techniques and fundamentals. *Ecological Applications* 2(1): 30-46.

Hedrick, P. W., and P. Miller. 1994. Rare alleles, MHC and captive breeding (pp. 187-204) *in* Loeschcke et al., *op. cit.*

Helmuth, B., Viet, R. R., and R. Holberton. 1994. Long-distance dispersal of a subantarctic brooding bivalve (*Gaimardia trapesina*) by kelp-rafting. *Marine Biology* 120:421-6.

Heltzer, M., and D. Eitam. 1987. *Olive Oil in Antiquity*. Shemen Industries, Haifa, Israel.

Hempel, G. 1979. *Early Life History of Marine Fish*. University of Washington Press, Seattle, London.

Henderson, L. E. 1968. First record of the Emperor Penguin in New Zealand. *Notornis* 15(1)34-5.

Henderson R. W., Noeske-Hallin T., Crother B. I., and A. Schwartz. 1988. The diets of Hispaniolan Colubrid Snakes II: Prey Species, Prey size, and phylogeny. *Herpetologica* 44(1)55-70.

Hendrickson, R. 1983. *More Cunning than Man*. Dorset Press, New York.

Hengeveld, R. 1989. *Dynamics of Biological Invasions*. Chapman and Hall, London, New York.

Herbig-Sandreuter, A.,von. 1964. Neue beobachtung am venezolanischen Dreizehenfaultier, *Bradypus infuscatus flaccidus*, Gray 1849. *Acta Tropica* 21(1): 97-113.

Hervey, C. 1953. A feed lot for $15 a head. *Farm Journal* 77(April 1953)106.

Hewson, R. 1995. Use of salmonid carcasses by vertebrate scavengers. *Journal of Zoology (London)* 235:53-65.

Hickey, T. 1973. Automated Caging Systems (pp. 28-32) *in* Mohr, J. (ed). Symposium on Newer Developments in Animal Containment Systems/ Automated Animal Caging Systems. *Lab Animal* 2: No. 31.

Hickey, T. E. 1978. Automated Systems (pp. 191-5) *in* ILAR (Institute of Laboratory Animal Resources) (ed).) *Laboratory Animal Housing*. National Academy of Science, Washington, D.C.

Hill, A. V. S., Yates, S. N. R., Allsopp, C. E. M., Gupta, S., Gilbert, S. C., Lalvani, A., Aidoo, M., Davenport, M., and M. Plebanski. 1994. Human leukocyte antigens and natural selection by malaria. *Philosophical Transactions of the Royal Society of London* B346:379-385.

Hill, J. E., and J. D. Smith. 1984. *Bats: a Natural History*. University of Texas Press, Austin.

Hill, W. C. O. 1964. The maintenance of langurs (Colobidae) in captivity: experiences and some suggestions. *Folia Primatologica* 2:222-231.

Hillenius, W. J. 1994. Turbinates in Therapsids: Evidence for Late Permian origins of mammalian endothermy. *Evolution* 48(2): 207-229.

Hindar, K. 1994. Alternative life histories and genetic conservation (pp. 333-6) *in* Loeschcke, *op. cit.*

Hinton, H. E. 1951-2. A new Chironomid from Africa, the larva of which can be dehydrated without injury. *Proceedings of the Zoological Society of London* 121:371-380.

Hintz, H. F. 1983. *Horse Nutrition: a Practical Guide*. Arco Publishing Co., New York.

Hintz, H. F., and R. G. Loy. 1966. Effects of pelleting on the nutritive value of horse rations. *Journal of Animal Science* 25:1059-1062.

Hintz, H. F., Schryver, H. F., and M. Halbert. 1973. A note on the comparison of digestion by New World camels, sheep, and ponies. *Animal Production* 16:303-5.

Hirshfield, M. F., Feldmeth, C. R., and D. L. Soltz. 1980. Genetic changes in physiological tolerances of Amargosa pupfish (*Cyprinodon nevadensis*) populations. *Science* 27(4434): 999-1001.

Hitchcock, F. C. 1959. *"Saddle Up"*. Stanley Paul, London.

Hoese, H. D. 1960. Biotic changes in a bay associated with the end of a drought. *Limnology and Oceanography* 5:326-336.

Hoelzel, A. R., Halley, J., O'Brien, S. J., Campagna, C., Arnbom, T., LeBoef, B., Ralls, K., and G. A. Dover. 1993. Elephant seal genetic variation and the use of simulation models to investigate historical population bottlenecks. *Journal of Heredity* 84:443-9.

Hoke, J. 1976. *Discovering the World of the Three-toed Sloth*. Franklin Watts, New York.

Hoke, J. 1987. Oh, it's so nice to have a sloth around the house. *Smithsonian* 18(1): 88-99.

Holder, C. F. 1903. Where olives grow. *Scientific American* 88(12)209.

Holsheimer, J. P. 1981. Nutrition of birds in theory and practice (pp. 153-165) *in* Risser et al., *op. cit.*

Holter, P. 1983. Effect of earthworms on the disappearance of cattle droppings (pp. 49-57) *in* J. E. Satchell (ed.) *Earthworm Ecology*. Chapman and Hall, London, New York.

Hong, S. W., Na, S. S. A., Hyun, B. S., Hong, S. Y., Gong, D. S., Kang, K. J., Suh, S. H., Lee, K. H., and Y. G. Je. 1994. Safety Investigations of Noah's Ark in a Seaway. *Creation Ex Nihilo Technical Journal* 8(1): 26-36.

Hoosier, Van G. L., and W. C. Ladiges. 1984. Biology and diseases of hamsters (pp. 123-147) *in* Fox, J. G., Cohen, B. J., and F. M. Loew, eds., *Laboratory Animal Medicine*. Academic Press, Orlando, San Diego.

Hopkins, A. 1913. *Modern Farm Buildings*. McBride, Nast, and Co., New York.

Hopkins, C. S. 1990. Carnivorous and insectivorous bats (pp. 171-184) *in* Hand, *op. cit.*

Hopkinson, R. G., Petherbridge, P., and J. Longmore. 1966. *Daylighting*. Heinemann, London.

Horn, M. H. 1972. The amount of spece available for marine and freshwater fishes. *Fishery Bulletin (of the U. S. Department of Commerce)* 70(4): 1295-7.

Howard, D. J. 1993. Small populations, inbreeding, and speciation (pp. 118-142) *in* Thornhill, *op. cit.*

Howe, G. F. 1968. Seed germination, sea water, and plant survival in the Great Flood. *Creation Research Society Quarterly* 5(3): 105-112.

Howe, H. H. 1984. Constraints on the evolution of mutualisms. *American Naturalist* 123(6): 764-777.

Howe, H. H. 1986. Seed-dispersal by fruit-eating birds and mammals (pp. 123-189) *in* Murray, D. R., ed., *Seed Dispersal*. Academic Press, Sydney, Orlando.

Howell, A. B. 1920. Contribution to the life-history of the California Mastiff Bat. *Journal of Mammalogy* 1(3): 111-117.

Howes, J. R. 1966. On-site composting of poultry manure (pp. 68-9) *in* Anon., *Proceedings of the National Symposium on Animal Waste Management*. ASAE (American Society of Agricultural Engineers) Publication No. SP-0366.

Hubbard, R. C. 1968. Husbandry and laboratory care of pinnipeds (pp. 299-358) *in* Harrison, J., ed., *The Behaviour and Physiology of Pinnipeds*. Appleton-Century Crofts, New York.

Hubbs, C. L. 1955. Hybridization between fish species in nature. *Systematic Zoology* 4(1): 1-20.

Hudson, R. 1965. The spread of the Collared Dove in Britain and Ireland. *British Birds* 58(4): 105-139.

Hudson, R. 1972. Collared Doves in Britain and Ireland during 1965-70. *British Birds* 65:139-155.

Huey, R. B., and J. G. Kingsolver. 1993. Evolution of resistance to high temperature in ectotherms. *American Naturalist* 142 (Supplement), pp. 521-546.

Huff, T. A. 1980. Captive propagation of the subfamily Boinae with emphasis on the genus *Epicrates* (pp. 125-134) *in* Murphy and Collins, *op. cit.*

Hughes, A. L. 1991. MHC polymorphisms and the design of captive breeding programs. *Conservation Biology* 5(2): 248-251.

Hughes, A. l., Hughes, M. K., and D. I. Watkins. 1993. Contrasting roles of interallelic recombination at the *HLA-A* and *HLA-B* loci. *Genetics* 133:669-680.

Hughes, A. L., Hughes, M. K., Howell, C. Y., and M. Nei. 1994. Natural selection at the class II major histocompatibility complex loci of mammals. *Philosophical Transactions of the Royal Society of London* B346:359-367.

Hughes, L. 1989. The World of Wood (pp. 144-184) *in* Walker, A., ed., *The Encyclopedia of Wood*. Facts on File, Oxford, New York.

Hulet, W. H., Masel, S. J., Jodry, L. H., and R. G. Wehr. 1967. The role of calcium in the survival of marine teleosts in dilute sea water. *Bulletin of Marine Science* 17(3): 677-688.

Hume, I. D., and C. Esson. 1993. Nutrients, antinutrients, and leaf selection bym captive koalas (*Phascolarctos cinereus*). *Australian Journal of Zoology* 41:379-392.

Humphrey-Smith, I. 1982. Survival of captive Microchiroptera feeding on prey attracted to artificial lights (pp. 164-172) *in* Evans. 1982. *op. cit.*

Hurd, L. M., and I. R. Bierly. 1947. Saving steps and time in caring for hens. *Poultry Science* 26(1): 25-29.

Huttermann, A. 1991. The ecological message of the Torah: a biologist's interpretation of the Mosaic Law. *Israel Journal of Botany* 40:183-195.

IES (Illumination Engineering Society). 1950. *Recommended Practice of Daylighting*. New York.

ILAR (Institute of Laboratory Animal Resources). 1978. *Guide for the Care and Use of Laboratory Animals*. NIH (National Institutes for Health) Publication Number 78-23, Bethesda, Maryland.

Immelman, K. 1973. Role of the environment in reproduction as source of "predictive" information (pp. 121-147) *in* Farner, D. S., ed., *Breeding Biology of Birds*. National Academy of Sciences, Washington, D. C.

Ingram, J. S., and J. R. O. Humphries. 1972. Cassava storage—a review. *Tropical Science* 14(2): 131-148.

Inns, F. M. 1980. Animal power in agricultural production systems. *World Animal Review* 34:2-10.

Inskipp, J. P. 1975. *All Heaven in a Rage: a Study into the Importation of Birds into the United Kingdom*. Royal Society for the Protection of Birds, London.

Irvine, G. 1992. Koalas all over—down under. *Good Housekeeping* 215(2): 96.

Iverson, J. B. 1979. Behavior and ecology of the rock Iguana *Cyclura carinata*. *Bulletin of the Florida State Museum (Biological Sciences)* 24(3): 175-358.

Jackson, G. G. 1927. *The Ship under Steam*. T. Fisher Unwin Limited, London.

Jacobs, M. R. 1955. *Growth Habits of the Eucalypts*. Australian Department of the Interior.

Jaeger, E. C. 1948. Does the poor-will "hibernate"? *Condor* 50(1): 45-6.

Jaenike, J. 1993. Rapid evolution of host specificity in a parasitic nematode. *Evolutionary Ecology* 7:103-108.

James, P., and N. Thorpe. 1994. *Ancient Inventions*. Ballantine Books, New York.

Jameson, R. E. 1965. Food consumption of hibernating and nonhibernating *Citellus lateralis*. *Journal of Mammalogy* 46(4): 634-640/

Janis, C. M. and M. Carrano. 1992. Scaling of reproductive turnover in archosaurs and mammals: why are large terrestrial mammals so rare? *Annales Zoologica Fennici* 28:201-216.

Janson, K. 1987. Genetic drift in small and recently founded populations of the marine snail *Littorina saxatalis*. *Heredity* 58:31-7.

Janssens, P. A. 1964. The metabolism of the aestivating African lungfish. *Comparative Biochemistry and Physiology* 11:105-117.

Janzen, D. H., and P. S. Martin. 1982. Neotropical anachronisms: the fruits the gomphotheres ate. *Science* 215:19-27.

Jedele, D. G. 1967. Exposure factor curves applied to swine-building ventilation design. *Transactions of the ASAE (American Society of Agricultural Engineers)* 10:619-621.

Jelley, J. V. 1989. Sea waves: their nature, behaviour, and practical importance. *Endeavour* 13(4): 148-156.

Jenkins, F. A. and D. M. Walsh. 1993. An early caecilian with limbs. *Nature* 365: 246-250.

Jennings, L. F. 1974. Housing requirements—large animals (pp. 87-94) *in* Melby and Altman, *op. cit.*

Jensen, L. B. 1949. *Meat and Meat Foods*. Ronald Press Co., New York.

Jett, S. C. 1971. Diffusion versus independent development: the bases of controversy (pp. 5-54) *in* Riley, C. L., Kelley, J. C., Pennington, C. W., and R. L. Rands., eds., *Man Across the Sea*.

Jewell, P. 1978. Successful start for the seaweed eaters. *Oryx* 14(3): 204-5.

Jewett, S. G., and H. W. Dobyns. 1929. The Virginia opossum in Oregon. *Journal of Mammalogy* 10(4): 351.

Jinchu, H., and W. Fuwen. 1990. Development and progress of breeding and rearing Giant Pandas in captivity within China (pp. 322-5) *in* Jinchu, H., ed., *Research and Progress in Biology of the Giant Panda*. Sichuan Publishing House, Beijing.

Job, S. V. 1959. The metabolism of *Plotosus anguillaris* (Bloch) in various concentrations in various concentrations of salt and oxygen in the medium. *Indian Academy of Sciences Proceedings* 50B:267-288.

Johnels, A. G., and G. S. O. Svensson. 1955. On the biology of *Protopterus annectens*. *Arkiv for Zoologi* (Band 7) 7:131-164.

Johnson, A. 1991. *Factory Farming*. Blackwell Scientific Publishing Company, Oxford, England.

Johnson, D. L. 1978. The origin of island mammoths and the Quaternary land bridge history of the North Channel Islands, California. *Quaternary Research* 10:204-225.

Johnson, G. E. 1931. Hibernation in mammals. *Quarterly Review of Biology* 6(4): 439-461.

Johnson, R. B. 1986. Human disease and evolution of pathogen virulence. *Journal of Theoretical Biology* 122(1):19-24.

Johnson, H. S., and S. F. Ridlen. 1972. Gases and odors from poultry manure. *Poultry Digest* 31(364): 295-6.

Johnson, K. G., Wei, W., Reed, D. G., and H. Jinchu. 1993. Food habits of Asiatic Leopards (*Panthera fusea*) in Wolong Reserve, Sichuan, China. *Journal of Mammalogy* 74(3): 646-650.

Johnson, R. F., and R. K. Selander. 1964. House sparrows: rapid evolution of races in North America. *Science* 144:545-550.

Johnstone, P. 1980. *The Sea-craft of Prehistory*. Harvard University Press, Cambridge, Massachussetts.

Jokiel, P. L. 1989. Rafting of reef corals and other organisms at Kwajalein Atoll. *Marine Biology* 101:483-493.

Jokiel, P. L. 1990a. Transport of reef corals into the Great Barrier Reef. *Nature* 347: 665-7.

Jokiel, P. L. 1990b. Long-distance dispersal by rafting: reemergence of an old hypothesis. *Endeavour* 14(2): 66-73.

Jones, A. J. 1972a. A general analysis of the Biblical "kind" (*min*). *Creation Research Society Quarterly* 9:(2): 53-57.

Jones, A. J. 1972b. Boundaries of the min: an analysis of the Mosaic lists of clean and unclean animals. *Creation Research Society Quarterly* 9:(2): 114-123.

Jones, A. J. 1973. How many animals on the Ark? *Creation Research Society Quarterly* 10:(2): 102-108.

Jones, A. J. 1982. The genetic integrity of the "kinds" (baramins): a working hypothesis. *Creation Research Society Quarterly* 19:(1): 13-18.

Jones, B. 1987. Death of South West Africa's/Namibia's coastal lions. *African Wildlife* 41(6): 297.

Jones, D. M. 1985. The care of exotic animals. *Symposium of the Zoological Society of London* 54:89-101.

Jones, P. H. 1969. Theory and future outlook of animal waste treatment in Canada and the United States (pp. 23-36) *in* Anon., *Animal Waste Management*. Cornell University Press, New York.

Jones, R. M., and S. S. Hillman. 1978. Salinity adaptations in the salamander *Batrachoseps*. *Journal of Experimental Biology* 76: 1-10.

Jordan, P. A., Shelton, P. C., and D. L. Allen. 1967. Isle Royale Wolf Population. American Zoologist 7:233-252.

Joya, M. 1912. The lore and legend of Japanese fire-flies. *Strand Magazine* 44(259): 72-7.

Junk, W. J. 1973. Investigations on the ecology and production-biology of the "floating meadows" (*Paspalo-echinochloetum*) on the middle Amazon. *Amazoniana* 4(1): 9-102.

Jury, S. H., Kinnison, M. T., Howell, W. H., and W. H. Watson III. 1994. The behavior of lobsters in response to reduced salinity. *Journal of Experimental Marine Biology* 180:23-37.

Kadlec, J. E., Morris, W. H. M., Bache, D., Crawford, R., Jones, H., Pickett, R., Judge, M. D., Dale, A. C., Peart, R. M., Friday, W. H., Haelterman, E. O, and P. N. Boehm. 1966. A comparison of swine growing-finishing building systems. *Purdue University Agricultural Experiment Station Research Bulletin* No. 816.

Kaplan, H. M. 1974. Reptiles in laboratory animal science (pp. 285-406) *in* Melby and Altman, *op. cit.*

Kappen, I., and E. I. Friedmann. 1983. Ecophysiology of lichens in the dry valleys of southern Victoria Land, Antarctica. *Polar Biology* 1:227-232.

Karl, S. A., Bowen, B. W., and J. C. Avise. 1995. Hybridization among the ancient mariners: characterization of marine turtle hybrids with molecular genetic assays. *Journal of Heredity* 86:265-8.

Karoly, K. 1992. Pollinator limitation in the facultatively autogamous annual *Lupinus nanus* (Leguminosae). *American Journal of Botany* 79(1): 49-56.

Karpevich, A. F. 1977. Physiological principles of acclimatization of aquatic organisms (pp. 28-35) *in* Karzinkin, *op. cit.*

Karzinkin, G. S. 1977. *Metabolism and Biochemistry of Fishes*. Indian National Scientific Documentation Center, New Delhi.

Kasahara, M., Klein, D., Fan, W., and J. Gutnecht. 1990. Evolution of the class II major histocompatibility complex alleles in higher primates. *Immunological Reviews* 113:65-82.

Katz, U. 1973. Studies on the adaptation of the toad *Bufo viridis* to high salinities: oxygen consumption, plasma concentration and water content of the tisues. *Journal of Experimental Biology* 58: 785-796.

Kaufman, J., Volk, H., and H.-J. Wallny. 1995. A "minimal essential Mhc" and an "unrecognized Mhc": two extremes in selection for polymorphism. *Immunological Reviews* 143:63-88.

Kayser, Ch. 1961. *The Physiology of Natural Hibernation*. Pergamon Press, Oxford, New York.

Kear, J. 1975. Breeding of endangered wildfowl as an aid to their survival (pp. 49-61) *in* Martin, R. D., ed., *Breeding Endangered Species in Captivity*. Academic Press, London, New York.

Keeling, 1984. *Where the Lion Trod: a Study of Forgotten Zoological Gardens*. Clam Publications, Surrey, England.

Kellems, R. O., Miner, J. R., and D. C. Church. 1979. Effect of ration, waste composition, and length of storage on the volatilization of ammonia, hydrogen sulfide, and odors from cattle waste. *Journal of Animal Science* 48(3): 436-445.

Kelly, C. F., Bond, T. E., and N. R. Ittner. 1953. Engineering design of a livestock physical plant. *Agricultural Engineering* 34(9): 6-1-7.

Kemp T. S. 1982. *Mammal-like Reptiles and the Origin of Mammals*. Academic Press, London, New York.

Kendall, A. W., and F. J. Schwartz. 1968. Lethal temperature and salinity tolerances of the White Catfish Ictalurus catus, from the Patuxent River, Maryland. *Chesapeake Science* 9(2): 103-108.

Kennard, D. C., and V. D. Chamberlin. 1938. Time and labor saving equipment for the laying house. *Ohio Agricultural Experiment Station (Wooster) Special Circular* No. 51.

Kerley, G. H. I. 1983. Relative population sizes and trends, and hybridization of fur seals Arctocephalus tropicalis and *A. gazella* at the Prince Edward Islands, Southern Ocean. *South African Journal of Zoology* 18:388-392.

Kerr, G. R. 1972. Nutritional requirements of subhuman primates. *Physiological Reviews* 52(2)415-467.

Keup, L., and J. Bayless. 1964. Fish distribution at varying salinities in Neuse River Basin, North Carolina. *Chesapeake Science* 5(3): 119-123.

Keymer, I. F. 1972. The unsuitability of non-domesticated animals as pets. *Veterinary Record* 91:378-381.

Khlebovich, V. V. 1969. Aspects of animal evolution related to critical salinity and internal state. *Marine Biology* 2:338-345.

Khlebovich, V. V., and V. P. Velikanov. 1982. Osmotic and ionic regulation in Green Toad (*Bufo viridis* Laur.) from Sarikamish Lake. *Soviet Journal of Ecology* 12(4): 228-231.

Kidd, F. 1914. The controlling influence of carbon dioxide in the maturation, dormancy, and germination of seeds, Parts I and II. *Proceedings of the Royal Society of London* B:408-421 snf 609, 625.

Kielan-Jaworowska, Z., Bown, T. M., and J. A. Lillegraven. 1979. Eutheria (pp. 221-258) *in* Lillegraven, J., Kielan-Jaworowska Z., and W. A. Clemens, eds., *Mesozoic Mammals*. University of California Press, Berkeley.

Kien, T. 1984. Breeding of cobras in Vietnam. *Acta Zoologica et Pathologica Antverpiensia* 78:215-8.

Kilby, J. D. 1955. The fishes of two Gulf Coast marsh areas of Florida. *Tulane Studies in Zoology* 2(8): 175-247.

Kiley-Worthington, M. 1990. *Animals in Circuses and Zoos*. Little Eco-Farms, Essex, England.

Kimbark, J. 1968. Deep manure pit kills cage house odors. *Poultry Digest* 27(315): 254-5.

King, G. M., and B. S. Rubidge. 1993. A taxonomic revision of small dicynodonts with postcanine teeth. *Zoological Journal of the Linnean Society* 107: 131-154.

King, M. W., and E. H. Roberts. Maintenance of recalcitrant seeds in storage (pp. 53-89) *in* Chin, H. F., and E. H. Roberts, eds., *Recalcitrant Crop Seeds*. Tropical Press, Kuala Lumpur, Malaysia.

Kinne, O. 1964. The effects of temperature and salinity on marine and brackish water animals. *Oceanography and Marine Biology Annual Review* 2:281-339.

Kirchshofer, R. 1968. *The World of Zoos*. Viking Press, New York.

Kirkwood, J. K. 1991. Energy requirements for maintenance and growth of wild mammals, birds, and reptiles in captivity. *Journal of Nutrition* 121: S29-S34.

Kirkwood, J. K., and K. Stathatos. 1992. *Biology, Rearing, and Care of Young Primates*. Oxford University Press, Oxford, New York, Tokyo.

Kirmiz, J. P. 1962. *Adaptation of Biota to Desert Environment*. Butterworth's, London.

Kivilan, A., and R. S. Bandurski. 1973. The ninety-year period for Dr. Beal's seed viability experiment. *American Journal of Botany* 60(2): 140-5.

Kivilan, A., and R. S. Bandurski. 1981. The one hundred-year period for Dr. Beal's seed viability experiment. *American Journal of Botany* 68(9): 1290-2.

Kjorsvik, E., Davenport, J., and S. Lonning. 1984. Osmotic changes during the development of eggs and larvae of the lumpsucker *Cyclopterus lumpus* L. *Journal of Fish Biology* 24:311-321.

Klein, J. 1986. *Natural History of the Major Histocompatibility Complex*. John Wiley and Sons, New York, Chichester.

Klein, J. 1987. Origin of major histocompatibility complex polymorphism: the trans-species hypothesis. *Human Immunology* 19:155-162.

Klein, J., and C. O'hUigin. 1995. Class II B Mhc motifs in an evolutionary perspective. *Immunological Reviews* 143:89-111.

Klein, J., O'hUigin, C., Figueroa, F., Mayer, W., E., and D. Klein. 1993. Different modes of *MHC* evolution in primates. *Molecular Biology and Evolution* 10(1): 48-59.

Klein, J., Takahata, N., and F. J. Ayala. 1993. MHC polymorphism and human origins. *Scientific American* 269(6): 78-83.

Klerks, P. L., and J. S. Levinton. 1989. Rapid evolution of metal resistance in a benthic oligochaete inhabiting a metal-polluted site. *Biological Bulletin* 176:135-141.

Knox, C. M., Hattingh, J., and J. P. Raath. 1992. Physiological responses of boma-confined impala to repeated capture. *South African Journal of Wildlife Research* 22(1): 1-6.

Koop, B. F., and L. Hood. 1994. Striking sequence similarity over almost 100 kilobases of human and mouse T-cell receptor DNA. *Nature Genetics* 7:48-53.

Kornegay, J. R., Schilling, J. W., and A. C. Wilson. 1994. Molecular adaptation of a leaf-eating bird stomach lysozome of the hoatzin. *Molecular Biology and Evolution* 11(6): 921-8.

Kornfield, I. L. 1978. Evidence for rapid speciation in African cichlid fishes. *Experientia* 34:(3): 335-336.

Kornhonen, H., Harri, M., and E. Hohtola. 1985. Response to cold in the blue fox and raccoon dog as evaluated by metabolism, heart rate, and muscular shivering: a re-evaluation. *Comparative Biochemistry and Physiology* 82A(4): 959-964.

Kowalski, Z. 1969. A note on bear hybrids. *International Zoo Yearbook* 8:89.

Kristoffersson, R., and A. Sivo. 1964. Hibernation of the hedgehog (*Erinaceus europaeus*). *Annales Academiae Scientiarum Fennicae* Series A, IV, 80:1-22.

Krogh, A. 1939. *Osmotic Regulation in Aquatic Animals*. Cambridge University Press, Cambridge.

Kronenberg, M., Brines, R., and J. Kaufman. 1994. MHC evolution: a long term investment in defense. *Immunology Today* 15(1): 4-6.

Kruesi, W. K. 1985. *The Sheep Raiser's Manual*. Williamson Publishing Co., Vermont.

Krutzsch, P. H., and S. E. Sulkin. 1958. The laboratory care of the Mexican free-tailed bat. *Journal of Mammalogy* 39(2): 262-5.

Krzanowski, A. 1985. Timber used as food by bats. *Bat Research News* 26(4): 47.

Kurta, A. 1990. Torpor patterns in food-deprived *Myotis lucifugus* (Chiroptera: Vespertilionidae) under simulated roost conditions. *Canadian Journal of Zoology* 69:255-7.

Lack, D. 1954. *The Natural Regulation of Animal Numbers*. Clarendon Press, Oxford.

Lack, D. 1966. *Population Studies of Birds*. Clarendon Press, Oxford.

Lahlou, B., Henderson, I. W., and W. H. Sawyer. 1969. Sodium exchanges in goldfish (*Carassius auratus L.*) adapted to a hypertonic saline solution. *Comparative Biochemistry and Physiology* 28:1427-1433.

Lambert, W. D. 1991. Altriciality and its implications for dinosaur thermoenergetic physiology. *Neues Jahrbuch fur Geologie und Palaontologie Abhandlungen* 182(1): 73-84.

Lammerts, W. E. 1975. Concerning the natural vs. the supernatural: a reply to Henry M. Morris. *Creation Research Society Quarterly* 12(1): 75-77.

Lande, R. 1980. Genetic variation and phenotypic evolution during allopatric speciation. *American Naturalist* 116(4): 463-479.

Lande, R. 1988. Genetics and demography in biological conservation. *Science* 241:1455-1460.

Landry, S. O. 1970. The Rodentia as Omnivores. *Quarterly Review of Biology* 45:351-372.

Langerwerf, B. A. W. A. 1980. The successful breeding of lizards from temperate regions (pp. 37-46) *in* Townson, S., Millichamp, N. J., Lucas, D. G. D., and A. J. Millwood, eds. *The Care and Breeding of Captive Reptiles*. British Herpetological Society.

Langerwerf, B. 1984. Techniques for large-scale breeding of lizards from temperate climates in greenhouse enclosures (Breeding many species of lizards in captivity, aiming the maintenance of populations of each species outside their natural habitat). *Acta Zoologica et Pathologica Antverpiensia* 78:163-176.

Lawler, S. H., Sussman, R. W., and L. L. Taylor. 1995. Mitochondrial DNA of the Mauritian macaques (*Macaca fascicularis*): an example of the founder effect. *American Journal of Physical Anthropology* 96:133-141.

Laws, R. M., Parker, I. S. C., and R. C. B. Johnstone. 1975. *Elephants and their Habitats*. Clarendon Press, Oxford.

Lawson G. H. K., and J. V. S. McAllister. 1966. Toxic gases from slurry. *Veterinary Record* 79(7): 274.

Layne, J. N. 1958. Notes on mammals of southern Illinois. *American Midland Naturalist* 60(1): 219-254.

Leberg, P. L. 1992. Effects of population bottlenecks on genetic diversity as measured by allozyme electrophoresis. *Evolution* 46(2)477-494.

Leck, M. A., Parker, V. T., and R. L. Simpson. 1989. *Ecology of Soil Seed Banks*. Academic Press, San Diego, New York.

Lee, K. E. 1985. *Earthworms*. Academic Press, Sydney, Orlando.

Lee, A. K., and F. N. Carrick. 1989. Phascolarctidae (pp. 740-754) *in* Anon., 1989. *Fauna of Australia*, Volume 1B, Australian Government Publishing Service, Canberra.

Lee, A. K., and P. Martin. 1988. *The Koala: a Natural History*. New South Wales University Press, Kerrington, Australia.

Lee, A. K., and E. H. Mercer. 1967. Cocoon surrounding desert-dwelling frogs. *Science* 157:87-8.

Lee, D. S., and M. K. Clark. 1993. Arizona's Night Visitors. *Bats* 11(2): 3-5.

Lekule, F. P., Mtenga, L. A., and A. Just. 1988. Total replacement of cereals by cassava and rice polishings in diets of growing-finishing pigs. *Tropical Agriculture* 65(4): 321-4.

Leopold, A. 1933. *Game Management*. Charles Scribner's Sons, New York.

Lesel, R., and P. Debrenne. 1975. Introducing animals to Iles Kerguelen. *Polar Record* 17(110): 485-494.

Leslie, R. F. 1970. *Wild Pets*. Crown Publishers, New York.

Lester, L. P., and R. G. Bohlin. 1989. *The Natural Limits to Biological Change*, 2nd Edition. Baker Book House, Michigan.

Levathes, L. 1994. *When China Ruled the Seas*. Simon and Schuster, New York, London.

Levi, W. M. 1957. *The Pigeon*. R. L. Bryan, Columbia, South Carolina.

Levi, W. M. 1984. *Making Pigeons Pay*. R. L. Bryan, Columbia, South Carolina.

Levi-Strauss, C. 1966. *The Savage Mind*. University of Chicago Press, Chicago and London.

Lewis, F. 1931. The koala, or Australian teddy bear. *National Georgaphic Magazine* 60:346-355.

Lewis, J. B. 1940. Mammals of Amelia County, Virginia. *Journal of Mammology* 21(4): 422-8

Lewis, L. D., Morris, M. L., and M. S. Hand. 1987. *Small Animal Clinical Nutrition III*. Mark Morris Associates, Kansas.

Liat, L. B. 1990. Venomous land snakes of Malaysia (pp. 387-417) *in* Gopalakrishnakone, P., and L. M. Chou, eds., *Snakes of Medical Importance (Asia-Pacific Region)*. National University of Singapore.

Licht, P., Feder, M. E., and S. E. Bledsoe. 1975. Salinity tolerance and osmoregulation in the salamander *Batrachoseps*. *Journal of Comparative Physiology* 102: 123-134.

Licht, P., Hoyer, H. E., and P. G. W. J. van Oordt. 1969. Influence of photoperiod and temperature on testicular recrudensence and body growth in the lizards, *Lacerta sicula* and *Lacerta muralis*. *Journal of Zoology (London)* 157:469-501.

Lindley, E. P. 1978. Forage conservation (pp. 29-196) *in* G. Williamson and W. J. A. Payne, eds., *An Introduction to Animal Husbandry in the Tropics*. Longman, London, New York.

Linhart, Y. B., and P. Feinsinger. 1980. Plant-hummingbird interactions: Effects of island size and degree of specialization on pollination. *Journal of Ecology* 68:745-760.

Lint, K. C., and A. M. Lint. 1981. *Diets for Birds in Captivity*. Blandford Press, Poole, Dorset, England.

Lister, A. M. 1989. Rapid dwarfing of red deer on Jersey in the Last Interglacial. *Nature* 342:539-542.

Litchfield, L. 1992. Panda politics. *Zoo Life* 3(3): 72-9.

Lithgow, K. A. 1982. Koalas feeding on Monterey Pine. *Victorian Naturalist* 99:259.

Littauer, M. A., and J. H. Crowell. 1979. *Wheeled Vehicles and Ridden Animals in the Ancient Near East*. Volume 1, Part 2B. E. J. Brill, Leiden.

Lockley, M. G. 1994. Dinosaur ontogeny and population structure (pp. 347-365) *in* Carpenter, K., Hirsch, K. F., and J. R. Horner, eds., *Dinosaur Eggs and Babies*. Cambridge University Press, Cambridge, New York.

Loehr, R. 1977. *Pollution Control for Agriculture*. Academic Press, New York.

Loeschcke, V., Tomiuk, J., and S. K. Jain. 1994. *Conservation Genetics*. Birkhauser Verlag, Basel, Switzerland.

Loeschcke, V., and J. Tomiuk. 1991. Epilogue (pp. 277-281) *in* Seitz and Loeschcke, *op. cit.*

Lomnicki, A. 1980. Regulation of population density due to individual differences and patchy environment. *Oikos* 35: 185-193.

Long, J. L. 1981. *Introduced Birds of the World*. Universe Books, New York.

Loosli, J. K. 1991. History of the development of animal nutrition (pp. 25-60) *in* Putnam, P. A., ed., *Handbook of Animal Science*, Academic Press, San Diego, New York.

Loosli, J. K., and L. R. McDowell. 1985. The role of ruminants in warm climates (pp. 1-19) *in* McDowell, L. R. (ed). *Nutrition of Grazing Ruminants in Warm Climates*. Academic Press, Orlando, San Diego.

Loreti, F. 1988. International Symposium on Vegetative Propagation of Woody Species. *Acta Horticulturae* No. 227/

Loudon, A. S. I. 1985. Lactation and neonatal survival of mammals. *Symposium of the Zoological Society of London* No. 54:183-207.

Loumbourdis, N. S., and A. Hailey. 1991. Food consumption of the lizard *Agama stellio stellio*. *Journal of Arid Environments* 21:91-7.

Lowe-McConnell, R. H. 1987. *Ecological studies in tropical fish communities*. Cambridge University Press, Cambridge, London, New York.

Ludington, D. C., Sobel, A. T., and B. Gormel. 1971. Control of odors through manure management. *Transactions of the ASAE (American Society of Agricultural Engineers)* 14(4): 771-4, 780.

Ludington, D. C., Sobel, A. T., and A. G. Hashimoto. 1971. Odors and gases liberated from diluted and undiluted chicken manure. *Transactions of the ASAE (American Society of Agricultural Engineers)* 14:855-9.

Luoma, J. R. 1987. *A Crowded Ark*. Houghton Mifflin Co., Boston.

Lyman, C. P., Willis, J. S., Malan, A., and L. C. H. Wang. 1982. *Hibernation and Torpor in Mammals and Birds*. Academic Press, New York, London.

Lynch, M. 1988. The rate of polygenic mutation. *Genetical Research* 51:137-148.

MacArthur, R. H. 1972. *Geographical Ecology*. Harper and Row, New York.

MacCluer, J. W., VandeBerg, J. L., Read, B., and O. A. Ryder. 1986. Pedigree analysis by computer simulation. *Zoo Biology* 5:147-160.

MacDonald, D. W. 1983. Predation on earthworms by terrestrial vertebrates (pp. 393-414) *in* Satchell, J. E., ed., *Earthworm Ecology*. Chapman and Hall, London, New York.

MacDonald, F. W., and H. R. Davis. 1966. BOD of captive wild animal wastes. *Water and Sewage Works* 113(2): 64-7.

MacDonald, G. A. 1972. *Volcanoes*. Prentice Hall, Englewood Cliffs, New Jersey.

Maceina, M. J., Nordlie, F. G., and J. V. Shireman. 1980. The influence of salinity on oxygen consumption and plasma electroytes in grass carp, *Ctenopharyngodon idella* Val. *Journal of Fish Biology* 16:613-619.

Madsen, D. B. 1989. A grasshopper in every pot. *Natural History* (July 1989) pp. 22-5.

Maier, F., and J. Page. 1990. *Zoo: the Modern Ark*. Facts on File Publications, New York.

Malhotra, A., and R. S. Thorpe. 1994. Parallels between island lizards suggests selection on mitochrondrial DNA and morphology. *Proceedings of the Royal Society of London* B257:37-42.

Mani, G. S. 1984. Darwinian theory of enzyme polymorphism (pp. 242-298) *in* Mani, G. S., ed., *Evolutionary Dynamics of Genetic Diversity*. Springer-Verlag, Berlin, Heidelberg, New York.

Mann, I. 1960. Meat handling in underdeveloped countries. *FAO (Food and Agriculture Organization of the UN) Development Paper* No. 70.

Mann, R. W., Bass, W. M., and L. Meadows. 1990. Time since death and decomposition of the human body: variables and observations in casc and experimental field studies. *Journal of Forensic Sciences* 35(1): 103-111.

Marcus, L. C. 1981. *Veterinary Biology and Medicine of Captive Amphibians and Reptiles*. Lea and Febiger, Philadelphia.

Markow, T., and 6 others. 1993. HLA polymorphism in the Havasupai: Evidence for balancing selection. *American Journal of Human Genetics* 53:943-952.

Markowitz, H. 1982. *Behavioral Enrichment in the Zoo*. Van Nostrand Reinhold, New York.

Martin, D. P. 1986. Infectious diseases (pp. 669-673) *in* Fowler, *op. cit*.

Martin, F. D. 1968. Intraspecific variation in osmotic abilities of *Cyprinodon variegatus* Lacepede from the Texas coast. *Ecology* 49(6): 1186-8.

Martin, R. D. 1975. General principles for breeding small mammals in captivity (pp. 143-167) *in* Martin, R. D., ed., *Breeding Endangered Species in Captivity*. Academic Press, London, New York.

Martin, T. J. 1990. Osmoregulation in three species of Ambassidae (Osteichthyes: Perciformes) from estuaries in Natal. *South African Journal of Zoology* 25(4): 229-234.

Martin, R. D., Rivers, J. P. W., and U. M. Cowgill. 1976. Culturing mealworms as food for animals in captivity. *International Zoo Yearbook* 16:63-70.

Maruyama, T., and P. A. Fuerst. 1985. Population bottlenecks and nonequilibrium models in population genetics. II. *Genetics* 111:675-689.

Masatomi, H. 1991. Population dynamics of red-crowned cranes in Hokkaido since the 1950's (pp. 297-9) *in* Harris, *op. cit.*

Mason, E. A. 1938. Determining sex in breeding birds. *Bird-Banding* 9:46-8.

Mason, C. F., and S. M. MacDonald. 1986. *Otters*. Cambridge University Press, Cambridge, London.

Mason, J., and P. Singer. 1990. *Animal Factories*. Harmony Books, New York.

Mason, R. T., Hoyt, R. F., Pannell, L. K., Wellner, E. F., and B. Demeter. 1991. Cage design and configuration for arboreal reptiles. *Laboratory Animal Science* 41(1): 84-5.

M'atee, W. L. 1925. Notes on drift, vegetable balls, and aquatic insects. *Ecology* 6(3): 288-302.

Mathews, R. K. 1971. *Wild Animals as Pets*. Doubleday and Co., New York.

Mathur, G. B. 1967. Anaerobic respiration in a Cyprinoid fish *Rasbora daniconius* (Ham). *Nature* 214:318-319.

Maton, A., Daelemans, J., and J. Lambrecht. 1985. *Housing of Animals: Construction and Equipment of Animal Houses*. Elsevier, Amsterdam, New York.

Matthew, W. D. 1915. Climate and evolution. *Annals of the New York Academy of Sciences* 24:171-318.

Matthews, W. J., and L. G. Hill. 1977. Tolerance of the red shiner, *Notropis lutrensis* (Cyprinidae) to environmental parameters. *Southwestern Naturalist* 22(1): 89-98.

Maurer, B. A., Brown, J. H., and R. R. Rusler. 1992. The micro and macro in body size evolution. *Evolution* 46(4): 939-953.

May, R. M. 1978. The dynamics and diversity of insect faunas (pp. 188-204) *in* Mound, L. A., and N. Waloff, eds. *Diversity of Insect Faunas*. Blackwell Scientific Publishing Company, Oxford, London.

May, R. M. 1991. The role of ecological theory in planning re-introduction of endangered species. *Symposium of the Zoological Society of London* No. 62: 145-163.

May, R. M. 1994. Conceptual aspects of the quantification of the extent of biological diversity. *Philosophical Transactions of the Royal Society of London* B345:13-20.

Mayer, W. E., and 5 others. 1988. Nucleotide sequences of chimpanzee MHC class I alleles: evidence for *trans*-species mode of evolution. *The EMBO Journal* 7(9): 2765-2774.

McAdam, S. N., and 6 others. 1994. A uniquely high level of recombination at the *HLA-B* locus. *Proceedings of the National Academy of Sciences (USA)* 91:5893-7.

McAdam, S. N., and 6 others. 1995. Chimpanzee MHC Class I *A* locus alleles are related to only one of the six families of human *A* locus alleles. *Journal of Immunology* 154:6421-9.

McAllister, D. E., and B. W. Coad. 1978. A test between relationships based on phenetic and cladistic taxonomic methods. *Canadian Journal of Zoology* 56:2198-2210.

McBane, S. 1993. *Keeping Horses*, Second Edition. Blackwell Scientific Publishing Company, London.

McBean, R. L., and L. Goldstein. 1970. Renal function during osmotic stress in the aquatic toad *Xenopus laevis*. *American Journal of Physiology* 219(4): 1115-1123.

McClure, F. A. 1943. Bamboo as panda food. *Journal of Mammology* 24(2)267-8.

McClure, M. R., and J. D. McEachran. 1992. Hybridization between *Prionotus alatus* and *P. paralatus* in the northern Gulf of Mexico (Pisces: Triglidae). *Copeia* 1992(4): 1039-1046.

McCracken, G. F. 1988. Who's endangered and what can we do? *Bats* 6(3)5-9.

McCullough, D. R. 1978. Case histories—the Tulk elk (pp. 173-185) *in* International Union for Conservation of Nature and Natural Resources, *Threatened Deer*. Morges, Switzerland.

McDonald, J. F. 1989. The potential evolutionary significance of retroviral-like transposable elements in peripheral populations (pp. 190-206) *in* Fontdevila, *op. cit.*

McDonald, J. F. 1995. Transposable elements: possible catalysts of organismic evolution. *TREE (Trends in Ecology and Evolution)* 10(3): 123-6.

McDowell, J. 1975. *More Evidence that Demands a Verdict*. Campus Crusade for Christ, San Bernardino, California.

McGee, H. 1984. *On Food and Cooking*. Charles Scribner's Sons, New York.

McGowan, C. 1984. *In the Beginning: a Scientist Shows Why the Creationists are Wrong*. Prometheus Books, New York.

McGrath, T. A., Shalter, M. D., Schleidt W., and P. Sarvella. 1972. Analysis of distress calls of chicken–pheasant hybrids. *Nature* 237:47-8.

McIntosh, J. S. 1992. Sauropoda (pp. 345-401) *in* Wieshampel et al., *op. cit.*

McKown, D. B. 1993. *The Mythmaker's Magic*. Prometheus Books, Buffalo, New York.

McLellan, B. N., and F. W. Hovey. 1995. The diet of grizzly bears in the Flathead River drainage of southeastern British Columbia. *Canadian Journal of Zoology* 73:704-712.

McWhirter, N. 1985. *Guinness 1985 Book of World Records*. Bantam Books, Toronto, New York.

Meagher, S., and T. E. Dowling. 1991. Hybridization between the Cyprinid fishes *Luxilus albeolus*, *L. cornutus*, and *L. cerasinus* with comments on the proposed hybrid origin of *L. albeolus*. *Copeia* 1991(4): 979-991.

Meier, B., Albignac, R., Peyrieras, A., Rumpler, Y., and P. Wright. 1987. A new species of *Hapalemur* (Primates) from South East Madagascar. *Folia Primatologica* 48:211-5.

Meijer, F. 1986. *A History of Seafaring in the Classical World*. Croom Helm, London, Sydney.

Melby, E. C., and N. H. Altman. 1974. *Handbook of Laboratory Animal Science*, Volume 1. CRC Press, Cleveland, Ohio.

Melland, F. 1938. *Elephants in Africa*. Country Life Ltd., London, New York.

Melville, E. G. K. 1994. *A Plague of Sheep*. Cambridge University Press, Cambridge.

Mencuccini, M., Fontanazza, G., and L. Baldoni. 1988. Effect of basal temperature cycles on rooting of olive cultivars (pp. 263-5) *in* Loreti, *op. cit.*

Mendelssohn, H. 1965. On the biology of the venomous snakes of Israel, II. *Israel Journal of Zoology* 14:185-212.

Menotti-Raymond, M., and S. J. O'Brien. 1993. Dating the genetic bottleneck of the African cheetah. *Proceedings of the National Academy os Sciences (USA)* 90:3172-6.

Mentzer, J. E., Hinkle., C. N., Jones, H. W., and J. E. Kadlec. 1969. A winter comparison of bedded and nonbedded open-front growing-finishing swine buildings. *Transactions of the ASAE (American Society of Agricultural Engineers)* 12:389-396.

Merenlender, A. M., Woodruff, D. S., Ryder, O. A., Kock, R., and J. Vahala. 1989. Allozyme variation and differentiation in African and Indian Rhinoceroses. *Journal of Heredity* 80:377-382.

Merola, M. 1994. A reassessment of homozygosity and the case for inbreeding depression in the Cheetah, *Acinonyx jubatus*: implications for conservation. *Conservation Biology* 8(4): 961-971.

Merrell, D. J. 1981. *Ecological Genetics*. University of Minnesota Press, Minneapolis.

Merrick, J. R. 1990. Freshwater fishes (pp. 7-15) *in* Hand, *op. cit.*

Merrien, J. 1954. *Lonely Voyagers*. G. P. Putnam's Sons, New York.

Mertens, R. von. 1968. Uber reptilienbastarde IV. *Senckenbergiana Biologia* 49(1): 1-12.

Merz, A. 1991. *Rhino*. Harper Collins Publishers, London, Glasgow.

Micklin, P. P. 1994. The Aral Sea Problem. *Proceedings of the Institution of Civil Engineers and Civil Engineering* 102:114-121.

Micol, T., and P. Jouventin. 1995. Restoration of Amsterdam Island, South Indian Ocean, following control of feral cattle. *Biological Conservation* 73:199-206.

Miller, E. C., and E. F. Hodges. 1970. One man feeds 5,000 cattle or 60,000 broilers. *Yearbook of Agriculture* (USA) for 1970.

Miller, P. S., and P. W. Hedrick. 1991. MHC polymorphism and the design of captive breeding programs: simple solutions are not the answer. *Conservation Biology* 5(4): 556-8.

Miller, S. D., and D. D. Everett. 1986. *Cats of the World*. National Wildlife Federation, Washington, D. C.

Mills, J. R. 1960. The largest Chinese junk and its displacement. *Mariner's Mirror* 46:147-8.

Mills, M. G. L. 1991. Conservation management of large carnivores in Africa. *Koedoe* 34(1): 81-90.

Minelli, A. 1993. *Biological Systematics*. Chapman and Hall, London.

Minnich, J. 1977. *The Earthworm Book*. Rodale Press, Pennsylvania.

Mitchell, A. 1990. *The Fragile South Pacific*. University of Texas Press, Austin.

Mitchell, B. L., Shenton, J. B., and J. C. M Uys. 1965. Predation on large mammals in the Kafue National Park, Zambia. *Zoologica Africana* 1(1): 297-318.

Mitchell, P. C. 1911. On longevity and relative viability in mammals and birds. *Proceedings of the Zoological Society of London* 1911:425-548.

Mitchell, P. C., and R. I. Pocock. 1907. On the feeding of serpents in captivity. *Proceedings of the Zoological Society of London* 1907:785-794.

Mitchell-Jones, A., J., Jefferies, D. J., Stebbings, R. E., and H. R. Arnold. 1986. Public concern about bats (Chiroptera) in Britain: an analysis of enquiries in 1982-3. *Biological Conservation* 36:315-328.

Mitton, J. B. 1993. Theory and data pertinent to the relationship between heterozygosity and fitness (pp. 17-41) *in* Thornhill, *op. cit.*

Mitton, J. B., and M. G. Raphael. 1990. Genetic variation in the marten, *Martes americana*. *Journal of Mammalogy* 71(2): 195-7.

Mobbs, A. J. 1982. *Hummingbirds*. Triplegate Ltd., Surrey, England.

Mohr, E. 1933. The muskrat, *Ondatra zibethica* (Linnaeus), in Europe. *Journal of Mammalogy* 14(1): 58-63.

Mollison, D. 1986. Modelling biological invasions: chance, explanation, prediction. *Philosophical Transactions of the Royal Society of London* B314:675-693.

Mondolfi, E., and R. Hoogesteijn. 1986. Notes on the biology and status of the Jaguar in Venezuela (pp. 85-125) *in* Miller and Everett, *op. cit.*

Monfort, S. L., Williamson, L. R., Wemmer, C. M., and D. E. Wildt. 1993. Intensive management of the Burmese brow-antlered deer *Cervus eldi thamin* for effective captive breeding and conservation. *International Zoo Yearbook* 32:44-56.

Monroe, B. L. 1991. *Ten-year index to the Auk (volumes 98-107), 1981-1990.* American Ornithologist's Union, Washington.

Montgomery, G. G., and M. E. Sunquist. 1975. Impact of sloths on neotropical forest energy flow and nutrient cycling (pp. 69-98) *in* Golley, F. B., and E. Medina, eds., *Tropical Ecological Systems.* Springer-Verlag, Berlin, Heidelberg, New York.

Montgomery, G. G., and M. E. Sunquist. 1978. Habitat selection and use by two-toed and three-toed sloths (pp. 329-359) *in* Montgomery, G. G., ed., *The Ecology of Arboreal Folivores.* Smithsonian Institution Press, Washington, D. C.

Montgomery, S. 1989. Operation Bicornis. *African Wildlife* 43(5): 229-233.

Mooney, H. A., and M. West. 1964. Photosynthetic acclimation of plants of diverse origin. *American Journal of Botany* 51(8): 825-7.

Moore, C. P., and J. H. Cock. 1985. Cassava forage silage as a feed source for Zebu calves in the tropics. *Tropical Agriculture* 62(2): 142-4.

Moore, D. E., and R. Smith. 1990. The red wolf as a model for carnivore re-introductions. *Symposium of the Zoological Society of London* 62:263-278.

Moore, J. A. 1949. Geographic variation of adaptive characters in *Rana pipiens* Schreber. *Evolution* 3(2): 1-24.

Moore, L. A. 1964. Symposium on forage utilization: nutritive value of forage as affected by physical form, part I. General principles involved with ruminants and effect of feeding pelleted or wafered forage to dairy cattle. *Journal of Animal Science* 23:230-8.

Moore, R. A. 1983. The impossible voyage of Noah's Ark. *Creation/Evolution* 11:1-43.

Moore, R. A. 1995. From Pentecostal Christianity to Agnosticism (pp. 275-282) *in* Babinski, E. T., ed., *Leaving the Fold: Testimonies of Former Fundamentalists.* Prometheus Books, New York.

Moreau, R. E. 1966. *The Bird Faunas of Africa and its Islands.* Academic Press, New York.

Morell, V. 1994. Serengeti's big cats going to the dogs. *Science* 264:1664.

Moreng, R. E., and J. S. Avens. 1985. *Poultry Science and Production.* Reston Publishing Co., Virginia.

Moriyama, E. N., and T. Gojobori. 1991. Molecular evolution of human and simian immunodeficiency viruses (pp. 291-301) in M. Kimura and N. Takahata, eds., *New Aspects of the Genetics of Molecular Evolution*. Japan Scientific Society Press, Tokyo.

Morris, H. M. 1976. *The Genesis Record*. Creation-Life Publishers, San Diego.

Morris, H. M. 1995. *The Defender's Bible*. Institute for Creation Research.

Morris, M. L. 1976. Prepared diets for zoo animals in the USA. *International Zoo Yearbook* 16:13-17.

Morris, R., and D. Morris. 1981. *The Giant Panda*. Penguin Books, England.

Morrison, A. 1947. The Chinese aviculturist. *Avicultural Magazine* 53(1): 1-3

Morrison, P., Rosenmann, M., and J. A. Estes. 1974. Metabolism and thermal regulation in the sea otter. *Physiological Zoology* 47:218-229.

Morrison, S. R., V. E. Mendel, and T. E. Bond. 1966. Sloping floors for beef-cattle feedlots (pp. 41-3) *in* ASAE. 1966., *op. cit.*

Morse, D. H. 1975. Ecological aspects of adaptive radiation in birds. *Biological Reviews* 50:167-214.

Morton, G. R. 1995. *Foundation, Fall, and Flood: A Harmonization of Genesis and Science*. DMD Publishers, Dallas, Texas.

Morton, J. F. 1971. The Wax Gourd, a year-round Florida vegetable with unusual keeping quality. *Proceedings of the Florida State Horticultural Society* 84:104-9.

Morton, S. R. 1980. Ecological correlates of caudal fat storage in small mammals. *Australian Mammalogy* 3:81-6.

Moss, C. 1992. *Echo of the Elephants*. William Morrow and Co., New York.

Mottershead, G. S. 1967. Penguin exhibit at Chester Zoo. *International Zoo Yearbook* 7:29.

Mowka, E. 1981. *The Seawater Manual*. Aquarium Systems Inc., Mentor, Ohio.

Mrosovsky, N., and K. C. Fisher. 1970. Sliding set points for body weight in ground squirrels during the hibernation season. *Canadian Journal of Zoology* 48:241-7.

Muehling, A. J. 1969. *Swine Housing and Waste Management*. University of Illinois (Urbana).

Muehling, A. J., and D. G. Jedele. 1964. A confinement swine building with partially slotted floors. *Agricultural Engineering* 45(3): 140-1, 144.

Muguerza, A. 1944. Various ways of propagating the olive. *Horticultural Abstracts* 14:8.

Mukherjee, S. K., and P. K. Majumder. 1973. Vegetative propagation of tropical and sub-tropical fruit crops. *ICAR (Indian Council of Agricultural Research) Technical Bulletin* No. 45.

Mullan, B., and G. Marvin. 1987. *Zoo Culture*. Weidenfeld and Nicolson, London.

Muller, K. A. 1976. Maintaining insectivorous bats in captivity. *International Zoo Yearbook* 16:32-38.

Muller, K. A., and L. J. Clayton. 1972. Maintaining and breeding owlet-nightjars *Aegotheles cristatus* at Sydney Zoo. *International Zoo Yearbook* 12:138-140.

Munsey, L. D. 1972. Salinity tolerance of the African pipid frog *Xenopus laevis*. *Copeia* 1972(3)584-6.

Murdoch, A. J., Roberts, E. H., and C. O. Goedert. 1989. A model for germination responses to alternating temperatures. *Annals of Botany* 63:97-111.

Murdoch, W. W., and A. Oaten. 1975. Predation and population stability. *Advances in Ecological Research* 9:1-131.

Murphy, J. B., and J. A. Campbell. 1987. Captive maintenance (pp. 165-182) *in* Seigel, R. A., Collins, J. T., and S. S. Novak., eds., *Snakes: Ecology and Evolutionary Biology*. MacMillan, New York, Toronto.

Murphy, J. B., and J. T. Collins. 1980. *Reproductive Biology and Diseases of Captive Reptiles*. SSAR (Society for the Study of Amphibians and Reptiles) Contributions to Herpetology No. 1.

Murrish, D. E. 1982. Acid-base balance in three species of Antarctic penguins exposed to thermal stress. *Physiological Zoology* 55(2): 137-143.

Myers, K., Parer, I., Wood, D., and B. D. Cooke. 1994. The rabbit in Australia (pp. 108-157) *in* Thompson, H. V., and C. M. King, eds., *The European Rabbit*. Oxford University Press, Oxford, New York.

Myers, N. 1985. The end of the lines. *Natural History*. 94(2): 2-12.

Naether, C. 1955. *Soft-Billed Birds*. All-pet Books, Inc., Wisconsin.

Naether, C. 1969. Understanding birds in captivity. *Avicultural Magazine* 75(1): 27-31.

Nagel, P. 1986. Die methode der arealsystemanalyse als beitrag zur rekonstruktion der landschaftsgenese im tropischen Africa. *Geomethodica* 11:145-176.

Magy, K. A. 1982. Energy requirements of free-living iguanid lizards (pp. 49-59) *in* G. M. Burghardt and A. S. Rand, eds., *Iguanas of the World*. Noyes Publications, New Jersey.

Nagy, K. A. 1987. Field metabolic rate and food requirement scaling in mammals and birds. *Ecological Monographs* 57(2): 111-128.

Nagy K. A., and C. C. Peterson. 1988. Scaling of water flux rate in animals. *University of California Publications in Zoology* No. 120.

Nakagawa, S. 1967. Penguin exhibit at Tokyo Zoo. *International Zoo Yearbook* 7:39-40.

NAS (National Academy of Sciences). 1973. *Nonhuman Primates: Standards and Guidelines*, 2nd Edition. Washington, D. C.

NAS (National Academy of Sciences). 1975. *Underexploited Tropical Plants with Promising Economic Value*. Washington, D. C.

Needham, J. 1962. *Science and Civilization in China*. Volume 4, Part 1. Cambridge University Press, England.

Needham, J. 1971. *Science and Civilization in China*. Volume 4, Part 3. Cambridge University Press, England.

Needham, J., and W. Ling. 1965. *Science and Civilization in China*. Volume 4, Part 2. Cambridge University Press, England.

Neel, J. V., and 6 others. 1986. The rate with which spontaneous mutation alters the electrophoretic mobility of polypeptides. *Proceedings of the National Academy of Sciences (USA)* 83:389-393.

Nei, M., Maruyama, T., and R. Chakraborty. 1975. The bottleneck effect and genetic variability in populations. *Evolution* 29(1): 1-10.

Neill, W. T. 1958. The occurrence of amphibians and reptiles in saltwater areas. *Bulletin of Marine Science of the Gulf and Caribbean* 8(1): 1-97.

Nelson, G. S. 1982. Carrion-feeding cannibalistic carnivores and human disease in Africa. *Symposium of the Zoological Society of London* 50:181-198.

Nelson, R. A. 1980. Protein and fat metabolism in hibernating bears. *Federation Proceedings* 39:2955-8.

Nelson, R. A.,, and five others. 1983. Behavior, biochemistry, and hibernation in black, grizzly, and polar bears. *Fifth International Conference on Bear Research and Management* 5:284-290.

Neubuser, H. 1968. The work of the zoo inspector (pp. 164-171) *in* Kirchshofer, *op. cit.*

Nevo, E., Filipucci, M. G., Redi,, C., Korol, A., and A. Beiles. 1994. Chromosomal speciation and adaptive radiation of mole rates in Asia Minor correlated with increased ecological stress. *Proceedings of the National Academy of Sciences (USA)* 91:8160-8164.

Newberne, P. M., and K. C. Hayes. 1979. Semipurified diets for nonhuman primates (pp. 99-119) *in* Hayes, K. C., *Primates in Nutrition Research*. Academic Press, New York, London.

Newcott, W. R. 1993. Lightning—nature's high-voltage spectacle. *National Geographic* 184(1): 83-103.

Newsome, A. E., and I. R. Noble. 1986. Ecological and physiological characters of invading species (pp. 1-20) *in* Groves and Burdon, *op. cit.*

Newton, G. L., Booram, C. V., Hale, O. M., and B. G. Mullinex. 1980. Effect of four types of floor slats on certain feet characteristics and performance of swine. *Journal of Animal Science* 50(1): 7-20.

Nichol, A. A. 1969. Culture and care of Arizona native cacti (pp. 205-7) *in* Benson, L., ed., *The Cacti of Arizona*, 3rd Edition, University of Arizona Press, Tucson.

Nichol, J. 1987. *The Animal Smugglers*. Facts on File Publications, New York, Oxford.

Niekerk, B. D. H. van. 1985. Advances in intensive ruminant nutrition. *South African Journal of Animal Science* 15(3): 63-71.

Nilsson, G. 1981. *The Bird Business*, 2nd Edition. Animal Welfare Institute, Washington, D. C.

Nordstrom, G. A., and J. B. McQuitty. 1976. Manure Gases in the Animal Environment. *Department of Agricultural Engineering (University of Alberta) Research Bulletin* 76-1.

Norton, P. M., Lawson, A. B., Henley, S. R., and G. Avery. 1986. Prey of leopards in four mountainous areas of south-western Cape Province. *South African Journal of Wildlife Research* 16: 47-52.

Norton, V. M., and K. B. Davis. 1977. Effect of abrupt change in the salinity of the environment on plasma electrolytes, urine volume, and electrolyte excretion in Channel Catfish, *Ictalurus punctatus. Comparative Biochemistry and Physiology 56A:425-431.*

Noton, N. H. 1982. *Farm Buildings*. College of Estate Management, Reading, England.

Nowak, R. M., and J. L. Paradiso, 1983. *Walker's Mammals of the World,* 4th Edition (Volume 1) John Hopkins University Press, Baltimore and London.

NRC (National Research Council). 1990. *Saline Agriculture*. National Academy Press, Washington, D. C.

NRC (National Research Council). 1991. *Microlivestock*. National Academy Press, Washington, D. C.

Oard, M. J. 1995. Polar dinosaurs and the Genesis Flood. *Creation Research Society Quarterly* 32(1): 47-56.

Oates, J. F. 1977. The Guereza and man (pp. 419-467) *in* Rainier, P., and G. H. Bourne, eds., *Primate Conservation*. Academic Press, New York, San Francisco.

Oberholtzer, J. W., and L. S. Hardin. 1945. Simplifying the work and management of hog production. *Purdue Agricultural Experiment Station Bulletin* 506.

O'Brien, H. R. 1953. Self-feed your silage. *Country Gentleman* 123(June 1953): 40.

O'Brien, S. J. 1994. Genetic and phylogenetic analyses of endangered species. *Annual Review of Genetics* 28:467-489.

O'Brien, S. J., and nine others. 1987. Evidence for African origins of founders of the Asiatic lion species survival plan. *Zoo Biology* 6:99-116.

Ocana, G., Rubinoff, I., Smythe, N., and D. Werner. 1988. Alternatives to destruction: research in Panama (pp. 370-7) *in* Wilson, E. O., and F. M. Peter. 1988. *Biodiversity*. National Academy Press, Washington, D. C.

O'Donovan, P. B., Chen, M. C., and P. K. Lee. 1972. Conservation methods and feeding value for ruminants of pineapple bran mixtures. *Tropical Agriculture* 49(2): 135-141.

O'hUigin, C. 1995. Quantifying the degree of convergence in primate Mhc-DRB genes. *Immunological Reviews* 143:123-140.

Ogilvie, M., and C. Ogilvie. 1986. *Flamingos*. Alan Sutton, New Hampshire.

O'Neill, D. H., and V. R. Phillips. 1991. A review of the control of odor nuisance from livestock buildings: Part I, Influence of the techniques for managing waste within the building. *Journal of Agricultural Engineering Research* 50:1-10.

Oliveira, M. E., Paillette, M., Rosa, H. D., and E. G. Crespo. 1991. A natural hybrid between *Hyla arborea* and *Hyla meridionalis* detected by mating calls. *Amphibia-Reptilia* 12:15-20.

Olivo, P. D., van de Walle, M. J., Laipis, P. J., and W. W. Hauswirth. 1983. Nucleotide sequence evidence for rapid genotypic shifts in the bovine mitochrondrial DNA D-loop. *Nature* 306:400-2.

Orr, R. T. 1954. Natural history of the pallid bat *Antrozous pallidus* (LeConte). *Proceedings of the California Academy of Sciences (4th Series)* 28(4): 165-246.

Orr, R. T. 1958. Keeping bats in captivity. *Journal of Mammalogy* 39(3): 339-344.

Orti, G., Bell, M., Reimchen, T. E., and A. Meyer. 1994. Global survey of mitochondrial DNA sequences in the threespine stickleback: evidence for recent migrations. *Evolution* 48(3): 608-622.

Orville, R. E., and D. W. Spencer. 1979. Global lightning flash frequency. *Monthly Weather Review* 107:934-943.

Osawa, R. 1993. Dietary preference of koalas, *Phascolarctos cinereus* (Marsupialia: Phascolarctidae) for *Eucalyptus* spp. with a specific reference to their simple sugar contents. *Australian Mammalogy* 16(1): 85-7.

Osburn, R. C. 1911. Notes on fur seal in captivity. *Zoological Society Bulletin* (of NY) 48:817-8.

Ostrander, C. E. 1971. Poultry waste handling systems. *Poultry Digest* 30(357): 529-532.

Overcash, M. R., F. J. Humenik, and J. R. Miner. 1983. *Livestock Waste Management*, Volume I. CRC Press, Baton Rouge, Louisiana.

Owen, J. 1983. *Cattle Feeding*. Farming Press Limited, Suffolk, England.

Owen R. B., Crossley R., Johnson T. C., Tweddle D., Kornfield I., Davison S., Eccles D. H., and D. E. Engstrom. 1990. Major low levels of Lake Malawi and their implications for speciation rates in cichlid fishes. *Proceedings of the Royal Society of London* B240:519-553.

Owens, M., and D. Owens. 1984. *Cry of the Kalahari*. Houghton, Mifflin and Co., Boston.

Padhye, A. D., and H. V. Ghate. 1992. Sodium chloride and potassium chloride tolerance of different stages of the frog, *Microhyla ornata*. *Herpetological Journal* 2:18-23.

Pahl, L. I., and I. D. Hume. 1990. Preferences for *Eucalyptus* species of the New England Tablelands and initial development of an artificial diet for koalas (pp. 123-128) *in* Lee, A. K., Handasyde, K. A., and G. D. Sanson, eds., *Biology of the Koala*. Surrey Beatty and Sons, Sydney, Australia.

Panati, C. 1987. *Extraordinary Origins of Everyday Things*. Harper & Row, New York.

Panwar, H. S., and W. A. Rodgers. 1986. The reintroduction of large cats into wildlife protected areas. *Indian Forester* 112(10): 939-944.

Parham, P., Adams, E. J., and K. L. Arnett. 1995. The origins of HLA-A, B, C polymorphism. *Immunological Reviews* 143:171-180.

Parin, N. V. 1984. Oceanic ichthyologeography: an attempt to review the distribution and origin of pelagic and bottom fishes outside continental shelves and neritic zones. *Archiv fur FischWissereiwissenschaft* 35(1): 5-41.

Parker, B. F. 1953. Nomographs and data for determining winter ventilating rates for poultry laying houses. *Agricultural Engineering* 34(10): 689-692, 708.

Parker, W. S., and W. S. Brown. 1974. Mortality and weight changes of Great Basin rattlesnakes (*Crotalus viridis*) at a hibernaculum in northern Utah. *Herpetologica* 30(3): 234-9.

Parkin, D. T., and S. R. Cole. 1985. Genetic differentiation and rates of evolution in some introduced populations of house sparrow *Passer domesticus* in Australia and New Zealand. *Biological Journal of the Linnean Society* 23(4):287-302.

Parks, R. R. 1950. Mechanized poultry feeding. *Agricultural Engineering* 31(1): 23-25.

Parrish, F. A., and R. B. Moffitt. 1993. Subsurface fish handling to limit decompression effects on deepwater species. *Marine Fisheries Review* 54(3): 29-32.

Parry, G. 1966. Osmotic adaptation in fishes. *Biological Reviews* 41:392-444.

Parsons, P. A. 1987. Features of colonizing animals: phenotypes and genotypes (pp. 133-154) *in* Gray, A. J., Crawley, M. J., and P. J. Edwards, eds, *Colonization, Succession, and Stability*. Blackwell Scientific Publishing Company, Oxford, London.

Pease, L. R. 1985. Diversity in H-2 genes encoding antigen-presenting molecules is generated by interactions between members of the major histocompatibility complex gene family. *Transplantation* 39(3): 227-231.

Peczkis, J. 1988. Predicting body-weight distribution of mammalian genera in families and orders. *Journal of Theoretical Biology* 132:509-510.

Peczkis, J. 1989. Trends in the description of extinct genera among mammalian orders. *Journal of Paleontology* 63(6): 947-950

Peczkis, J. 1995. Implications of body-mass estimates for dinosaurs. *Journal of Vertebrate Paleontology* 14(4): 520-533.

Peel, C. V. A. 1903. *The Zoological Gardens of Europe*. F. E. Robinson and Co., London.

Pengelley, E. C., and K. C. Fisher. 1963. The effect of temperature and photoperiod on the yearly hibernating behavior of captive golden-mantled ground squirrels (*Citellus lateralis tescorum*). *Canadian Journal of Zoology* 41:1103-1120.

Pengelley, E. C., and K. C. Fisher. 1968. Ability of the ground squirrel, *Citellus lateralis*, to be habituated to stimuli while in hibernation. *Journal of Mammalogy* 49(3): 561-2.

Pennycuik, P. R., and A. H. Reisner. 1990. The founding population: the effect of differences in the size, nature, and season of establishment on the subsequent dynamics of populations of house mice, *Mus musculus* L. *Australian Journal of Zoology* 38:479-492.

Perrins, C. M. 1985. The effect of man on the British avifauna (pp. 5-29) *in* Bunning, L. J., ed., *Proceedings of the Birds and Man Symposium*. Witwatersrand Bird Club, Johannesburg.

Perry, D. A., and J. G. Harrison. 1970. The deleterious effect of water and low temperature on germination of pea seed. *Journal of Experimental Botany* 21(67): 504-512.

Peters, F. E., and P. A. Wills. 1956. Dried breadfruit. *Nature* 178:1252.

Peters, R. H. 1983. *The Ecological Implications of Body Size*. Cambridge University Press, Cambridge, London.

Peterson, R. S., LeBoeuf, B. J., and R. L. DeLong. 1968. Fur seals from the Bering Sea breeding in California. *Nature* 219:899-901.

Petter, J. J. 1975. Breeding of Malagasy lemurs in captivity (pp. 187-203) *in* Martin, R. D., ed., *Breeding Endangered Species in Captivity*. Academic Press, London, New York.

Phillips, J. C. 1928. Wild birds introduced or transplanted in North America. *United States Department of Agriculture Technical Bulletin* 61.

Pickering, S., Creighton, E., and B. Stevens-Wood. 1992. Flock size and breeding success in flamingos. *Zoo Biology* 11:229-234.

Pienaar, U. du V. 1969. Predator-prey relationships amongst the large mammals of the Kruger National Park. *Koedoe* No. 12.

Pierce, B. A. 1985. Acid tolerance of amphibians. *BioScience* 35:239-243.

Pigozzi, G. 1991. The diet of the European badger in a Mediterranean coastal area. *Acta Theriologica* 36(3-4): 293-306.

Pilliner, S. 1992. *Horse Nutrition and Feeding*. Blackwell Scientific Publishing Co., London.

Pimm, S. L. 1988. Rapid morphological change in an introduced bird. *Trends in Ecology and Evolution* 3(11): 290-1.

Pimm, S. L., Jones, H. L., and J. Diamond. 1988. On the risk of extinction. *American Naturalist* 132(6): 757-785.

Pingale, S. V., and V. Balu. 1955. Grain storage practices in India. *Tropical Agriculture* 32(2): 88-94.

Platte. 1982. Bulk transport of livestock by sea with particular reference to instruction, procedure, and problems (pp. 177-184) *in* Moss, R., ed., *Transport of Animals Intended for Breeding, Production, and Slaughter*. Martinus Nishoff Publishers, the Hague, Boston.

Player, I. 1967. Translocation of White Rhinoceros in South Africa. *Oryx* 9(2): 137-150.

Plimer, I. R. 1994. *Telling Lies for God*. Random House Australia, New South Wales.

Poiley, S. M. 1974. Housing requirements—general considerations (pp. 21-61) *in* Melby and Altman, *op. cit.*

Poore, B. B., Herren, K., and W. F. Buchelle. 1968. Field wafering: an evaluation. *Agricultural Engineering* 49:526-7.

Porges, F. 1982. *Handbook of Heating, Ventilation, and Air Conditioning*, 8th Edition. Butterworth's, London, Boston.

Porter, H. D. 1905. Olive and "wild olive" in America. *Biblical World* 26(1): 59-63.

Porter, R. H. 1949. Recent developments in seed technology. *Botanical Review* 15(4): 221-344).

Porterfield, I. D., Longhouse, A. D., and H. O. Henderson. 1957. Choose comfortable stalls for your dairy cows. *West Virginia University Agricultural Experiment Station Bulletin* 410.

Portsmouth, J. I. 1962. *Commercial Rabbit Meat Production*. Ilife Books, London.

Potts, R., and A. K. Behrensmeyer. 1992. Late Cenozoic terrestrial ecosystems (pp. 419-541) *in* Behrensmeyer, A. K., Damuth, J. D., DiMichele, W. A., Potts, R., Sues, H. D., and S. L. Wing, eds. *Terrestrial Ecosystems Through Time*. University of Chicago Press, Chicago and London.

Pough, F. H. 1973. Lizard energetics and diet. *Ecology* 54:837-844.

Pough, F. H. 1977. The relationship between body size and blood oxygen affinity in snakes. *Physiological Zoology* 50:77-87.

Pough, F. H. 1980. The advantages of ectothermy for tetrapods. *American Naturalist* 115:(1): 92-112.

Pough, F. H. 1989. Amphibians: a rich source of biological diversity (pp. 245-277) *in* Woodhead, A. D., and K. Vivirito, eds. *Nonmammalian Animal Models for Biomedical Research*. CRC Press, Florida.

Poulsen, H. 1960. Colour feeding of flamingos. *Avicultural Magazine* 66(2): 48-51.

Powers, S. 1911. Floating islands. *Popular Science Monthly* 79:303-7.

Powledge, T. M. 1993. The genetic fabric of human behavior. *BioScience* 43(6): 362-7.

Pragar, E. M., and 8 others. 1993. Mitochrondrial DNA sequence diversity and the colonization of Scandinavia by house mice from East Holstein. *Biological Journal of the Linnean Society* 50:85-122.

Prager, E. M., and A. C. Wilson. 1975. Slow evolutionary loss of the potential for insterspecific hybridization in birds: a manifestation of slow regulatory evolution. *Proceedings of the National Academy of Sciences (USA)* 72(1): 200-4.

Prakash, I. 1991. Ecology of artiodactyls in the Thar Desert (pp. 243-250) *in* J. A. McNeely and V. M. Neronov, eds., *Mammals in the Palaearctic Desert*. Moscow.

Prater, S. H. 1965. *The Book of Indian Animals*, 2nd Edition. Diocesan Press, Madras.

Pratt, A. 1937. *The Call of the Koala*. Robertson and Mullens, Melbourne, Australia.

Pray, L. A., and C. J. Goodnight. 1995. Genetic variation in inbreeding depression in the red flour beetle *Tribolium castaneum*. *Evolution* 49(1): 176-188.

Prescott, W. H. 1855. *History of the Conquest of Mexico*, Vol. II., Phillips, Sampson, and Co., Boston.

Preston, T. R., and M. B. Willis. 1975. *Intensive Beef Production*, 2nd Edition. Pergamon Press, Oxford, New York.

Price, E. O. 1984. Behavioral aspects of animal domestication. *Quarterly Review of Biology* 59(1): 1-32.

Priestley, D. A. 1986. *Seed Aging*. Cornell University Press, Ithaca and New York.

Prins, R. A., and M. A. Dornhof. 1984. Feed intake and cell wall digestion by okapi (*Okapia johnstoni*) and Giraffe (*Giraffa camelopardis reticulata*) in the zoo. *Der Zoologische Garten* 54(1/2): 131-4.

Privolnev, T. I. 1977. Effect of environmental salinity on water metabolism in freshwater fish (pp. 371-9) *in* Karzinkin, *op. cit.*

Proctor, E. 1949. Temperature changes in hibernating hedgehogs. *Nature* 163:108-9.

Promislow, D. E. L., and P. H. Harvey. 1990. Living fast and dying young: a comparative analysis of life-history variation among mammals. *Journal of Zoology (London)* 220:417-437.

Pugh, P. J. A. 1994. Non-indigenous Acari of Antarctica and the subantarctic islands. *Zoological Journal of the Linnean Society* 110:207-217.

Quiring, R., Walldorf, U., Kloter, U., and W. J. Gehring. 1994. Homology of the *eyeless* gene of *Drosophila* to the *small eye* gene in mice and *Aniridia* in humans. *Science* 265:785-9.

Rabb, G. B. 1994. The changing roles of zoological parks in conserving biological diversity. *American Zoologist* 34(1): 159-164.

Rabinowitz, H. 1972. Dietary Laws (pp. 26-46) *in Encyclopedia Judaica* (Volume 1).

Racey, P. A. 1970. The breeding, care, and management of vespertilionid bats in the laboratory. *Laboratory Animals* 4:171-183.

Rainey, A. 1971. Sacrifice (pp. 600-7) *in Encyclopedia Judaica* (Volume 14).

Ralls, K., Brugger, K., and J. Ballou. 1979. Inbreeding and juvenile mortality in small populations of ungulates. *Science* 206:1101-3.

Ralls, K., Ballou, J. D., and A. Templeton. 1988. Estimates of lethal equivalents and the cost of inbreeding in mammals. *Conservation Biology* 2(2): 185-193.

Ramage, M. C. 1947. Notes on keeping bats in captivity. *Journal of Mammalogy* 28(1)60-2

Ramirez, W. B. 1970. Host specificity of fig wasps (Agaonidae). *Evolution* 24:680-691.

Randall, W. C., and A. J. Martin. 1930. Predetermination of daylighting by the fenestra method. *Illumination Engineering Society Transactions* 25:262-281.

Ranker, T. A. 1994. Evolution of high genetic variability in the rare Hawaiian Fern *Adenophorus periens* and implications for conservation management. *Biological Conservation* 70:19-24.

Ransome, R. 1990. *The Natural History of Hibernating Bats*. Christopher Helm, London.

Rao, P. S. S., and S. G. Inbaraj. 1980. Inbreeding effects on fetal growth and development. *Journal of Medical Genetics* 17:27-33.

Rashid, S. M. A. 1991. A note on the occurrence of the roofed turtle, *Kachuga tecta* in saline water in southern Bangladesh. *British Herpetological Society Bulletin* 37:39.

Rasweiler, J. J. 1973. Care and management of the long-tongued bat, *Glossophaga soricina* (Chiroptera: Phyllostomatidae), in the laboratory, with observations on estivations induced by food deprivation. *Journal of Mammalogy* 54(2): 391-404.

Rasweiler, J. J. 1977. The care and management of bats as laboratory animals (pp. 519-577) *in* Wimsatt, W. A., ed., *Biology of Bats*, Volume 3. Academic Press, New York, London.

Rasweiler, J. J., and H. deBonilla. 1972. Laboratory maintenance methods for some nectarivorous and frugivorous phyllostomatid bats. *Laboratory Animal Science* 22(5): 658-663.

Ratcliffe, H. L. 1956. *Adequate Diets for Captive Wild Animals*. Penrose Research Laboratory, Zoological Society of Philadelphia.

Ratner, V. A., and L. A. Vasilyeva. 1989. Mobile genetic elements and quantitative characters in *Drosophila*: fast heritable changes under temperature treatment.(pp. 163-190) *in* Fontdevila, *op. cit.*

Ray, C. E. 1960. *Trichecodon huxleyi* (Mammalia:Odobenidae) in the Pleistocene of southeastern United States. *Bulletin of the Museum of Comparative Zoology* (Harvard University) 122(3): 127-145.

Ray, C., and M. S. R. Smith. 1968. Thermoregulation of the pup and adult Weddell Seal, *Leptonychotes weddelli* (Lesson), in Antarctica. *Zoologica* (NY) 53(1): 33-48.

Reeder, W. G., and R. B. Cowles. 1951. Aspects of thermoregulation in bats. *Journal of Mammalogy* 32(4): 389-402.

Rees, P. A. 1982. Gross assimilation efficiency and food passage time in the African elephant. *African Journal of Ecology* 20:193-8.

Regal, P. J. 1967. Voluntary hypothermia in reptiles. *Science* 155:1551-3.

Regal, P. J. 1985. Common sense and reconstructions of the biology of fossils: *Archaeopteryx* and feathers (pp. 67-74) *in* M. K. Hecht, ed., *The Beginnings of Birds*. Eichstatt, Germany.

Reig, O. A. 1989. Karyotypic repatterning as one triggering factor in cases of explosive speciation (pp. 246-289) *in* Fontdevila, *op. cit.*

Reinertsen, R. E. 1983. Nocturnal hypothermia and its energetic significance for small birds living in the arctic and subarctic regions: a review. *Polar Research* 1:269-284 (New Series).

ReMine, W. J. 1993. *The Biotic Message*. St. Paul Science, Minnesota.

Renfro, W. C. 1959. Survival and migration of fresh-water fishes in salt water. *Texas Journal of Science* 11(2): 172-180.

Renfro, W. C. 1960. Salinity relations of some fishes in the Aransas River, Texas. *Tulane University Studies in Zoology* 8(3): 83-91.

Reuther, R. T. 1969. Growth and diet of young elephants in captivity. *International Zoo Yearbook* 9:168-178.

Ruvolo, M., and 5 others. 1994. Gene trees and hominoid phylogeny. *Proceedings of the National Academy of Sciences (USA)* 91:8900-4.

Rickett M. J. 1984. Contaminants in foodstuffs (pp. 43-50) *in* Partridge, J. (ed.), *The Management of Cranes, Storks, and Ratites in Captivity*. ABWAK (Association of British Wild Animal Keepers), Bristol, England.

Ricketts, E. F. 1968. *Between Pacific Tides*. Stanford University Press, Stanford, California.

Ricklefs. R. E. 1973. Patterns of growth in birds II. *Ibis* 115(2): 177-201.

Ricklefs, R. E. 1974. Energetics of reproduction in birds (pp. 152-292) *in* Paynter, R. A., ed., *Avian Energetics*. Nutall Ornithological Club, Cambridge, Massachusetts.

Ridley, H. N. 1930. *The Dispersal of Plants throughout the World*. Ashford, England.

Ridpath, M. G. 1991. Feral mammals and their environment (pp. 169-191) *in* Haynes, C. D., Ridpath, M. G., and M. A. J. Williams, eds., *Monsoonal Australia*. A. A. Balkema, Rotterdam.

Riedman, M. 1990. *The Pinnipeds*. University of California Press, Berkeley.

Riggs, T. J. 1966. Notes on Hummingbirds. *American Cage-Bird Magazine*, May 1966, pp. 38-40.

Riley, H. W. 1929. Natural draft dairy stable ventilation. *Agricultural Engineering* 10(4): 125-7.

Ripley, L. S. 1991. Concerted mutagenesis: its potential impact on interpretation of evolutionary relationships. *NATO ASI Series* H59:63-94.

Risser, A. C., Baptista, L. F., Wylie, S. R., and N. B. Gale. 1981. *Proceedings of the 1st International Birds in Captivity Symposium*. Seattle, Washington.

Ritland, S. 1982. The Allometry of the Vertebrate Eye (4 Volumes). *University of Chicago Phd Dissertation*.

Roberts, E. H., and R. H. Ellis. 1989. Water and seed survival. *Annals of Botany* 63:39-52.

Roberts, S. 1973. *Bird Keeping and Bird Cages: a History*. Drake Publishers, New York.

Roberts, T. J., and S. E. Landfried. 1987. Hunting pressures on cranes migrating through Pakistan (pp. 139-145) *in* Archibald and Pasquier, *op. cit.*

Robinson, T. W. 1961. *The Handling of Hog Manure from Confined Systems of Management*. Master's Thesis, Purdue University.

Rodriguez, W. C., and W. M. Bass. 1985. Decomposition of buried bodies and methods that may aid in their location. *Journal of Forensic Sciences* 30(3): 836-852.

Rogers, A. R., and L. B. Jorde. 1995. Genetic evidence on modern human origins. *Human Biology* 67(1)1-36.

Romspert, A. P. 1976. Osmoregulation of the African Clawed Frog, *Xenopus laevis*, in hypersaline media. *Comparative Biochemistry and Physiology* 54A:207-210.

Ronov, A. B. 1982. The earth's sedimentary shell, part 2. *International Geology Review* 24(12): 1365-1388.

Roonwal, M. L., and S. M. Mohnot. 1977. *Primates of South Asia*. Harvard University Press, Cambridge, Massachussetts.

Roots, B. I. 1956. The water relations of earthworms, II. *Journal of Experimental Biology* 33:29-44.

Roots, C. 1970. *Softbilled Birds*. Arco Publishing Co., Inc., New York.

Roots, C. 1989. *The Bamboo Bears*. Hyperion Press, Winnipeg, Canada.

Rosen, B. 1994. Mammoths in Ancient Egypt? *Nature* 369:364.

Roser, B., and C. Colaco. 1993. A sweeter way to fresher food. *New Scientist* 138(1873): 24-8.

Ross, H. 1990. Noah's floating zoo. *Facts and Faith* 4(3): 4-5.

Ross, H. 1994. *Creation and Time*. NavPress, Colorado Springs, Colorado.

Ross, S. T., and J. A. Baker. 1983. The response of fishes to periodic spring floods in a southeastern stream. *American Midland Naturalist* 109(1): 1-14.

Roth, V. L. 1990. Insular dwarf elephants: a case study in body mass estimation and ecological inference (pp. 151-179) *in* Damuth, J., and B. J. MacFadden, eds., *Body Size in Mammalian Paleobiology*. Cambridge University Press, Cambridge and London.

Ruben, J. 1995. The evolution of endothermy in mammals and birds. *Annual Review of Physiology* 57:69-95.

Ruckebusch, Y. 1972. Comparative aspects of sleep and wakefulness in farm animals (pp. 23-33) *in* Chase, M. H., ed., *The Sleeping Brain*. University of California Press, Los Angeles.

Ruf, T., Stieglitz, A., Steinlechner, S., Blank, J. L., and G. Heldmaier. 1993. Cold exposure and food restriction facilitate physiological responses to short photoperiod in Djungarian hamsters (*Phodopus sungorus*). *Journal of Experimental Zoology* 267:104-112.

Rugini, E., Bazzoffia, A., and A. Jacoboni. 1988. A simple *in vitro* method to avoid the initial dark period and to increase rooting in fruit trees (pp. 438-440) *in* Loreti, *op. cit.*

Ruibal, R. 1959. The ecology of a brackish water population of *Rana pipiens*. *Copeia* 1959(4): 315-322.

Russell, R. C. H. 1953. *Waves and Tides*. Philosophical Library, New York.

Russell, R. H. 1975. The food habits of polar bears of James Bay and southwest Hudson Bay in summer and autumn. *Arctic* 28:117-129.

Russell, W. 1989. Geomatrix matting proven helpful in combating avian foot problems. *Animal Keeper's Forum* 16:195-7.

Ryberg, O. 1947. *Studies on Bats and Bat Parasites*. Bokforlaget Svensk Natur, Stockholm.

Rydell, J. 1990. The northern bat of Sweden. *Bats* 8(2): 8-11.

Ryg, M. 1983. Regulation of annual weight cycles in reindeer and other cervids. *Polar Research* 1:249-257 (New Series).

Saether, B.-E., and I. J. Gordon. 1994. The adaptive significance of reproductive strategies in ungulates. *Proceedings of the Royal Society of London* B256:263-8.

Safford, J. W., and A. S. Hoversland. 1960. A study of lamb mortality in a western range flock. I. Autopsy findings on 1051 lambs. *Journal of Animal Science* 19:265-273.

Sainsbury, D., and P. Sainsbury. 1979. *Livestock Health and Housing*. Bailliere Tindall, London.

Salter, J. 1857. On the vitality of seeds after prolonged submersion in the sea. *Journal of the Proceedings of the Linnean Society of London (Botany)* 1:140-2.

Salter, R. M., and C. J. Schollenberger. 1939. Farm manure. *Ohio Agricultural Experiment Station Bulletin* 605.

Salvadori, F. B., and P. L. Florio. 1978. *Wildlife in Peril*. Westbridge Books, Devon, England.

Samson, F. B., Perez-Trejo, F., Salwasser, H., Ruggiero, L. F., and M. L. Schaffer. 1985. On determining and managing minimum population size. *Wildlife Society Bulletin* 13(4): 425-433.

Sandlund, O. T., Hindar, K., and A. H. D. Brown. 1992. *Conservation of Biodiversity for Sustainable Development*. Scandinavian University Press.

Sauey, R. T., and B. Brown. 1977. The captive management of cranes. *International Zoo Yearbook* 17:89-92.

Saville-Kent, W. 1897. *The Naturalist in Australia*. Chapman and Hall, London.

Schafer, W. 1972. *Ecology and Palaeoecology of Marine Environments*. University of Chicago, Chicago, London.

Schaller, G. B. 1972. *The Serengeti Lion*. University of Chicago Press, Chicago, London.

Schaller, G. B. 1993. *The Last Panda*. University of Chicago Press, Chicago, London.

Schaller, G. B., Dang, N. X., Thuy, L. D., and V. T. Son. 1990. Javan Rhinoceros in Vietnam. *Oryx* 24(2): 77-80.

Scheffer, V. B. 1951. The rise and fall of a reindeer herd. *Scientific Monthly* 13:356-362.

Schemske, D. W. 1983. Limits to specialization and coevolution in plant-animal mutualisms (pp. 67-109) *in* Nitecki, M. H., ed., *Coevolution*. University of Chicago Press, Chicago, London.

Schenkel, R., and L. Schenkel-Hulliger. 1969. *Ecology and Behaviour of the Black Rhinoceros (Diceros bicornis L.)*. Verlag Paul Parey, Hamburg, Berlin.

Scherer, S. 1986. On the limits of variability (pp. 219-241) *in* Andrews E. H., Gitt W., and W. J. Ouweneel, eds. *Concepts in Creationism*. Evangelical Press, Welwyn, Herts, England.

Scherer, S. 1993. Basic types of life (pp. 1-19) *in* Scherer, S., ed. *Studium Integrale*. Pascal-Verlag, Berlin.

Shikaputo, C. 1986. Properties and end-uses of Zambezi Teak (pp. 350-7) *in* Piearce, G. D., ed., *The Zambezi Teak Forests*. Zambia Forest Department, Ndola, Zambia.

Schmich, J. 1978. The Ark, its course and destination. *Creation Research Society Quarterly* 15(3): 161-3.

Schneour, E. A. 1986. Occam's Razor. *Skeptical Inquirer* 10(4): 310-313.

Schneider, E. C. 1955. Mechanizing the feeding of dairy cows. *Agricultural Engineering* 36(2): 95-99.

Schober, W. 1984. *The Lives of Bats*. Croom Helm, London.

Scholander, P. F., Hock, R., Walters, V., Johnson, F., and L. Irving. 1950. Heat regulation in some arctic and tropical mammals and birds. *Biological Bulletin* 99(2): 237-258.

Scholander, P. F., Flagg, W., Walters, V., and L. Irving. 1953. Climatic adaptation in arctic and tropical poikilotherms. *Physiological Zoology* 26(1): 67-92.

Schulz, A. H. 1960. Basic requirements for beef cattle housing, feeding, and handling. Agricultural Engineering 41:615-7.

Schwaner, T. D. 1989. A field study of thermoregulation in black tiger snakes (*Notechis ater niger*: Elapida) on the Franklin Islands, South Australia. *Herpetologica* 45(4): 393-401.

Schwartz, O. A., Bleich, V. C., and S. A. Holl. 1986. Genetics and conservation of mountain sheep *Ovis canadensis nelsoni*. *Biological Conservation* 37:179-190.

Scott, M. L. 1973. Nutrition in reproduction—direct effects and predictive functions (pp. 46-59) *in* D. S. Farner, ed., *Breeding Biology of Birds*. National Academy of Science, Washington, D. C.

Seal., U. S., and N. R. Flesness. 1981. Noah's Ark—sex and survival (pp. 301-317) *in* Risser et al., *op. cit.*

Seidensticker, J. C., Hornocker, M. G., Wiles, W. V., and J. P. Messick. 1973. Mountain lion social organization in the Idaho primitive area. *Wildlife Monographs* No. 35.

Seitz, A., and V. Loeschke. 1991. *Species Conservation: A Population-Biological Approach*. Birkhauser Verlag, Basel, Boston.

Sekkar, A. C., and A. S. Gulati. 1988. Suitability Indices of Indian timber for industrial and engineering uses. *Indian Forest Records* 2(1): 1-61.

Seligman, D. 1992. *A Question of Intelligence*. Carol Publishing Group, New York.

Selwood, L. 1982. Brown antechinus *Antechinus stuartii*: management of breeding colonies to obtain embryonic material and pouch young (pp. 31-8) *in* Evans. 1982. *op. cit.*

Senft, D. 1991. Update for an ancient watering strategy. *Agricultural Research* 39(7)25.

Serventy, V., and C. Serventy. 1975. *The Koala*. E. P. Dutton and Co., Inc., New York.

Seth-Smith, D. 1943. The Bird House in the London Zoo in war time. *Avicultural Magazine* 8(5): 129-130.

Seymour, R. S. 1987. Scaling of cardiovascular physiology in snakes. *American Zoologist* 27:97-109.

Sharp, J. G. 1953. *Dehydrated Meat*. Her Majesty's Stationary, London.

Sheail, J. 1971. *Rabbits and Their History*. David and Charles, Devon, England.

Sheat, W. G. 1965. *Propagation of Trees, Shrubs, and Conifers*. MacMillan and Co., Ltd., New York.

Shepherdson, D., Brownback, T., and A. James. 1990. Mealworm dispenser for meerkats. *Animal Keeper's Forum* 17:298-300.

Sherman, H. B. 1954. Raccoons of the Bahama Islands. *Journal of Mammalogy* 35(1): 126.

Shields, E. B. 1974. *Raising Earthworms for Profit.*, 11th ed. Privately Printed, USA.

Shields, W. M. 1993. The natural and unnatural history of inbreeding and outbreeding (pp. 143-169) *in* Thornhill, *op. cit.*

Shine, R. 1991. Intersexual dietary divergence and the evolution of sexual dimorphism in snakes. *American Naturalist* 138(1): 103-122.

Shine R., and A. E. Greer. 1991. Why are clutch sizes more variable in some species than in others? *Evolution* 45(7): 1696-1706.

Shingoethe, P. J. 1988. Nutrient needs of ruminants versus monogastric species (pp. 448-455) *in* D. C. Church, ed., *The Ruminant Animal*. Prentice-Hall, New Jersey.

Shirai, K. 1967. Penguin exhibit at Nagasaki Aquarium. *International Zoo Yearbook* 7:35-6.

Shoemaker V. H. and K. A. Nagy. 1977. Osmoregulation in amphibians and reptiles. *Annual Review of Physiology* 39:449-471.

Short, A. K. "Dad." 1938. *Ancient and Modern Agriculture*. Naylor Company, San Antonio, Texas.

Shull, G. H. 1914. The longevity of submerged seeds. *Plant World* 17:329-337.

Sicwaten, J. B., and D. Stahl. 1982. *A Complete Handbook on Backyard and Commercial Rabbit Production*. CARE. Phillipines.

Sikes, S. K. 1968. Observations on the ecology of arterial disease in the African elephant (*Loxodonta africana*) in Kenya. *Symposium of the Zoological Society of London* 21: 253-273.

Sikes, S. K. 1971. *The Natural History of the African Elephant*. American Elsevier Publishing Co., New York.

Simkin, T., and R. S. Fiske. 1983. *Krakatau 1883*. Smithsonian Institution Press, Washington, D. C.

Simkin, T., and L. Siebert. 1994. *Volcanoes of the World*. 2nd ed. Geoscience Press, Tucson, Arizona.

Simmonds, R. C. 1991. Standards: the guide for the care and use of laboratory animals (pp. 184-8) *in* Ruys, T., ed. *Handbook of Facilities Planning*.(Volume 2). Van Nostrand Reinhold, New York.

Sinervo, B., and S. C. Adolph. 1994. Growth plasticity and thermal opportunity in *Sceloporus* lizards. *Ecology* 75(3): 776-790.

Singer, M. C., Thomas, C. D., and C. Parmesan. 1993. Rapid human-induced evolution of insect-host associations. *Nature* 366:681-3.

Skehan, J. W. 1986. *Modern Science and the Book of Genesis*. National Science Teachers Association.

Slatis, H. M. 1960. An analysis of inbreeding in the European Bison. *Genetics* 45:275-287.

Slavens, R. L. 1988. *Inventory, longevity, and breeding notes—reptiles and amphibians in captivity*. Privately printed, Seattle, Washington.

Smith, A. P. 1915. Birds of the Boston Mountains, Arkansas. *Condor* 17:41-57.

Smith, C. E. G. 1982. Major factors in the spread of infections. *Symposium of the Zoological Society of London* 50:207-235.

Smith, G. A. 1983. Surgical sexing of birds: some observations. *Aviculture Magazine* 89(1): 29-31.

Smith, G. R. 1992. Introgression in fish: significance for paleontology, cladistics, and evolutionary rates. *Systematic Biology* 41(1): 41-57.

Smith, H. W. 1930. Metabolism of the lung-fish, *Protopterus aethiopicus*. *Journal of Biological Chemistry* 88(1): 97-130.

Smith, J. M. B. 1990. Drift disseminules on Fijian beaches. *New Zealand Journal of Botany* 28:13-20.

Smith, J. M. B. 1991. Tropical drift disseminules on southeast Australian beaches. *Australian Geographic Studies* 29(2): 355-369.

Smith, D. G., Lorey, F. W., Suzuki, J., and M. Abe. 1987. Effect of outbreeding on weight and growth rate of captive infant rhesus macaques. *Zoo Biology* 6:201-212.

Smith, E. N., and S. C. Hagberg. 1984. Survival of freshwater and saltwater organisms in a heterogenous flood model experiment. *Creation Research Society Quarterly* 21(1): 33-7.

Smith, G. R., and R. E. Ballinger. 1994. Thermal tolerance in the tree lizard (*Urosaurus ornatus*) from a desert population and a low montane population. *Canadian Journal of Zoology* 72:2066-2069.

Smith, H. D., Hamilton, A. B., and S. H. DeVault. 1947. Labor utilization in dairy buildings. *Maryland Agricultural Experiment Station Bulletin* No. A46.

Smith, K., and P. Hallock. 1992. Dormancy in benthic foraminifera: response to prolonged darkness in an algal/foraminiferal symbiosis. *Geological Society of America Abstracts with Programs* 24(7): A76.

Snow, D. W. 1981. Tropical frugivorous birds and their food plants: a world survey. *Biotropica* 13(1): 1-14.

Sobel, A. T. 1966. Physical properties of animal manures associated with handling (pp. 27-31) *in* ASAE, *op. cit.*

Sobel, A. T. 1969. Removal of water from animal manures (pp. 347-362) *in* Anon., *Animal Waste Management*. Cornell University, New York.

Soest, P. J., van. 1982. *Nutritional Ecology of the Ruminant*. Cornell University Press, New York.

Sokol, O. M. 1967. Herbivory in lizards. *Evolution* 21:192-4.

Solounias, N., and S. M. C. Moelleken. 1993. Dietary adaptations of some extinct ruminants determined by premaxillary shape. *Journal of Mammalogy* 74(4): 1059-1071.

Soroka, L. G., and C. L. Nelson. 1983. Physical constraints on the Noachian Deluge. *Journal of Geological Education* 31:135-9.

Soule, M. E. 1986. *Conservation Biology*. Sinauer Associates, Publishers, Massachusetts.

Soule, M. E., and L. S. Mills. 1992. Conservation genetics and conservation biology: a troubled marriage. (pp. 55-69) *in* Sandlund et al., *op. cit.*

South, G. R., and A. Whittick. 1987. *Introduction to Phycology*. Blackwell Scientific Publication, Oxford, London.

Southwood, T. R. E. 1987. Species-time relationships in human parasites. *Evolutionary Ecology* 1:245-6.

Speakman, J. R., P. I. Webb, and P. A. Racey. 1991. Effects of disturbance on the energy expenditure of hibernating bats. *Journal of Applied Ecology* 28:1087-1104.

Speck, F. G. 1923. Reptile lore of the northern Indians. *Journal of American Folklore* 36:273-280.

Spinney, L. 1994. Animals seeking oblivion. *New Scientist* 143(1945): 29.

Spinney, L. 1995. The way of all flesh. Supplement to *New Scientist*, No., 1971, pp. 12-15.

Spira, T. P., and L. K. Wagner. 1983. Viability of seeds up to 211 years old extracted from adobe brick buildings of California and northern Mexico. *American Journal of Botany* 70(2): 303-7.

Spotila, J. R., O'Connor M. P., Dodson P., and F. V. Paladino. 1991. Hot and cold running dinosaurs: body size, metabolism and migration. *Modern Geology* 16:203-227.

Srinivasan, T. K. 1955. Crustaceans in relation to underwater timber structures. *Current Science* 24:342.

Starr, J. 1990. Koalas (pp. 83-90) *in* Hand, *op. cit.*

Stearns, S. C. 1983. The evolution of life-history traits in mosquitofish since their introduction to Hawaii in 1905: Rates of evolution, heritabilities, and developmental plasticity. *American Zoologist* 23:65-75.

Stebbings, R. E. 1988. *Conservation of European Bats*. Christopher Helm, London.

Stegeman, L. C. 1938. The European Wild Boar in the Cherokee National Forest, Tennessee. *Journal of Mammalogy* 19(3): 279-290.

Steiner, K. E. 1993. Has Ixianthes (*Scrophulariaceae*) lost its special bee? *Plant Systematics and Evolution* 185:7-16.

Stephens, S. G. 1966. The potentiality for long range oceanic dispersal of cotton seeds. *American Naturalist* 100(912): 199-210.

Stevenson, R. D. 1985. Body size and limits to the daily range of body temperature in terrestrial ectotherms. *American Naturalist* 125:102-117.

Stewart, E. A. 1928. Mechanical power in agriculture. *Agricultural Engineering* 9(11): 349-351.

Stewart, J. S. 1989. Techniques for sex identification in reptiles (pp. 99-104) *in* Gowen, *op. cit.*

Stewart, C.-B., Schilling, J. W., and A. C. Wilson. 1987. Adaptive evolution in the stomach lysozomes of foregut fermenters. *Nature* 330:401-4.

Steyn, P. 1982. *Birds of Prey of Southern Africa*. David Philip, Cape Town, Republic of South Africa.

Stone, I. 1972. *The Healing Factor*. Grosset and Dunlap, New York.

Stonehouse, B. 1967. The general biology of penguins. *Advances in Ecological Research* 4:131-196.

Stonehouse, B. 1978. Introduction (pp. 2-8) *in* Bardzo, J.,ed., *Management of Polar Birds and Mammals in Captivity*. ABWAK (Association of British Wild Animal Keepers).

Stonehouse, B. 1989. *Polar Ecology*. Blackie, Glasgow and London.

Stones, R. C., and J. E. Wiebers. 1965. A review of the temperature regulation in bats. *American Midland Naturalist* 74(1): 155-167.

Stowell, R. R., and W. G. Bickert. 1993. Design features of naturally ventilated free stall dairy barns and their effect on warm season thermal environment (pp. 395-402) *in* E. Collins and C. Boon, eds., *Livestock Environment IV*. American Society of Agricultural Engineers, Michigan.

Street, P. 1956. *The London Zoo*. Odhams Press Limited, London.

Strumwasser, F. 1960. Some physiological principles governing hibernation in *Citellus beecheyi*. *Bulletin of the Museum of Comparative Zoology (Harvard University)* 124:285-320.

Subbarayappa, B. V. 1982. Glimpses of science and technology in ancient and mediaeval India. *Endeavour* 6(4): 117-182.

Sugisaki, R., and K. Mimura. 1994. Mantle hydrocarbons: Abiotic or biotic? *Geochimica et Cosmochimica Acta* 58(11):2527-2542.

Sukumar, R. 1989. *The Asian Elephant*. Cambridge University Press, Cambridge, New York.

Sullivan, J. T. 1973. Drying and storing herbage and hay (pp. 1-31) *in* Butler, G. W., and R. W. Bailey, eds., *Chemistry and Biochemistry of Herbage*, Volume 3. Academic Press, London, New York.

Summers-Smith, J. D. 1988. *The Sparrows: a Study of the* Genus Passer. T & AD Poyser, Calton, England.

Sumner, F. B. 1905. The physiological effects of changes in the density and salinity of water. *Bulletin of the Bureau of Fisheries (USA)* 25:55-108.

Sunquist, F. 1986. Secret energy of the sloth. *International Wildlife* 16(1): 4-11.

Swengel, S. 1987. A proposed management plan for captive red-crowned cranes (pp. 513-523) *in* Archibald and Pasquier, *op. cit.*

Swennen, C. 1977. *Laboratory Research on Sea-Birds*. Institute for Sea Research, Texel, the Netherlands.

Taiganides, E. P. 1977. *Animal Wastes*. Applied Science Publishers Ltd., London.

Taiganides, E. P. 1987. Animal waste management and wastewater treatment (pp. 91-153) *in* D. Strauch (ed.). *Animal Production and Environmental Health*. Elsevier, Amsterdam, Oxford.

Taiganides, E. P., and R. K. White. 1969. The menace of noxious gases in animal units. *Transactions of the ASAE (American Society of Agricultural Engineers)* 12:359-362.

Takahata, N. 1993a. Evolutionary genetics of human paleo-populations (pp. 1-21) *in* Takahata, N., and A. G. Clark, eds., *Mechanisms of Molecular Evolution*. Sinauer Associates, Sunderland, Massachusetts.

Takahata, N. 1993b. Allelic geneology and human evolution. *Molecular Biology and Evolution* 10(1): 2-22.

Takahata, N. 1994. Polymorphism at MHC loci and isolation by the immune system in vertebrates (pp. 233-246) *in* Golding, B., ed., *Non-Neutral Evolution*. Chapman and Hall, New York, Bonn.

Takahata, N. 1995. MHC diversity and selection. *Immunological Reviews* 143:225-247.

Tangley, L. 1984. The zoo Ark—charting a new course. *BioScience* 34(10): 606-610, 612.

Tannenbaum, M. G., and E. B. Pivorun. 1984. Differences in daily torpor patterns among three southeastern species of *Peromyscus*. *Journal of Comparative Physiology* B154:233-6.

Tardif, S. D., Clapp, N. K., Henke, M. A., Carson, R. L., and J. J. Knapka. 1988. Maintenance of cotton-top tamarins fed an experimental pelleted diet versus a highly sweetened diet. *Laboratory Animal Science* 38(5): 588-591.

Tarpy, C. 1993. New zoos: taking down the bars. *National Geographic* 184(1): 2-37.

Tatarenkov, A., and K. Johannesson. 1994. Habitat related allozyme variation on a microgeographic scale in the marine snail *Littorina mariae* (Prosobranchia: Littorinacea). *Biological Journal of the Linnean Society* 53:105-125.

Tatarinov, L. P. 1986. Certain aspects of the theory of speciation. *Paleontological Journal* 20:(2): 1-8.

Taylor, C. R. 1968. The minimum water requirements of some East African bovids. *Symposium of the Zoological Society of London* 21:195-206.

Taylor, E. H. 1943. A new ambylystomid salamander adapted to brackish water. *Copeia* 1943(3): 151-6.

Teeple, H. M. 1878. *The Noah's Ark Nonsense*. Religion and Ethics Institute, Inc., Evanston, Illinois.

Tegetmeier, W. B. 1880. The koala, or native bear of Australia. *The Field (London)*. May 22, 1880, p. 653.

Temple, R. 1986. *The Genius of China*. Simon and Schuster, New York.

Temple, R. 1995. Technological wonders of the past. *Nature* 374:418-9.

Temple, S. A. 1977. Plant-animal mutualism: Coevolution with dodo leads to near extinction of plant. *Science* 197(4306): 885-886.

Templeton, A. R. 1980. The theory of speciation via the founder principle. *Genetics* 94:1011-1038.

Templeton, A. R. 1986. Coadaptation and outbreeding depression (pp. 105-116) *in* Soule, *op. cit*.

Templeton, A. R. 1987. Inferences on natural population structure (pp. 257-272) *in* Chepko-Sade, B. D., and Z. T. Halpin, eds., *Mammalian Dispersal Patterns*. University of Chicago Press, Chicago, London.

Templeton, A. R. 1991a. Genetics and conservation biology (pp. 15-29) *in* Seitz and Loeschcke, *op. cit.*

Templeton, A. R. 1991b. Off-site breeding of animals and implications for plant conservation strategies (pp. 182-194) *in* Falk, D. A., and K. E. Holsinger, eds., *Genetics and Conservation of Rare Plants*. Oxford University Press, New York, Oxford.

Templeton, A. R. 1994. Biodiversity at the molecular genetic level: experiences from disparate macroorganisms. *Philosophical Transactions of the Royal Society of London* B345:59-64.

Templeton, A. R. 1996. Translocation in conservation (pp. 315-325), *in* Szaro, R., ed., *Biodiversity in Managed Landscapes*. Oxford University Press, New York, Oxford.

Templeton, A. R., Davis, S. K., and B. Read. 1987. Genetic variability in a captive herd of Speke's Gazelle (*Gazella spekei*). *Zoo Biology* 6:305-313.

Templeton, A. R., Hemmer, H., Mace, G., Seal, U. S., Shields, W. M., and D. S. Woodruff. 1986. Local adaptation, coadaptation, and population boundaries. *Zoo Biology* 5:115-125.

Templeton, A. R., and B. Read. 1983. The eliminating of inbreeding depression in a captive herd of Speke's Gazelle (pp. 241-61) *in* Schonewald-Cox, C. M., Chambers, S., MacBryde, B., and W. L. Thomas, eds. *Genetics and Conservation*. Benjamin/Cummings Publishing Co., London, Amsterdam.

Templeton, A. R., and B. Read. 1994. Inbreeding—One word, several meanings, much confusion (pp. 91-105) *in* Loeschcke et al., *op. cit.*

Templeton, G. S. 1968. *Domestic Rabbit Production*. Interstate Printers and Publishers, Illinois.

TenBoom, C. 1971. *The Hiding Place*. Bantam Books, New York.

Terborgh, J. 1986. Keystone plant resources in the tropical forest (pp. 330-344) *in* Soule, 1986, *op. cit.*

Tercafs, R. R., and E. Schoffeniels. 1962. Adaptation of amphibians to salt water. *Life Sciences* 1:19-23.

Tessier-Yandel, J. 1971. Rediscovery of the pygmy hog. *Animals* 13(20): 956-8.

Thomas, D. W. 1995. Hibernating bats are sensitive to nontactile human disturbance. *Journal of Mammalogy* 76(3): 940-946.

Thomas, J. H. 1993. Thinking about genetic redundancy. *Trends in Genetics* 9(11): 395-8.

Thompson, D. R. 1983. Strategies for captive reproduction of psittacine birds (pp. 193-203) *in* International Foundation for the Conservation of Birds (IFCB), eds. *Proceedings of the Jean Delacour/IFCB Symposium on Breeding Birds in Captivity*.

Thompson, K., and J. P. Grime. 1983. A comparative study of germination responses to diurnally-fluctuating temperatures. *Journal of Applied Ecology* 20:141-156.

Thompson, K., Grime, J. P., and G. Mason. 1977. Seed germination in response to diurnal fluctuations of temperature. *Nature* 267:147-9.

Thorne, S. 1986. *The History of Food Preservation*. Barnes and Noble Books, New Jersey.

Thornhill, N. W. 1993. *The Natural History of Inbreeding and Outbreeding*. University of Chicago Press, Chicago and London.

Thornton, I. W. B., and T. R. New. 1988. Krakatau invertebrates: the 1980's fauna in the context of a century of recolonization. *Philosophical Transaction of the Royal Society of London* B322:493-522.

Till-Bottraud, I., Wu, L., and J. Harding. 1990. Rapid evolution of life history traits in populations of *Poa annua* L. *Journal of Evoiutionary Biology* 3:205-224.

Titus-Trachtenberg, E. A., Rickards, O., DeStefano, G. F., and H. A. Erlich. 1994. Analysis of HLA Class II haplotypes in the Cayupa Indians of Ecuador: a novel DRB1 allele reveals evidence for convergent evolution at position 86. *American Journal of Human Genetics* 55:160-7.

Toleman, W. J. 1967. Handling Manure: Poultry farm manure handling. *Cornell Poultry Pointers* 19(1): 5-6.

Tollefson, C. I. 1982. Nutrition (pp. 220-249) *in* Petrak, M. L., ed., *Diseases of Cage and Aviary Birds*. Lea and Febiger, Philadelphia.

Tomich, P. Q. 1986. *Mammals in Hawaii*, 2nd Edition. Bishop Museum Press, Honolulu.

Toynbee, A. 1973. *Animals in Roman Life and Art*. Cornell University Press, New York.

Traub, R. 1985. Coevolution of fleas and mammals (pp. 295-437) *in* Kim, K. C., ed. *Coevolution of Parasitic Arthropods and Mammals*. John Wiley and Sons, New York, Chichester.

Tramer, E. J. 1977. Catastrophic mortality of stream fishes trapped in shrinking pools. *American Midland Naturalist* 97(2): 469-478.

Trow-Smith, R. 1957. *A History of British Livestock Husbandry to 1700*. Routledge and Kegan Paul, London.

Tryon, B. W. 1984. Snake hibernation: in and out of the zoo. *British Herpetological Society Bulletin* No. 10, pp. 22-29.

Tucker, V. A. 1966. Diurnal torpor and its relation to food consumption and weight changes in the California pocket mouse *Perognathus californicus*. *Ecology* 47(2): 245-252.

Turnbull, J. E. 1967. European experience with removal of cattle manure from slotted floor barns. *Canadian Agricultural Engineering* 9(1): 33-36,53.

Turelli, M., and L. R. Ginzburg. 1983. Should individual fitness increase with heterozygosity? *Genetics* 104:191-209.

Turrill, W. B. 1957. Germination of Seeds: 5. *Gardener's Chronicle*, Series 3, 142(2): 37.

Tuttle, M. D. 1979. Status, causes of decline, and management of endangered bats. *Journal of Wildlife Management* 43(1): 1-17.

Tuttle, M. D. 1991. How North America's bats survive the winter. *Bats* 9(3): 7-12.

Tuttle, M. D. 1994. The lives of Mexican free-tailed bats. *Bats* 12(3): 6-14.

Twente, J. J., Twente, J., and V. Brack. 1985. The duration of hibernation of three species of vespertilionid bats. II. Laboratory studies. *Canadian Journal of Zoology* 63:2955-2961.

Twente, J. J., and J. Twente. 1987. Biological alarm clock arouses hibernating big brown bats, *Eptesicus fuscus*. *Canadian Journal of Zoology* 65:1668-1674.

Uman, M. A. 1992. Physics of lightning phenonena (pp. 5-21) *in* Andrews, C. J., and 3 others, eds., *Lightning Injuries*. CRC Press, Boca Raton (Florida).

Uri, M. Ben. 1975. Interest in Creation Week and in the Flood in Israel. *Creation Research Society Quarterly* 12(2): 83.

USDA (United States Department of Agriculture). 1948. Woody-plant seed manual. *USDA Miscellaneous Publication* No. 654.

USDA (United States Department of Agriculture). 1973. Storing vegetables and fruits. *Home and Garden Bulletin* No. 119.

Valdes, A. M., Slatkin, M., and N. B. Freimer. 1993. Allele frequencies at microsatellite loci: the stepwise mutation model revisited. *Genetics* 133:737-749.

Vance, V. J. 1990. *Exploring Zoos*. Kendall Hunt Publishing Co., Dubuque, Iowa.

Vandenbeld, J. 1988. *Nature of Australia*. Facts on File, New York, Oxford.

Varro 36BC. *M. Terenti Varronis Rerum Rusticum Libri Tres (Varro on Farming)*, Translated (1912) by L. Storr-Best, G. Bell and Sons, London.

Vazquez-Yanes, C., and H. Smith. 1982. Phytochrome control of seed germination in the tropical rain forest pioneer trees. *New Phytologist* 92:477-485.

Velebil, M. 1977. Collection, storage, and transport of cattle wastes (pp. 157-165) *in* Taiganides. 1977, *op. cit.*

Vermeij, G. J. 1987. *Evolution and Escalation*. Princeton University Press, New Jersey.

Viljoen, P. J., and J. du P. Bothma. 1990. Dailey movements of desert-dwelling elephants in the northern Namib Desert. *South African Journal of Wildlife Research* 20(2): 69-72.

Vogel, S., and C. Westerkamp. 1991. Pollination: an integrating factor of biocenoses (pp. 159-170) *in* Seitz and Loeschke, eds, *op. cit.*

Voigt, J. W. 1972. Diminutive Deserts. *Outdoor Illinois* 11(2): 29-30.

Vorontsov, N. N., and E. A. Lyapunova. 1989. The ways of speciation (pp. 221-246) *in* Fontdevila, *op. cit.*

Vos, A., De., Manville, R. H., and R. G. Van Gelder. 1956. Introduced mammals and their influence on native biota. *Zoologica* (NY) 41:163-194.

Voss, G. 1968. Difficult animals in the zoo (pp. 151-163) *in* Kirchshofer *op. cit.*

Vossen, H. A. M Van Der. 1979. Methods of preserving the viability of coffee seed in storage. *Seed Science and Technology* 7:65-74.

Vriends, M. M. 1985. *Breeding Cage and Aviary Birds.* Howell Book House, New York.

Vuorinen, J., Naesje, T. F., and O. T. Sandlund. 1991. Genetic changes in a vendance *Coregonus albula* (L.) population, 92 years after introduction. *Journal of Fish Biology* 39(Supplement A):193-201.

Waal, B. M., de. 1989. The myth of a simple relation between space and aggression in captive primates. *Zoo Biology Supplement* 1:141-8.

Wachsmann, S. 1990. Ships of Tarshish to the land of Ophir. *Oceanus* 33(1): 70-82.

Wackernagel, H. 1968. Substitution and prefabricated diets for zoo animals. *Symposium of the Zoological Society of London* 21:1-12.

Wade, O. 1930. The behavior of certain spermophiles with special reference to aestivation and hibernation. *Journal of Mammalogy* 11(2): 160-188.

Wainwright, S. J. 1980. Plants in relation to salinity. *Advances in Botanical Research* 8:221-261.

Walker, C. 1982. Desert dwellers. *Elephant* 2(1): 135-9.

Walker, E. P. 1942. Care of captive animals. *Annual Report of the Smithsonian Institution* 1941: 305-366.

Wall, D. A., Davis, S. K., and B. M. Read. 1992. Phylogenetic relationships in the subfamily Bovinae (Mammalia: Artiodactyla) based on ribosomal data. *Journal of Mammalogy* 73(2): 262-275.

Wallace, D. C. 1987. Maternal genes: mitochondrial diseases (pp. 137-190) *in* McKusick, V. A., Roderick, T. H., Mori, J., and N. W. Paul., eds. *Medical and Experimental Mammalian Genetics: a Perspective.* 1987 March of Dimes Birth Defects Foundation.

Wallace, M. E., and R. J. Berry. 1978. Excessive mutational occurrences in wild Peruvian house mice. *Mutation Research* 53(2): 282-3.

Wallach, J. D., and W. J. Boever. 1983. *Diseases of Exotic Animals.* Saunders, Philadelphia.

Walsh, J. H. 1869. *The Horse.* Porter and Coates, Philadelphia.

Walton, H. V., and D. C. Sprague. 1951. Air flow through inlets used in animal shelter ventilation. *Agricultural Engineering* 32(4): 203-5.

Ward, D. L., and D. B. Carter. 1988. Carrion feeding in *Varanus varius*—notes from a field study.

Ward, G. R., and M. Brookfield. 1992. The dispersal of the coconut: did it float or was it carried to Panama? *Journal of Biogeography* 19:467-480.

Warnell, K. J., Crissey, S. D., and O. T. Oftedahl. 1989. Utilization of bamboo and other fiber sources in red panda diets (pp. 51-6) *in* Glatston, *op. cit.*

Watanabe, K. 1989. Fish: a new addition to the diet of Japanese Macaques on Koshima Island. *Folia Primatologica* 52:124-131.

Wathes, C. M. 1981. Insulation of animal houses (pp. 379-414) *in Clark, J. A., ed., Environmental Aspects of Housing for Animal Production*. Butterworths, London, Boston.

Watkins, D. I., and 12 others. 1992. New recombinant *HLA-B* alleles in a tribe of South American Amerindians indicate rapid evolution of MHC class I loci. Nature 357:329-333.

Watts, M. E. T. 1982. Bulk transport of farm animals by air and vehicular ferries (pp. 147-166) *in* R. Moss, ed. *Transport of Animals Intended for Breeding, Production, and Slaughter*. Martinus Nishoff Publishers, The Hague, Boston.

Wedekind, C., Seebeck, T., Bettens, F., and A. J. Paepke. 1995. MHC-dependent mate preferences in humans. *Proceedings of the Royal Society of London* B260:245-9.

Weigelt, J. 1989. *Recent Vertebrate Carcasses and their Paleobiological Implications*. University of Chicago Press, London.

Weiner, J. 1995. Evolution made visible. *Science* 267:30-33.

Welch, D. 1982. Dung properties and defecation characteristics in some Scottish herbivores. *Acta Theriologica* 27: 191-212.

Welch, G. J., and A. P. Hooper. 1988. Ingestion of feed and water (pp. 108-116) *in* Church, D. C., ed., *The Ruminant Animal*. Prentice-Hall, New Jersey.

Weller, J. B., and S. L. Willets. 1977. *Farm Wastes Management*. Crosby Lockwood Staples, London.

Wellnitz, M. von. 1979. Noah and the Flood: the apochryphal traditions. *Creation Research Society Quarterly* 16(1): 44-6.

Werff, P. H. van der. 1980. Thoughts on the structure of the Ark. *Creation Research Society Quarterly* 17(3): 167-8.

Wesson, G., and P. F. Wareing. 1967. Light requirements of buried seeds. *Nature* 213:600-1.

Wheeler, W. M. 1916. Ants carried in a floating log from the Brazilian mainland to San Sebastian Island. *Psyche* 23(6): 180-3.

Whitaker, T. W., and G. F. Carter. 1954. Oceanic drift of gourds—experimental observations. *American Journal of Botany* 41(9): 697-700.

Whitcomb J. C. 1988. *The World that Perished*, Revised Edition, Baker Book House, Michigan.

Whitcomb J. C., and H. M. Morris. 1961. *The Genesis Flood*. Presbyterian and Reformed, New Jersey.

White, F. N. 1973. Temperature and the Galapagos marine iguana—insights into reptilian thermoregulation. *Comparative Biochemistry and Physiology* 45A:503-513.

White, J. W. 1886. On the germination of seeds after prolonged submersion in salt. *Proceedings of the Linnean Society of London* 1886, pp. 108-110.

White, W. 1994. Painted out. *Nature* 370:604.

Wieland, C. 1994a. Diseases on the Ark. *Creation Ex Nihilo Technical Journal* 8(1): 16-17.

Wieland, C. 1994b. Diseases on the Ark. *Creation Ex Nihilo Technical Journal* 8(2): 153-4.

Wienker, W. R. 1986. Giraffe squeeze cage procedure. *Zoo Biology* 5:371-7.

Wiepkema, P. R. 1985. Control systems for coping at critical densities (pp. 230-8) *in* Zayan, R., ed., *Social Space for Domestic Animals*. Martinus Nijhoff Publishers, Dordrecht, Boston.

Wierenga, II. K. 1983. The influence of the space for walking and lying in a cubicle system on the behaviour of dairy cattle (pp. 171-181) *in* Baxter, S. H., Baxter, M. R., and J. A. D. MacCormack, eds., *Farm Animal Housing and Welfare*. Martinus Nijhoff Publishers, Boston, The Hague.

Wiesenfeld, S. L. 1967. Sickle-cell trait in human biological and cultural evolution. *Science* 157: 1134-1140.

Wieshampel, D. B., Dodson P., and H. Osmolska. 1992. *The Dinosauria*. University of California Press, Berkeley.

Wilkins, M. J., and J. P. Moreland. 1995. *Jesus under Fire*. Zondervan Publishing Co., Michigan.

Williams, G. C. 1992. *Natural Selection*. Oxford University Press, Oxford, New York.

Williams, N. 1995. Chernobyl: Life abounds without people. *Science* 269:304.

Williams, W. D., and I. C. Campbell. 1987. The inland aquatic environment and its fauna (pp. 156-183) *in* Anon. *Fauna of Australia*, Volume 1A. Australian Government Publishing Service, Canberra.

Williams, H., and A. R. McBirney. 1969. Floating pumice as a means of biological dispersal (pp. 113-116) *in* Williams, H., and A. R. McBirney, eds., Geology and Petrology of the Galapagos Islands. *Geological Society of America Memoir* 118.

Williamson, M. 1981. *Island Populations*. Oxford University Press, Oxford, New York.

Willoughby, D. P. 1975. *Growth and Nutrition in the Horse.* A. S. Barnes and Co., New Jersey.

Wilmer, J. M. W., Melzer, A. M., Carrick, F., and C. Moritz. 1993. Low genetic diversity and inbreeding depression in Queensland koalas. *Wildlife Research* 20:177-188.

Wilson, D. E. 1988. Maintaining bats for captive studies (pp. 247-263) *in* Kunz, T. H., ed., *Ecological and Behavioral Methods for the Study of Bats.* Smithsonian Institution Press, Washington, D. C.

Wilson, E. O. 1984. *Biophilia.* Harvard University Press, Cambridge, London.

Wilson, A. C., Maxson, L. R., and V. M. Sarich. 1974. Two types of molecular evolution. Evidence from studies of interspecific hybridization. *Proceedings of the National Academy of Sciences (USA)* 71(7): 2843-7.

Wilson J. D. E., and D. M. Reeder. 1993. Introduction (pp. 1-12) *in* Wilson, D. E., and D. M. Reeder, eds. *Mammal Species of the World.* Smithsonian Institution Press, Washington, D. C.

Wimsatt, W. A., and A. Guerriere. 1961. Care and maintenance of the common vampire in captivity. *Journal of Mammalogy* 42(4): 449-455.

Witten, G. J. 1985. Relative growth in Australian agamid lizards: adaptation and evolution. *Australian Journal of Zoology* 33:349-362.

Wittwer, S., Youtai, Y., Han, S., and W. Lianzheng. 1987. *Feeding a Billion.* Michigan State University Press, East Lansing.

Witzel, S. A., Jorgenson, N. A., Johannes, R. F., Larsen, H. J., and C. O. Cramer. 1967. Cold deep-bedded packs vs. cold free stalls. *Agricultural Engineering* 48:86-7.

Wolf, D. C. 1965. Developments in hog-manure disposal. *Transactions of the ASAE (American Society of Agricultural Engineers)* 8(1): 107-9.

Wolf, J. O., and G. C. Bateman. 1978. Effects of food availability and ambient temperature on torpor cycles of *Perognathus flavus* (Heteromyidae). *Journal of Mammalogy* 59(4): 707-716.

Wolfheim, J. H. 1983. *Primates of the World.* University of Washington Press, Seattle and London.

Wood, G. L. 1982. *The Guinness Book of Animal Facts and Feats.* Guinness Superlatives, Middlesex, England.

Wood, A. J., Nordan, H. C., and I. McT. Cowan. 1961. The care and management of wild ungulates for experimental purposes. *Journal of Wildlife Management* 25(3): 295-302.

Wood-Jones, F. 1923. *The Mammals of South Australia,* Part I. R. E. E. Rogers, Adelaide, Australia.

Wood-Jones, F. 1924. *The Mammals of South Australia,* Part II. R. E. E. Rogers, Adelaide, Australia.

Woodmorappe, J. 1993. *Studies in Flood Geology.* Institute for Creation Research, San Diego.

Woodmorappe, J. 1995. The Biota and Logistics of Noah's Ark. *in* Walsh, R. E., and C. L. Brooks, eds., *Proceedings of the Third International Conference on Creationism*, Pittsburg.

Woodward, F. I. 1987. *Climate and Plant Distribution*. Cambridge University Press, Cambridge, New York.

Wooten, M. C., and M. H. Smith. 1985. Large mammals are genetically less variable? *Evolution* 39(1): 210-212.

Worcester, G. R. G. 1947. *The Junks and Sampans of the Yangtze.*, Vol. I., Statistical Department, Shanghai.

Worcester, G. R. G. 1966. *Sail and Sweep in China*. Her Majesty's Stationery Office, London.

Wright, A. I., Osborne, A. D., Penny, R. H. C., and E. M. Gray. 1972. Foot-rot in pigs: experimental production of the disease. *Veterinary Record* 90:93-9.

Wright, B. S. 1951. A walrus in the Bay of Fundy; the first record. *Canadian Field Naturalist* 65:61-4.

Wright, G. R. H. 1985. *Ancient Building in South Syria and Palestine*, Volume 1. E. J. Brill, Leiden.

Wright, S. 1980. Genic and organismic selection. *Evolution* 34(5): 825-843.

Wyles, J. S., Kunkel, J. G., and A. C. Wilson. 1983. Birds, behavior, and anatomical evolution. *Proceedings of the National Academy of Sciences (USA)* 80: 4394-7.

Xueming, Y., and T. Junchang. 1991. Preliminary studies on the breeding habits and domestication of the Demoissale crane (pp. 79-81) *in* Harris, *op. cit.*

Xuqi, J., and M. Kappeler. 1986. *The Giant Panda*. G. P. Putnam's Sons, New York.

Y. 1842. Progress of practical and theoretical mechanics and chemistry. *Journal of the Franklin Institute*, 3rd Series, Vol. 3:320-5.

Yabushita, S., and N. Hatta. 1994. On the possible hazard on the major cities caused by asteroid impact in the Pacific Ocean. *Earth, Moon, and Planets* 65:7-13.

Yeh, H., Liu, P., Briggs, M., and C. Synolakis. 1994. Propagation and amplification of tsunamis at coastal boundaries. *Nature* 372:353-5.

Yelamos, N. K., and 8 others. 1995. Targeting of non-Ig sequences in place of the V segment by somatic hypermutation. *Nature* 376:225-229.

Yom-Tov, Y., Ashkenazi, S., and O. Viner. 1995. Cattle predation by the Golden Jackal *Canis aureus* in the Golan Heights, Israel. *Biological Conservation* 73:19-22.

Young, D. A. 1977. *Creation and the Flood*. Baker Book House, Grand Rapids, Michigan.

Young, D. A. 1995. *The Biblical Flood*. Wm. Eerdmans Publishing Co., Grand Rapids, Michigan.

Young, T. P. 1994. Natural die-offs of large mammals: implications for conservation. *Conservation Biology* 8(2): 410-418.

Young, T. P., and L. A. Isbell. 1994. Minimum group size and other conservation lessons exemplified by a declining primate population. *Biological Conservation* 68:129-134.

Youngblood, R. 1980. *How it all Began*. G. L. Publications, Ventura, California.

Yund, P. O., and M. Feldgarden. 1992. Rapid proliferation of historecognition alleles in populations of a colonial ascidian. *Journal of Experimental Zoology* 263:442-452.

Zaneveld, J. S. 1959. The utilization of marine algae in tropical south and east Asia. *Economic Botany* 13:59-131.

Zangenberg, G., Huang, M.-M., Arnheim, N., and H. Erlich. 1995. New HLA-DPB1 alleles generated by interallelic gene conversion detected by analysis of sperm. *Nature Genetics* 10:407-414.

Zenten, Van B. O. 1983. Possibilities of long-range dispersal in bryophytes with special reference to the southern hemisphere (pp. 49-64) *in* Kubitzki, K., ed., *Dispersal and Distribution*. Sonderbande des Naturwissenschaftlichen, Hamburg.

Zerfoss, G. E. 1947. Hay density in relation to various factors. *Agricultural Engineering* 28(5): 205-7.

Zimmerman, E. C. 1960. Possible evidence of rapid evolution in Hawaiian moths. *Evolution* 14(1): 137-8.

Zimmerman, L. C., and C. R. Tracy. 1989. Interactions between the environment and ectothermy and herbivory in reptiles. *Physiological Zoology* 62(2): 374-409.

Zink, F. J. 1935. Specific gravity and air space of grains and seeds. *Agricultural Engineering* 16(11): 439-440.

Zobel, D. B., and J. A. Antos. 1992. Survival of plants buried for eight growing seasons by volcanic tephra. *Ecology* 73(2): 698-701.

Zohary, D., and P. Spiegel-Roy. 1975. Beginnings of fruit growing in the Old World. *Science* 187:319-327.

Zullinger, E. M., Ricklefs, R. E., Redford, K. H., and G. M. Mace. 1984. Fitting sigmoidal equations to mammalian growth curves. *Journal of Mammalogy* 65(4): 607-636.

Study Questions

Following: In parentheses are the page number(s) in the book where the answer can be located.

1. Was *every type* of animal life on the Ark? (p. 4)

2. Was each *species* of animal on the ark? (pp. 6-7)

3. Does belief in rapid origin of new species mean that creationists are accepting organic evolution? (p. 7)

4. Were insects and other invertebrates on the Ark? (p. 4)

5. How could dinosaurs (including the largest sauropods) have all fit on the Ark? (p. 4, pp. 67-68)

6. Was the median size of animals on the Ark sheep-sized, or much smaller? (p. 13)

7. Based on actual laboratory-animal housing standards, how much Ark floor space was necessary to house the 16,000 animals? (p. 16)

8. Must the diets of captive wild animals, for the most part, closely resemble their diets in nature? (p. 17)

9. As the Ark moved, would the water have sloshed out of the drinking containers? (p. 21)

10. Is it possible to have designed an arrangement in which the twelve tons of daily animal waste was not handled by the eight-person crew at all? (pp. 25-30, 34-35)

11. What prevented vermin from being a serious problem on the Ark? (p. 30)

12. Would the methane emanating from the decomposing manure have caused an explosion, destroying the Ark? (p. 32)

13. Is the slotted Ark window an adequate design for ventilation? (p. 38-39)

14. Considering all of the animals, provender, etc., was the ark overloaded? (p. 47)

15. Were the ancient peoples capable of building only boats and small ships? (pp. 48-50)

16. Is it not physically impossible to build a *wooden* ship of Ark dimensions? (pp. 50-51)

17. If petroleum was used as the pitch to seal the Ark, where did it originate on the antediluvian earth? (p. 51)

18. What kinds of experience did the ancients have in managing large numbers of wild animals simultaneously? (p. 58)

19. How could Noah have dealt with fearful or recalcitrant animals, especially the large ones? (pp. 60-63)

20. How could Noah have distinguished males from females in the case of animals whose genders appear identical? (pp. 63-64)

21. Is the taking of the young of large animals on the Ark impractical because of the high death rate of juvenile animals? (p. 64)

22. Based on realistic situations, how many animals can be cared for by one person? (pp. 71-72)

23. Do actual animal-care labor studies substantiate the conclusion that eight people could care for 16,000 animals? (pp. 72-81)

24. How could exercise be provided for large numbers of animals in a short period of time? (p. 81)

25. When compared with modern animal housing, was the Ark overcrowded? (pp. 83-86)

26. Would not the floors have caused fatal hoof injuries? (p. 87)

27. Were bathing and burrowing facilities necessary on the Ark? (p. 88-89)

28. If the Ark got wet inside, would the food have spoiled? (p. 91)

29. Is there any vegetable which can stay fresh for a year, without refrigeration or preservatives? (p. 92)

30. Was there not an impossibly large volume of hay on the Ark? (p. 95-98)

31. How could meat-eaters and fish-eaters have been expeditiously fed on the Ark? (pp. 99-103)

32. Were fresh flowers on the Ark necessary for the nectar-eating birds and bats? (p. 103)

33. Were fresh fruits on the Ark necessary for primates, as well as for frugivorous bats and birds? (pp. 103-105)

34. How could snakes have been maintained on the Ark without the need for laboriously raising live foods (e.g., mice)? (p. 105-106)

35. Were live insects necessary on the Ark for those birds and bats which only eat live insects in nature? (pp. 106-110)

36. How could certain highly-specialized eaters (leaf-eating monkey, 3-toed sloth, panda, and koala) be maintained on the Ark? (pp. 111-117)

37. Must the tropical animals on the Ark have been supplied with a source of heat? (pp. 119-120)

38. Must the polar animals on the Ark have been supplied with refrigerated enclosures? (pp. 120-123)

39. If the preFlood earth had been warm, how could the strongly cold-adapted and heat-adapted animals have survived on the Ark? (pp. 119-123)

40. If there were no deserts in the preFlood world, where did the desert-adapted creatures live then? (pp. 123-124)

41. How could the narrow temperature tolerances of many bats and reptiles have been met on the Ark? (pp. 124-125)

42. Can animals go into hibernation only under highly exacting conditions? (pp. 128-130)

43. Would the constant motion of the Ark have prevented the Ark animals from hibernating? (p. 131)

44. If awakened during hibernation, would the Ark animals die, especially if awakened repeatedly? (p. 135)

45. Must hibernation of animals have been highly effective in order to have significantly reduced the time necessary to care for them on the Ark? (p. 135)

46. Would the oceans have gotten intolerably hot for marine life as a result of volcanic action during the Flood? (pp. 139-140)

47. Were the waters on earth much too muddy during the Flood for anything to have survived in them? (pp. 141-142)

48. Since most freshwater fish do not tolerate saltwater, and most marine fish do not tolerate freshwater, how could both kinds of fish have survived the Flood? (pp. 143-149)

49. Since amphibians are very fragile creatures, how could they have survived the Flood? (pp. 151-152)

50. Would any salt left behind on land (after the floodwaters had drained off) have posed a problem for plant growth? (p. 153)

51. Since most seeds do not float, how could plants have survived the Flood? (pp. 153-156)

52. If the seeds became soaked during the Flood, would not the plants all have germinated prematurely, and suffocated? (pp. 156-157)

53. How could plants that have specialized pollinators reproduce after the Flood? (pp. 159-162)

54. Once the roof covering of the Ark had been removed by Noah, were the animals exposed to the hostile elements? (p. 163)

55. What is one obvious reason for God having re-instilled the fear of man in animals (Genesis 9:2-3)? (p. 164)

56. What are some advantages of the Ark having landed in a mountainous region instead of on a plain? (pp. 164-165)

57. What was there for animals to eat (besides each other) once they got off the Ark? (pp. 167-170)

58. How long did it take for the first food chains to re-establish themselves after the Flood? (pp. 171-172)

59. How could animals that breed only when in flocks have reproduced themselves from single-pair founders released from the Ark? (pp. 175-176)

60. Can single-pair founders give rise to lasting populations? (pp. 176-179)

61. Is the "Created Kind" an arbitrary concept? (pp. 179-180)

62. Can it be substantiated that the genera of animals released from the Ark could have given rise to new species in only a few thousand years? (pp. 180-182)

63. Since Noah's surviving family consisted of only eight people, would not inbreeding among Noah's immediate descendants have caused serious problems? (pp. 183-185)

64. Does the *"50/500 rule"* of conservation biology rule out single-pair founders having sufficient genetic diversity for their descendants to survive? (p. 187-189)

65. What role did supergenes play in postFlood genetics? (pp. 189-190)

66. Was a miracle necessary to restore genetic diversity among the postFlood populations? (pp. 191-192)

67. Could those Ark animals have been selected which bore an unusually high genetic diversity? (pp. 193-195)

68. Is it possible for animal populations to regain heritable genetic variance in only a few thousand years? (p. 197)

69. If certain animals lost most of their genetic diversity because of the Flood, were they necessarily doomed to extinction? (pp. 197-198)

70. Do the frequencies of alleles in modern animals show any hallmarks of a recent Ark release? (pp. 198-199)

71. What is the significance of "jumping genes" in the rapid restoration of genetic diversity among living things? (pp. 201-202)

72. How can so-called pseudogenes be easily explained in a creationist context? (p. 202)

73. Are there any lines of evidence which point to the existence of built-in mechanisms, in organisms, for the rapid recovery of lost genetic diversity? (p. 202)

74. Does the close similarity between the human and chimp HLA complex demonstrate that neither humans nor chimps could have undergone a recent drastic reduction in population size? (pp. 202-206)

75. How rapidly could HLA diversity have been recovered after the Flood? (pp. 207-209)

76. How can the mitochondrial-DNA "clock" (which includes the "African Eve") be compressed to less than 5000 years? (pp. 211-212)

77. Did Noah's family have to carry the entire load of parasites and pathogens which humans can be afflicted with? (pp. 215-216)

78. Could host-specific parasites and pathogens have been carried *only* by their current hosts while on the Ark? (pp. 215-216)

Index